The Turkish E

Its Growth and Decay

Baron G. Shaw-Lefevre Eversley

Alpha Editions

This edition published in 2024

ISBN : 9789362516206

Design and Setting By
Alpha Editions
www.alphaedis.com
Email - info@alphaedis.com

As per information held with us this book is in Public Domain.
This book is a reproduction of an important historical work. Alpha Editions uses the
best technology to reproduce historical work in the same manner it was first
published to preserve its original nature. Any marks or number seen are left
intentionally to preserve its true form.

Contents

PREFACE ....- 1 -

PART I THE GROWTH OF EMPIRE ....- 5 -

OTHMAN 1288-1326 ....- 7 -

II ORCHAN 1326-59 ....- 13 -

III MURAD I 1359-89 ....- 22 -

IV BAYEZID I 1389-1403 ....- 32 -

V MAHOMET I 1413-21 ....- 44 -

VI MURAD II 1421-51 ....- 48 -

VII MAHOMET II, 'THE CONQUEROR' 1451-81 ....- 55 -

VIII BAYEZID II 1481-1512 ....- 74 -

IX SELIM I 1512-20 ....- 78 -

X. SOLYMAN THE MAGNIFICENT 1520-66 ....- 87 -

XI GRAND VIZIER SOKOLLI 1566-78 ....- 104 -

PART II THE DECAY OF EMPIRE ....- 115 -

XII THE RULE OF SULTANAS 1578-1656 ....- 117 -

XIII THE KIUPRILI VIZIERS 1656-1702 ....- 130 -

XIV TO THE TREATY OF PASSAROWITCH 1702-18 ....- 149 -

XV TO THE TREATY OF BELGRADE 1718-39 ....- 158 -

XVI TO THE TREATY OF KAINARDJI 1739-74 ....- 164 -

XVII TO THE TREATY OF JASSY 1774-92 ....- 173 -

XVIII TO THE TREATY OF BUCHAREST 1792-1812 .....- 185 -

XIX MAHMOUD II 1808-39 ....- 199 -

XX THE RULE OF ELCHIS 1839-76 ....- 224 -

XXI ABDUL HAMID II 1876-1909 ....- 247 -

XXII THE YOUNG TURKS 1909-14 ....- 276 -

XXIII A RETROSPECT..- 290 -

APPENDIX GENEALOGY OF THE OTTOMAN SULTANS..- 299 -

FOOTNOTES: ....- 301 -

PREFACE

THE favour with which, two years ago, my book on *The Partitions of Poland* was received by the public has induced me to devote the interval to a study of the history of another State which, in modern times, has almost disappeared from the map of Europe—namely Turkey.

The subject is one in which I have for many years past taken great interest. In the course of a long life, I have witnessed the greater part of the events which have resulted in the loss to that State of all its Christian provinces in Europe and all its Moslem provinces in Africa, leaving to it only its capital and a small part of Thrace in Europe, and its still wide possessions in Asia.

So long ago, also, as in 1855 and 1857, I spent some time at Constantinople and travelled in Bulgaria and Greece, and was able to appreciate the effects of Turkish rule. As a result, I gave a full support, in 1876, to Mr. Gladstone in his efforts to secure the independence of Bulgaria, and in 1879 was an active member of a committee, presided over by Lord Rosebery, which had for its object the extension of the kingdom of Greece so as to include the provinces inhabited by Greeks still suffering under Turkish rule.

In 1887 and 1890 I again visited the East and travelled over the same ground as thirty years earlier, and was able to observe the immense improvements which had been effected in the provinces that had gained independence, and how little change had taken place at Constantinople.

In view of these experiences and of the further great changes portended in Turkey after the conclusion of the present great war, I have thought it may be of use to tell, in a compact and popular form, the story of the growth and decay of the Turkish Empire.

History may well be told at many different lengths and from different points of view. That of the Ottoman Empire, from the accession of Othman in 1288 to the treaty of Kainardji in 1774, which secured to Russia a virtual protectorate in favour of the Christian subjects of Turkey, has been told at its greatest length by the German professor, Von Hammer, in eighteen volumes. He is the only historian who has explored for this long period both Greek and Turkish annals.

The British historian, Knolles, writing in 1610, told the story of the growth of the Turkish Empire in two bulky folio volumes, much admired by two such different authorities as Dr. Johnson and Lord Byron. The work is based on a few only of the Greek annals. It is very discursive and imperfect, but it contains many most terse and striking passages. Gibbon, the historian of the Roman Empire, and Sir Edwin Pears, in his most interesting book on the

Destruction of the Greek Empire, have also relied on Greek authorities up to the capture of Constantinople by the Turks in 1453, before which date there were no Turkish historians. Very recently, in 1916, Mr. Herbert Gibbons, of the Princeton University, published a very valuable work on the foundations of the Ottoman Empire, dealing with its first four great Sultans. He has again examined with very great care the numerous and conflicting early Greek authorities, and has thrown much new light on the subject.

Other historians of Turkey, writing in English and French, such as Creasy, Lane Poole, La Jonquière, and Halil Ganem (a Young Turk), have drawn their facts mainly from Von Hammer's great work. Their books are all of interest and value. But these writers, and especially Sir Edward Creasy, in his otherwise admirable *History of the Ottoman Empire*, written at the time of the Crimean War, to which I have been much indebted, took what would now be considered too favourable a view of Turkish rule in modern times, and were over sanguine, as events have shown, as to the maintenance and regeneration of the Empire. I have followed their example in basing my narrative mainly on Von Hammer's work, correcting it in some important respects from the other sources I have named, compressing it into much smaller compass than they have done, treating it from a somewhat different point of view, and bringing it down to the commencement of the present great war in 1914.

It would have been easier to tell the story at double the length, so as to include much other important and interesting matter, but, in such a case, the lesson to be drawn from it would have been obscured by the maze of detail. My book does not aim at a full history of the long period dealt with. I have proposed only to explain the process by which the Turkish Empire was aggregated by its first ten great Sultans, and has since been, in great part, dismembered under their twenty-five degenerate successors, and to assign causes for these two great historic movements.

I will only add that I commenced my recent studies under the impressions derived in part from some of the histories to which I have referred and with which I was familiar, and in part from the common tradition in Western Europe—dating probably from the time of the Crusaders—that the Turkish invasions and conquests in Europe were impelled by religious zeal and fervour and by the desire to spread Islam. I have ended them with the conviction that there was no missionary zeal whatever for Islam in the Turkish armies and their leaders who invaded Europe, and that their main incentive was the hope of plunder by the sack of cities, the sale of captives as slaves or for harems, and the confiscation of land and its distribution among soldiers as a reward for bravery. I have also concluded that the decay of the military spirit and the shrinkage of Empire was largely due to the absence of these motives and rewards when the Turks were on the defensive.

If I have expressed my views freely on this subject, and on the misrule of the Turks in modern times, I have endeavoured to state the facts on which they are based with perfect fairness as between the Crescent and the Cross.

I have purposely refrained from expressing an opinion as to the future of Turkey, after the conclusion of the existing great war. The problems which will then have to be solved are of a different order to those of the past which have been dealt with in this book. The Turkish Empire, in the sense of the rule of an alien race over subject races, has practically ceased to exist in Europe. It survives in Asia and at its capital, Constantinople, under very different conditions.

With respect to the numerous works I have consulted for the latter part of my book, I desire specially to acknowledge my indebtedness to Mr. Lane Poole's admirable *Life of Lord Stratford de Redcliffe*.

I have to thank Lord Bryce, Lord Fitzmaurice, and Sir Edwin Pears for their valuable suggestions, and Lady Byles and Mr. Laurence Chubb for their kind help.

E.

June 1, 1917.

- 4 -

PART I

THE GROWTH OF EMPIRE

OTHMAN
1288-1326

TOWARDS the middle of the thirteenth century a small band or tribe of nomad Turks migrated from Khorassan, in Central Asia, into Asia Minor. They were part of a much larger body, variously estimated at from two to four thousand horsemen, who, with their families, had fled from their homes in Khorassan under Solyman Shah. They had been driven thence by an invading horde of Mongols from farther east. They hoped to find asylum in Asia Minor. They crossed into Armenia and spent some years in the neighbourhood of Erzerum, plundering the natives there. When the wave of Mongols had spent its force, they proposed to return to Khorassan. On reaching the Euphrates River Solyman, when trying, on horseback, to find a ford, was carried away by the current and drowned. This was reckoned as a bad omen by many of his followers. Two of his sons, with a majority of them, either returned to Central Asia or dispersed on the way there.

Two other sons, Ertoghrul and Dundar, with four hundred and twenty families, retraced their course, and after spending some time again near Erzerum, wandered westward into Asia Minor. They came into a country inhabited by a kindred race. Successive waves of Turks from the same district in Central Asia, in the course of the three previous centuries, had made their way into Asia Minor, and had taken forcible possession of the greater part of it. They formed there an Empire, known as that of the Seljukian Turks, with Konia, the ancient Iconium, as its capital. But this Empire, by the middle of the thirteenth century, was in a decadent condition. It was eventually broken up, in part, by assaults of a fresh swarm of invaders from Central Asia; and in14 part by internal civil strife, fomented by family disputes of succession.

When Ertoghrul's band appeared on the scene, Sultan Alaeddin ruled at Konia over what remained to him of the Seljukian State. Other remnants of it survived under independent Emirs at Karamania, Sarukhan, Mentsche, and numerous other smaller States. Between them they possessed nearly the whole of Asia Minor, with the exception of a few cities in its north-west, such as Brusa, Nicæa, and Nicomedia and the districts round them, and a belt of territory along the Bosphorus, the Sea of Marmora, and the Hellespont, to which the Byzantine Emperors, formerly the owners of nearly the whole of Anatolia, were now reduced. Two small Christian States also still existed there—Trebizond, in the north-east, and Little Armenia, in Cilicia, in the south-east. Though divided among many independent Emirs, the people of Asia Minor, with the exception of the Greeks and Armenians, were fairly welded together. The invading Turks had intermixed with the native population, imposing on them the Turkish language, and had themselves adopted the religion of Islam. Ertoghrul and his nomad tribe, before entering this country, were not Moslems, but they were not strangers in language. Whatever their religion, it was held lightly. They were converted to Islam after a short stay in the country and, as is often the case with neophytes, became ardent professors of their new faith.

The oft-told story of the first exploit of Ertoghrul and his four hundred and twenty horsemen, on coming into the country of the Seljuks, as handed down by tradition, though savouring somewhat of a myth, is as follows: They came unexpectedly upon a battle in which one side was much pressed. They knew nothing of the combatants. Ertoghrul spoke to his followers: "Friends, we come straight on a battle. We carry swords at our side. To flee like women and resume our journey is not manly. We must help one of the two. Shall we aid those who are winning or those who are losing?" Then they said unto him: "It will be difficult to aid the losers. Our people are weak in number and the victors are strong!" Ertoghrul replied: "This is not the speech of bold men. The manly part is to aid the vanquished." Thereupon the whole body of them fell upon the Mongols, who were the winning side, and drove them into flight. The side to which they brought aid and victory proved to be that of Sultan Alaeddin of Konia. In return for this providential aid, Sultan Alaeddin made a grant of territory to Ertoghrul to be held as a fief under the Seljuks. It consisted of a district at Sugut, about sixty miles south-east of Brusa, and a part of the mountain range to the west of it.

Ertoghrul and his horsemen were a welcome support to Alaeddin's waning fortunes. In a later encounter with a small Byzantine force they came off victorious, and Alaeddin made a further addition to their territory on the borders of his own, over which he had a very nominal sovereignty. Thenceforth Ertoghrul lived an uneventful pastoral life as the head of his clan or tribe of Turks in the ceded territory, till his death in 1288, nearly fifty years from the date of his leaving Khorassan. His son, Othman, who was born at Sugut in 1258, was chosen by the clan to succeed him, and soon commenced a much more ambitious career than that of his father. When of the age of only sixteen he had fallen in love with the beautiful daughter of Sheik Idebali, a holy man of great repute in Karamania. It is evidence of the small account then held of Ertoghrul and his son that the Sheik did not think the marriage good enough for his daughter. It was only after a long and patient wooing by Othman, and as the result of a dream, which foretold a great future of empire for his progeny, that Idebali gave consent to the marriage.

There were no contemporary Turkish histories of the early Ottoman Sultans. It was not till many years after the capture of Constantinople in 1453 that Turkish historians wrote about the birth of their State. They had to rely upon traditions, which must be accepted with much reserve. This, however, is certain, that Othman, in his thirty-eight years of leadership, increased his dominion from its very narrow limits at Sugut and Eski-Sheir to a territory extending thence northward to the Bosphorus and Black Sea, a distance of about a hundred and twenty miles by an average breadth of sixty miles, an area of about seven thousand square miles. There are no means of estimating its population. It was probably sparse, except on the coast of the Marmora and Black Sea. It included only one important city, Brusa, which was surrendered by its garrison and citizens shortly before the death of Othman in 1326, after being hemmed in and cut off from communication with Constantinople for many years. Considerable as these additions were, the nascent State could not even yet be considered as important in size. It was exceeded by several of the larger Turkish Emirates in Asia Minor, such as Karamania, Sarukhan, and others.

It is notable that Othman, from the outset of his career, devoted his efforts, not against the Turkish Moslem States lying to the south and west of him, but against the territory to the north in possession of the Byzantine Empire, or which had recently been more or less emancipated from it, and inhabited chiefly by Christians. It is to be inferred from this that the motive of Othman was partly a religious one, to extend Islam. This was not effected by any signal victories over the armies of the Greek Empire. There was only one recorded battle against any army of the Emperor, that at Baphœon, near Nicomedia, where Othman, who by this time reckoned four thousand horsemen among his followers, defeated the inconsiderable body of two thousand Byzantine troops. In the following year, 1302, the Greek Emperor, Michael Palæologus, alarmed at the progress of Othman, crossed in person into Asia Minor at the head of a small army of mercenary Slavs. But he brought no money with him to pay his soldiers. They would not fight without pay. They dispersed, and Michael was obliged to return to his capital. This was his last attempt to defend his remaining territory in that district. He was hard pressed in other directions by other Turkish Emirs in Asia Minor, and in the first decade of the fourteenth century the Greek Empire lost all its possessions in the islands of the Ægean Sea.

The extensions of territory by Othman, during his long reign of thirty-eight years, were effected by a slow process of attrition, by capturing from time to time petty fortresses and castles and annexing the districts round them. He acted in this respect, in the earlier stages, as fief of the Seljuk State; but later, when that Empire came to an end, Othman declared his independence, and thenceforth his accretions of territory were on his own behalf. It would seem that, as these additions were made, their populations, or the greater part of them who were Christians, adopted Islam, not under compulsion—for there is no record of the massacre of captives or of the sale of them as slaves — but because they were abandoned by their natural protectors, the Greeks of Constantinople. The important fact, clearly shown by Mr. Gibbons in his recent work, is that the new State thus created by Othman did not consist purely of Turks. It had a very large mixture of Greeks and Slavs, who were welded with Turks by the religion of Islam. They were, from an early period, very distinct from the people of other Turkish States. They called themselves Osmanlis. The term 'Turk' was used by them rather as a term of contempt for an inferior people, as compared with themselves. It was only in later years, when the other Turkish States of Asia Minor were incorporated in the Empire, that the term 'Turk' was applied to its people, in the first instance by outsiders, and eventually by themselves.

To Othman, therefore, is due the credit of this inception of a new State and a new and distinct people. He did not, however, assume the title of Sultan. He was simply an Emir, like so many other rulers of petty States in Asia Minor. He was not a great general. He had no opportunity of conducting a great campaign. He was a brave soldier and a sagacious leader, who inspired confidence and trust in his followers and subjects. He pursued with great persistency the policy of enlarging his domain. He was also a wise and capable administrator, and was assisted in this by his father-in-law, Idebali, who acted as his Vizier. He meted out equal justice to all his subjects, irrespective of race and religion. He was simple and unostentatious in his habits. There is no record of his having more than one wife or more than two sons. He did not amass wealth. He divided the loot of war equally among his soldiers, setting apart a portion for the poor and orphans.

Othman had a vein of cruelty in his character, as had so many of his descendants, the Ottoman Sultans. When, on one occasion, he propounded to his war council a scheme of further aggression on his neighbours, his uncle, Dundar, a nonagenarian, who had been companion in arms to Ertoghrul, ventured to raise objection to the policy of further extension. Othman, instead of arguing the question with him, took up his cross-bow and shot his uncle dead on the spot, and in this way closured the discussion and put down, at the outset, opposition in the council.

Von Hammer, in relating this story, says:—

This murder of the uncle marks with terror the commencement of the Ottoman dominion, as the brother's murder did that of Rome, only the former rests on better historical evidence. Idris (the Turkish historian), who, at the beginning of his work, declares that, passing over in silence all that is reprehensible, he will only hand down to posterity the glorious deeds of the royal race of Othman, relates, among the latter, the murder of Dundar. If then such a murderous slaughter of a relative be reckoned by the panegyrists of the Osmanlis among their praiseworthy acts, what are we to think of those which cannot be praised and of which their history therefore is silent?[1]

We must judge of Othman, however, not by the standard of the present time, but by that of his contemporaries. By that standard he was reckoned a humane and merciful sovereign. This view is expressed in the prayer which has been used in the religious ceremony, on the accession of every one of his successors to the throne, when he is girt with the double-edged sword of the founder of the Empire, "May he be as good as Othman."

In his old age, when Othman was incapable of taking the field himself, his son, Orchan, took his place as the leader of the army, and just before the death of Othman, Brusa surrendered to him. It was then, as now, one of the most important cities in Asia Minor.

When Othman was on his deathbed, after a reign of thirty-eight years, his son Orchan, in terms of affection and lamentation, addressed him: "Oh, Othman! Thou fountain of Emperors, Lord of the World, Thou conqueror and subduer of Nations." The dying king replied:—

Lament not, oh my sons: delight! for this my last conflict is the lot of all human kind, common to young and old, who equally breathe the air of this malignant world. Whilst I now pass to immortality, live thou glorious, prosperous, and happy. Since I have thee for successor, I have no cause to grieve at my departure. I will give thee my last instructions, to which be attentive. Bury the cares of life in oblivion. I conjure thee, crowned with felicity, lean not to tyranny, nor so much as look towards cruelty. On the contrary, cultivate justice and thereby embellish the earth. Rejoice my departed soul with a beautiful series of victories, and when thou art become conqueror of the world, propagate religion by thy arms. Promote the learned to honour, so the divine law shall be established, and in what place soever thou hearest a learned man, let honour, magnificence, and clemency attend him. Glory not in thy armies, nor pride thyself in thy riches. Keep near thy person the learned in the law, and, as justice is the support of kingdoms, turn from everything repugnant thereto. The Divine law is our sole arm, and our progress is only in the paths of the Lord. Embark not in vain undertakings or fruitless contentions. For it is not our ambition to enjoy the empire of the world, but the propagation of the faith was my peculiar desire, which therefore it becomes thee to accomplish. Study to be impartially gracious to all, and take care to discharge the public duties of thy office, for a king not distinguished by goodness belies the name of a king. Let the protection of thy subjects be thy constant study, so shalt thou find favour and protection from God.[2]

It is probable that much of this was the invention of some historian, writing many years later. It may be taken, however, as a summary, based on tradition, of the principles which had actuated the dying chief during his long reign.

Othman died shortly after receiving the welcome news of the surrender of Brusa, and by his last wish was buried there. He was the progenitor of a royal race who, for nine more generations, continued the career of conquest which he inaugurated, till the Empire, in the middle of the sixteenth century, two hundred and seventy-eight years from the accession of Othman, under Solyman the Magnificent, the greatest of his race, reached its zenith. It was only after ten generations of great Sultans that the race seemed to be exhausted, and thenceforth, with rare exceptions, produced none but degenerates down to the present time.

II
ORCHAN
1326-59

OTHMAN, on his deathbed, designated as his successor the younger of his two sons, Orchan, aged forty-two, who had been brought up as a soldier under his father's eye, and had shown capacity in many campaigns, and especially in that resulting in the surrender of Brusa. Alaeddin, the elder brother, was not a soldier. He had led a studious life, devoted to religion and law, both founded on the Koran, under the guidance of Idebali.

The Turkish historians agree in stating that Orchan was most unwilling to act on his father's wishes and take precedence over his elder brother, and that he proposed to divide the heritage of state between them, but that Alaeddin declined the offer. Orchan is then reported to have said: "Since, my brother, thou wilt not take the flocks and herds which I offer thee, be the shepherd of my people. Be my Vizier." Alaeddin agreed to this, and devoted himself to the administration of the growing State and to the organization of the army, under the rule of his brother.[3]

Orchan followed closely the example of his father. He pursued the same method of slow, but sure and persistent, aggrandizement of his State. It will be seen that he succeeded in adding to it a territory nearly three times greater than that which he inherited. Two-thirds of this were in the north-west corner of Asia Minor, along the shore of the Marmora and the Dardanelles, and the remaining third in Europe, where he was the first to make a lodgment for the Ottomans. He made Brusa his capital, and there, after a time, he assumed the title of Sultan. He coined money with the inscription, "May God cause to endure the Empire of Orchan, son of Othman." The phrase must be taken rather as a measure of his ambition than as a description of his existing State, for it was then inferior in size to several of the Turkish Emirates in Asia Minor and to most of the Balkan States. Orchan led a most active and simple life. He was always on the move. When not in the field with his troops, he spent his time in visiting his many petty strongholds, seldom remaining more than a month in any one of them.

The immediate objects of Orchan's ambition, on his accession, were the Greek cities of Nicæa and Nicomedia, with their surrounding districts, the last important possessions of the Byzantine Empire in Asia. Nicæa was then a great city. It had attained greater importance during the sixty years when the Latins were in occupation of Constantinople and the Greek Emperors were relegated to Asia and made it their capital. It was well fortified. It could only be captured, as Brusa had been, by cutting off its communications with Constantinople, and depriving its people of the means of subsistence. The Greek Emperor, Andronicus III, made an effort to relieve it. He hastily raised an army of mercenaries, in 1326, and led them across the Bosphorus. He fought a battle against Orchan at Pelecanon, on the north shore of the Gulf of Nicomedia. According to the Greek historians, the Ottomans had much the worst of it, losing a great number of men, while the losses of the Greeks were trivial. However that may have been, Andronicus decided on a retreat. But a scrimmage occurred in the night between his bodyguard and the enemy, in which the Emperor himself was slightly wounded. He thereupon fled precipitately, and was conveyed in a litter to the Bosphorus and thence to Constantinople. His army, dispirited by this abandonment by their Emperor, was defeated and dispersed. As a result, Nicæa surrendered in the following year, 1327, on favourable terms. The majority of its garrison and citizens followed the example of those of Brusa and adopted Islam. Very few availed themselves of the offer to transfer themselves to Europe. This ill-starred campaign and cowardly flight of Andronicus was the last effort of the Byzantine Emperors to save their possessions in Asia. What remained of them, chiefly the city of Nicomedia, were left to their own resources, without further aid from Europe. Nicomedia was well fortified and was apparently a tough job for the Ottomans, for it held out till 1337, or possibly 1338, and eventually surrendered in the same way, and on the same terms, as Brusa and Nicæa.

In the interval of ten years between the capture of Nicæa and Nicomedia, Orchan was further engaged in extending his State elsewhere in Asia, not towards Angora, in the south, as stated by some historians, but to the north-west, in the ancient Mysia, by the conquest of the Emirate of Karasi, which lay immediately to the north of Sarukhan and with a frontage to the sea opposite to the island of Mytilene. The Emir of this State died in 1333. His two sons disputed the succession. The younger one was favoured by the Ottomans, and when he was put to death by his brother, Orchan sent an army ostensibly to avenge him. The Emir was driven into exile and his State was promptly annexed by Orchan. The same fate befell some other petty Emirates on the southern borders of the Marmora and the Hellespont, rounding off the boundary of the Ottoman State in the north-west corner of Anatolia. The population of Karasi and the smaller States was mainly Turkish, but there must have been many Greeks on the coast who probably adopted Islam, as had the majority of the Greeks of Brusa and Nicæa. After these acquisitions, and that of Nicomedia in 1338, there were no further additions to the Ottoman State in Asia Minor during Orchan's reign.

There followed, after the capture of Nicomedia, a few years of peace, and it may well be that, during this time, Orchan completed the scheme for the organization of his State and his army. Hitherto, when Othman and Orchan were involved in disputes with their neighbours, and it was necessary to use armed force in resistance or attack, an appeal was made for the voluntary service of all the male members of their petty State or clan capable of bearing arms; and the appeal was responded to without question. When the occasion for their service was at an end, the warriors returned to their homes and to their usual vocations. With a rapidly expanding territory and with great ambitions for further conquests, it was evidently thought necessary to constitute a permanent and well-disciplined force, and Orchan, whether adopting, or not, the plans of his brother Alaeddin, determined to effect this. On the one hand, he enrolled a considerable body of infantry for continuous service. They were subject to strict discipline and were well paid, and it will be seen that they could be sent beyond the realm to assist the Greek Emperor or otherwise.[4] On the other hand, a large body of horsemen was provided, not under continuous service, but under obligatory service, when occasion arose for calling them out.

For this purpose the country districts were divided into fiefs, the holders of which were bound to serve in the event of war, and to come provided with horses and equipment, or to find substitutes in proportion to the extent of their fiefs. It was, in fact, the adoption of the feudal system, then almost universal in Europe, with this marked difference, that the fiefs were small in extent and were not, as a rule, hereditary. They were given for life as rewards for military service, and on the death of their holders were granted to other soldiers, though in some cases hereditary claims were recognized. When new territories were acquired by conquest from non-Moslems, large parts of them were divided into new fiefs, and were granted to the soldiers who had distinguished themselves in the war. Military service, whether in the new infantry or in the feudal cavalry, was strictly confined to Moslems. Christians, who were thus exempted from military duty, were subjected to a heavy capitation tax from which Moslems were free.

This new organization of the army, commenced by Orchan and extended and perfected by his son Murad, who also, it will be seen, created the famous corps of Janissaries, converted the nascent Ottoman State into a most powerful engine for war, and gave an immense impetus to the conquest of non-Moslem countries. Most splendid rewards were held out to the Moslem soldiers for victory and bravery. In the event of victory they benefited not only from the ordinary booty in money and chattels, on the sack of cities and the pillage of country districts. They also received as their share four-fifths of the proceeds of the sale of captives as slaves, the other fifth being reserved as the share of the Sultan. The captives were not only the enemies' soldiers taken in battle, but in many cases the inhabitants of the conquered districts. The strong and the young of both sexes were carried off and were sold, the men as slaves, the fairer women for wives or concubines, or for harems. The soldiers further received, as has been shown above, a large share of the confiscated lands to be held as military fiefs in reward for bravery in battle. As these fiefs were granted for life only, there was a further distribution among the soldiers of the fiefs held by their comrades who were killed in battle, and often, it is said, the same fiefs changed hands many times in the course of a campaign.

The Moslem inhabitants of a conquered territory were not sold off as slaves, nor were their lands confiscated. These measures were reserved for Christians or non-Moslems. In some cases the Christians were given the option of embracing Islam in order to avoid slavery and the confiscation of their land. But these exceptions were rare in the conquests in Europe, and it is obvious that, to whatever extent they took place, the rewards obtained by the soldiers were reduced.

It has been shown that hitherto in the Ottoman conquests in Asia Minor at the expense of the Byzantine Empire a great proportion of the Christian population embraced Islam; and it may well have been that the spread of Islam and the conversion of infidels to the true faith were in part the incentives for the expansion of the Ottoman Empire. But henceforth, after the organization of the army by Orchan and Murad and the great rewards held out to the soldiers for the conquest of non-Moslem territories, it does not appear that the Ottoman armies were inspired by any missionary zeal for the spread of Islam. The main, if not the sole motives, were loot and plunder, the sale of captives as slaves, and the confiscation of land and its distribution among the soldiers as fiefs; and these objects were attained to a far greater extent by the invasion of Christian States in Europe than by the extension of the Empire over Moslem countries in Asia.

In the year 1354 Orchan, after completing the organization of his army, turned his attention for the first time to Europe. Thenceforth, till his death in 1359, his restless ambition was directed against the Byzantine Empire. Advancing age prevented his taking the field himself at the head of his army. But his eldest son, Solyman, who had all the great qualities of his race, and who was the idol of the army, took his place in command of the invading forces.

It may be well to point out here that, at this time, the middle of the fourteenth century, the Byzantine Empire was already reduced to very insignificant proportions, compared to its ancient grandeur. The territories subject to it, which for centuries had extended to the Danube in Europe, and in Asia over Anatolia and Syria, had been already greatly diminished when the leaders of the fourth Crusade, in 1204, in one of the most disgraceful episodes in history, turned aside from their avowed object of attacking the Moslems in

Palestine and, in lieu thereof, attacked and captured Constantinople, and compelled the Byzantine Emperor to transfer the seat of his government to Nicæa, in Asia Minor. There followed the brief period of the Latin Empire. But in 1261 the Byzantine Greeks reconquered Constantinople, and the ephemeral Latin Empire disappeared from history. The Byzantines were then able to recover a small part only of their old dominions in Europe and Asia. At the time when Orchan, who had driven them from Asia, decided to attack them in Europe, they held there no more than Thrace with Adrianople, a part of Macedonia with Salonika, and the greater part of the Morea in Greece. To the north of them Serbia, under Stephen Dushan, the most eminent of its rulers, had asserted supremacy over the greater half of the Balkan peninsula, was threatening Salonika, and had ambition to possess himself of Constantinople. Bulgaria, though it had lost territory to Serbia, still possessed the smaller half of the Balkans. The Republics of Venice and Genoa owned many commercial ports and islands in the Ægean Sea and Adriatic, and were madly jealous of one another. The position was such as to afford a favourable opportunity to new invaders like the Ottomans, for there was no probability of a combination among these Christian communities to resist them.

The story of the first entry of the Ottomans into Europe, as told by the early Turkish historians and adopted by Von Hammer and others, is shortly this. In the year 1356 Solyman, the son of Orchan, at the head of a small body of Ottoman troops, variously estimated at from seventy-five to three hundred, under the inspiration of a dream, stealthily crept, it is said, across the Hellespont in boats, and succeeded in surprising and overcoming the Greek garrison of the small fortress of Tzympe, on the European side of the Straits, and having thus gained possession of it, increased the invading force to three thousand. Mr. Gibbons, on the other hand, has unravelled from the Byzantine historians a much fuller and more reliable story of the successive entries of Ottoman troops into Europe from 1345 downwards. It may be briefly epitomized as follows, in explanation of the great historic event—the first entry of the Ottomans into Europe—a story which is most discreditable to the Byzantine Greeks:—

On the death, in 1338, of the Greek Emperor Andronicus III, the most feeble and incompetent of the long line of Palæologi, his Grand Chancellor, Cantacuzene, was appointed, under his will, guardian of his son, John Palæologus, and as co-regent with his widow, the Empress Anna. Cantacuzene, not satisfied with this arrangement, and ambitious to secure supreme power in the Empire, had himself proclaimed Emperor at Nicotika in 1343. This was bitterly resented and opposed by the Empress Anna. Civil war broke out. Both Anna and Cantacuzene appealed to Orchan, their new and powerful neighbour across the Straits, for aid against the other. Cantacuzene offered his young daughter, Theodora, in marriage to Orchan

- 17 -

in return for the aid of six thousand Ottoman troops. Orchan apparently thought this a better offer than that of the Empress Anna, whatever that may have been. He was perhaps flattered by the prospect of a family connection with a Byzantine Emperor. He closed with the offer and sent six thousand soldiers into Europe, in 1345, in support of Cantacuzene, who made use of them by investing Constantinople, of which the Empress had obtained possession. After a year's siege, Cantacuzene effected an entry into the city by the aid of his partisans there, who treacherously opened its gates to him. The Empress was thereupon compelled to come to terms. She agreed that Cantacuzene and his wife should be crowned as Emperor and Empress, together with herself and her son. This union was further cemented by the marriage of the young Emperor John, at the age of sixteen, with another daughter of Cantacuzene. Orchan, in pursuance of his agreement with the new Emperor, was married in 1346 at the ripe age of sixty-two to the young Theodora, who was to be allowed to remain a Christian.

It may be assumed that the six thousand soldiers lent to Cantacuzene returned to Asia. But the loan of them soon became a precedent for other transactions of the same kind. In 1349 the Serbians, under Stephen Dushan, were seriously threatening Salonika, and had ultimate designs on Constantinople itself. Orchan was again appealed to for aid by the two Emperors, his father-in-law and brother-in-law, and at their instance he sent twenty thousand soldiers into Europe for the relief of Salonika. With their aid Cantacuzene was able to defeat the Serbians, and to extinguish for ever their hope of replacing the Byzantine Empire at Constantinople. On this occasion, again, it appears that the Ottoman troops, having effected their purpose, returned to Asia. But four years later another opportunity befell Orchan of sending troops across the Straits, and this time of effecting a permanent lodgment in Europe. Cantacuzene, not satisfied with being only a co-Emperor with his son-in-law and the Empress Anna, attempted, in 1353, to usurp the supreme power in the State. His son-in-law, John Palæologus, now of full age, strongly opposed this. Civil war again broke out. For a third time Cantacuzene appealed to his son-in-law Orchan for aid. In return for the loan of twenty thousand soldiers he offered to hand over to the Ottomans a fortress on the European side of the Hellespont. Orchan agreed to this. The Ottoman soldiers were sent into Europe, under Solyman, and were employed by Cantacuzene in fighting against his other son-in-law, the co-Emperor John. They were successful in this, and occupied Demotika. Meanwhile the insignificant fortress of Tzympe was handed over to Orchan and was occupied by Ottoman troops with the full consent of Cantacuzene.

Shortly after this an earthquake occurred in the Thracian Chersonese—not an unfrequent event there. It did great damage to many cities, among others to Gallipoli, the most important fortress on the European side of the

Hellespont, and at no great distance from Tzympe. Its walls and ramparts were in great part tumbled down and destroyed, so that entrance to it was made easy. The Ottoman troops at the neighbouring Tzympe, under Solyman, when this opportunity was afforded to them of getting possession of such an important fortress, determined to avail themselves of it. The Greek garrison of Gallipoli, under the belief that the earthquake and the tumbling down of the walls indicated the Divine will, made no resistance, and the Ottomans established themselves there without opposition. Cantacuzene complained of this to Orchan as a gross breach of their treaty, and demanded that Gallipoli should be restored to him. He offered also to pay a fair price for Tzympe. Orchan, though willing enough to take money for Tzympe, refused point-blank to give up Gallipoli. "God," he said, "having manifested His will in my favour by causing the ramparts to fall, my troops have taken possession of the city, penetrated with thanks to Allah." It will be seen that Greeks and Turks took the same view of the Divine intervention, the one to excuse their failure to defend the fortress, the other to justify their seizure of it.

This action of Orchan roused great indignation at Constantinople. Cantacuzene now began to see how grave an error he had committed when inviting the Turks into Europe. Public opinion compelled him to declare war against Orchan. He appealed to the Czars of Serbia and Bulgaria to assist him in driving the Ottomans back to Asia. They flatly refused to do so. The Czar of Bulgaria replied: "Three years ago I remonstrated with you for your unholy alliance with the Turks. Now that the storm has burst, let the Byzantines weather it. If the Turks come against me we shall know how to defend ourselves"—a very unfortunate prediction as events ultimately proved! The whole course of history might have been altered if these two Balkan States had joined with the Byzantines in preventing this lodgment of the Turks in Europe. Want of union of the Christian Powers was then, as on many other later occasions, mainly responsible for the extension of the Ottoman Empire in that continent.

Cantacuzene was soon to reap the just reward for his treachery to his country. So far everything had gone well with him. He had ousted the Palæologi from the throne, of which, it must be admitted, they were quite unworthy. He had proclaimed his son Matthew as co-Emperor with himself. But when the full effect of his policy of inviting the Turks into Europe was understood there was a revulsion of feeling against him at Constantinople. The Greek Patriarch refused to crown Matthew. A revolution took place in the city. Cantacuzene found himself without friends. He was everywhere accused of having betrayed the Empire to the Turks. He was compelled to abdicate. He became a monk and retired to a monastery in Greece. He spent the remaining thirty years of his life in seclusion there, and in writing a history of his times, which, though very unreliable, tells enough of his own misdeeds to justify the conclusion that, by inviting the Ottomans into Europe, he proved to be a traitor to his country. The Empress Irene, his wife, became a nun.

John Palæologus was recalled by the people of Constantinople, and, after defeating Matthew, not without difficulty, was established there as sole Emperor. His reign lasted for fifty years, a period full of misfortune for the Empire. He was no more able to compel or induce the Turks to evacuate Europe and return to Asia than his father-in-law. The twenty thousand soldiers who had been invited to Europe by Cantacuzene remained there as enemies of the State they had come to assist. Under the command of Solyman, they advanced into Thrace and captured Tchorlu, within a few miles of Constantinople. Though the occupation of this city and of Demotika was only temporary, the Ottomans firmly established themselves in the southern part of Thrace. The Emperor John was eventually compelled to sign a treaty with Orchan, which recognized these Ottoman conquests in Thrace. Thenceforth the Byzantine Empire became subservient to, and almost the vassal of, the Ottoman Sultan. Solyman brought over from Asia many colonies of Turks and settled them in the Thracian Chersonese and other parts of Thrace.

In 1358 Solyman, who had shown great capacity when in command of the Ottoman army, met with his death by a fall from his horse when engaged in his favourite sport of falconry. His father, Orchan, died in the following year at the age of seventy-two. He had enormously increased the Ottoman dominions. He had achieved the first great object of his ambition, that of driving the Byzantines from their remaining possessions in Asia. He had rounded off his boundaries in the north-west corner of Anatolia by annexing Mysia. He had invaded Europe and had extended Ottoman rule over a part of Thrace. He had reduced the Byzantine Emperor almost to vassalage. These great results had been achieved not so much by force of arms as a general, for he is not credited with any great victory in the field, or by successful assaults on any great fortresses, as by crafty diplomacy and intrigue, backed up by superior force, and by taking advantage of the feebleness and treachery of the Byzantines. He also forged the military weapon by which his son, Murad, was able to effect far greater territorial conquests, both in Europe and Asia.

London: T. Fisher Unwin. Ltd.   *Stanford's Geog.¹ Estab.¹ London.*

SOUTH EASTERN EUROPE
AND ASIA MINOR
AT THE TIME OF THE ENTRY OF THE OTTOMANS INTO
EUROPE
1353.

III
MURAD I
1359-89

MURAD succeeded his father, Orchan, at the age of forty. He soon proved himself to be eminently qualified to rule by his untiring activity and vigour, his genius for war, and his wise and sane statesmanship. He was illiterate. He could not even sign his name. There is extant in the archives of the city of Ragusa a treaty with its petty republic, which Murad, in 1363, signed by dipping his hand in ink and impressing it with his finger marks. The 'tughra' thus formed became the official signature of subsequent Sultans of Turkey. Osman and Orchan between them created the Ottoman dynasty and State, but Murad must be credited with having founded the Empire in the sense of imposing Ottoman rule on subject races.

On Murad's accession his territory, though greatly increased by Orchan, was less in extent than some other Turkish Emirates in Anatolia. It consisted of an area on both sides of the Sea of Marmora, two hundred miles in length by about one hundred in depth. It included both shores of the Dardanelles, but only one side of the Bosphorus. Constantinople, on the other side, though nearly hemmed in by the Ottomans, was nominally independent, and its communications with the Greek province of Thrace were still open. Deducting the area of the Sea of Marmora, the territory under Murad's rule was not of greater area than twenty thousand square miles. Its population probably did not amount to a million in number. It is difficult to understand how Murad from this small territory so enormously increased his Empire in Europe. It may be surmised that large numbers of Turks from other parts of Anatolia flocked to his standard in search of adventure and booty in Europe.

The ownership of both sides of the Dardanelles did not, in the days before the invention of gunpowder, give command of the Straits, and as Murad was without a navy, the passage of his armies between Asia and Europe was at the mercy of any naval Power. The Genoese, who had important commercial settlements on the shores of the Black Sea and on the Bosphorus at Galata, and who maintained a large naval force in the Ægean Sea, might easily have barred the way of the Ottomans to Europe, but they hated the Greeks and were greedy of money, and they could be relied on to convey Murad's armies across the Straits for a full consideration. It will be seen that Murad, during his reign of thirty years, increased by more than fivefold the Ottoman possessions, and at one point brought them up to the Danube. He compelled other States also, including the Greek Empire itself, to accept the position of tributaries to his Empire. His fame in Ottoman history must be regarded as on a level with that of Mahomet, the Conqueror of Constantinople, and of Solyman the Magnificent, who raised the Empire to its zenith.

Murad's great extensions of his Empire may more conveniently, than in a chronological order, be treated under three distinct heads:—

1. His conquest of the possessions of the Greek Empire in Thrace and Bulgaria and the reduction of that decadent Empire to the humiliating position of vassalage. 2. His great conquests in Bulgaria, Macedonia, and Serbia. 3. His extensions in Anatolia by the absorption of Turkish Emirates or parts of them.

1. THE CONQUESTS IN THRACE.

The Greek Empire, under John Palæologus V, the most unfortunate and incompetent of men, on the accession of Murad, was in a perilous and decadent condition. We have already shown how small were its remaining possessions in Europe. It had no friends on whom it could rely to stem the advance of the Moslems. The old spirit of the early Crusaders in Europe was almost extinct. There was a bitter feud between the Latin and Greek Churches. They hated one another more than they feared the Turks. It was a condition of any assistance of the Latin Christians that the Greeks should come into the fold of the Pope of Rome. The Greeks, on their part, flatly refused this, even for the purpose of saving their Empire from extinction by the Moslem Turks.

It was under these conditions that Murad, in the first year of his reign, determined to follow up the designs of his father by conquests in Europe. Leaving Brusa, the then capital of his State, he crossed the Dardanelles, and at the head of a great army marched into Thrace. His generals, Evrenos and Lalashahin, commanded the two wings of it. Evrenos advanced on the left, recaptured the fortress of Tchorlu, five miles from Constantinople, massacred its garrison, and razed its walls. Lalashahin, on the right, captured Kirk Kilisse, and thus protected the army from a possible landing of the enemy from the Black Sea. Murad then advanced with the centre of his army, formed a junction with the two wings, and fought a great battle at Eski Baba, in 1363, in which he completely defeated the Byzantine army opposed to him, with the result that Adrianople surrendered without a struggle and almost the whole of Thrace fell into Murad's hands. Lalashahin then advanced up the Maritza Valley into Bulgaria and captured Philippopolis, a Byzantine possession south of the Balkans.

As a result of this successful invasion the Greek Emperor found himself compelled to enter into a treaty with Murad, by which he bound himself to refrain from any attempt to recover what he had lost in Thrace, to abstain from giving aid to the Serbians and Bulgarians in resisting a further advance of the Ottomans in Europe, and to support Murad against his Anatolian enemies, the Turkish Emirs. Murad thereupon returned to Brusa to cogitate over new enterprises and to organize his forces. He was soon recalled to Europe by most serious events. The Christian Powers had shown no disposition to help the Greeks against the Ottoman invasion, while their possessions in Asia and Europe were being invaded, but the advance into Bulgaria seems to have caused alarm to them. Pope Urban V stirred up Louis, the King of Hungary, and the Princes of Serbia, Bosnia, and Wallachia to resist. They combined together and sent an army of twenty thousand men into Thrace, with the avowed object of driving the Turks out of Europe. Murad hastened to confront them, but before he could arrive on the scene of action his general, Lalashahin, led an army against the allies. The two armies met on the River Maritza, not far from Adrianople, in 1363. Ilbeki, in command of the Ottomans, made a sudden night attack, when the Christian troops were heavy with sleep after a festive revel. A stampede took place. The Turkish historian says of the allied army: "They were caught even as wild beasts in their lair. They were driven as flames are driven before the wind, till, plunging into the Maritza, they perished in its waters."

The Christian army was practically exterminated. The King of Hungary escaped by a miracle. It was the first conflict of the Ottomans with the Hungarians, who were destined to bar the way into Europe for a hundred and fifty years. As a result of this battle all the country south of the Balkan Mountains was incorporated in the Ottoman Empire. Ilbeki, who devised the night attack, and so successfully carried it out, was made away with by poison, at the instance of Lalashahin, who was madly jealous of his great victory.

The battle of the Maritza was a crushing blow to the Christians. One result of it was that Murad decided in favour of a scheme of conquest in Europe rather than in Asia. In this view he transferred the seat of his government from Brusa to Thrace, and made Demotika the capital of his Empire. Three years later he transferred it to Adrianople, which for ninety years, till after the capture of Constantinople, held this position, and from thence he organized his great invasion of the Balkan States. Another result was that the Greek Emperor, John Palæologus V, was forced into a further step towards subjection to the Ottomans. He agreed to become a tributary to the Sultan and to send a contingent to the Ottoman army in future wars.

After a time the Emperor fretted under this position of vassalage, and in 1369 he went on a mission to Rome, in the hope of inducing the Pope to stir up the Christian Powers of Europe to another crusade against the Ottomans. He left his eldest son, Andronicus, in charge of the government at Constantinople during his absence. Arriving at Rome, he submitted to the most humiliating conditions with the object of gaining the support of the

Pope Urban V. He abjured at St. Peter's, before the High Altar, the principles of the Greek Church, so far as they differed from those of Rome. He admitted the ecclesiastical supremacy of the Pope. He was then permitted to bend his knee, and to kiss the Pope's feet and hands. He was privileged also to lead the Pope's mule by the bridle. He obtained, however, no return for these abject humiliations. The Pope was unable to induce the Christian Powers again to take up arms against the Ottomans.

The Emperor's concessions to the Pope were also disavowed by the Hierarchs of the Greek Church at Constantinople. There never was any prospect of a reunion of the two Churches. The Emperor, John Palæologus, embarked on his homeward journey having nothing to show for his pains. On his way back, when passing through Venice, he was arrested, at the instance of his Venetian creditors, who had lent him money to defray the cost of his mission. Not having the means to pay, he could not discharge the legal process. Andronicus had no wish that his father should ever return to Constantinople. He made no effort to raise money for the release of the Emperor. He pleaded the poverty of the Treasury. A younger son, Manuel, however, with more filial piety, raised the necessary sum, by selling all his property, and obtained the release of his father. Shortly after his return to Constantinople the Emperor, as was to be expected, deprived Andronicus of all his appointments, and replaced him by Manuel, whom he also made co-Emperor with himself.

The son of Andronicus, of the same name, furious at this treatment of his father, entered into a mad conspiracy with Saoudji, the youngest son of Sultan Murad, with the object of dethroning both Emperor and Sultan and reigning in their place. Saoudji, being in command of the Sultan's army in Europe, during the absence of Murad in Asia, was able to tamper with the loyalty of the Ottoman troops. He assembled a considerable force in the neighbourhood of Constantinople, where he was joined by a large number of the sons of Greek nobles and by many soldiers.

Murad, when he heard, at Brusa, of this mad outbreak, returned with all haste to Europe, and organized resistance to it, in concert with the Greek Emperor. They agreed that the two rebels, when captured, should be deprived of their eyesight. Murad thereupon, taking what soldiers he could get together, marched to meet Saoudji's army. When within hearing of it, he called out to the soldiers by night, urging them to return to their duty and promising pardon to them. The soldiers, hearing the voice of the Sultan, who had so often led them to victory, repented of their treachery and deserted the cause which they had so foolishly taken up. Saoudji and Andronicus and the band of Greek nobles, thus deserted by the rank and file of the army, took refuge in the fortress of Demotika. Murad had no difficulty in capturing this place, and with it the two rebel princes and the Greek nobles. In pursuance of his agreement with the Emperor, he then deprived his own son of his eyesight and, going beyond his promise, had the young man executed. He caused the Greek nobles to be bound, two and three together, and thrown into the Maritza, while he stood on the bank and revelled in the sight of their drowning struggles. In some cases he insisted on parents themselves putting their sons to death in his presence. When they refused, the parents were drowned in the river together with their sons. In this instance Murad showed that he had in him the vein of cruelty which was conspicuous, more or less, in all the descendants of Othman. Andronicus was handed over to the Greek Emperor, who partially, but not completely, carried out his promise of depriving his grandson of eyesight.

As a result of these events, the Emperor John Palæologus found himself compelled to enter into another treaty with Murad, by which, in order "that he might enjoy up to the end of his life in peace his last possession," he recognized himself as vassal of the Sultan, promised to do military service in the Ottoman army, and gave his son Manuel in charge of Murad as a hostage.

2. THE CONQUESTS IN MACEDONIA, BULGARIA, AND SERBIA.

The conquest of Thrace by the Ottomans and the defeat of the allied Christians at the Maritza were as great blows to the Bulgarians as to the Greek Empire, though they had given no assistance to the allies. The occupation of Adrianople and Philippopolis opened the way to a further advance into Bulgaria and Macedonia. It was not, however, till 1366 that Murad availed himself of this advantage, and commenced the series of attacks which ultimately made him master of Macedonia and of a great part of Bulgaria and Serbia. The position of affairs in the peninsula at this time was very favourable to him. The Bulgarians, Serbians, Bosnians, and Greeks were madly jealous of one another; each of them preferred the extension of the Ottoman rule to that of their rivals. Bulgaria alone, if united, might have successfully resisted Murad. But in 1365 its Czar, Alexander, died, and his kingdom was divided between his three sons. Sisman, the elder, got the largest share. The other two gave no assistance to their brother when the Ottomans invaded his country. Between 1366 and 1369, Murad advanced into Bulgaria, and took possession of the Maritza Valley, as far as the Rhodope Mountains. In 1371 Lalashahin encountered an army of Bulgarians and Serbians at Samakof, not far from the city of Sofia, and completely defeated it, with the result that Bulgaria, up to the Balkan range, was annexed to the Ottoman Empire. It remained so for over five hundred years, till its release in our own times.

After this great victory at Samakof, Lalashahin was instructed by Murad not to pursue his conquest of Bulgaria north of the Balkan range, but to proceed westward, and, in concert with Evrenos, to invade Macedonia as far as the

River Vardar. This occupied the two generals in the years 1371-2. Kavalla, Druma, and Serres fell into their hands. In 1372 they crossed the Vardar River and penetrated into Old Serbia, Albania, and Bosnia. The main part of Serbia, however, remained in the hands of Lazar, its prince. But he was compelled to acknowledge the suzerainty of the Sultan. As regards the part of Bulgaria not annexed, its prince, Sisman, was allowed to retain his independence. His daughter entered the harem of Murad, with the understanding that she was not to be compelled to adopt the Moslem religion. It was not till 1381 that a further advance was made by Murad. He then sent his armies across the Vardar River and captured Monastir. He also took possession of Sofia, and in 1386 of Nisch, after a fierce struggle with the Serbians.

3. MURAD'S ACQUISITIONS IN ASIA MINOR.

Between the years 1376 and 1380 Murad found himself able to turn his attention in the direction of Asia Minor. In the first of these years he induced the Emir of Kermia, doubtless by threats of war, to give a daughter in marriage to Bayezid, his eldest son. She brought with her as dowry a considerable part of Kermia and the fortress of Kutayia, a position of great strategic importance. In 1377 he followed this up by inducing the Emir of Hamid to sell a great portion of his Emirate lying between Tekke, Kermia, and Karamania, including the district of Ak-Sheir. The effect of this acquisition was to make his frontier conterminous with that of Karamania. Again, in 1378, he declared war against the Emir of Tekke, and annexed a part of his territory, leaving to him Adalia.

Murad made no further effort to extend his dominion in Asia till 1387, when he led a large army against Alaeddin, the Emir of Karamania. For this purpose he called upon the Greek Emperor and the Princes of Serbia and Bulgaria as vassals of the Empire to send their contingents. His two sons, Bayezid and Yacoub, commanded the wings of this army. With a view to conciliate the peasantry of the district he passed through, and to ensure full supplies of food to his army, he gave strict orders that there was to be no pillage, and that the lives and property of the country people were to be respected. Among his troops were two thousand Serbians, whom the Prince of Serbia was bound by his recent treaty to supply. These men refused to obey Murad's order, and committed atrocious depredations on the route of the army. Murad inflicted severe punishment on them, and directed many of them to be put to death as a warning to the others. The army then marched to meet the Karamanians. A battle again took place on the plain of Angora. Bayezid especially distinguished himself by the fierceness of his cavalry charges and earned for himself the sobriquet of 'the Thunderbolt.'

There are different versions as to the issue of this battle. Some historians describe it as a great victory for Murad, and claim that he treated the vanquished Emir of Karamania with great generosity, insisting only on a token of submission. Murad, however, was not in the habit of neglecting to take full advantage of any successes of his armies. It is very certain that, in this case, he did not succeed in extending his Empire. Karamania retained its independence for many years to come, and did not even submit to a nominal vassalage. It seems more probable, therefore, that this battle was indecisive, and that Murad withdrew, without having effected his purpose.

Murad, who was now near the age of seventy, would have been glad to end his life in repose, but he was recalled to Europe by an outbreak of the Serbians. It appeared that the Serbian soldiers, on their return to their homes, after the campaign against the Karamanians, told the story of the execution of their comrades by order of Murad. It caused universal indignation among the Serbians. They could not understand a war conducted without the levy of booty from the enemy's country. The whole of Serbia rose in rebellion. An alliance was formed with Bulgaria, Bosnia, and Albania. Assistance was obtained from Hungary and Wallachia. Murad again took the field in command of an Ottoman army, and, crossing the Balkans, captured Schumla and Tirnova, and then marched towards the Danube. Sisman, the King of Bulgaria, shut himself up in Nicopolis, on the Danube, but was soon compelled to come to terms. He agreed to give up Silistria to the Turks, and to pay a tribute in the future.

Lazar, the King of Serbia, in spite of this defection, continued the struggle against the Ottomans, and Sisman himself broke the treaty almost before the ink was dry. He refused to give up Silistria, and sent a contingent in aid of the Serbians. Murad sent part of his army, under Ali Pasha, against Sisman, who was again shut up in Nicopolis. This fortress was captured. Murad was again generous in sparing Sisman's life, but this time he deprived the southern part of Bulgaria of its autonomy, and insisted on its being completely incorporated in the Turkish Empire.

Lazar, the King of Serbia, continued the war. Murad, in spite of his seventy years, led his army, supported, as in Asia Minor, by his two sons. The decisive battle took place on the plain of Kossova, at the point of junction between Serbia and Bulgaria. It was fiercely contested. At a critical point of it a Serbian noble, Milosch Kobilowitch, who on the previous day had been falsely charged in the Serbian camp with disaffection and treason, gave signal proof of his patriotism by riding boldly into the Turkish lines, as though he was a deserter, and claiming that he had a most important message to deliver to the Sultan. He was allowed to approach Murad, and, while kneeling before him, plunged a dagger into his heart, causing a mortal wound. Milosch then made a desperate rush to escape, but in vain. He was captured and brought to the

Sultan's tent. Meanwhile Murad, in spite of his approaching death, was able to give orders for the charge of his reserves, which decided the battle in favour of the Ottomans. The Serbians and their allies were completely defeated and routed. Lazar was taken prisoner and was brought to the Sultan's tent. Murad lived long enough to direct the execution in his presence of Lazar and Milosch. He then expired.

To complete the tragedy of the day, Bayezid, on hearing of the death of his father, and his own consequent accession to the throne, gave immediate orders for the murder of his brother Yacoub, who had been his valiant companion in arms in so many battles. This was effected in the presence of the dead body of the father. The brutal deed was justified by a verse from the Koran, "Rebellion is worse than execution." It was assumed by Bayezid that his brother would claim the throne against him. This was the first recorded case of fratricide in the Othman royal race. Thenceforth it became the settled practice for a Sultan of Turkey, on his accession to the throne, immediately to put to death his brothers and other collaterals, lest they should dispute the succession with him. By the law of succession the eldest living male of the reigning family, and not the eldest son of a defunct Sultan, was entitled to the throne. This supplied an additional motive for the practice of fratricide, for the new Sultan, by murdering his brothers and uncles, ensured the succession, after his own death, to his eldest son free from competition. In later times, however, when public opinion would no longer justify fratricide, and when the law of succession of the oldest male in the family was more fully recognized, the Sultan, on his accession to the throne, directed the close confinement of his next heir, generally his brother. It followed from this practice that the heir to the throne, instead of being employed on State affairs, or as a general, and gaining experience, was treated as a prisoner, and was forbidden to take any part in public affairs. It will be seen that this practice of forced seclusion of the heir to the throne during the lifetime of the reigning Sultan was one of the main causes of the degeneracy of the Othman dynasty.

Reverting to Murad, it has been shown how important an epoch his reign was in the growth of the Ottoman Empire. During the twenty-four years of war, in which he led his armies in the field, he never met with a reverse. He extended the Empire for the first time into vast territories inhabited not by Turks or by Byzantines, but by sturdy Christian races, such as the Bulgarians, Serbians, and Bosnians. For the first time also the Turks came into conflict with the Hungarians, and defeated them. The influence of the Empire was extended practically to the Danube. Some of the intervening territory was not treated as conquered country and added to the Empire, but was allowed to retain the position of tributary or vassal States, as in the case of Serbia.

Other parts, such as Thrace, Macedonia, and Bulgaria, were fully incorporated in the dominion of the Sultan.

Murad, when not engaged in war, devoted himself to perfecting the organization of his army on the lines laid down by his father, Orchan. He also created a new standing corps of soldiers, recruited from the Christian population of the provinces conquered in Europe. This was the renowned corps of Janissaries—the new army. Von Hammer and other historians following him, and more recently Sir Edwin Pears, give very full details as to the constitution of this corps and the motives of its founder. They state that one thousand lads, between the ages of ten and twelve, were in every year conscripted from amongst the children of Christian parents. The most physically strong and intelligent of them were taken. They were forcibly converted to Islam, and were trained with great care for military careers under the immediate direction of the Sultan. After six years of training they were drafted into a special corps, which reached, after a few years, a maximum of twelve thousand men. The discipline of this corps was very severe. It formed the most efficient and reliable body in the Ottoman army. The men looked on their regiment as their home. Their lives were devoted to it. They were not allowed to own property. What they acquired belonged to the regiment. They were not, till a later period in the history of the Empire, allowed to marry. They formed the backbone of the Ottoman armies in war; and in many a hard-fought battle, when disaster and defeat were imminent, they saved the army by their intrepid and persistent stand against the enemy. The object which Murad aimed at is said to have been not merely the strengthening of his army by a standing force of this kind, but that it should, by its personal devotion to the Sultan, act as a check on his other turbulent forces.[5]

Sir Edwin Pears says of this force:—

Take a number of children from the most intelligent portion of the community; choose them for their strength and intelligence; instruct them carefully in the art of fighting; bring them up under strict military discipline; teach them to forget their childhood, their parents, and friends; saturate them with the knowledge that all their hope in life depends upon their position in the regiment; make peace irksome and war a delight, with the hope of promotion and relaxation from the hardship and restraints of the barracks; the result will be a weapon in the hands of a leader such as the world has rarely seen. Such a weapon was the army of the Janissaries.[6]

The levy of children was regarded by the Christians as a blood tax of a terrible kind. The corps thus formed was a most valuable instrument in the hands of Sultans who were strong enough to control it. But later, in the times of degenerate Sultans, it became a kind of Prætorian Guard. It dictated the deposition of Sultans and the nomination of their successors. It often insisted on a policy of war. In 1648, under Mahomet IV, the restriction of the force to Christian children was removed, and the sons of Janissaries and other Moslems were admitted. Later the levy of Christian children was abandoned, and none but sons of Moslems were admitted to the corps. After the time of Solyman its numbers were greatly increased. It became a danger to the State. It will be seen that in 1826 Mahmoud II took vengeance on it for the humiliations he and previous Sultans had undergone, and extinguished it in ruthless scenes of blood.

There cannot be a doubt, however, that Murad, by creating this corps of Janissaries and recruiting it from the Christian population in Europe, forged a weapon which for two hundred years to come played a dominant part in the aggrandizement of the Ottoman Empire.

Knolles, in his graphic history of the Turkish Empire, sums up the character of Murad in the following sentences, which could not be improved upon:—

Murad was more zealous than any other of the Turkish kings; a man of great courage and in all his attempts fortunate; he made greater slaughter of his enemies than both his father and grandfather; his kingdom in Asia he greatly enlarged by the sword, marriage, and purchase; and using the discord and cowardice of the Grecian princes to his profit, subdued a great part of Thracia, with the territories adjoining thereto, leaving unto the Emperor of Constantinople little or nothing more in Thracia than the imperial city itself, with the bare name of an emperor almost without an empire; he won a great part of Bulgaria and entered into Serbia, Bosnia, and Macedonia; he was liberal and withal severe; of his subjects both beloved and feared; a man of very few words, and one that could dissemble deeply.[7]

IV

BAYEZID I
1389-1403

BAYEZID succeeded his father, Murad, at the age of thirty-four. He reigned as Sultan for only fourteen years, the last of which was spent in captivity. No one of the Othman race passed through such vicissitudes, with such a brilliant career of victory during nearly the whole of his reign, but ending with overwhelming and crushing defeat. He had all the courage and military capacity of his three predecessors. He excelled them greatly in cruelty and brutality. In his private life he descended to depths of sensuality and unmentionable and degrading vice which were unknown to them.

Early in his reign he adopted a much bolder attitude toward the Christian Powers of Europe than Murad had thought prudent. To a deputation from Italy asking for a renewal of commercial privileges, he replied that when he had conquered Hungary he intended to ride to Rome, and there give feed to his horse with oats on the altar of St. Peter's. His treatment of his Christian subjects was much harsher than that of his predecessors.

Bayezid followed up his father's great victory at Kossova over the Serbians, and compelled Stephen, the successor of Lazar, to sue for peace. The terms of the treaty then agreed to were very moderate. Instead of being incorporated in the Ottoman Empire as Bulgaria had been, Serbia was to be an autonomous State, under vassalage to the Ottoman Empire, paying tribute in money, and bound to provide and maintain a contingent of five thousand soldiers at the disposal of the Sultan. Stephen, its prince, also gave his sister, Despina, to the Sultan as an additional wife. He most loyally carried out his promises to Bayezid. In the great battles of Nicopolis against the Hungarians and the crusaders from Western Europe, and of Angora against Timur, the Serbian contingent fought with the utmost bravery, and there were no more loyal soldiers in the Ottoman ranks.

Having come to terms with Serbia, Bayezid marched southwards with his army, and took up a menacing position near to Constantinople, where the aged and feeble John Palæologus still reigned, supported by his son Manuel as co-Emperor. By threatening to promote the cause of Andronicus, whose eyesight had not been quite extinguished, after his mad rebellion against the Emperor, the Sultan compelled the two Emperors to sign a treaty, under which the remnant of the Greek Empire became an abject vassal State to that of the Ottomans. The Emperors promised to pay an annual tribute of thirty thousand pieces of gold and to supply a contingent of twelve thousand men to the Ottoman army to be at the disposal of the Sultan for any purpose he might design. They also undertook to surrender to the Ottomans the stronghold of Philadelphia, the only remaining possession of the Byzantine Empire in Asia Minor. When the officer in command of that city refused to surrender it, Bayezid insisted on the Greek Emperor employing his contingent in capturing his own city, and on his leading the assault on it, with the aid of his son Manuel, for the purpose of handing it over to himself, their nominal ally, but crafty and designing foe. It would be difficult to imagine a lower depth of humiliation and cowardice than that to which the Emperor and his son thus descended. These public humiliations were aggravated by a domestic one. Bayezid, having captured at sea a vessel bringing a foreign princess as a bride for Manuel, took a great fancy for the lady, and insisted on her entering his own harem.

Bayezid next turned his attention to Asia Minor, where he was mainly ambitious to add to his Empire. His first effort there was directed against Aidin. After defeating its Emir and annexing the State, he dealt in the same way with the Emirs of Sarukhan and Mentsche. He then made an attack on the city of Smyrna, at that time in possession of the Knights of St. John of Jerusalem. The Knights made a vigorous resistance, and Bayezid, not having command of the sea, was compelled, after six weeks, to withdraw from the siege. He next, in 1391, attacked the Emir of Tekke, and took from him what had been left under his rule by Murad, including the important city of Adalia. The Ottoman frontier was now conterminous with that of Karamania, whose Emir, Alaeddin, was brother-in-law to the Sultan. This family connection was no protection to him. Bayezid invaded and laid siege to Konia. He withdrew on Alaeddin agreeing to give up a slice of his Emirate, including the city of Ak-Sheir.

Having achieved these annexations, for which there was no justification other than mere greed for the extension of his Empire, Bayezid returned to Adrianople, leaving his general, Timurtash, in command of the conquered provinces. The Greek Emperor John, meanwhile, had been engaged in putting his capital into a state of defence, and for this purpose had demolished three of the most beautiful churches of Constantinople, intending to use their masonry for the erection of new forts. The Sultan, when he heard of this, sent word to the Emperors ordering them to desist from any such work, and threatening to deprive Manuel of his eyesight. The Emperor had no alternative but to obey. But this humiliation was the last he had to endure. He died very shortly afterwards, under the weight of his cares and anxieties, as some historians say, but according to others of gout and debauchery. His son, Manuel, who was detained at the Court of the Sultan, acting as a kind of Groom of the Chamber, on hearing of his father's death, secretly fled and reached Constantinople, where he was installed as the successor to his father. Bayezid by way of reprisal for this directed a blockade by land of Constantinople. There commenced what was virtually a siege by land of the city, which lasted for seven years, till the invasion of Asia Minor by Timur caused a diversion and brought it to an end.

Leaving a part of his forces to conduct this blockade, and with instructions to harass the Greek garrison by day and night, Bayezid, with the larger part of his army, marched through Bulgaria, and compelled the Prince of Wallachia to submit as a vassal of the Ottoman Empire. A part of his army then penetrated into Syrmia and engaged in war with the Hungarians. It was defeated and driven back, and Sigismund, the Hungarian King, was able to make a counter-attack, and to capture the important stronghold of Nicopolis. He, in turn, was forced to abandon the city, mainly by the assistance given to Bayezid by the Wallachians. It was during his retreat through the Duchy of Hunyadi that Sigismund met and became enamoured with Elizabeth Moronay. The offspring of this liaison was the celebrated Hungarian hero Hunyadi the Great, who later took such an active part against the Turks.

In 1393, Bayezid sent an army, under command of his eldest son, Solyman, to invade the northern part of Bulgaria, which still enjoyed an autonomous existence. Tirnova, its capital, was taken by storm after a siege of three weeks. Its inhabitants were sent into Asia Minor as slaves. He then decided to incorporate the northern part of Bulgaria in the Ottoman Empire in the same manner as the southern part had already been treated. This completed the servitude of the Bulgarian people. Sisman, their prince, disappeared from the scene, and the ruling family became extinct. The land was confiscated, except in a few cases where the owners were allowed to become Moslems. It was parcelled out to Turks under a feudal system involving military service, while the cultivators of the soil were reduced to serfdom.

About this time the fortresses of Nicopolis, Widdin, and Silistria fell into the hands of the Ottomans and opened the way into Hungary. Bayezid commenced a system of raids into that country, not for the purpose, at that time, of acquiring its territory, but for plunder. His Turkish 'akinjis,' or irregulars, spread terror over wide districts, burning and destroying villages and carrying off their inhabitants for sale as slaves. He fitted out ships also with the same object in the newly acquired ports in Asia Minor, and ravaged the islands of Chios and Negropont and districts on the coast of Greece.

Bayezid was now compelled by an outbreak in his recent acquisitions in Asia Minor, fomented by the Emir of Karamania, to suspend operations on his northern frontier in Europe and to transfer his army to Asia. He received at Brusa an envoy from his brother-in-law, Alaeddin of Karamania, suing for peace. Bayezid replied that the sword alone could determine the issue between them. He sent an army at once, under Timurtash, against the Karamanians. It encountered Alaeddin on the plain of Ak-Tchai. The

Turkish army was completely successful. Alaeddin and his two sons were captured, and without waiting for authority from Bayezid, Timurtash had them hanged. When Bayezid heard of this treatment of his brother-in-law, he affected to be greatly distressed and incensed, but he soon consoled himself by a text from the Koran, "The death of a prince is less regrettable than the loss of a province," and he gave practical application of the verse by orders to his army to occupy and annex the whole of Karamania. There was no resistance. Konia and other cities in the eastern part of the State were taken. In spite of this, however, Karamania was not at this time finally incorporated in the Ottoman Empire. After the invasion of Asia Minor by Timur it recovered its independence, and it was not till seventy years later that it was finally subjected and incorporated.

About the same time, 1393-4, Bayezid made further important conquests in Asia Minor—namely, Samsun, Cæsarea, and Sivas, the last of the most important fortresses on the frontier of Armenia. These great successes both in Europe and Asia were followed by a period of repose, during which Bayezid gave himself up to a life of gross debauchery. He was recalled from this by threats of war on the part of Sigismund, King of Hungary, and he soon showed that he had lost none of his vigour and dash.

Sigismund had fretted under the constant raids on his kingdom, above referred to, and had for some time past been contemplating war against the Ottomans for the recovery of the fortresses on the Danube, which were so great a menace to him. For this purpose he appealed, in 1395, to the Christian Powers of Europe for assistance. He was backed up by Pope Boniface IX, who preached another crusade against the infidels. Through the efforts of the King of France, Charles VI, a large number of leading nobles of France were induced to band together, under the Comte de Nevers, son of the Duke of Burgundy, a young man of twenty-two years, without any military experience. A thousand horsemen, chevaliers of good birth and position, and six thousand attendants and mercenaries were enrolled in France for this adventure. Others came from England and Scotland, and from Flanders, Lombardy, and Savoy. On their march through Germany to Hungary they were joined by great numbers of German knights, under Count Frederick of Hohenzollern, the Grand Prior of the Teutonic Order, and by a large force of Bavarians, under the Elector Palatine. Later they were reinforced by a number of the Knights of St. John of Jerusalem, under the command of de Naillac, their Grand Master. When joined by the Hungarian army, under Sigismund, and by the contingents from Wallachia and Bosnia, they made up a total force of about sixty thousand men. The expedition was in the nature of a crusade, but was more secular than religious in its aims and methods, and was regarded, it seems, by most of those engaged in it rather as a kind of picnic than as a serious campaign. The composite force collected together at

- 35 -

Buda, in Hungary, in the summer of 1396, and thence marched down the Danube to Nicopolis, capturing Widdin and Sistova on the way. When passing through Serbia they ravaged wide districts inhabited by innocent Christians, and emulated, if they did not exceed, the Ottomans in cruel devastation, as though they were in an enemy's country. They established their camp before Nicopolis in September, but for sixteen days they refrained from assaulting the fortress, which was bravely defended by an Ottoman garrison, thus giving time to Bayezid to collect his army and to advance against the allied forces.

The Christian camp was the scene of riotous living and gambling. Large numbers of courtesans had accompanied the crusaders. The whole army was in a state of indiscipline and disorder. The French knights were boastful. They spoke with contempt of the Turkish troops, and could not believe that there was any danger from them. Bayezid, whose army was full of confidence in its superiority, was allowed to approach within striking distance, without any attempt to harass his advance. Even then the Christians did not believe there was danger. The Turks suddenly came into contact with them. The knights were compelled to abandon their gaming tables and their women, and to face the enemy whom they had so much despised.

The Ottoman army was preceded by large numbers of scouts and irregulars. The leaders of the chevaliers, knowing nothing of the numbers of the Ottomans or of their methods in war, and utterly despising them, most rashly proposed an immediate attack by the whole force of their splendid cavalry. The King of Hungary, who had had experience of the Ottomans and who knew their method of masking the main body of their army by irregulars, was more cautious, and advised that the foot soldiers of Hungary and Wallachia should be first employed to meet the attack of the Turkish irregulars, and that the cavalry should be reserved to meet the main body of the Ottomans. The chevaliers were furious at this suggestion. They suspected Sigismund of playing for his own hand, and of wishing to rob them of the glory of a great victory. They insisted on an immediate attack. Sigismund, on hearing of this decision, said, "We shall lose the day through the great pride and folly of these French." And so it turned out.

The chevaliers advanced in splendid array and had no difficulty in dispersing and slaughtering the mob of Turkish irregulars. But this impetuous charge spent their energy and tired their horses. When they were confronted by the main body of the Ottomans, sixty thousand in number, they were powerless to resist. They were surrounded and were compelled to surrender. The main body of Hungarian foot soldiers, when they came in contact with the Ottomans, were not more fortunate. The Wallachians, who formed one of the wings of the army, when they saw how the battle was going, retired from the field without a fight. The centre of the Hungarian army, under Sigismund, supported by the Bavarians, made a most gallant fight, and might have been successful if it had not been that the Serbian army, under Prince Stephen, came at a critical time, in support of the Ottomans, and turned the scale in their favour. After a battle of only three hours the Christian allies were completely defeated with great slaughter on both sides. Ten thousand of the Christians, including most of the surviving chevaliers, were taken prisoners. Those who escaped across the Danube suffered terribly in their retreat through Wallachia. They were beaten and maltreated by the peasantry, for whom they had shown no consideration in their advance.

Sigismund and the Grand Prior of Rhodes, at a late stage of the battle, abandoned the army to its fate. They escaped in a small boat down the Danube, and were taken on board by a Venetian vessel, which conveyed them to Germany through the Black Sea, the Dardanelles, and the Adriatic. On passing the Straits the Turks paraded before their eyes the knights made captives at Nicopolis. One of these prisoners thus described what took place:—

The Osmanlis took us out of the towers of Gallipoli and led us to the sea, and one after the other they abused the King of Hungary as he passed, and mocked him and called to him to come out of the boat and deliver his people; and this they did to make fun of him, and skirmished a long time with each other on the sea. But they did not do him any harm, and so he went away.[8]

On the morning of the battle of Nicopolis, Bayezid, when told of the heavy losses of his own army, and that in the early part of the battle the chevaliers had massacred a number of Turks who had surrendered on promise of life, was greatly incensed. He gave orders that all the Christian prisoners to the number of ten thousand were to be put to death in his presence. He made an exception only in favour of twenty-four of the knights, including de Nevers, their leader, for whose release a heavy ransom might be expected. But they were compelled to witness the execution of their comrades in arms.

On taking leave of them a year later at Brusa, Bayezid addressed de Nevers in these proud and insolent terms:—

John, I know thee well, and am informed that you are in your own country a great lord. You are young, and in the future I hope you will be able to recover with your courage from the shame of the misfortune which has come to you in your foul knightly enterprise, and that in the desire of getting rid of the reproach and recovering your honour you will assemble your power to come against me and give me battle. If I were afraid of that and wanted to, before your release, I would make you swear upon your oath and religion that you would never bear arms against me, nor those who are in your company here. But no; neither upon you nor any other of those here will I impose this oath, because I desire, when you have returned to your home, and will have leisure, that you assemble your power and come against me. You will find me always ready to meet you and your people on the field of battle. And what I say to you, you can say in like manner to those to whom you will have the pleasure of speaking about it, because for this purpose was I born, to carry arms and always to conquer what is ahead of me.[9]

Before their final departure, Bayezid treated these knights to a day's sport on a regal scale; seven thousand falconers were employed on the occasion, and five thousand men led dogs to pick up the game. The historian does not state what was the bag resulting from this great battle.

Of the twenty-four knights only one, Marshal Boucicaut, took up the parting challenge of Bayezid and returned to the East to make war against him. The others showed no desire to wipe out the disgrace of their defeat.[10]

After this great battle at Nicopolis the Ottoman army made irruptions into Wallachia, Styria, and Hungary. The city of Peterwardein was captured and eighteen thousand of its inhabitants were sold into slavery. Another division invaded Syrmia, and devastated the country between the Drave and the Danube. The fortresses on the river taken by the crusaders were recaptured. The raid into Wallachia was a failure. The Turks engaged in it were defeated and driven back. Bayezid himself threatened Buda, in Hungary, but his progress was checked by a long and painful fit of gout. Gibbon moralizes on this in the following sentence: "The disorders of the moral are sometimes corrected by those of the physical world; and an acrimonious humour falling on a single fibre of one man may prevent or suspend the misery of nations."[11] The invasion of Hungary on this occasion was a failure.

After this campaign Bayezid returned to Adrianople, and there occupied himself by inflicting further humiliations on the Greek Empire. He forced Manuel to resign and imposed John, the son of Andronicus, as its Emperor. He then issued forth again with his army, in 1397, and fell like a thunderbolt on Greece, without any warning or cause of complaint. He marched with his army through Thessaly, capturing on the way Larissa and Pharsalia. He passed through Thermopylæ. The mere passage of his army sufficed to subdue Doris and Locris. His two generals, Yacoub and Evrenos, then invaded the Peloponnesus. The latter captured and pillaged Argos. Its inhabitants, to the number of thirty thousand, were sold as slaves and deported to Asia. Colonies of Turks were planted in the Morea. Theodore Palæologus, who acted as despot there on behalf of the Greek Empire, agreed to become tributary of the Sultan.

Returning to Adrianople, Bayezid determined to obtain immediate possession of Constantinople. The Greek Empire had been already deprived of nearly all territory outside the walls of its capital. The Sultan opened proceedings against it by sending an envoy to the Emperor with this insulting message:—

When I dethroned your predecessor, Manuel, it was not in your interest but in mine. If, then, you want to remain my friend, you must surrender your crown. I will give you any other government you may wish for. If you do not consent, I swear by God and the Prophet I will not spare a soul in your city; I will exterminate all of them.

The citizens of Constantinople, rather than experience the terrible fate which they knew would befall them in the event of a successful assault by the Ottoman army, were willing to come to terms. But the Emperor, who was buoyed up by hope of assistance from the Christian Powers, refused to acquiesce in a pusillanimous surrender. He replied to the ambassador in dignified terms: "Tell your master that, feeble as we are, we know no other power to whom to address ourselves if it be not God, Who protects the feeble and humbles the powerful. Let the Sultan do what he pleases."

At this stage, and before he could give effect to his threats, Bayezid was compelled by great events in Asia to raise the siege of Constantinople. Hitherto, in twelve years of incessant war, Bayezid had been uniformly successful. He had annexed the greater part of Asia Minor, Macedonia, Northern Bulgaria, and Thessaly. He had reduced to vassalage the Greek Empire itself and Serbia, Wallachia, Bosnia, and a great part of Greece. He had defeated the feudal chivalry of Europe in the great battle of Nicopolis. He had not met with a single reverse. The next two years, the last of his reign, were to result in disastrous and overwhelming defeat to him, in his capture and death, and in the temporary crumpling up of the Turkish Empire. He came into conflict for the first time with Timur, a general and a conqueror more resolute, crafty, able, and cruel than himself.

Timur the Tartar, better known to us as Timurlane —Timur the lame, for he had met in early life with an accident which lamed him—was the greatest, the most ruthless, and the most devastating of warriors recorded in all history. Born in 1333, a descendant through his mother of the great Gengis Khan, he began life as a petty chief of a Tartar tribe in the neighbourhood of Samarkand. It was not till he had reached the age of thirty-five that he achieved eminence over other neighbouring Tartar States. He then conceived the ambition of universal conquest. "As there was only one God in heaven," he said, "so there should be only one ruler on earth"—that one was to be himself. He went a long way towards gaining this object of his ambition, for he embarked on a career which, in rather less than thirty-five years, resulted in an empire extending from the Great Wall of China to the frontier of Asia Minor, and from the Sea of Aral to the River Ganges and the Persian Gulf. He had, by this time, conquered twenty-seven separate States and

- 39 -

extinguished nine dynasties. He effected his purpose, not only by force of arms, but by a deliberate policy of terrorism. After victory he was of settled purpose ruthless in cruelties on the greatest scale.

It was obvious that, sooner or later, he would come into conflict with what was, at that time, the only other growing military Power in the world—the Ottoman Empire. The two potentates had already become neighbours, and causes of dispute and antagonism were often arising between them. Each had sheltered refugee princes, whose territories had been absorbed by the other, and who were engaged in intrigues to stir up war between the two rivals, in the hope of regaining their possessions. Insolent messages passed between the two potentates.

What is the foundation of thy insolence and folly? [wrote Timur to Bayezid]. Thou hast fought some battles in the woods of Anatolia; contemptible trophies! Thou hast obtained some victories over the Christians of Europe; thy sword was blessed by the Apostle of God; and thy obedience to the precepts of the Koran in waging war against the infidel is the sole consideration that prevents us from destroying thy country, the frontier and bulwark of the Moslem world. Be wise in time; reflect; repent; and avert the thunder of our vengeance which is yet suspended over thy head. Thou art no more than an ant; why wilt thou seek to provoke the elephants? Alas, they will trample thee under their feet.

Bayezid replied in terms of the greatest indignation. He protested that Timur had never triumphed unless by his own perfidy and the vices of his foes.

Thy armies are innumerable: be they so; but what are the arrows of the flying Tartars against the scimitars and battle-axes of my firm and invincible Janissaries? I will guard the princes who have implored my protection; seek them in my tents. The cities of Arzingan and Erzerum are mine; and unless the tribute be paid I will demand the arrears under the walls of Tauris and Sultania.

And he added an insult of a yet grosser kind which, by its allusion to the harem, was the worst that could be devised by a Moslem:—

If I fly from thy arms may my wives be thrice divorced from my bed; but if thou hast not courage to meet me in the field, mayest thou again receive thy wives after they have thrice endured the embrace of a stranger.

After this interchange of abuse Timur determined, in 1400, to attack and invade Asia Minor from Armenia, at the head of a horde of armed men, estimated by historians at not less than eight hundred thousand. He laid siege to Sivas, in Cappadocia, on the Armenian frontier, which had only been captured by Bayezid about three years previously. It was now defended by a garrison of Turks, under command of Ertoghrul, the eldest son of Bayezid. The fortifications were immensely strong, but Timur was ready to sacrifice any number of men in assaulting and capturing the city. He employed six thousand miners in undermining its defences with galleries and propping up the walls temporarily with timber smeared with pitch. When the mines were completed, fire was applied to the timber, and the walls gradually sank into the cavities laid open to them, and afforded entrance to the assaulting columns. The city was captured. Four thousand of its defenders were buried alive by order of Timur, and Ertoghrul was executed.

Bayezid, thus challenged, advanced, in 1401, with an army of one hundred and twenty thousand men to avenge the disaster at Sivas. Timur, however, after the capture of that city, refrained from advancing farther into Asia Minor. He passed into Syria and captured Damascus, and thence into Mesopotamia for the capture of Bagdad. It was not till the next year, 1402, that he determined to return to Asia Minor and to humble Bayezid. He retraced his steps to Sivas, and thence, after a further exchange of insolent messages with the Ottoman Sultan, he went in search of him towards Angora, taking the route of Cæsarea and Kir Sheir.

Bayezid had also collected a great army in the east of Asia Minor, and had finally concentrated it in the neighbourhood of Angora. He showed none of his previous skill as a general, though all of his insolence and bravado. His army was discontented by his avarice, and by his neglect to pay them out of the well-filled treasury. He refused to follow the advice of his best generals, who warned him against meeting Timur's vast hosts on a field where they could deploy their whole strength. The two armies met at last on the plain of Angora, the site of many previous famous battles. It is almost inconceivable that Bayezid, in arrogant contempt of his foe, employed his army, in the face of the enemy, in a great hunt for game, which led them into a district devoid of water, where his soldiers suffered terribly, and five thousand are said to have died of thirst.

On return to their camp they found that Timur had diverted the stream which supplied it with water. Bayezid was forced to fight at a disadvantage. The Tartars, who formed a fourth part of the Ottoman army, were not to be relied on in this battle. Their sympathies were with their fellow-Tartars under Timur. Bayezid had committed the fatal error of placing them in the front line, after his usual tactics of meeting the first encounter of the enemy with inferior troops. But in this case the Tartars deserted on the field of battle. The Serbian contingent, under Prince Stephen, and other Christian vassal troops fought with the utmost gallantry and loyalty. But it was in vain. The whole Ottoman army was outnumbered, overwhelmed, and routed with great slaughter. Bayezid with his bodyguard made a last stand. "The

Thunderbolt," says the Turkish historian, "continued to wield a heavy battle-axe. As a starving wolf scattering a flock of sheep he scattered the enemy. Each blow of his redoubtable axe struck in such a way that there was no need of a second blow." But in the end he was overpowered and taken prisoner.

Bayezid for some time after his capture was treated with unwonted generosity by Timur, who was impressed by his dignified bearing, in spite of his overwhelming defeat and humiliation. But after an attempt to escape he was more rigidly guarded, and was put into fetters at night. The treatment of him became more cruel and contemptuous. He was carried by day in the train of Timur, when on the march, in a litter, which was in effect a cage[12] with open bars, exposed to the derision and contempt of the Tartars. His wife, Despina, the Serbian princess, was compelled to serve Timur with drink at his meals in a state of nudity, and with other women of Bayezid's harem was taken into that of the conqueror. Timur is also said to have made a footstool of his conquered foe.

Bayezid died of a broken heart after eight months of humiliation, at the age of forty-eight. During that time Timur overran the greater part of Asia Minor, capturing Nicæa and Brusa and many other strongholds from the Ottomans, and Smyrna from the Knights of St. John of Jerusalem. The walls of Smyrna were undermined in the same way as those of Sivas. In two weeks Timur effected a capture which Bayezid had failed to do in three times that length of time. The Knights, when they found that the city was no longer tenable, fought their way down to their galleys against the crowd of despairing inhabitants. Most of them escaped to Rhodes and effected there another settlement. Those who failed to escape were put to death by Timur, who built a pyramid of their heads. Everywhere there was ruthless cruelty. When approaching the city of Ephesus, children came out to meet him singing songs to appease his wrath. "What is this noise?" he asked. When told, he ordered his horsemen to ride over the children. They were trampled to death.

Timur reinstated in their former territories, as tributaries to his own Empire, most of the petty princes who had been dispossessed by the Turks, including the Emir of Karamania. He eventually returned to Samarkand, where he made preparations for the invasion of China, but before this could be realized he died, at the age of seventy-one, two years after the death of Bayezid. As a result of his raid into Asia Minor the Ottoman Empire there, for the time being, completely collapsed. But the Tartars disappeared without leaving any trace behind them.

If Bayezid's physical downfall was overwhelming and humiliating, his moral decadence was even worse, and, as it turned out, was more permanently injurious to the people of his Empire by the evil example it set. In the brief periods of peace, spent at Brusa and Adrianople, he gave way to self-indulgence and vice of a deplorable kind. He was the first of his race to break the laws of the Prophet and to drink too freely of wine. In company with his Grand Vizier, Ali, he was addicted to drunken orgies. Still worse, he was tempted by that boon companion to give way to vice of unmentionable depravity, condemned by all the world. The Empire was ransacked for good-looking boys, the sons of Christian parents, who were compelled to embrace Islamism and to enter the service of the Court, nominally as pages, but really to pander to the degrading desire of the Sultan. In adopting such practices, Bayezid set the fashion to others of his entourage. The moral infection then spread widely among the upper classes of society, especially among the judges and ulemas. There can be little doubt that immorality infected the upper society of the Empire and was one of the causes which ultimately led to decadence and ruin.

It is to be noted of Bayezid that in his short but strenuous career of conquest he did not show any falling off of vigour and courage as a result of his excesses. But in his final campaign against Timur his conduct was so fatuous as to give rise to the belief that his gross debauchery had resulted in softening of the brain. However that may have been, he met in Timur a greater man than himself who, even at the age of seventy, had lost none of his vigour of mind and body, and who, as master also of bigger battalions, was practically invincible.

V

MAHOMET I
1413-21

ON the death of Sultan Bayezid, in captivity, it seemed as though the Ottoman Empire was doomed to extinction. Asia Minor had already passed out of its hands, and was either in possession of the Emirs who had been reinstated in their territories by Timur, and who had sworn allegiance to him, or was still in the occupation of the invading Tartars. It was not to be expected that the Empire in Europe would survive when it could no longer draw support from Asia. The Christian populations of Bulgaria, Bosnia, and Wallachia would soon reassert their independence, and the Greek Empire might be expected to recover some of its lost provinces. The Turkish Empire, however, showed a most unexpected vitality. It survived not only the invasion of Timur, but civil war, which after the death of Bayezid broke out between four of his sons. An interregnum of ten years occurred, during which there was internecine war between these claimants to his throne. The Empire emerged from these stupendous difficulties, under the able rule of the youngest of them, Mahomet I, as strong as ever, and without the loss of a single province.

Timur's hosts, after ravaging the whole of Asia Minor, departed like a swarm of locusts which has denuded a district of its produce and then seeks fresh ground. They returned to Central Asia. They left nothing behind in Asia Minor of Tartar rule, either of an army or of an administration. The field was left open to the Ottomans to fight among themselves and their former vassals and neighbours for such a settlement as could be achieved by the strongest of them.

Of the six sons of Bayezid, five fought with him at Angora in command of divisions of his army. One of them, Mustapha, was supposed to be among the slain; another, Musa, was taken prisoner and shared the captivity of his father. The other three escaped. The eldest of them, Solyman, accompanied by the Grand Vizier, Ali, and Hassan, the Agha of the Janissaries, made his way to Adrianople, where, on the death of Bayezid, he had himself proclaimed Sultan, and exercised power as such over the European provinces of the Empire. Issa, a younger son, fled to Brusa, where he also claimed to be successor to his father, and Mahomet, the youngest son, but by far the ablest, retired to Amasia, a small principality in the north-east of Asia Minor. He there assumed authority over the district. After the death of their father these three claimants for succession to his Empire fought it out between themselves, and, later on, a fourth claimant was added to the list in Musa,

- 44 -

who had been set free by Timur, in order that he might convey the dead body of his father for interment at Brusa.

The earliest conflict was between Mahomet and Issa. Mahomet offered to divide between them the Ottoman possessions in Asia. Issa refused and claimed the whole of them. He was defeated and fled to Europe, where he sought the assistance of Solyman, who had firmly established himself in the Ottoman dominions there, and who was now able to lead an army into Asia Minor in support of Issa. Mahomet was hard pressed by Solyman. He sent Musa across the Straits to effect a diversion by raising revolt against Solyman in Europe. This had the desired effect, and Solyman was compelled to return to Adrianople. After his departure Mahomet succeeded in defeating Issa again, and the latter disappeared and was heard of no more.

In Europe, Solyman and Musa were now in deadly conflict. Solyman was much the same type of man as his father—of great vigour and courage in action, but given to orgies of drink and debauchery. The Agha of the Janissaries in vain tried to rouse him from the apathy to which he was often reduced after these bouts. He threatened to shave the Agha's beard with his sword. He was often severe and even cruel to his soldiers, and finally the Janissaries, incensed by his brutal treatment, his dissolute habits, and his inability to rouse himself to action, rebelled against him, at the instance of Hassan, and put him to death. They then took service under Musa, who became master of the position in Europe and assumed the title of Sultan.

After an expedition to Serbia for the purpose of avenging what he considered their treachery to him in supporting Mahomet, and where he committed the most revolting cruelties, Musa returned to Adrianople, and opened a campaign against the Emperor Manuel, who, after the death of Bayezid, had superseded Andronicus on the Greek throne and who supported Mahomet.

The Emperor appealed to Mahomet for assistance. Mahomet, with a Turkish army, supported by the Serbian contingent, crossed the Bosphorus in answer to this appeal, and the strange sight was witnessed of a Turkish army, under command of one of the Othman race, defending Constantinople against another Turkish army.

Musa eventually retreated from his lines in front of Constantinople, and was pursued by Mahomet. When, later, the two armies came into close touch on the borders of Serbia, a conflict was avoided by a revolt of Musa's troops. The Agha, Hassan, addressed the Janissaries in the very presence of Musa. "Why," he said to them, "do you hesitate to go over to the ranks of the most just and virtuous of the Othman princes? Why subject yourselves to be outraged by a man who can take care neither of himself nor of others?"

Musa, on hearing this harangue to his troops, rushed at Hassan and slew him. The companion of Hassan struck at Musa with his sword and wounded him in the hand. The troops, when they saw that their general was seriously wounded, were seized with panic. They deserted and went over to Mahomet. Musa fled with three attendants, and, later, his dead body was found in a marsh.

Mahomet was now in undisputed command of the Empire as Sultan. He reigned as such for only eight years. He showed, during that time, infinite skill and patience, as a statesman equally as a general, in restoring, consolidating, and maintaining his Empire. He was ardently desirous of peace. To the representatives of Serbia, Wallachia, and Albania he said: "Forget not to tell your masters that I grant peace to all, and that peace I will accept from all. May God be against the breakers of peace."

He kept on the best of terms with the Greek Emperor, with whom he had made a defensive alliance, and restored to him certain cities on the coast of the Black Sea and in Thessaly. He had frequent causes, however, for the use of his army, and for showing his skill as a general. He compelled the Emirs of Karamania, Kermia, and other principalities in Asia Minor, who had promised allegiance to Timur, to renew their vassalage to the Ottoman Empire. Two or three times the Karamanian prince revolted and endeavoured to assert complete independence. As often Mahomet defeated him, but contented himself with asserting supremacy, and did not insist upon the incorporation of his territory with the Empire. He also defeated an attempt of a Turkish upstart to create an independent State at Smyrna and Aidin. He put down a dangerous revolt of Dervishes and extinguished the sect. He came into conflict at sea with the Republic of Venice, and though he was worsted, and his fleet of galleys was destroyed, he succeeded in making an honourable peace.

As a ruler of his Empire he showed many great qualities. He gained the appellation which is best translated into English as the "Great Gentleman"— and right well he deserved it. He was magnanimous and just. He strictly observed his promises. He knew that his Empire could not be maintained by force alone, but that justice and clemency were necessary. His Christian subjects were everywhere treated with consideration. He would not tolerate cruelty to them. He was a liberal patron of literature, and in his short reign the Ottomans first showed a bent for poetry. It was a blot on his fame that he caused his youngest brother to be deprived of his sight, and that he put to death his nephew, the son of Solyman, lest either of them should dispute the throne with himself or his son after him. His experience of his brothers and the history of his family doubtless convinced him that no member of the Othman race would be content with any position short of the Sultanate. This may not be a moral justification, but it is an explanation which, in view of the ethics of the times, must prevent too severe a judgment. Though Mahomet in his short reign, after attaining full command of the Empire, made no extension of it, he must be regarded practically as one of its founders and as among its most eminent and successful rulers. He owed his success over his brothers to his moral ascendancy and to the great reputation which he achieved with his troops for his high qualities as a ruler even more than to his prowess as a general. The emergence of the Empire from the extreme difficulties into which it fell from the Mongolian invasion must have been due to the fact that the Ottomans at that time were much superior to the Greeks and the other Christian communities in all the qualities which tend to make a stable government.

Mahomet died of apoplexy in 1421 at the early age of forty-seven. He was buried at Brusa in a mausoleum near to the splendid building known as the Green Mosque, which he had himself erected.

VI

MURAD II
1421-51

MURAD succeeded his father in the Sultanate as second of the name. He reigned for thirty years, including two short periods when he abdicated and retired into private life. But on each occasion he was compelled by the exigencies of the State, and the youth and inexperience of his son and successor, to resume the throne. He much resembled his father in vigour and capacity as a general and in his desire to act justly.

At the very commencement of Murad's reign the Greek Emperor Manuel, by an almost incredible act of folly, hoping to take advantage of Murad's youth and inexperience, let loose from confinement a man who claimed, whether rightly or not was never clearly established, to be Mustapha, the son of Sultan Bayezid, who had disappeared after the battle of Angora. Manuel entered into a treaty with this claimant to the Ottoman throne, by which, in the event of his succeeding in establishing his succession, the city of Gallipoli and all the cities on the shores of the Black Sea, taken from the Greek Empire by the Turks, were to be restored to it.

In spite of this scandalous treachery to Islam, the so-called Mustapha succeeded in raising a large army in Europe, with which he defeated the troops who adhered to Murad. He then crossed the Dardanelles into Asia with his army in vessels supplied by the Emperor Manuel. Murad showed all the vigour and capacity of his race in dealing with this emergency. He won over the greater part of Mustapha's army, who were disaffected. He defeated what remained. Mustapha was driven across the Straits again to Gallipoli, where he was besieged, captured, and hanged, as the best proof, it was said, that he was an impostor.

Murad, having defeated this claimant to his throne, determined to avenge the perfidy of the Emperor Manuel and to put an end to the Greek Empire by the capture of Constantinople. For this purpose he collected an army of veterans. He invested the city, making a long line of great earthworks from the Golden Horn to the Sea of Marmora. From this he bombarded the city walls by cannon, then for the first time used by the Ottoman army, but which were not as yet very effective. He also used movable towers, from which assaults could be made on the walls of the city. He proclaimed that the great wealth of the capital would be the prize of the soldiers if the assault on it were successful. He made a special promise to a band of five hundred Dervishes, who were to lead the assault, that all the nuns in the city would be given to them as concubines. In spite of these great inducements to victory, the assault was unsuccessful. The Greeks defended the walls of the city with the utmost heroism, assisted, it was said, by a timely apparition of the Holy Virgin, which stimulated their efforts and depressed the assailants. Murad would probably have been successful with the overwhelming forces at his disposal if he had persisted in the siege, but he was compelled to raise it by a diversion cleverly contrived by the Greek Emperor.

A rival to the Sultan was set up in Asia in another Mustapha, a younger brother of Murad, who had not been put to death in pursuance of the fratricidal policy of his family. This new claimant was supported by the Karamanians and Kermians, and with their aid he defeated an Ottoman army in Asia Minor. Murad found it necessary to abandon the siege of Constantinople, and to transfer his main army to Asia Minor for the purpose of dealing with this danger to his throne. He came to close quarters as quickly as possible with Mustapha's army, and defeated it. Mustapha was taken prisoner and was hanged at once by his captors, without giving an opportunity to Murad to exercise his clemency in favour of his brother, had he so willed it. Murad then occupied himself by reducing the Karamanian and other Emirs to complete subjection to his Empire.

Meanwhile the Emperor Manuel died, and was succeeded by John Palæologus. Murad, in lieu of renewing the siege of Constantinople, was content to make another treaty with the new Emperor, imposing on him a heavy tribute and stripping him of almost every possession beyond the walls of his capital. The Empire thus obtained a reprieve for a few brief years.

In the case of Salonika, which had been recently sold by the Greek Emperor to the Republic of Venice, now desirous of effecting a lodgment in Macedonia, Murad refused to recognize the right of the Emperor to transfer to a foreign Power a city which at one time had been under Ottoman rule. It had three times in the last hundred years been captured by the Ottomans, and had as often been recaptured by the Greeks. Murad led an army, in 1430, to attack it, and, after a vigorous resistance by the Venetians, captured it by assault, and finally annexed the city and its district to the Turkish Empire. It was thought that Murad showed great clemency in not allowing his soldiers to indulge in a wholesale massacre. The Greek inhabitants, however, were sold into slavery, and their numbers were so great that a good-looking girl was sold for the price of a pair of boots.

The suppression of rebellion in Asia Minor, the subjection of the Greek Emperor to the position of a humble vassal, and the capture of Salonika had occupied Murad for some years. Later he was involved in long struggles with his neighbours, the Hungarians, on the northern boundaries of his Empire. The Ottomans were engaged in constant raids across the Danube, where vast districts were devastated, and thousands of their population were carried off as captives for sale as slaves. There arose about this time in Hungary a national hero, the celebrated Hunyadi, a natural son of the late King Sigismund. He was a born leader of men, not a great general, but a most valiant fighter. He had gained great distinction in war in other directions. He now became the soul of hostility against the Ottomans. He was known as the White Knight, on account of his silver armour, which always shone in the van of the impetuous charges of his cavalry. He was rightly regarded by his countrymen as a patriot and a national hero. None the less, he was a bloodthirsty ruffian. He made a practice of massacring all the prisoners taken in battle. He found pleasure in having this effected, in his presence, at banquets, where the guests were entertained by the shrieks of the dying men.

Hunyadi for twenty years was a terror to the Ottoman armies. His first encounter with them was at Hermannstadt, north of the Danube, which was invested by an army of eighty thousand Ottomans. He led an army of twenty thousand Hungarians against them, in relief of the fortress, and inflicted a severe defeat on them, in despite of great disparity of numbers. Twenty thousand of the Ottomans were killed, including the general. The others were dispersed. Murad sent another army of eighty thousand men against him, under another Pasha. Hunyadi again defeated it with great slaughter at Varsag.

These notable victories roused great enthusiasm in Europe. It was determined to take the offensive against the Ottomans, and to make another effort to drive them out of Europe. A coalition was formed for the purpose between Hungary and Poland, then united under King Ladislaus, and Wallachia and Bosnia. Serbia, which under its king, Stephen Lazariwitch, had been the firm ally of the Ottomans, and had supported them in many campaigns in Asia and Europe, was now induced to abandon this alliance and, under Stephen's successor, George Brancowitch, to join the confederacy against the Ottomans. The Pope, Eugenius, was most active in support of this combination. His legate, Cardinal Julian Cesarini, led an armed force in support of it. Money was raised for the purpose of the war by a great sale of indulgences to the faithful in every part of Europe. A large contingent of French and German knights joined the allied army. It was, in fact, another crusade, prompted by religious zeal on behalf of Christianity against Islam. The allied army was under the nominal command of Ladislaus, but Hunyadi was its real leader.

The Republics of Venice and Genoa gave their support, and as, at this time, the Ottomans had no naval force, it was hoped that these Powers, by means of their numerous and powerful galleys, would prevent the transfer to Europe of Murad's main army, which was again engaged in conflict with the Karamanians in Asia Minor.

The allied army, under these favourable circumstances, crossed the Danube in 1443. It defeated an Ottoman army on the banks of the Masova and again at Nisch. It then crossed the Balkan range in winter—an operation of extreme difficulty, which has since only twice been effected, by General Diebitsch and General Gourko—and again defeated the Turks in a battle at the foot of these mountains. Strange to say, instead of marching onwards to Adrianople, as Diebitsch did in 1829, Hunyadi was content with the laurels already achieved, and returned with his army to Buda, where he displayed his trophies and received a triumph.

Murad, on hearing of the retreat of the Hungarians across the Balkans, determined to come to terms with them, and not to pursue them again across the Danube. With some difficulty, and in spite of the sullen opposition of Cardinal Julian and the French contingent, a treaty was agreed to, at Szegeddin, with Ladislaus, by which Serbia was to be freed from dependence on the Ottoman Empire and Wallachia was to be ceded to Hungary. The treaty was to be in force for ten years. It was solemnly sworn to on the Gospel and the Koran by Ladislaus and Murad.

While this treaty was being negotiated Murad, weary of war, and desirous of spending the remainder of his life in sensual enjoyments which had so long been denied to him, decided to abdicate his throne. He was still in the full vigour of life at the age of forty-one, though he was said to be growing rather fat. He did not propose, like the Emperor Charles V, to retire to a monastery, but rather, like Diocletian the Roman Emperor, to a luxurious palace, surrounded by beautiful gardens, which he had prepared for his retreat at Magnesia. On the ratification of the treaty of Szegeddin, in 1444, he carried out this purpose, and his son Mahomet, at the age of fourteen, was proclaimed Sultan in his place.

When this became known to the Hungarians a revulsion of opinion took place against the recent treaty with the Turks. The Hungarian Diet determined, at the instance of Cardinal Julian, backed up by the Pope, to break the treaty. News had arrived of a fresh outbreak of the Karamanians. The fleets of Genoa, Venice, and Burgundy were masters of the Hellespont and would, it was believed, prevent the Ottoman army in Asia Minor from crossing into Europe. The opportunity for crushing the Turks and driving them out of Europe seemed to be most favourable.

Is it now [said Cardinal Julian to the Hungarian Diet] that you will desert expectations and your own fortunes? Is it to your God and your fellow-Christians that you have pledged your faith? That prior obligation annihilates a rash and sacrilegious oath to the enemies of Christ. His vicar on earth is the Roman Pontiff, without whose sanction you can neither promise nor perform. In his name I absolve your perjury and sanctify your arms. Follow my footsteps in the path of glory and salvation; and, if you still have scruples, devolve on my head the punishment and the sin.

"This mischievous casuistry," says the historian Gibbon, "was seconded by his respectable character and the levity of popular assemblies." The Hungarian Diet resolved on war, and King Ladislaus, in spite of his recent oath, determined to break the treaty. Hunyadi was, in the first instance, strongly opposed to this, but his assent was obtained by the promise of the throne of Bulgaria, in the event of the defeat of the Ottomans and the conquest of that province. The Prince of Serbia, who had regained his independence by the treaty, was persuaded to join with the allies by the promise of an addition to his kingdom.

It was decided to send an army at once against the Ottomans. But it was a much reduced one in comparison with that which had so recently crossed the Balkans. Most of the French and German knights and their attendants had already gone home. Not more than ten thousand remained under Hunyadi. They were joined by five thousand Wallachians. They invaded Bulgaria, and then, instead of crossing the Balkans, descended the Danube to the coast and thence marched to Varna. Meanwhile the Ottomans, in great alarm and fearing the incompetence of the young Mahomet to conduct a great war, induced Murad to emerge again from his retreat. He hastily gathered together an army in Asia Minor. He bribed the Genoese, at the rate of a ducat for each man, to convey it across the Hellespont. He arrived in front of Varna unexpectedly, before the Christian army knew of his intentions. His army greatly outnumbered that of King Ladislaus. In spite of this, the two wings of it were driven back with great slaughter. Murad, in command of the centre of his army, for the moment and for the only time in his life, lost his presence of mind and was disposed to fly. But the Beglerbey of Anatolia laid hold of the70 bridle of his horse and urged him to fight it out. The battle was renewed. The Janissaries stood firm and successfully repulsed the main body of the Christians. Ladislaus was unhorsed and asked for quarter. But he was put to death on the field. His head was stuck upon a lance and was held up by the side of another lance which bore on high a copy of the violated treaty. The Christians, when they saw the head of their dead king in its soldier's helmet thus held aloft, were struck with panic and fled precipitately. Hunyadi escaped with difficulty. Cardinal Julian expiated by death on the field his sin in advising the breach of the treaty. Two other bishops shared his fate. Never was defeat and disaster more richly deserved. Two-thirds of the Christian army were slain in the battle, and even greater numbers, though a less proportion, of the Ottomans shared their fate.

Murad, having won this great victory, again, a second time, abdicated his throne and returned to his retreat at Magnesia, and again the young Mahomet was invested as Sultan. Though history supplies cases of great kings seeking retirement from the cares of office, and of some of them being induced to resume their thrones, it records no other case of a second abdication and a second resumption. Murad was very soon recalled from his abode of pleasure. A serious outbreak of the Janissaries occurred at Adrianople. They ravaged the city and committed great atrocities. The ministers of the young Sultan were greatly alarmed. They felt that only a strong hand could keep a check on the unruly Janissaries. Murad was again summoned from his retreat. The young Mahomet was induced to go on a hunting expedition. In his absence Murad again made his appearance at Adrianople and resumed power. Mahomet, on his return from hunting, found that his father was again in the saddle. Murad was received by his troops with a great ovation, and even the unruly Janissaries gave in their submission to him. He did not again seek retirement at Magnesia. He reigned for seven more years—another period of almost incessant war. He first made an invasion of the Morea, which the Greek Emperor's brothers had divided between them and governed as petty princes, or despots, as they were called. Murad had no difficulty in storming and capturing the fortification by which the isthmus of Corinth was defended. He com71pelled the two despots to accept the position of vassals under the Empire.

Murad then again turned his attention to Serbia and Hungary. He defeated the combined forces of Hungary, Serbia, and Bosnia, under Hunyadi, on the field of Kossova, where in 1389 Murad I had first subdued the Serbians. As a result of this great battle Serbia lost its independence and was finally incorporated as an integral part of the Ottoman Empire. Bosnia became a tributary State.

Murad was less fortunate in his efforts to subdue the Albanians. These people were under the leadership of George Castriota—commonly called Scanderbeg—who had been brought up at Murad's Court as a Mussulman, and had learned the art of war from him, but who had abjured Islam, with a view to leadership of the Albanians. He carried on a guerrilla war against the Ottoman invaders with great success, and Murad was unable to complete the conquest of the State. This was practically the only failure of Murad's adventurous life. His generals met with many defeats at the hand of Hunyadi, but Murad retrieved them in the two battles in which he came in conflict with the great Hungarian hero. He died of apoplexy in 1451.

Looking back at his career, it does not appear that he made war with ambitious objects to aggrandize his Empire. War was, in almost every case, forced upon him. Three times the Prince of Karamania declared war against him, and three times Murad defeated him, and was content with insisting on the vassalage of the province and not on its extinction and incorporation with the Empire. It has been shown how perfidious was the conduct of the Greek Emperor, and how fully justified Murad was in reducing his territory to the narrowest limits. Murad's attack on Salonika when in the hands of the Venetian Republic was equally justified, for the Greek Emperor had no right to sell it, and thus invite a foreign Power to make a lodgment there. The wars on the northern frontier were forced upon him by the Hungarians and the Christian Powers in alliance with them. They appealed to arms, and victory decided against them. It will be seen that as a net result of Murad's reign the Ottoman Empire was extended during these thirty years by the acquisition of many petty principalities in Asia Minor, by the complete subjection of Serbia72 and Bosnia, the conquest of Salonika and its district, and by the conversion of the Morea into a tributary State. It was, however, reduced by the loss of Wallachia as a vassal State.

Gibbon, quoting from a Turkish historian, says:—

Murad was a just and valiant prince, of a great soul; patient of labour, learned, merciful, religious, charitable; a lover and encourager of the studious and of all who excelled in any art or science. No man obtained more or greater victories. Belgrade alone withstood his attacks. Under his reign the soldier was ever victorious, the citizen rich and secure. If he subdued any country, his first care was to build mosques and caravansaries, hospitals, and colleges.

Though, *more suo*, Gibbon suggests doubts whether such praise could be justified in the case of a Sultan "whose virtues are often the vices most useful to himself or most agreeable to his subjects," he admits that

the justice and moderation of Murad are attested by his conduct and acknowledged by Christians themselves, who consider a prosperous reign and a peaceful death as the reward of his singular merits. In the vigour of his age and military power he seldom engaged in war till he was justified by a previous and adequate provocation. In the observance of treaties his word was inviolate and sacred.[13]

73

VII

MAHOMET II, 'THE CONQUEROR' 1451-81

IF Mahomet, the eldest son of Murad, at the age of fourteen, had been reckoned too feeble to cope with the emergencies of the State, it is very certain that he soon made wonderfully rapid progress. At the age of twenty-one, when he again mounted the throne on the death of his father, he was amply, and almost precociously, endowed with many of the best, and many also of the worst, qualities of an autocrat, and was quite able alone to take command of the State. He was undoubtedly the ablest man that the house of Othman had as yet produced, not only as a general, but as a statesman. He had also great intellectual capacity and literary attainments. He spoke five languages fluently. He was the most proud and ambitious of his race and the most persistent in pursuing his aims. He combined with these high qualities, however, extreme cruelty and perfidy and sensuality of the grossest and vilest kind. He differed from his predecessors in his craving for absolute power, free from control by his ministers, and in his reckless disregard of human life. Hitherto, from Othman to Murad II, the Sultans had been in intimate association with their viziers and generals, and had shared their meals with them. They were accessible to their subjects, high and low. Mahomet was very different. He was the true despot after the Oriental fashion. He held himself aloof. He took his meals alone. He made no confidants. He treated his viziers and pashas as though they were his slaves. He had no regard for their lives. There were men in his personal service who were adepts at striking off heads by single blows of their scimitars. Two at least of Mahomet's Grand Viziers were put to death in this way in his presence74 without warning or compunction. This levelling process was not apparently objected to by his subjects.

On hearing at Magnesia of the death of his father, Mahomet, who was eager to resume power, mounted at once an Arab horse, and exclaiming, "Let all who love me follow!" he rode to the Hellespont, and thence crossed to Gallipoli and made his way to Adrianople. He was there again acclaimed as Sultan, not, however, without having to submit to onerous presents to the Janissaries, a bad precedent which was later always followed on the accession of a Sultan. The first act of his reign was to direct that his brother, an infant son of Murad, by his latest wife, a Serbian princess, should be put to death. He feared that the child, when grown up, might dispute the throne with him, on the ground that its mother was a legitimate wife of royal descent, while he himself (Mahomet) was only the son of a slave. A high officer of the Court was directed to drown the child in a bath. This was effected at the very moment when the mother was engaged in offering her congratulations to the new Sultan on his accession. The foul deed created a very bad impression, and Mahomet found it expedient to disown the act. He did so by directing the execution of the officer who had carried out his order. He compelled the mother, in spite of her royal rank, to marry a slave, an outrageous insult to the Serbian prince and to the memory of his father.

From the earliest moment of his accession it became clear that Mahomet intended to signalize his reign by the capture of Constantinople. With this view, he came to terms for a three years' truce with Hunyadi and the Hungarians. He chastised and then gave easy terms to the Karamanians, and accepted as a wife the daughter of their prince. He sent an army to the Peloponnesus to prevent the two brothers of the Greek Emperor, who were ruling there, from lending their aid to the Greeks of Constantinople. He directed the erection of a great fortress on the European side of the Bosphorus, at its narrowest point opposite to another, which had been erected by Bayezid, very near to the capital, so as to command the Straits. When the Greek Emperor sent an envoy to protest against this, Mahomet replied:—

I make no threats against your city. By assuring the safety of my country I am not infringing any treaty. Have you forgotten the 75extremity to which my father was reduced when your Emperor, in league with the Hungarians, endeavoured to prevent his crossing to Europe by closing the Straits against him? Murad was compelled to ask for the assistance of the Genoese. I was at Adrianople at the time and was very young. The Mussulmans were in great alarm and you Greeks insulted them. My father took an oath at the battle of Varna to erect a fort on the European side. This oath I will fulfil. Have you the right or the power to prevent my doing what I wish on my own territory? The two sides of the Straits are mine—that of Asia Minor because it is peopled by Ottomans, that of Europe because you are unable to defend it. Tell your master that the Sultan who now reigns in no way resembles his predecessors. My power goes beyond their vows. I permit you now to withdraw, but in the future I will have flayed alive those who bring me such messages.[14]

No more envoys were sent to him after this by the Greeks. Their Emperor, Constantine—the last of his line—had succeeded his brother three years before the accession of Mahomet. He was a brave and conscientious prince, who gave lustre to the last days of the Empire. But he was most unwise and provocative in his conduct to the new Sultan, evidently under the belief that he had to deal with the inexperienced youth who had been displaced by Murad six years previously. He threatened to let loose, as a rival claimant to the Ottoman throne, Orkhan, a grandson of Bayezid, who was under his charge, if a larger allowance was not given for his maintenance. Mahomet

- 56 -

contemptuously rejected the claim. The Grand Vizier, Khalil, who was suspected of being in the pay of the Greeks, warned the Emperor of his extreme folly. "Your madness," he said to the Greek ambassador, "will put Constantinople in the hands of the Sultan. Proclaim Orkhan Sultan in Europe, call in the Hungarians to your aid, retake what provinces you can, and you will speedily see the end of the Greek Empire."

The new fortress was completed in the autumn of 1452. It was then seen that, in combination with the fortress on the opposite shore, it gave complete command of the Straits to the Ottomans. Venetian vessels which attempted to pass were captured and their crews were sawn in halves. Mahomet then declared his intention to attack Constantinople. In an address to his principal pashas, after describing the conquests made by his predecessors in 76Europe and Asia, he pointed out that the great barrier to further progress was this city and the army of the Emperor.

The opposition [he said] must be ended; these barriers must be removed. It was for them to complete the work of their fathers. They had now against them a single city, one which could not resist their attacks; a city whose population was greatly reduced and whose former wealth had been diminished by Turkish sieges, and by the continued incursions made by his ancestors upon its territories; a city which was now only one in name, for in reality its buildings were useless and its walls abandoned and for the great part in ruins. Even from its weakness, however, they knew that from its favourable position, commanding both land and sea, it had greatly hindered their progress and could still hinder it, opposing their plans and being always ready to attack them. Openly or secretly it had done all it could against them. It was the city which had brought about the attack by Timerlane and the suffering which followed. It had instigated Hunyadi to cross the Danube, and on every occasion and in every possible manner had been their great enemy. The time had now come when, in his opinion, it should be captured or wiped off the face of the earth. One of two things: he would either have it within his Empire or he would lose both. With Constantinople in his possession, the territories already gained could be safely held and more would be obtained; without it, no territory that they possessed was safe.[15]

In the ensuing winter (1452) Mahomet made every preparation at Adrianople for a campaign in the next year. Having no means of casting cannons, which at that time were coming into use in European armies, he tempted a Wallachian, who was experienced in such work, and who was in the service of the Greeks, to come over to his side for higher pay, and devised with him a cannon of enormous size, firing stone balls of 2-1/2 feet in diameter, and many other smaller, but still large, guns throwing balls of 150 lb. weight, for use against the walls of Constantinople. He also constructed a large fleet of war vessels propelled by oars, biremes and triremes, to be used in the siege of the city. He was most active and eager, working day and night in concerting plans with his generals for his great purpose. Early in the following year (1453) he collected in front of the walls of Constantinople an army, estimated at a hundred and fifty thousand men, including twelve thousand Janissaries, and a vast number of irregulars and camp followers eager for the sack of the great city.

77

Constantine, on his part, was equally engaged in making preparations for the defence of his capital. He collected supplies of every kind. He did his best to repair and strengthen the walls of the city, which had been neglected and badly repaired by fraudulent Greek contractors. He invited the aid of the Christian princes of Western Europe for the coming struggle. In this view, and in the hope of getting full support from the Pope, he agreed to a scheme of union between the Greek and Latin Churches, in which everything was conceded to the latter. A great service was held at St. Sophia to ratify this union. Cardinal Isidore, the legate of the Pope, a Greek by birth, presided. It was attended by the Emperor and all his Court, clergy, and the officers of State. This gave great offence to the main body of the Greek clergy, and to the great majority of the people of Constantinople. There was implacable hatred between the members of the two Churches, and not even the grave peril of the State could induce them to compose their differences. St. Sophia was deserted by its congregation. It was thought to be polluted by the service.[16] The Grand Duke Notaras, the second person in the State after the Emperor, in command of all the forces, was specially offended. He even went the length of saying in public that he would rather see the turban of the Turks at Constantinople than the hat of a cardinal. It resulted that the Greeks were divided into two parties. Priests refused to give the sacrament to dying men not of their party. The Churches refused to contribute out of their vast wealth to necessities of the State. Constantine was seriously embarrassed and weakened by the division among his people. Of a total population of the city, reduced as it was, as compared with the past, and estimated at a hundred thousand, not more than six thousand took up arms in support of Constantine against the Turks.

The appeals to the Western Powers resulted in a certain, but very insufficient, number of volunteers from Southern Europe giving their services to support the Greek cause in its final struggle with the Moslems. Seven hundred Genoese came under the command of Giustiniani, an able 78soldier of fortune, who proved to be the main support of Constantine. Others had come with Cardinal Isidore, at the instance of the Pope, and with some small amount of money from the same quarter. There were Catalans and Aragonese from Spain, but the number of these recruits from Western Europe did not exceed three thousand. The total force under the command of Constantine for the defence of the city amounted to no more than eight thousand. It is strange that there were no volunteers from France and Germany, or from Hungary and Poland, from whence so many crusaders had volunteered in previous years to drive the Turks out of Europe. Nor was there any valid assistance in men and money from the numerous Greeks in the Levant. The unfortunate Constantine was not only very deficient in men, but his resources in money were very low. He had, however, in his service twenty powerful galleys well manned, and three galleys had come from Venice.

It would seem that the cause of Constantine did not much interest Europe, and did not even meet with an effective support among the Greeks themselves.

The city of Constantinople, as it then existed, was situate between the Golden Horn, its great harbour, and the sea of Marmora. Its land frontage, distant about nine miles from the entrance to the harbour, was four miles in length. It was protected by a triple line of walls, the two inner of which were very massive, flanked by towers at distances of 170 feet. There was a space of 60 feet between these walls. The third and outer wall was a crenelated breastwork on the other side of a fosse, of a width of 60 feet. This powerful line of defence had been devised by the Emperor Theodosius II about a thousand years ago and had protected the city in twenty sieges. Before the invention of cannon it was practically impregnable.[17] There were also fortifications extending for about nine miles on the side of the Golden Horn. The eight thousand men were too few even for effective defence of the four miles of walls, which were to be attacked directly by the Ottoman army, to say nothing of the fortifications along the side of the Golden Horn. The defence, however, with these limited means, was a spirited one. It showed that if the Greek Emperor had been adequately supported by the Western Powers Mahomet might not have been able to capture the city.

The siege was commenced by Mahomet on April 6, 1453. Much time had been occupied in conveying the cannon from Adrianople. There were two very interesting incidents in the siege which are worth recording. The one was the breaking of the close blockade of the port by four powerful and well-manned Genoese galleys, bringing provisions and stores to the beleaguered city from Chios. They sailed across the Marmora and up the Bosphorus with a strong breeze in their favour. The Sultan sent against them a hundred and forty of his fleet of smaller vessels propelled by oars. They found great difficulty in stemming the heavy sea. The four larger Genoese vessels came down on the smaller craft, crashing against them and shivering their oars. Their crews hurled big stones on the Turkish galleys and emitted against others the inextinguishable fire of which the Greeks had the secret. The Turkish boats could make no headway against the superior weight of the bigger vessels. A large number of them were sunk with serious loss of life. When near to the entrance of the harbour the wind died off and the Genoese vessels were in imminent peril, surrounded as they were by the numerous Turkish craft. But at the last moment an evening breeze sprang up. The Genoese vessels were able to force their way through. The chain which prevented ingress to the harbour was lowered, and the relieving vessels were admitted.

The Sultan had watched the naval battle from the shore. He spurred his horse some distance into the shallow sea in the hope of animating his sailors to greater efforts. He was bitterly disappointed at this first engagement of his new fleet. The next morning he sent for the admiral, Balta Oghlou, a sturdy Bulgarian by birth, and bitterly reproached him for his failure. He directed the admiral to be laid on the ground and held there by four strong men, while he was bastinadoed. Some historians state that the Sultan himself belaboured the unfortunate admiral with his mace.

The other incident, growing out of the naval defeat, was that Mahomet, on finding that his small craft, propelled only by oars, were of little effect against the powerful vessels at the disposal of the Greeks, determined to transfer a large number of them from the Bosphorus to the upper part of the harbour, where the bigger vessels could not engage them, owing to the shallow depth of water, and where they would be of use against the inner defence of the city. For this purpose Mahomet directed the construction of a broad plank road from Tophane, on the Bosphorus, across the hill intervening between it and the head of the Golden Horn. This road was well greased with tallow, and the vessels were dragged up it with windlasses and oxen. The descent on the other side of the hill was easy enough. The scheme was not quite a novelty, as an operation of the same kind, though on a smaller scale, had been attempted elsewhere. It was carried out with striking success; and in one night eighty of the Turkish galleys were transferred in this way to the upper harbour. Mahomet also constructed a pontoon bridge across the harbour, on which batteries were erected. The two schemes together enabled him to attack the Greek defences along the line of the harbour, and compelled Constantine to withdraw many men from the defence of the landward walls, where the main attack was made.

The young Sultan took a most active part in the siege work. He traced the lines of fourteen batteries from which the walls were bombarded. The first great cannon was a failure. It burst at the first shot and blew to pieces the Wallachian who had cast it. It was recast, however, and two others of the same size were also cast. About two hundred smaller guns were used. They threw stone balls[18] against the walls and towers of the city, and ultimately succeeded in effecting a breach. There can be no doubt that the capture of the city was mainly due to the provision of these great guns, which were far above anything previously used against fortresses. The Greeks also used cannons in defence, but the parapets of the walls were not wide enough to allow of the recoil of the guns, and where it was possible to use them the walls suffered from the concussion. Gunpowder was also deficient.

After seven weeks of siege the bombardment effected breaches in the walls at three points such as to give Mahomet every hope of success in a final assault. The principal breach was at St. Romanus, where the outer of the two main walls was practically levelled for a length of four hundred yards, and four of the flanking towers were destroyed. The broad ditch was filled in part by the débris of the wall and in part by fascines. The Sultan decided that the assault should take place on May 29th. This became known to the Greeks in the city, and both sides made every preparation for a supreme effort.

On the 28th, Mahomet ordered a proclamation to be made to his troops, to the effect that when the city was captured it would be given up to them to sack at their will for three days. The Sultan, it said, had sworn by the everlasting God, by the four thousand prophets, by Mahomet, and by his own soul that the whole population of the city, men, women, and children, should be given over to them. This was received by the troops with tumultuous expressions of delight.

On the same day the Sultan reviewed his army in three divisions, each of fifty thousand men, and afterwards received in his tent all the leaders, military and naval. He made a speech to them in which he announced his intention to make a final assault on the city on the next day, explained to them the method of attack, and gave his final orders. He enlarged on his promise to give to the troops the plunder of the city.

In the city [he said] there was an infinite amount and variety of wealth of all kinds—treasure in the palaces and private houses, churches abounding in furniture of silver, gold, and precious stones. All were to be theirs. There were men of high rank and in great numbers who could be captured and sold as slaves; there were great numbers of ladies of noble families, young and beautiful, and a host of other women who could either be sold or taken into their harems. There were boys of good family. There were houses and beautiful gardens. "I give you to-day a grand and populous city, the capital of the ancient Romans, the very summit of splendour and of glory, which has become, so to say, the centre of the world. I give it over to you to pillage, to seize its incalculable treasure of men, women, and boys, and everything that adorns it. You will henceforward live in great happiness and leave great wealth to your children. The great gain to all the sons of Othman would be the conquest of a city whose fame was great throughout the world. The greater its renown, the greater would be the glory of taking it by assault. A great city which had always been their enemy, which had always looked upon

- 61 -

them with a hostile eye, which in every way had sought to destroy the Turkish power, would come into their possession. The door would be open to them by its capture to conquer the whole of the Greek Empire."[19]

We have quoted this speech of Mahomet as further proof that plunder and the capture of men, women, and boys for sale or for their harems, and not religious fanaticism, was the main incentive to Moslem conquest.

The night before the assault was spent by the Turks in rejoicing. Their camp was illuminated. Very different was the action of the Greeks on this last day of their Empire. There was a religious procession through the city, in which every one whose presence was not required in defence of the walls took part and joined in prayer, imploring God not to allow them to fall into the hands of the enemy. Eikons and relics were paraded. At the close of the procession the Emperor Constantine addressed a gathering of nobles and military leaders. He called attention to the impending assault. He said:—

It had always been held the duty of a citizen to be ready to die either for his faith, his country, his sovereign, or his wife and children. All these incentives to heroic sacrifice were now combined. The city was the refuge for all Christians, the pride and joy of every Greek, and of all who lived in Eastern lands. It was the Queen of Cities, the city which, in happy times, had subdued nearly all the lands under the sun. The enemy coveted it as his chief prize. He had provoked the war. He had violated all his engagements in order to obtain it. He wished to put the citizens under his yoke, to take them as slaves, to convert the holy churches, where the divine Trinity was adored and the most holy Godhead worshipped, into shrines for his blasphemy, and to put the false prophet in the place of Christ. As brothers and fellow-soldiers it was their duty to fight bravely in the defence of all that was dear to them, to remember that they were the descendants of the heroes of ancient Greece and Rome, and so conduct themselves that their memory should be as fragrant in the future as that of their ancestors.... For himself, he was determined to die in its defence.... He and they should put their trust in God, and not, as did their enemy, in the multitude of his hordes.

In the evening a solemn service was held at St. Sophia, memorable as the last Christian service before its conversion into a Turkish mosque. The Emperor and his followers partook of the Sacrament and bade farewell to the Greek Patriarch. It was a memorable scene—a requiem service for the Empire which was about to expire. Later the Emperor paid a last visit to his palace and bade farewell there to its staff. It was a most touching occasion. One who was present there wrote of it: "If a man had been made of wood or stone, he must have wept at the scene." It is very certain that the Emperor had no hope of saving the city from capture by its mortal foes.

Very early in the morning of the next fateful day, the 29th May, 1453, the final assault was delivered by the Turkish army. The scheme of the Sultan was to attack the walls of the city at many points, from both land and sea, but to make the main assault on the part of the wall which had been so much injured by the cannon in the Lycus Valley, near the gate of St. Romanus, and then, by successive waves of his vastly greater army, to overwhelm the defenders, using first his inferior troops, and reserving his best for the last attack, when the enemy would be wearied by long fighting. The first assault was made by an immense horde of irregulars, armed with bows and arrows, and with slings throwing stones and iron balls. Gunpowder, though already used for cannon, was not yet applied to muskets. The men advanced with scaling-ladders for the assault, and a cloud of arrows darkened the sky. No more than two thousand Greeks could be spared to defend this part of the long line of fortifications. They were collected in the *peribolus* between the two walls. The gates in the inner wall were closed, so that these men had no opportunity of shirking the defence and retreating into the city. They had to fight for their very lives between the two walls.

The Sultan directed the great cannon to be brought to the edge of the fosse, and a shot from it broke down the stockade which had been erected in place of the outer wall. Under cover of the dust the Turks made the assault. They were bravely met by the defenders, and were driven back with heavy loss. A second assault was then made by the Anatolian infantry, a very superior force to the irregulars. But they were no more successful. The Sultan, thinking that the Greeks must be exhausted by these two assaults, then personally led a third great body of men to a third assault. It consisted of his Janissaries. He led them to the edge of the fosse, and thence directed their attack. The cannon was used again against the stockade, and again under cover of the dust caused by it the Janissaries made their assault. Some of them succeeded in getting over the stockade, and a hand-to-hand fight occurred between them and the Greeks. The defenders seemed to have the best of it. But at this crisis a grave misfortune occurred to the Greeks. Giustiniani, who commanded them, was severely wounded. Blood flowed freely from his wounds. He decided to leave the field of battle and return to his ship in the harbour, for medical relief. The Emperor Constantine, who was near by, in vain implored him to remain, pointing out to him the damaging effect his departure would have on the soldiers who remained. Others thought that the wounds were not very serious and that the general was not justified in leaving the field. But he insisted on doing so, and demanded the key of the gate in the inner wall. With him departed some of his Genoese soldiers. This defection caused dismay and depression among the troops. Their resistance to the Turks slackened.

Some Greek historians accuse Giustiniani of cowardice in deserting the battle at so critical a moment, and Gibbon lends the weight of his great authority to this. The reputation, however, of the famous Italian soldier has been vindicated by later historians, such as Mr. Finlay and Sir Edwin Pears. They have shown that Giustiniani died of his wounds within a few days of the capture of Constantinople, the best proof of their serious and fatal character. All the same, he may not have sufficiently appreciated the effect of his withdrawal on the soldiers. It might have been better to have died there rather than on board his ship. However that might have been, all are agreed that the departure of the general was the turning-point of the day, and that it had the worst effect on the soldiers engaged in the defence.

The Emperor did his utmost to retrieve the position. He took upon himself the charge vacated by Giustiniani, and led the defence. Mahomet, on his part, had observed from the other side of the fosse the slackening of the defence. He called out to the Janissaries: "We have the city! It is ours! The wall is undefended!" He urged them to a final effort. They rushed the stockade and effected an entry into the *peribolus*. Soon great swarms of others followed, and overwhelmed the defenders with their vast numbers. The Emperor, despairing of success, threw aside his imperial mantle. He called out, "The city is taken and I am still alive!" Drawing his sword, he threw himself into the mêlée. He died fighting gloriously for his city and his Empire. His body was never found, though search was made for it by order of the Sultan. The Greek and Italian soldiers in the *peribolus* were now completely outnumbered. There was no exit through the inner wall by which they could escape. They were in a trap between the two walls. They were massacred to a man. The Janissaries, having effected this, found no difficulty in making their way through the inner wall, which, as we have explained, was not defended owing to the want of men.

All attacks on other parts of the city were failures. This one alone succeeded. Victory here was due in part to the good generalship of Mahomet and to his indomitable persistency, and in part to the ill-fortune of the Greeks in the withdrawal of Giustiniani at the critical moment of the defence. The defenders of the city had nobly performed their duty. Their numbers were quite insufficient. They had received no adequate support from Western Europe, or even from the neighbouring Christian States. It is quite certain that a few thousand more soldiers would have saved the city. Thirty galleys sent by the Pope with reinforcements were on their way when the city fell. They had been detained at Scio by adverse wind. "Auxilium deus ipse negavit," says the Greek historian.

When the Turks entered the city they began to massacre all the persons they met in the streets, without distinction of age or sex. But there was practically no resistance. There were no armed men left in the city. The population was cowed and panic-stricken, as well they might be in face of the overwhelming misfortune which now came upon them. After a short period of massacre the Turks turned their attention to the more practical business of looting and taking captives for sale. They effected this in a deliberate and systematic way. One great band of soldiers devoted themselves to plundering the palaces of the wealthy, another to the churches, and a third to the shops and smaller houses. Everything of value was gathered together for subsequent division among the soldiers. Of the inmates of the palaces and houses the older people were put to death; the stronger and younger of both sexes were carried off in bands as prisoners, bound together with ropes, with a view to ultimate sale as slaves.

The Turkish historian, Seadeddin, in words which seem to smack of pleasure at the scene, says:—

Having received permission to loot, the soldiers thronged into the city with joyous hearts, and there, seizing the possessors and their families, they made the wretched unbelievers weep. They acted in accordance with the precept, "Slaughter their aged and capture their youth."[20]

The gravest misfortunes fell upon the wealthier and more cultured classes in the city. Their daughters and sons were torn from them to be sold to harems in Asia Minor, or for other vile purposes. The parents, if still strong, were sold as slaves. Numbers of them fled from their houses and crowded into St. Sophia and other churches, hoping that their foes would respect places of worship, or expecting that a miracle of some kind would save them. But it was in vain. St. Sophia acted as a kind of drag-net in which all the best in the city were collected, and were carried off thence in gangs. Virgins consecrated to God were dragged from this and other churches by their hair and were ruthlessly stripped of every ornament they possessed. A horde of savage brutes committed unnameable barbarities.

The city was cleared of everything of value and was all but denuded of its population. By the lowest estimate, fifty thousand persons, mostly the strong and the young of both sexes, were made captives, and later were sold as slaves and deported to Asia Minor. Some few escaped from the city into the country districts. Others found refuge in the Greek and Genoese galleys in the harbour, which were able to get away and escape because the crews of the Turkish vessels blockading the port had deserted in order to take part in the sack. Some were able to hide themselves in the city, and emerged later when the scene of horrors was at an end. Others, we know not how many, were ruthlessly massacred because they were of no value for sale. The proceeds of the sack and of the sale of captives brought wealth to every soldier in the Turkish army. No such dire misfortune to a city had occurred since the destruction of Carthage.

After three days and nights of these orgies the Sultan intervened and proclaimed an end of them. Meanwhile, on the day of the last assault, when his troops were in possession of the city, the Sultan rode into it. He went direct to St. Sophia, and, dismounting, entered the great church. He took pains at once to prevent any destruction of its contents, and himself struck down a soldier engaged in this work, telling him that buildings were reserved for himself. He instructed a mollah to call people to prayer from the pulpit. He thus inaugurated the conversion of the splendid Christian church into a mosque.

After this he sent for Notaras, who had been in command of the Greek forces under the Emperor, and affected to treat him with generosity. He obtained a list of all the leading men in the city and offered a large reward for their heads.

On the next day the Sultan made an inspection of the city and paid a visit to the Imperial Palace. On entering it he quoted the lines from a Persian poet:—

The spider's web hangs before the portal of Cæsar's palace,

The owl is the sentinel on the watch-tower.

Later he presided at a great banquet, where he appears to have imbibed too freely of wine. When half-drunk he directed the chief eunuch to go to Notaras and demand of him his youngest son, a handsome lad of fourteen. Notaras refused, preferring death to dishonour for his son. The Sultan thereupon ordered Notaras and all his family to be put to death at once. Their heads were struck off and brought to the banquet and placed before the Sultan as a decoration of his table.

It was said that the Sultan's ferocity was stimulated by the last favourite of his harem, with whom he was much enamoured, and that she, on her part, was instigated by her father, a Greek renegade. Under this influence the Sultan ordered the execution of all the persons to whom on the previous day he had promised liberty. The Papal legate, Cardinal Isidore, escaped recognition and was sold as a slave by a soldier for a mean price. He was later ransomed. Orkhan, the grandson of Bayezid, who had been brought up as a Christian at the Imperial Court, committed suicide rather than be sold as a slave.

Although many cruel deeds were committed by the Sultan and his soldiers, and a terrible calamity fell upon the whole community of Greeks, it cannot be said that the capture of Constantinople was the scene of such infamous orgies as took place in 1204, when it was captured by the Crusaders. After the first few hours of entry there was on this occasion no general massacre. There was not much incendiarism. The Sultan did his best, successfully, to save the churches and other buildings.

Although the young Sultan was most brutal in some of his actions, he showed in others remarkable foresight and statesmanship. One of his earliest acts, after putting an end to the sack of the city, was to proclaim himself as protector of the Greek Church. A charter was granted to the Orthodox members of that Church securing to the use of it some of the churches in the capital, and authority to celebrate in them religious rites according to their ancient usage. It also gave to them a certain amount of autonomy in civil matters. It recognized their laws of marriage and of succession to property and gave jurisdiction to the Patriarch and to Ecclesiastical Courts to enforce them.

The most eminent survivor of the Greek clergy, Gennadius, was sought for. He had been sold as a slave after the sack of the city to a pasha at Adrianople. He was brought back to Constantinople and was invested by the Sultan with the office of Patriarch of the Greek Church. Mahomet, in doing so, said: "I appoint you Patriarch. May Heaven protect you. In all cases and all occasions count on my friendship and enjoy in peace all the privileges of your predecessors." This was a most wise and opportune act of policy. The Sultan had been advised by fanatics among the Turks to order a general massacre of Greeks and others who would not embrace Islam. Mahomet's record shows that he would have sanctioned this if he had thought it for the interest of the State, and he would probably have revelled in it. In pursuance of a deliberate policy of enlightened statecraft he rejected this advice. It was necessary to repeople his capital and to attract others than Turks to it. Mahomet was also ambitious of further conquests in Europe. He recognized that the attempt to force a wholesale change of religion on the vanquished would stimulate their resistance, while a wise tolerance might weaken it. When the Prince of Serbia asked Hunyadi, the Hungarian patriot, what he would do with the Orthodox Greek Church if he made himself master of that province, the reply was, "I will establish everywhere Catholic churches." The reply of Mahomet to a similar question was, "By the side of every mosque a church shall be erected in which your people will be able to pray."

This great act of tolerance of Mahomet was far ahead of the political ethics of the Christian Powers of Europe at that time. His example was not followed by the Spaniards, when they drove from their country the Moslem Moors, who had refused to adopt the religion of their victors. The action of Mahomet is another proof that the Turkish invasion of Europe was not actuated by religious fanaticism or the desire to spread Islam. There seems to have been no attempt to induce or compel the Greeks and others of the conquered city to embrace Islam.

Mahomet also set to work, at an early date, to repeople Constantinople. For a long time previous to the conquest its population had been dwindling. In proportion as the Greek Empire was reduced by the loss of its territories, so the importance of the capital was diminished. Mahomet invited all who had fled after the capture to return, promising protection to their property and religion. He directed the transfer of families of Greeks, Jews, and Turks from many parts of his Empire. When he took possession of Trebizond and the Morea, many thousands of Greeks were forcibly removed to Constantinople. The same was the case with many islands in the Ægean Sea. At the end of his reign Constantinople was far more populous and flourishing than it had been under the last Greek Emperor.

Although the capture of Constantinople was the principal feat in Mahomet's long reign, and that on which his fame in history chiefly rests, it was, in fact, only the first of a long list of conquests which earned for him from his countrymen the title *par éminence* of 'the Conqueror.' During the thirty years of his reign he was almost always at war in personal command of his armies, and there were very few in which he did not add fresh territory to his Empire, either in Europe or Asia.

Bosnia and the Morea, which had become tributary States under previous Sultans, were now again invaded and were compelled to become integral parts of the Empire. Their princes were dethroned and put to death. Wallachia and the Crimea were forced to become vassal States. In Asia, Karamania, so long the rival and foe of the Ottomans, and which, after many wars, had agreed to pay tribute, was now forcibly annexed, and its Seljukian line of kings was put an end to by death. The great city of Trebizond and its adjoining province of Cappadocia, which had been cut off from the parent Empire, after the capture of Constantinople by the Crusaders, and formed into a miniature Empire, under the Comneni dynasty, was invaded and annexed by Mahomet, and at his instance its reigning family was put to death. The possessions of the Genoese on the coasts of the Black Sea were seized and appropriated.

Many islands in the Greek Archipelago, including Lesbos, Lemnos, and Cephalonia, were also attacked and annexed. The same fate befell Eubœa. It belonged to the Republic of Venice, which was also deprived of others of its possessions on the coast of the Morea. Besides all these enterprises, Mahomet in several successive years sent armies to ravage parts of Styria and Transylvania. He even sent an army across the frontier of Italy to ravage the region of Friuli, and other districts almost within sight of Venice, whose Republic was compelled to enter into an ignominious treaty, binding it to assist the Ottomans in other wars with a naval force. The last achievement of the ambitious Sultan was to send a force to the South of Italy, where it captured Otranto. The only captures which Mahomet attempted without success were those of Belgrade, in 1456, and the island of Rhodes in 1480. The case of Belgrade was of the greatest importance, for it long barred the way to the invasion of Hungary and Germany. The Sultan himself took command of the army of attack with a hundred and fifty thousand men and three hundred guns. He thought the capture of it would be an easy task after that of Constantinople. But Western Europe, which had rendered so little assistance to the Greek Empire in its extremities, was alarmed at the prospect of the invasion of Germany through the loss of Belgrade. The Pope preached another crusade, and a large body of knights volunteered for the defence of this frontier city.

Hunyadi led the Hungarians in this his last campaign. The lower town was taken by the Turks after great loss of life; but the upper town made a protracted resistance. The Christian knights in a notable sortie attacked the batteries of the enemy, captured all the guns, and wounded the Sultan himself. Mahomet was compelled to raise the siege after losing fifty thousand men. It was the last feat of the Hungarian patriot. He died twenty days after this signal success. It was fifty years before Belgrade was again attacked and captured and the road was opened for the invasion of Hungary and Vienna.

In all these campaigns Mahomet personally led his armies in the field, with the exception of those for the invasion of the Crimea, the attack on Rhodes, and the capture of Otranto, where he delegated the task to able generals, of whom he appears to have had an abundant supply. But there never was a great commander who more completely dominated the generals under him and maintained his supremacy in the State. He made no confidences as to his intended military operations, or what were his immediate objects of attack. There were no councils of war. His armies were collected, year after year, on one side or other of the Bosphorus, without any one knowing their destination. When, on one occasion, one of his generals asked him what was his next object, he replied that if a single hair of his beard knew what his intentions were he would pluck it out and cast it into the fire. He held secrecy and rapidity to be the first elements of success in war, and he acted on this principle. With the exception of the single case of the invasion of Wallachia, the provocation for war was in every case on the part of the Sultan. Invasion and attack were preceded by laconic messages calling upon the State or city aimed at to surrender, and the actual attack was made with the shortest possible delay.

Having determined on war and invasion, his object was pursued with the utmost vigour, and wholly regardless of the loss of life. As a rule, his campaigns were short; but the war with Venice was an exception. It lasted for many years. It consisted mainly of attacks on strongholds of the Republic in the islands of the Archipelago and the coasts of Greece and Albania, where the fleets of the two Powers played a large part. The conquest of Albania also was only effected after a struggle spread over many years, in which the patriot hero, Scanderbeg, defeated successive attacks by Ottoman armies enormously exceeding his native levies. It was not till after the death of this great chief, in 1467, that Mahomet was able to wear down opposition in Albania by sheer force of numbers.

Early in his reign Mahomet recognized the strategic value of Constantinople. It became the keystone of his Empire. He transferred the seat of his government to it from Adrianople. He fortified the Dardanelles by the erection of two castles on either side of it near to Sestos and Abydos, each with thirty guns, which commanded the Straits. This secured his capital from attack. It prevented the entrance of a hostile fleet into the Sea of Marmora and the Black Sea. He added greatly to his navy, and made it superior to that of any other single Power in the Mediterranean. It gave him absolute supremacy in the Black Sea and the Sea of Marmora. The possessions of the Genoese in the Black Sea were at his mercy. He sent a flotilla of small vessels up the Danube to assist in the siege of Belgrade.

Throughout all his campaigns Mahomet exhibited perfidy and cruelty on a scale almost without precedent. Princes, generals, and armies, who capitulated on the promises of safety of life and respect of property, were put to death without compunction, in gross breach of faith. The inhabitants of cities were sold into slavery or transferred forcibly to Turkish dominions, in total disregard of solemn pledges.

A notable case of this kind was that of Bosnia, where the final victory was achieved by the Ottoman Grand Vizier, in command of one of the armies engaged, under the supreme command of the Sultan. The Prince of Bosnia and his army capitulated on the distinct engagement in writing that their lives would be spared. Mahomet was full of wrath at this concession. It was his deliberate policy to extinguish by death the family of any reigning prince whom he vanquished in war. He consulted on the point the Mufti, with doubtless a strong hint as to what the answer should be. The Mufti issued a *fetva* which declared that no treaty of this kind with an infidel was binding on the Sultan. The holy man went so far as to offer himself to act as executioner. When the Bosnian king was summoned to the presence of the Sultan, and came before him trembling, with the treaty of capitulation in his hand, the Mufti himself struck off his head in the presence of the Sultan, exclaiming that it was a good deed to put an end to an infidel. The *fetva* in this case formed a precedent for numerous similar cases. The whole of the royal family of Comnenus, the Emperor of Trebizond, who, without a fight, surrendered his kingdom to Mahomet, upon the promise of life and private property to himself and his family, were put to death a few weeks later in Constantinople on the most flimsy pretence.

In a similar way, when the island of Euboea was captured from the Venetians in 1470 by the Sultan, the Venetian garrison, supported by the Greek population, made a most gallant defence and inflicted enormous losses on the Turks. Paul Evizzo, the Venetian general in command of the island, eventually surrendered on the promise of safety of life to himself and his army. Mahomet broke his word. He put to death the whole of the Venetian garrison by the cruel method of impaling. The gallant Evizzo was, by the Sultan's order, sawn in two. His daughter was summoned to Mahomet's tent, and when she refused to submit to his lust, was put to death by his order. The island was added to the Ottoman Empire in 1471.

It must be admitted that in all these conquests the Ottoman armies were very greatly superior in number and in armaments. In many cases they were also assisted by the disunion of their opponents. The subjection of Karamania was due to the death of its last king, Ibrahim, who left seven sons behind him. Six of them were sons of a wife of royal descent, the seventh the son of a slave. The father favoured the youngest, whom he declared his heir. The other six fought for their patrimony against the youngest and besieged him in Konia, the capital. Mahomet thought that this was a good opportunity to intervene and to annex the whole country. Without any cause of quarrel he marched an army of a hundred thousand men into the country and waged war against all the sons. The Grand Vizier, Mahmoud Pasha, was sent on in advance, and defeated Ishak, the youngest son of Ibrahim, in front of Konia. The terms of capitulation were thought by Mahomet to be too humane. He determined to punish Mahmoud for his leniency. The cords of his tent were cut while the Vizier was asleep. The tent fell on the luckless sleeper. This was a sign of disgrace. Mahmoud, who was a most able and successful general and statesman, was removed from his post and was put to death. The Karamanian dynasty, which for so long had been the rival of that of Othman, was now completely subdued. The country became a province of the Turkish Empire. Its two principal cities were depopulated and lost their splendour. It never again gave trouble to the Ottoman government.

The country which suffered most from the cruelties of Mahomet was Greece. Here, again, disunion was the main cause of its ruin. Two brothers of Constantine, the last Greek Emperor at Constantinople, Demetrius and Thomas, held sway as tributaries of the Sultan, the one at Argos, the other at Patras. Unmindful of the danger which threatened them, they fought one another for supremacy, after the death of Constantine, and were assisted in their internecine war by large numbers of turbulent Albanians, who transferred their services, now to one and now to another of these petty despots, and are said to have changed sides three times in the course of a single Sunday. Mahomet, in 1458, thinking that the disputes between the two brothers afforded a good occasion for getting full possession of the Morea, invaded it with a large force. The two brothers, instead of uniting to defend the country, continued to fight against one another, and attempted, at the same time, singly to fight against the Turks. There followed scenes of massacre and rapine as Mahomet's army passed through the country, besieging and capturing successively its many petty strongholds. In nearly every case, after vigorous resistance, capitulation was offered and agreed to on promise of life to the garrisons. In no case was the promise kept. As a rule, the fighting-men were massacred after surrender, their leaders were sawn in two, and the other inhabitants were sold into slavery, or were in some cases transferred *en masse* to Constantinople as colonists to fill the empty city. The two brothers were driven from the country. Demetrius appears to have made some kind of terms with the Sultan, one of which was that his daughter should enter Mahomet's harem. This promise was not kept; she was not thought worthy of it, and she was insulted by being deprived of the only eunuch who attended her. It is not stated what became of her. Thomas fled from the country, carrying with him, instead of treasure, a valuable relic, the head of St. Andrew, with which he disappeared from history. The Sultan possessed himself of the whole country, with the exception of two or three seaports in the hands of the Venetians. The memory of this cruel invasion of the Turks was deeply impressed on the minds of the people of Greece. But for 471 years, with a short interlude when it was held by the Venetians, it remained a Turkish province.

On his way back to Constantinople the Sultan passed by Athens, where one Franco reigned as Duke, but tributary to the Turks. He gave orders that Franco was to be strangled. As a special favour this operation was effected, not in the tent of the Turkish general, but in his own domicile, and thus the last spark of Greek independence passed away.

It is not perhaps fair to judge of Mahomet as regards his cruelties and perfidies by a high standard. His opponents, the chiefs of the countries he invaded and conquered, were, in many cases, not inferior to him in these respects. Scanderbeg, whose patriotic defence of Albania won for him the reputation of a saint in his own country, and a high place in history, was most cruel and vindictive whenever he had the opportunity. He habitually massacred the prisoners taken in his battles. The two despots of the Morea were not behindhand in this respect. The Prince, or Voivode as he was called, of Wallachia, Wlad by name, was one of the most cruel and bloodthirsty ruffians recorded in history. He was known by the name of "the Impaler." He revelled in the dying agonies of the prisoners and other victims whom he subjected to this cruel death. They were reserved for this purpose to enliven his banquets. When some guest expressed surprise that he could bear the odour emanating from the victims of this death, the prince directed the immediate execution of his guest, on a higher pale than the others, so that he might not be incommoded by the odour he complained of.

Mahomet invaded Wallachia, in 1462, with an army of two hundred thousand. In his pursuit of Wlad he came across a field where twenty thousand Turks and Bulgarians had been put to death, one-half of them by impalement and the other half by crucifixion. Mahomet defeated and drove into exile this ruffian, and installed in his place a favourite named Radul, who had been brought up at his Court as a page. On the death of this man Wlad turned up again, but was killed by a slave. Wallachia, which previously had been compelled to pay tribute by Mahomet, was now made a vassal State. The Sultan appointed its prince. It was not otherwise treated as a Turkish province.

The failure of the Turkish general to capture the island of Rhodes was said to be due to the fact that, just before the final assault, after long resistance by the Knights who held this island, the Turkish general issued an order to the army that there was to be no pillage of the city, wishing to reserve for the Sultan and himself the wealth which might be captured. This dispirited the Turkish soldiers, and they made no effort for success in the assault. The Knights again repulsed the attack and the siege was raised. It was not till 1520 that Rhodes was finally captured.

Great as Mahomet was as a warrior and general, he was not less conspicuous as an administrator and statesman. The organization and provisioning of his armies in his numerous campaigns were specially worthy of notice. His soldiers were always well fed and were amply equipped with guns and armaments. He was also the sole source of legislation for his Empire. He had supreme power over life and property of all his subjects. More than any of his predecessors and successors, he founded mosques, hospitals, colleges, and schools in Constantinople and other cities of his Empire. He fully recognized the importance of science in education. He cultivated the society of learned men and loved to converse with them. He had some reputation as a poet. With all this, he was notorious for evil and sensual life in a direction which is held to be infamous and degrading by all peoples. He was not only himself guilty of fratricide, but he prescribed it as a family law for his successors. He died at the age of fifty-one, after thirty years of reign. He had collected a great army for another campaign, but no one knew what his aims and intentions were, whether for another attack on Rhodes, or for the invasion of Candia, or to follow up his success in Calabria. His secret died with him. He was the first Sultan to be buried at Constantinople, in the famous mosque which he built there. In spite of his cruelties and perfidies and of his evil life, he has been held in honour by successive generations of his countrymen, and has been rightly designated as 'the Conqueror.'

VIII

BAYEZID II
1481-1512

MAHOMET left two sons, of whom the eldest, Bayezid, succeeded him as Sultan at the age of thirty-five. Von Hammer and other historians, who have founded their narratives on his great work, write of Bayezid in terms of disparagement because, unlike other early Sultans of the Othman race, he did not signalize his reign by any great additions to his Empire. If success as a ruler is only to be measured by territorial expansion, Bayezid must take rank in history below the other nine Sultans who created the Ottoman Empire and raised it to its zenith. A great Empire, however, such as that which the Ottomans had already achieved, may be better served by peace than by war for further conquests. It would certainly have been well for the Ottomans if no attempt had ever been made to extend their Empire northwards beyond the Danube. Bayezid, so far as we can gather his policy from his actual deeds, was not favourable to expansion of his Empire. If he was engaged for some years in war with Hungary, Venice, and Egypt, he was not the aggressor. He came to terms of peace with these Powers when it was possible to do so. He did not support the army which, under his predecessor, had invaded Italy and captured Otranto. He recalled the very able general, Ahmed Keduk, who commanded it. Khaireddin Pasha, who succeeded in command, after a most gallant defence, was compelled to capitulate; and never again was Italy invaded by a Turkish army. It would seem to have been a wise decision on the part of Bayezid not to pursue further the Italian adventure.

As it is not our intention to write a complete history of the Ottoman Sultans, but rather to describe the early expansion of their Empire and its later dismemberment, it will not be necessary to devote more than a very few pages to the comparatively uneventful reign of Bayezid. It may be well, however, briefly to note that he was of philosophic temperament, very austere in religion, and without his father's vices. Like many of his race he was devoted to literary studies, and he had a reputation as a poet. He was not wanting in energy and valour when occasion required. He was, however, the first of his race who did not habitually lead his armies into the field.

His younger brother Djem, who at the death of Mahomet was only twenty-two years of age, was a much more fiery, valorous, and ambitious soldier, and of more attractive personality. He was of a romantic disposition, and had a much greater reputation than Bayezid as a poet. His poems rank high in Turkish literature. His strange adventures and sad fate form one of the romances of Turkish history, which might well fill many chapters. It must suffice to record of him that, like other brothers of Sultans who were not at once put to death at the commencement of a new reign, he took up arms and claimed the throne against Bayezid. The latter fortunately was the first to arrive at Constantinople after the death of Mahomet. He there obtained the support of the Janissaries, not without large presents to them. With the aid of Ahmed Keduk, Bayezid, after vain efforts to come to terms with his brother, was successful in putting down two rebellions of a formidable character on behalf of Djem. After the second defeat Djem fled to Egypt, and thence, after many adventures, found his way to the island of Rhodes, where he claimed the hospitality of the Knights of Jerusalem. Their Grand Master, D'Aubusson, who had made such a gallant defence of the island against Mahomet, and who was a most brave warrior, was also a crafty and perfidious intriguer. On the one hand, he induced Prince Djem to enter into a treaty, by which very important concessions were promised to the knights in the event of Djem being able to gain the Ottoman throne. On the other hand, D'Aubusson negotiated a treaty with Bayezid under which he was to receive an allowance of 45,000 ducats a year, nominally for the maintenance of Djem, but really as an inducement to prevent the escape of that prince from Rhodes. On the strength of this, the unfortunate prince was detained as a virtual prisoner in Rhodes, and later in a castle at Sasesnage, in France, belonging to the order of the Knights, for not less than seven years. At the end of this time the King of France, Charles VIII, intervened in favour of the prince, and got him transferred into the keeping of the Pope at Rome. The Pope Callixtus was also not above making a good profit out of Djem. He came to terms with Sultan Bayezid under which he was to pocket the 45,000 ducats a year so long as Djem was kept out of mischief. On the death, some years later, of this Pope, his successor, Pope Alexander Borgia, of infamous memory, renewed the treaty with Sultan Bayezid, with the addition of a clause that he was to receive a lump sum of 300,000 ducats if Prince Djem, instead of being detained as prisoner, was put to death. After a short interval the Pope, fearing the intervention of the King of France, on behalf of Djem, and wishing to pocket the lump sum, contrived the death by poison of the prince. The menace to the Sultan was thus at last removed, and his Empire was spared another civil war, at a cost which by the ethics of the day was no doubt fully justified.

Of other incidents in Bayezid's reign it is only necessary to state that the most important of his achievements was the complete subjection, in the second year of his reign, of Herzegovina, which had been a tributary State under his predecessors, but was now again invaded. It was finally incorporated as a province of the Empire. There were also many years of desultory war with Hungary, in which frequent raids were made by the two Powers upon one another's territories, and where each vied with the other in atrocious cruelties. Everywhere children were impaled, young women were violated in presence of their parents, wives in presence of their husbands, and thousands of captives were carried off and sold into slavery. But there were no other results, and peace was eventually established between the two Powers.

In Asia there was war for five years with the Mameluke government of Egypt and Syria. The Mamelukes had sent an army in support of an insurrection in Karamania. The outbreak was put down, and the Karamanians were finally subjected, but the Mamelukes defeated the Turkish armies in three great battles. Peace was eventually made, but only on concession by the Turks of three important fortresses in Asia Minor.

There was also war with the Republic of Venice, in the course of which the Turks succeeded in capturing the three remaining Venetian fortresses in the Morea—Navarino, Modon, and Coron—an important success which extinguished the influence of Venice on the coasts of Greece. The success was largely due to a great increase of the Turkish navy, which in Mahomet's reign had achieved a supremacy in the Mediterranean over any other single naval Power. It now defeated the Venetian fleet in a desperate battle off Lepanto in 1499, and met on equal terms the combined fleets of Venice, Austria, and the Pope in 1500. It also went farther afield, and at the entreaty of the Moors of Grenada, who were severely pressed by the Christian army in Spain, ravaged the coasts of that country.

The last two years of Bayezid's fairly prosperous reign were obscured by another civil war, this time at the instance of his son and successor, Selim. Selim was the youngest of three surviving sons of Bayezid. All three had been invested with important posts as governors of provinces in Asia. Ahmed, the second of them, was the favourite of his father, who designated him for succession to the throne. But Selim was by far the ablest and most daring of them. He determined to anticipate the death of his father, who was ageing and in feeble health, by securing the throne for himself. Leaving his seat of government with a large suite, almost amounting to an army, he paid a visit, uninvited, to his father at Constantinople, and there fomented intrigues. He was the idol of the Janissaries, who were dissatisfied with the long inaction of Sultan Bayezid, and hoped for new conquests and loot under Selim. Bayezid, however, was supported for the time by a section of his army, and succeeded in defeating his son. Selim then fled to the Crimea, where he raised a new army and, later, again made his way to Constantinople by a forced march round the north of the Black Sea. On arriving there he was supported by the full force of the Turkish army.

The Janissaries, at the instance of Selim, stormed at the gates of the imperial palace and insisted on the Sultan receiving them in person. Bayezid gave way and admitted a deputation of them to an audience. Seated on his throne, he asked them what they wanted. "Our Padishah," they said, "is old and sickly; we will that Selim shall be Sultan." Bayezid, finding that he could not rely on any section of his army, submitted. "I abdicate," he said, "in favour of my son, Selim. May God grant him a prosperous reign." He only asked as a favour that he might be allowed to retire to the city of Asia Minor where he was born. His son thereupon conducted his father, the ex-Sultan, to the outskirts of the city with every mark of respect, and Bayezid departed on his journey. He died, however, three days later, not without grave suspicion of foul play. The deposition of Bayezid is interesting and important as showing the increasing power of the Janissaries. Only the strongest Sultan could thenceforth cope with them, and they became eventually one of the main causes of the decay of the Empire which they had done so much to call into existence.

Bayezid, like others of his race, in spite of his philosophic temperament and his love of ease, had a vein of cruelty. It has been shown that he caused his brother Djem to be poisoned. This was in accord with the family law. A more serious instance was that he put to death his great general, Ahmed Keduk, to whom he was deeply indebted for success in putting down the insurrection of Djem. Ahmed had deeply offended the Sultan by brusquely opposing his peaceful policy, and Bayezid forcibly removed the incautious critic.

The net result to the Turkish Empire of the thirty-one years of Bayezid's reign was, on the one hand, the incorporation of Herzegovina, and the expulsion of the Venetians from the Morea; on the other, the loss of three fortresses in Asia Minor to the Mamelukes of Egypt and the withdrawal from the South of Italy.

An incident worth recording was the first appearance of Russia in the field of Turkish diplomacy. An ambassador was sent to Bayezid by Czar Ivan III. He was instructed to refuse to bow his knee to the Sultan or to concede precedence to any other ambassadors. Bayezid meekly gave way on these points of etiquette. This was a presage of the attitude of Russia which two centuries later threatened the existence of the Turkish Empire.

IX

SELIM I
1512-20

ON the forced abdication of Bayezid, Selim was proclaimed Sultan at Constantinople, with the full support of the Janissaries. He reigned for only eight years, but he succeeded in this short time in more than doubling the extent of the Ottoman Empire. He made no additions to it in Europe, but he conquered and annexed the great provinces of Diarbekir and Khurdistan from Persia, and Egypt, Syria, and a great part of Arabia, including the holy cities, from the Mameluke government of Egypt. He commenced this career of war and conquest at the ripe age of forty-seven. He proved to be a ruler and general of indomitable will and vigour, the exact opposite to his father in his greed for expansion of his Empire. He was a most able administrator. He cared little for his harem or other pleasures of life. Sleeping but little, he spent his nights in literary studies. He delighted in theological discussions and in the society of learned men, and he appointed them to high offices in the State. They had no effect, however, in softening his evil nature. He had no regard for human life, whether in war or in peace. He was attended by men called mutes, who were ready at any moment to strangle or decapitate on the spot any person designated by him. His most trusted counsellors, his oldest friends and associates, were in constant danger of life. He met argument or protest against his schemes, or criticism of his past actions, by instant death, not unfrequently by his own hand. During his short reign seven of his Grand Viziers were decapitated by his orders. Numerous other officials and generals shared the same fate. They seldom enjoyed the sweets of office for more than a few months. One of them, in playful reminder of this to Selim, asked to be given a short notice of his doom, so that he might put his private affairs in order. The Sultan replied to him: "I have been thinking for some time of having thee killed, but I have at present no one to fill thy place, otherwise I would willingly oblige thee." Judges convicted of corruption were dealt with in the same way. By a malicious irony they were compelled to pass sentence on themselves, before being handed over to the executioner. Janissaries who dared to ask for an increase of pay were also condemned to death. The first recorded act of Selim's reign was to strike dead with his own sword a Janissary who was deputed by the corps to ask for the accustomed presents on his accession. It does not appear that these events cast gloom on Selim's Court. They soon lost the sense of novelty. There were plenty of applicants for the vacant posts, willing and eager to run the risks of office. Selim was agreeable in his conversation and life was gay. He did not indulge in refinements of cruelty like his grandfather Mahomet. He acted from a sense of public duty. If he spilled much blood, he restored and maintained discipline in the army and stemmed the course of corruption. He was distinctly popular with his subjects, with whom, as in most Eastern countries, affection was in part inspired by terror.

As was to be expected, Selim's two elder brothers, Khorkand and Ahmed, whose claims to the Sultanate had been set aside, and who were at the head of important governments in Asia Minor, took up arms against him. Selim, without loss of a moment, led an army to Brusa against them. Khorkand, taken unawares, was quickly defeated. He was allowed an hour's respite before being bow-strung. During this short interval he wrote a poem deprecating his brother's cruelty. Selim wept over the poem and ordered a State funeral for his brother. At Brusa a horrible scene of slaughter took place. Five nephews of Selim—possible claimants to the throne—were collected there. They were of varying ages, from five to twenty. They were all strangled by order of the Sultan—the eldest of them resisting with terrible struggles, the youngest with plaintive cries for mercy, while Selim from an adjoining room was a witness of the scene, and urged his mutes to hasten their task. Ahmed, the second and favourite son of Bayezid, made a longer resistance in the field, but a few months later he was defeated and put to death.

Selim, now safe on his throne, turned his attention to war with Persia. The principal cause of conflict arose out of a dispute on religion. From an early time the Mahommedan world had been divided into two hostile sects—the Sunnites and the Schiis. The point of difference was whether authority should be attributed to the writings of the four immediate descendants of the Prophet, as the Schiis contended, or whether the words of the Prophet alone should be conclusive on matters of dogma. It would seem that the smaller the difference in dogma between two sects of a religious body, the worse they hate one another; and just as the Christians of the Greek and Latin Churches hated one another more than they hated the followers of Mahomet, so the Sunnites and the Schiis hated one another to the point that they were each bent on exterminating the other—though the difference between them might seem to outsiders to be no greater than that between Tweedledum and Tweedledee.

Persia was the headquarters of the Schiis. In the Ottoman Empire the Sunnites greatly prevailed. But of late years the Schiis had gained ground in Asia Minor. Selim, who was a bigoted follower of Mahomet, determined to extirpate this heresy throughout his Empire. With devilish zeal he employed an army of spies to ferret out the heretics, and on a given day seventy thousand of them were arrested. Forty thousand of them were put to death, and the remainder were condemned to terms of imprisonment. This violent action does not seem to have aroused any popular indignation against Selim.

It earned for him in Turkey the title of 'the Just,' and diplomats of the day and historians wrote of it in laudatory terms. It was a proof of the possibility of extirpating a heresy if the means adopted were ruthlessly carried out. The Schii heresy was extinguished, once for all, in the Ottoman Empire. This exploit, however, added to the animosity already existing between the Persians and the Ottomans, and made war between them inevitable. The immediate clash was hastened by the Persians giving asylum to Murad, a son of Ahmed, who had not been included in the slaughter of his cousins at Brusa.

Persia, at this time, was under the rule of Shah Ismail, a most capable and successful ruler, who had renovated the kingdom, and added largely to it by the conquest and subjection of many minor adjoining States. The two potentates were well matched in vigour and ability. When war with Persia was propounded by Selim in his council, there was ominous silence. There was evidently fear of the undertaking. The Janissary guarding the entrance to the chamber broke down the suspense by throwing himself on his knees before Selim and expressing ardent support to the war. This precipitated a decision by the council, and the Janissary was at once promoted to high office.

Early in March, 1514, a hundred and forty thousand men and three hundred guns were collected on the Asian side of the Bosphorus, under command of the Sultan. Sixty thousand camels were provided to carry its baggage and munitions. The army commenced its march on April 20th. Its aim was Tabriz, then the capital of Persia, distant from Scutari, as the crow flies, by over one thousand miles of a mountainous country, in which there were no roads. The main difficulty was the supply of the army with food for men, horses, and camels. This was partly effected from Trebizond, to which the command of the Black Sea enabled Selim to send supplies from Constantinople.

Selim preluded his campaign by an insolent letter to Shah Ismail. In the course of it he said:—

It is only by the practice of the true religion that a man will prosper in this world and deserve eternal life in the world to come. As for thee, Emir Ismail, such a reward will never be thy lot; for thou hast deserted the path of salvation and of the holy commandment; thou hast denied the purity of the doctrine of Islam; thou hast dishonoured and cast down the altars of God; thou hast by base stratagem alone raised thyself and sprung from the dust— to a seat of splendour and glory; thou hast opened to Mussulmans the gate of tyranny and oppression; thou hast forced iniquity, perjury, and blasphemy to impiety, heresy, and schism; thou hast, under the cloak of hypocrisy, sown in all parts the seeds of trouble and sedition; thou hast raised the standard of ungodliness; thou hast given way to thy shameful passions and abandoned thyself without restraint to the most disgraceful excesses.... Therefore, as the first duty of a Mussulman, and above all of a pious prince, is to obey the commandment, "Oh ye faithful who believe, perform ye the decrees of the Lord"—the ulemas and our teachers of the law have pronounced death against thee, perjurer and blasphemer as thou art, and have laid upon every good Mussulman the sacred duty of taking arms for the defence of religion and for the destruction of heresy and impiety, in thy person and the persons of those who follow thee.

On the approach of Selim and his army to the frontier of Persia, Shah Ismail, instead of going out to meet his foe, laid waste the whole country and retreated towards his capital. This greatly increased the difficulty Selim had of supplying his army. The soldiers were exhausted by the long march. The Janissaries began to murmur. One of the generals, Hemdar Pasha, who had been brought up with Selim from his earliest childhood, and might be expected to have great influence with him, was persuaded by his brother officers to remonstrate with the Sultan against further prosecution of the invasion of Persia, through a country where every vestige of food was destroyed. The Sultan met the suggestion by ordering the instant decapitation of the pasha.

Selim endeavoured to provoke Ismail to meet him in battle by another insolent letter, written mainly in verse, taunting him with cowardice. "One who, by perjury," he wrote, "seizes sceptres, ought not to skulk from danger.... Dominion is a bride to be wooed and won by him only whose lip blanches not at the biting kiss of the sabre's edge." Ismail replied in a dignified letter denying the existence of any reason for war, and expressing willingness to resume peaceful relations. He suggested that Selim's letter, written in a style so unfitting the dignity of the Sultan, must have been the hasty production of a secretary, who had taken an overdose of opium. The taunt was a bitter one, for it was well known that Selim was addicted to opium. The letter was accompanied by the present of a box of opium to the supposed secretary.

Meanwhile Selim and his army marched on with ever-increasing difficulties of supplies. The soldiers at last broke out in open revolt and demanded to be led back to their homes. Selim took the bold course of riding into the midst of them and addressing them personally.

Is this [he said] your service to your Sultan? Does your loyalty consist of mere boast and lip worship? Let those among you who wish to go stand out from the ranks and depart. As for me, I have not advanced thus far merely to double back on my track. Let the cowards instantly stand aloof from the brave who have devoted themselves with sword and quiver, soul and hand to our enterprise.

He gave word of command to form columns and march, and not a single man dared to leave the ranks.

On the approach of the Ottoman army to Tabriz, Ismail was at last drawn from his reserve. He determined to give battle. The two armies met at Calderan, not far from the capital, on August 14th, 116 days from the commencement of the march, which must have covered nearly twelve hundred miles. This was a great performance on the part of the Turkish army. It was by this time reduced to one hundred and twenty thousand men, of whom eighty thousand were cavalry. The Persian army consisted of eighty thousand cavalry, splendidly mounted and equipped, and well trained. But there were no infantry and no guns. The Turkish soldiers were fatigued by their long march. They were ill-fed and the horses were stale and out of condition. The issue turned upon the success of the charges of the Persian cavalry. They attacked the Turks with great impetuosity in two bodies on either flank. That under command of Ismail himself was successful and broke and dispersed the opposing wing of the Turks. The other column was unsuccessful. The Ottomans fell back behind their guns. The Janissaries formed a solid front. The cannons opened a destructive fire, which was supported by the fire of the Janissaries, who were now armed with muskets. The Persians were shattered and destroyed. The defeat of the other wing of the Turkish army was retrieved. Twenty-five thousand Persian horsemen lay dead on the field. Ismail himself was badly wounded and escaped with difficulty.

After this victory Selim entered Tabriz, and remained there eight days. It was his wish to winter in Persia and to renew his campaign in the following spring, but his soldiers objected and insisted on being led home. This time Selim found himself unable to refuse. He turned homeward with his army. No terms of peace were concluded with Ismail, and the two countries continued nominally at war during the remainder of Selim's life. But the great provinces of Diarbekir and Khurdistan remained in the hands of the Turks. Selim left them in charge of the well-known Turkish historian, Idris, who spent the next year in organizing these two departments and in putting down any attempt at resistance. He was eminently successful in this, and the two provinces were permanently annexed to the Ottoman Empire. The whole campaign of Selim must be considered as a most striking success. To have marched a hundred and forty thousand men, with eighty thousand horses and three hundred guns, over twelve hundred miles, and to have defeated a powerful army, backed by all the resources of a great country, was an achievement which earned for Selim a place in the first rank of great generals. Selim does not appear to have been anxious to include Persia in his Empire.

- 82 -

His hatred of the Schii heresy was such that he aimed rather at isolation than annexation. He issued a firman forbidding any trade with Persia, and when a number of merchants were reported to him for having broken the law by entering into illicit trade with the Persians, he ordered them to be executed. He was only with difficulty induced to revoke the order by the Mufti Djemali.

On his return to Constantinople Selim, inflamed by his success in putting down the heresy of the Schiis and his victory over heretical Persia, determined to extirpate Christianity from his dominion. Again with the greatest difficulty he was dissuaded from this course by the courageous Mufti. But he insisted on depriving the Christians in Constantinople of all their churches, which he turned into mosques.

In the spring of 1516 Selim determined to extend his Empire by the conquest of Syria and Egypt. These countries had been for many years past under the rule of the Mamelukes, a body of soldiers recruited from Circassian slaves, and from whose ranks Sultans were elected for their lives. The existing Sultan, Kansar Ghowri, was eighty years of age, but was still able to take command in the field of his Mamelukes. The immediate pretext for war, as in the case of Persia, was a religious one. A claim was preferred by Selim for the protection of the holy cities of Mecca and Medina.

On June 26th Selim arrived at Konia, and thence sent an insolent missive of defiance to Ghowri, who was at Aleppo. In return, a mission was sent to the Turkish headquarters. It consisted of an envoy and a suite of ten Mamelukes in splendid military array and glittering with armour. Selim was indignant at this warlike demonstration. He directed the immediate execution of the ten members of the suite, and with difficulty was persuaded not to deal in the same way with the envoy. As an alternative the envoy was shorn of his beard and hair, his head was covered by a nightcap, and he was mounted on a broken-down donkey, and was returned in this ignominious way to Ghowri.

The two armies met in battle not far from Aleppo. The issue was not in doubt. The Egyptians had no guns. They also suffered from the defection of the Djellans, a section of Mamelukes of the second and inferior rank. An hour sufficed to ensure complete victory to the Turks. Ghowri fled and died, trampled to death, it was said, by the mass of fugitives. The victory caused the loss not only of Aleppo but of the whole of Syria. Selim, after a few days at Aleppo, went to Damascus, and there organized the invasion of Egypt. This involved the provision of many thousands of camels to carry water for the troops when crossing the desert. He sent five thousand men to Gaza, under Sinan Pasha, the brave general who had led the victorious wing of his army against the Persians. They met there an Egyptian army of about the same number, and a fierce battle ensued, which resulted in the defeat of the Mamelukes, mainly owing to the Ottoman artillery.

Selim left Damascus with his main army on December 16th. On arrival at Gaza he ordered the immediate slaughter of all its inhabitants. He also directed the execution of one of his own generals who ventured to point out to him the danger of an invasion of Egypt. On January 10th the arrangements for this expedition were complete. Ten days were occupied in crossing the desert between Syria and Egypt. The army was harassed by Arabs, but there was no attempt to resist on the part of the main Egyptian army. When, at one time, the Grand Vizier, thinking that the cloud of Arabs meant a more serious resistance, persuaded Selim to mount his war-horse, the Sultan, on finding it was a false alarm and that it was only an affair with Arabs, directed the execution of the Vizier.

On the last day of the year 1516 Selim arrived with his army within a few miles of Cairo. Meanwhile the Mamelukes had elected Tourman Bey as Sultan to succeed Ghowri. But there was much opposition to this on the part of those who favoured the claim of the son of Ghowri. As a result, there was dissension in the Egyptian army. Two of their leaders, Ghazali Bey and Khair Bey, entered into treasonable relations with Selim. Ghazali persuaded Tourman to send the guns, with which the Egyptian army was now provided, by the ordinary route, and then secretly sent information of this to Selim, who was able to avoid the guns by taking another route.

The two armies met near Ridania. The battle resulted in the complete defeat of the Egyptians, with a loss of twenty-five thousand men, owing to their want of guns. Selim then advanced on Cairo. There was no resistance at first, but later the Mamelukes reoccupied it and made a desperate resistance to the Turkish army. The streets were barricaded and every house was turned into a fortress. Selim spent three days in getting possession of the city. Eight hundred Mamelukes who surrendered on promise of their lives were put to death. A general massacre of the inhabitants then took place, and fifty thousand of them perished by the sword, or were thrown into the flames of the burning houses. As a result of this, and further military operations in the Delta, Egypt was completely subdued. The brave and generous Tourman was taken prisoner and, after denouncing the two traitors in the presence of Selim, was put to death.

Some months were then occupied by Selim in organizing the conquered country. It was not annexed as an integral part of Turkey. The Mamelukes, or rather the section of them who had been unfaithful to their Sultan, and who had survived the general slaughter, were entrusted with the administration of Egypt, subject to the superior control of a pasha appointed by the Turkish government. Ghazali and Khair Bey received the reward of their treason—Ghazali was appointed Governor of Syria and Khair Bey of Egypt. A garrison of five thousand Ottoman soldiers was left at Cairo. The Turkish army insisted on an early return to Constantinople. A war against

Moslems, where there was no opportunity of making captives for sale as slaves or for harems, had no charm for them. Selim had once more to give way.

It was not till September 17th that he was able to commence his homeward march. Having safely passed the desert, he said to his Grand Vizier, Younis Pasha, who was riding beside him, "Well, our backs are now turned on Egypt and we shall soon be at Gaza." Younis, who had originally been opposed to the expedition, could not resist the reply: "And what has been the result of all our trouble and fatigue, if it is not that half our army has perished in battle, or in the sands of the desert, and that Egypt is now governed by a gang of traitors?" This imprudent speech cost the Grand Vizier his life. His head was struck off as he rode by his master's side.

The conquest of Egypt entailed the acquisition of the interests of that country in a great part of Arabia, including the holy cities of Mecca and Medina. Selim was also able to induce the titular Caliph, who through many generations had inherited from the early successors of Mahomet a certain undefined authority in the religious world, and who held a shadowy Court at Cairo, to make over to him and his successors, as Sultans of Turkey, the barren office, together with its symbols, the standard and cloak of the Prophet. These symbols were removed to Constantinople, and thenceforth the Sultans assumed the title of Caliphs and Protectors of the Holy Places—and this may have added to their prestige in the Moslem world, though it may be doubted whether it contributed much to the strength of the Turkish Empire. Of more material advantage was the fact that an annual tribute was paid by the Egyptian government, which a few years later, under Solyman, was fixed at 80,000 ducats. It also contributed men and ships to wars undertaken by the Sultan. In the siege of Rhodes, in 1524, Egypt sent three thousand Mamelukes and twenty vessels of war.

Selim spent some time at Damascus and Aleppo on his way back in organizing his new acquisitions. Syria was incorporated in the Turkish Empire, and has remained so to the present time.

The campaign which ended in the conquest of Egypt and Syria was not less conspicuous in its result than that against Persia, more on account of the difficulties of organization, than for success on the field of battle. Treason and the want of artillery were more responsible for the defeat of the Mamelukes than the valour of the Ottoman troops. It is not easy for us to understand why Egypt was not incorporated in the Empire in the same way as Syria. The Mamelukes were as much strangers to the country as the Turks themselves. The minority of them, who survived the war and the bloody executions by Selim, had no claim to recognition as the ruling class in Egypt, other than their treachery to their fellow-Mamelukes and their Sultan and the aid which they had given to the invaders. It will be seen that these surviving Mamelukes soon regained full power in Egypt, and reduced the pashas appointed from Constantinople to puppets.

Selim returned to his capital in 1518. In the remaining two years of his life there were no further military exploits. He made great preparations for another campaign. He added greatly to the strength of his navy. He built a hundred and fifty ships of war, many of them of great size for those days. It was generally believed that he intended an attack on Rhodes to avenge the defeat of his grandfather, the acquisition of which, lying as it did across the route to Egypt, was of great importance. Before, however, any decision was arrived at, Selim died on his way to Adrianople, very near to the spot where his father had been poisoned by his orders. He left the reputation of being one of the ablest organizers of victory, but also the most cruel despot of the Othman line. It was for long a common expression with the Turks, by way of a curse, "May'st thou be a vizier to Sultan Selim."

X.

SOLYMAN THE MAGNIFICENT
1520-66

SELIM was succeeded by his only son, Solyman, at the age of twenty-six, who reigned for forty-six years, a period of unexampled splendour in the history of the Ottoman Empire—its culminating era. This was mainly due to the personal qualities of the new Sultan. He surpassed all his predecessors, and still more his degenerate successors, in dignity and graciousness. He was not behind the best of them in military capacity, vigour of action, and personal courage. He combined with these qualities statesmanship of high order. With rare exceptions he stood by his engagements and did not follow the precept of the Koran that faith need not be kept with infidels. He was great as an administrator and legislator. Before he mounted the throne he had been employed by his father as governor of three very important provinces, and had gained a high reputation for his determination to secure justice to his subjects, whatever their race or creed. His private life was free from scandal. He was noted for his clemency and kindness of heart. If massacres took place after victories or after capture of fortresses when he was in command, it was because he could not restrain his turbulent and bloodthirsty Janissaries; but the occasions of such scenes were comparatively rare. He had, however, a blend of cruelty in his character, as had most of his predecessors. Being an only son, he had no occasion, on mounting the throne, to carry out the fratricidal law of Mahomet II. But he was determined that there should be no possible rival in his family, however remote. After the surrender of Rhodes, two years later, on the promise of life and property to its defenders, he singled out, in breach of his promise, a son of Prince Djem, who was one of those included in the amnesty, and directed the immediate execution of him and his four sons. Worse also than fratricide was the murder by Solyman of two of his own sons. The eldest of them, Mustapha, was a most promising prince. He had already shown his capacity as governor of a province. He was endowed with all his father's best qualities. He was the idol of the army and the hope of his country.

Solyman was persuaded by his latest favourite concubine, a Russian lady, Ghowrem by name, who had unbounded influence over him and retained it till late in life, that Prince Mustapha was intriguing against him, and aimed at dethroning him, as Selim had done in the case of Bayezid. She hoped to secure the succession for her own son. Without a word of warning or any opportunity of defending himself, Mustapha, in the course of the second Persian campaign in 1553, on entering his father's tent, was seized by the mutes and was strangled while Solyman looked on at the foul deed. There was more excuse for putting to death another son, Bayezid, who had been goaded by an intrigue in the Sultan's harem into taking up arms, in 1561, against his brother Selim. He was defeated and fled to Persia, where he was at first received with great honour by Shah Talmasp, the successor to Ismail, with the distinct promise that he would not be given up. But Solyman obtained his extradition by threat of war and the promise of 400,000 pieces of gold. The unfortunate prince was treated with the greatest indignity. His hair and beard were shorn. He was handed over, together with his four sons, to an emissary of his brother Selim, who at once put to death the whole party.

As a result of the murders of these two sons of Solyman, a third one, the son of Ghowrem, was the only heir to the throne. He succeeded Solyman and was known as "Selim the Sot." It will be seen that this prince had none of the qualities of his race. He was the first of a long line of degenerates who eventually lost the greater part of the Empire which had been built up by Solyman and his predecessors.

Though the office of Grand Vizier was not so dangerous to its holders as under Selim I, it proved to be fatal to two of the nine men who held it during Solyman's reign. One of the most remarkable incidents of Solyman's life was his infatuation for Ibrahim, the second of his Grand Viziers. Ibrahim, a renegade Greek by birth, had been captured as a boy by corsairs and sold as a slave to a widow in Magnesia, who brought him up as a Mussulman. Recognizing his talents, this lady gave him an excellent education. Solyman, on a visit to that province, came across Ibrahim, and, attracted by his musical talent, took him into service, where he rose to be master of the pages and grand falconer. He soon acquired immense influence over his master, whose sister was given to him in marriage. He was rapidly promoted, and in 1523 was appointed Grand Vizier. The Sultan and his favourite became inseparable. They had their meals alone together. They concerted between them all the affairs of State. Ibrahim justified this preference, for he proved to be of great capacity, not inferior in any respect to his master, and his superior in education and knowledge of languages and history. He was appointed Seraskier, or Commander-in-Chief, when the Sultan was unable personally to command. In the earlier campaigns in Hungary and Persia, and in the siege of Vienna, he took a most active part, and was the main adviser to his master.

After thirteen years of implicit confidence in Ibrahim, suspicion arose in the mind of the Sultan and was fanned by the Sultana Ghowrem, who coveted the post of Grand Vizier for her son-in-law, Roostem Pasha. There does not appear to have been any ground for these suspicions, save that Ibrahim, intoxicated by his elevation, assumed the airs almost of an equal with the Sultan. A vizier suspected was very near to his doom. Entering the palace one day in 1536 to dine with the Sultan as usual, he was never seen alive again. The next morning his body was found in the palace. His immense wealth was confiscated to the State. It was said that Solyman in an adjoining room to that where this murder was perpetrated was smothered with kisses by Ghowrem so as to drown the cries of the dying Vizier.

In another case, the Grand Vizier Achmet was decapitated in the council chamber by order of Solyman, solely because he gave advice which displeased his master. Von Hammer gives a long list of other high officials who shared the same fate.

During the forty-six years of his reign Solyman added enormously to the Empire. Belgrade, Rhodes, nearly the whole of Hungary, the Crimea, the great provinces of Mossul, Bagdad, and Bassorah, and a part of Armenia taken from Persia, Yemen and Aden in Arabia, Algiers, Oran, and Tripoli, and an undefined extent of hinterland inhabited by Arabs in North Africa, and a wide extension of Egypt in the direction of Nubia, were the contributions which he transmitted to his successors. There were few years of his long reign in which he was not under arms. War with Hungary and Austria in the north alternated with war with Persia in the east and with Spain in the west. Solyman was often in command of his armies. He conducted personally thirteen campaigns, some of them, such as those against Persia, extending over two years. For the most part these wars were embarked on without any just or even plausible cause. They were stimulated by lust of conquest on the Sultan's part, and by craving for active service and for loot on the part of the Janissaries. Religious fanaticism seems to have had little concern with the motives or results of them.

Solyman's first campaign, in 1521, was directed against Belgrade, the city which had successfully defied Mahomet II. He marched against it at the head of an army of a hundred thousand men with three hundred guns. It was bravely defended by the Hungarians. But they had no guns. After seven days of bombardment the city was assaulted and captured. There was no massacre of the garrison or the inhabitants. Solyman converted the principal church into a mosque. The city was thenceforth garrisoned by a Turkish force. It constituted the principal stronghold of the Empire on the Danube, and was the gateway for many invasions of Hungary.

In the next year, 1523, Solyman followed up this success by an attack on the island of Rhodes, where Mahomet had also failed, and the capture of which had become more important since the conquest of Egypt, lying as it did on the direct route by sea from Constantinople. For this purpose Solyman sent a fleet of three hundred vessels with eight thousand Janissaries and a hundred siege guns. He marched at the head of a hundred thousand men through Asia Minor to the bay of Marmerice, opposite to Rhodes, whence they were conveyed to the island. The knights, six hundred in number, with only five

- 89 -

thousand trained soldiers and a *levée* of peasants on the island, made a heroic defence under their Grand Master, de Lisle Adam. It was only after a siege of nine months that they were at last compelled to capitulate. It was the first occasion on which a great fortress was approached by sap and spade work, so as to avoid gun fire, and in which bombs were used by the attacking army. Solyman's army is said to have lost fifty thousand men in casualties and as many more by disease. Under the terms of capitulation, the survivors of the garrison with all their personal property were to be conveyed to Crete, after twelve days, in their own galleys. After an interview with the Grand Master the Sultan is reported to have said, with great generosity, "It is not without regret that I force this brave man from his home in his old age." The arms of the knights are still to be seen carved on the houses they occupied in Rhodes. The Turks have always respected them in memory of the gallant defence. The terms of surrender were faithfully observed by Solyman with the exception already referred to. The knights eventually settled at Malta, at that time a nearly desert island. They made it the seat of their order and fortified it. Its central position in the Mediterranean made it a stronghold of the utmost importance. Solyman, in the last year but one of his long reign, thought it necessary for the expansion of his Empire, in the North of Africa, to oust the knights from their new nest. He sent an army and a fleet under command of Piale Reis to besiege it. There commenced another celebrated siege in which the knights, under command of their Grand Master, Lavallette, covered themselves with glory. The Turks were defeated in many assaults on the fortress, and were ultimately compelled to withdraw with heavy losses.

The two years after the conquest of Rhodes were spent by Solyman in organizing his kingdom. His inaction was greatly resented by the Janissaries, who hated their dull life in barracks and longed for war and for loot. They broke out in revolt and pillaged the houses of Ibrahim and other great functionaries. The outbreak was quelled, Solyman killing with his own hand three of the rebels. Their Agha and other leaders were put to death. But Solyman found it expedient to appease the mercenaries by generous presents, and in the next year—mainly at their instigation—embarked on another war. He was urged to invade Hungary by Francis I, King of France, who hoped to create a diversion from the ambitious projects of the Emperor Charles V. This may be considered as the first entry of the Turks into the maze of European politics. Hungary and Bohemia were at that time united under the rule of Louis II, a very young and inexperienced man.

In April, 1526, Solyman and his Grand Vizier, Ibrahim, with a hundred thousand men and three hundred guns, marched to Belgrade, and thence invaded Hungary. On August 27th, five months after their departure from Constantinople, they met the Hungarian army at Mohacz, not far from the Danube, and about half-way from Belgrade to Buda, then, as now, the capital of Hungary. The battle was quickly decided. The Ottoman army had the advantage of an overwhelming superiority both of men and guns. The Hungarians were defeated. Their King, eight bishops, a great majority of the Hungarian nobles, and twenty-four thousand men were killed. This decided the fate of Hungary. Before marching onwards, Solyman ordered all the prisoners he had taken—four thousand in number—to be put to death. He reached Buda on September 10th. The city surrendered. Solyman received there the submission of a number of Hungarian nobles who had survived the disaster of Mohacz. At his instance, Count Zapolya, one of the magnates of Hungary and Voivode of Transylvania, was elected by them as King of Hungary in succession to Louis II, who had left no heir. Solyman shortly after this—influenced in part by news of civil disturbance in Asia Minor—left Buda and retreated to the Danube, and thence returned to his capital. The temporary occupation of part of Hungary had been attended with fearful devastation and with great loss of life to its population. It was estimated that two hundred thousand men were massacred. The retreating army carried off an immense booty and drove before them about a hundred thousand captives of both sexes, who were eventually sold as slaves at Constantinople. Garrisons were left by the Turks in some of the frontier fortresses of Hungary.

The election of Count Zapolya as King of Hungary under the dictation of the Turks led to civil war in that country. Archduke Ferdinand, brother of Charles V, to whom the Emperor had transferred his Archduchy of Austria, claimed the throne of Hungary, by virtue of a treaty between the Emperor and the late King Louis. On the other hand, it was claimed by Zapolya and his adherents that, under an ancient law of Hungary, no one but a native could be elected as King. In spite of this, the nobles of Western Hungary met in Diet at Presburg and elected Ferdinand. Ferdinand appealed to arms, and was supported by the Austrians. He defeated his rival. Zapolya was driven from the country. He fled to Poland, and thence he appealed to the Sultan for aid in support of his claims in Hungary. Ferdinand, hearing of this, sent an envoy to the Sultan. Most unwisely, he not only claimed assistance in support of his claims to the throne of Hungary, but he demanded that Belgrade and other towns in Hungary in possession of the Sultan should be given up. Ibrahim, the Grand Vizier, who conducted the negotiations with the two rivals, was most arrogant. He claimed that every place where the hoofs of the Sultan's horses had once trod became at once and for ever part of the Ottoman Empire. "We have slain," he said, "King Louis of Hungary. His kingdom is now ours to hold or to give to whom we list. It is not the crown that makes the King, it is the sword. It is the sword that brings men into subjection; and what the sword has won the sword will keep."

The Sultan decided against Ferdinand and said to Zapolya's envoy, "I will be a true friend to thy master. I will march in person to aid him. I swear it by our Prophet Mahomet, the beloved of God, and by my sabre." To the rival's agent he said that he would speedily visit Ferdinand and drive him from the kingdom he had stolen. "Tell him that I will look for him on the field of Mohacz or even in Buda, and if he fail to meet me there, I will offer him battle beneath the walls of Vienna."

In pursuance of these threats, Solyman, in 1529, at the head of two hundred and fifty thousand men and with three hundred guns, again invaded Hungary and laid siege to Buda. The city surrendered at the instance of traitors among its defenders. Under the terms of capitulation life and property were to be preserved to the garrison and the citizens. The Janissaries, furious at the loss of loot, refused to recognize the terms. They massacred all the garrison as they issued from the fortress, and they carried off for sale most of the young women of the town. Zapolya was reinstated as a vassal King of that part of Hungary. Solyman then marched on to Vienna. He arrived there on September 27, 1529, with over two hundred thousand men. There ensued the first of the two memorable sieges of Vienna by the Ottomans.

Charles V, Emperor of Germany, was at this time the greatest and most powerful sovereign in Europe. He had inherited the kingdoms of Spain, the Netherlands, Naples and Sicily, as well as his possessions in Germany. Born six years later than Solyman, he was elected Emperor of Germany a year before the accession of Solyman as Sultan. He abdicated his throne and retired to a monastery ten years before the death of Solyman. For thirty-six years, therefore, their reigns were synchronous. It would be hard to say which of the two sovereigns was the more valiant in arms, or the more astute statesman. Judged by the extent of conquests, Solyman far surpassed his rival. Charles did little more than maintain the integrity of his immense inherited possessions in Europe. But he acquired by conquest Tunis in Africa, and Mexico and Peru in America.

When Solyman, instigated by Francis I of France, was invading Austria, Charles was deeply engaged in war against France in Italy, and could not send an army to meet the Ottomans in the field. Vienna was left to stand the brunt of invasion without a protecting army. Its garrison consisted of only sixteen thousand soldiers under Count de Salms. Its fortifications were only a continuous wall 5 feet in thickness and without bastions. Its guns were only seventy-two in number. Such weak defences seemed to offer little hope against the overwhelming numbers of the Ottomans. The tents of the Sultan and his army whitened the whole plain round the city. Irregular cavalry, called Scorchers, depending on loot for their food and pay, ravaged the country for miles round the city with incredible cruelty and rapacity. A Turkish flotilla of four hundred small vessels found its way up the Danube, after destroying all bridges, and lent assistance to the siege. It was all in vain. The Austrian and Spanish troops under the Count de Salms defended the weak lines with the utmost courage and tenacity. The Viennese citizens constructed lines of earthworks within the walls, against which the lighter guns of the Turks had little effect. The powerful siege guns of the Ottomans had been left behind *en route*, owing to heavy rains and the badness of roads. Numerous assaults were made by the Turks. The soldiers were at last dispirited by failure. In vain their officers drove them on by sticks and sabres. The men said they preferred death from their officers to death from the long arquebuses of the Spaniards. Twenty ducats a head were given or promised to them. It was to no purpose. Solyman, after three weeks of fruitless assaults, found himself compelled to raise the siege and to retreat with his great army. His irregulars had so ravaged the country that he had the utmost difficulty in feeding his men.

Before striking the camp all the immense booty taken in the campaign was burnt. The prisoners, most of them the peasantry of the district round Vienna, were massacred. Only the fairest of the young women were carried off captives to be sold as slaves. The Sultan returned to Constantinople. There was no pursuit of his army. It came back intact. It was a slur on the fame of Solyman that he endeavoured to conceal his failure to capture Vienna by lying accounts of success, and by a popular celebration of triumph, on return to his capital. There was this much to be said for him, that he had flouted the Austrians, by invading their country and devastating it up to the walls of Vienna, without any attempt, on their part, to meet him in the field or to follow him up on his retreat.

Three years later, in 1532, Solyman, with another immense army, again invaded Hungary, with the avowed object of marching to Vienna and attacking the army of the Emperor. Charles V, on this occasion, took command of the Austrian army. It was expected that a trial of strength would take place between the two potentates, and would decide which of them was the stronger. But Solyman's progress was delayed by the heroic defence for three weeks of the small fortress of Guns. After its capture Solyman made no further advance towards Vienna, but turned aside and devastated Styria, and then led his army homeward. The Emperor, on his part, made no effort to meet his foe and join conclusions with him. It was evident that both of them were anxious to avoid the issue of a great battle.

Though the Sultan had retreated and had returned to Constantinople, peace was not concluded, and a desultory war was continued for some years between Ferdinand and Zapolya. Peace was concluded in 1538, under which Zapolya was to retain the title of King of Eastern Hungary and Transylvania and Ferdinand was acknowledged ruler of the western half. In 1566 Solyman again invaded Hungary, on his thirteenth and last campaign, to which we will revert later.

We have thus described briefly the course of events between the Turks and the Hungarians, supported by Austria. Though the conquests of Solyman in this direction had been arrested by his failure to capture Vienna, he succeeded in securing virtual possession of the greater part of Hungary.

It is necessary to revert to Solyman's feats in other directions. In 1534 he entered upon his sixth campaign, this time against Persia. Shah Ismail was no longer alive, and had been succeeded by Shah Talmasp, a very weak personage. Solyman, as a prelude to his attack, gave orders for the execution of all the Persian prisoners at Gallipoli. Ibrahim was sent on, in advance, by some months, with a large army. Instead of marching by Aleppo to Bagdad, he took the route direct to Tabriz, which he occupied without resistance on the part of the Persians. He wintered there, and the next spring he was joined by Solyman with another army, and together they marched to Mossul and Bagdad, through a most difficult country, where the climate entailed great losses on the army. Bagdad was ultimately reached. It was treacherously surrendered by its commander. In fact, the Shah made no attempt to repel the invasion of the Ottoman army, and the two great provinces of Mossul and Bagdad were added to the Ottoman Empire, without any pitched battle on the part of Persia.

There were other campaigns in Persia in 1548, 1553, and 1554, in which the Turks often suffered more from the climate and from the difficulty of obtaining supplies than from the guerilla attacks of the Persians. But there was no pitched battle between the armies of the two Powers. The Turks maintained their conquests, and have done so to the present year (1917).

Not less remarkable during the long reign of Solyman than his conquests by his army were the exploits of his navy. It achieved victory in many hard-fought battles with Spain and Venice. There was no great disparity in naval force between the Turks and the Spaniards, but when the fleets of Venice and the Pope were combined with those of Spain, there was great superiority on their part in the number and size of vessels. In spite of this, in the two great battles where this combination was against them, the Turks were victorious, and generally, throughout Solyman's reign, his fleets maintained a supremacy in the Mediterranean. This enabled him to add to his Empire the provinces of Algiers, Oran, and Tripoli, and numerous islands in the Ægean Sea, taken from Venice.

The Mussulman States of North Africa, at the commencement of Solyman's reign, were in the hands of degenerate and incompetent Mahommedan rulers, who exercised little control over the Arabs of the hinterland. The cities on the coast were the haunts of pirates, who sometimes sailed under the flags of these States, but more often under no flag but their own. They preyed on the commerce of the Mediterranean, bringing their prizes into their ports and selling the captives as slaves, with the result that in Tunis alone there were twenty thousand Christian captives. These corsairs formed squadrons of ten or twenty galleys, under the command of admirals, chosen from the most daring and adventurous of them. They were called corsairs, but, in fact, they were mere pirates, knowing no law but their own, and that founded on robbery and murder. The sea-dogs in command of these pirates gained great experience in handling their ships and squadrons. They ravaged the coasts of Spain, Italy, and France, and even occasionally of England and Ireland, devastating the cities and villages and carrying away booty and captives.

It has been shown that Selim paid great attention to his navy, and increased his ships in number and size. Solyman followed the same course. But his admirals and captains did not compare in skill and daring with those of the pirate squadrons. When Solyman became aware of this, he most astutely invited the ablest and most experienced of these pirates to take service under the Ottoman flag, and to bring with them their ships and men. He gave high appointments to them, raised them to the rank of admirals and commanders-in-chief of his navy, over the heads of the officers of his regular service.

The first and most distinguished of these corsairs to take naval service under Solyman was Kheireddin, better known in history as Barbarossa. He was one of four brothers, of Greek descent, born in Mytilene, three of whom in early life took to piracy as a profession, under the pretence of legitimate commerce at sea. Two of them eventually lost their lives in the venture, but the third survived, prospered, and made money. He collected a squadron under his command and became the terror of the whole Mediterranean, capturing merchant vessels and devastating the coasts in all directions. Gathering strength in number of ships and men, he made war on his own account. He attacked Algiers and made himself master of that city and its surrounding district. But finding himself unequal to the task of maintaining an independent rule there, he recognized the supremacy of the Sultan of Turkey. He carried on his ships seventy thousand fugitive Moors from Andalusia, in Spain, and settled them at Algiers. Later, he was employed by Solyman in an attack on Tunis, which was then under the rule of Muley-Hasan, the twenty-second representative of the dynasty of Boni Hafss—a degenerate reprobate, who had murdered all but one of his forty-four brothers on his accession to the throne, and who spent his energies in recruiting a harem of four hundred good-looking lads. On the pretext of putting an end to this infamy, Barbarossa attacked the city of Tunis, and had no difficulty in getting possession of it and expelling the contemptible Sultan. He did not, however,

- 95 -

remain many months in possession of it. Muley-Hasan appealed to the Emperor Charles for aid.

The Emperor, in personal command of a fleet of five hundred vessels and an army of thirty thousand men, attacked and defeated Barbarossa in a battle before the walls of Tunis, captured his vessels lying there, and drove him into the interior of the country. Although he had come there at the invitation of the Sultan of Tunis, and the inhabitants of the city had given no assistance to Barbarossa in defending it against the Spanish attack, the Emperor allowed his soldiers to sack it after the capture. A scene of almost incredible cruelty and destruction took place. Thirty thousand of the innocent inhabitants were massacred, and ten thousand were sold into captivity. The mosques and all the principal buildings were burnt and destroyed. No worse deed was ever perpetrated by any victorious Moslem army in that age. It resulted that Tunis, for a time, was rescued from Barbarossa and from Ottoman rule. Muley-Hasan was reinstated there on terms of close dependence on Spain. It was not till 1574 that Tunis finally fell into the hands of the Turks.

Barbarossa had made a splendid defence of the city. His force was quite inadequate for the purpose. Solyman was at the time engaged in war with Persia and could not give adequate support. Shortly after this, when war broke out between the Ottomans and Spain, the Sultan invited Barbarossa to Constantinople, and made him Grand Admiral of the Turkish fleet. In this capacity he fought in 1538 a great naval battle off Prevesa against the combined fleets of Spain, Venice, and the Pope, under Admiral Andrea Doria, in which he achieved victory, in spite of great inferiority of numbers and size of vessels. He appears to have been the first to adopt the manœuvre of breaking the line of the enemy's fleet, for which three centuries later Nelson was so famous. The Turkish fleet numbered a hundred and thirty vessels, and that of the combined Christian Powers a hundred and sixty-seven. Six of the latter were captured and destroyed. The main body of the combined fleet drew off, under cover of the night. Later, Barbarossa accompanied Solyman in the attack on Corfu, which was heroically defended by the Venetians. The Sultan was compelled to withdraw from the island.

This failure at Corfu, and that before Vienna, were the only reverses which Solyman personally encountered in his numerous campaigns. Barbarossa, however, in the course of the war with the Venetians, succeeded in capturing from them all the many islands which they possessed in the Ægean Sea, with the exception of Crete and the few fortified places they held in the Morea. These were his last exploits. He died at Constantinople in 1546.

Others, however, of the same brood of corsairs or pirates succeeded Barbarossa in the Turkish navy, and maintained its reputation for successful daring. The most distinguished of them were Dragut (or Torghut) and Piale, both of them renegade subjects of Turkey who had taken to piracy as a profession. Dragut, a Croatian by birth, closely resembled Barbarossa in his career, in his prowess at sea, and in the terror which he created on the coasts of Italy and Spain. He had little respect for the allies of the Sultan, and captured their vessels as readily as those of his enemies. When called to account by the Porte for the destruction of some Venetian merchant ships, and summoned to Constantinople, he declined to go there, well knowing the fate in store for him. He betook himself, with his pirate squadron, to Morocco, which he made the base for piracy for some years. Later, Solyman, finding the need of such a daring spirit, invited him again to take service under the Ottoman flag, and promised to make him Governor of Tripoli, if he could capture it. Tripoli then belonged to the Knights of St. John at Malta. Dragut attacked and captured it, and annexed it to the Turkish Empire. Eventually Dragut was appointed Governor of Tripoli and, in this capacity, led a fleet in aid of the attack on Malta in 1565. He lost his life in an assault on the city.

Another such corsair was Piale, who, in his turn, after a long spell of piracy, was taken into the Ottoman naval service by Solyman, and rose to be commander-in-chief. He defeated the combined fleet of Spain, Venice, and the Pope, under command of Andrea Doria, sent to recapture Tripoli. He attacked and annexed for the Turks the province of Oran, on the African coast, westward of Algiers. He commanded the Turkish fleet in the attack on Malta in 1565, the last naval enterprise in Solyman's reign.

It was not only in the Mediterranean that Solyman's navy was active. A fleet was fitted out at Suez, under command of Piri Pasha. It secured to Turkey the command of the Red Sea and enabled the capture of Aden and Yemen. It extended its operations thence to the Persian Gulf and the coast of India, where it came into conflict with the Portuguese, who beat off the Ottoman ships.

The failure of the expedition to Malta, though he was not in personal command, appears to have weighed heavily on the mind of Solyman. It was his ambition to finish his career by a success as signal and important as that against Belgrade, in the first year of his reign. He determined to take command himself of the army which was to make another invasion of Hungary in 1566, in spite of his seventy-two years and the feeble state of his health.128 He was not able to mount his horse. He was carried in a litter at the head of his army. It was his special wish to capture Szigeth and Erlau, which had successfully resisted Ottoman attack on the last invasion. He appears to have directed the march of his army in the minutest detail. One of his pashas accomplished a march in one day which he was instructed to effect in two days. Solyman was incensed and directed the execution of the over-zealous pasha, and with difficulty was dissuaded from this by his Grand Vizier.

The great Sultan died unexpectedly in his tent from apoplexy during the siege of Szigeth, before the capture of this city and while the guns of his army were thundering against its citadel, most bravely defended by Nicholas Zriny—a fitting end to the old warrior. His death was for long concealed from the army. The Grand Vizier directed the execution of the Sultan's physician, lest he should divulge the secret. Solyman's body was embalmed and was carried in the royal litter during the remainder of the short campaign in Hungary, and orders were still given to the army in the name of the defunct Sultan. It was not till news came that Selim had arrived at Belgrade from his government in Asia Minor that the army, on its homeward march, was informed of the death of the great Sultan.

This was the last of Solyman's thirteen campaigns in which he led his armies personally on the field. There were others in which his generals commanded. It is to be observed of all of them that there was only one case in which a pitched battle of any great importance was fought on land. The single case was that of Mohacz, already referred to, where the Ottoman army greatly exceeded in number that of the Hungarians opposed to it, and was provided with a park of artillery, in which the enemy was wholly deficient. The result, therefore, was never in doubt. With that exception, there was no great battle either with the Hungarians, the Austrians, or the Persians. The campaigns consisted of invasions by great armies of the Ottomans, with heavy parks of artillery, and with large forces of irregular cavalry, who ravaged and devastated the invaded country. The generals opposed to them, not being able to meet the Turks in the field, spread their forces in numerous fortresses, more or less strong, and the campaigns consisted in besieging these fortresses. With rare exceptions, these sieges were successful. The Turks brought overwhelming forces to bear on them. Their siege guns completely overmatched the guns of the defence. It was a question of a few days or a few weeks how long these fortresses could resist. The wonder is that many of them resisted so long. The usual course of such campaigns was that the Turks, having captured the fortresses in the invaded districts, either annexed them to their Empire, as in the case of Eastern Hungary and Mesopotamia, or compelled the vanquished State to acknowledge the suzerainty of the Sultan and to pay tribute, as in the case of Western Hungary, or retired, leaving the ravaged country so destitute of supplies that the enemy could not follow up the retreating army.

Solyman was almost always successful in his campaigns—but they do not entitle him to a place in the first rank of great generals who have earned their laurels by defeating opponents not unequal in number in the open field. Practically, there was only one sovereign in Europe—namely the Emperor

Charles V—and no one in Asia, who could hope to meet Solyman on equal terms on the battlefield, and the Emperor evidently did not care to measure swords with him in the open.

If these considerations detract from the military fame of Solyman, they do not lessen his reputation as an empire-builder and as an organizer of campaigns of invasion. Seldom has an Empire been extended to such an extent as that of the Ottomans under his efforts, with so little expenditure of life or of the resources of the State. Solyman evidently made it his task to run no risk of failure, but to use such overwhelming force as made resistance all but impossible.

To put in the field these enormous armies, supported by large masses of cavalry and great parks of artillery, to transport them from Constantinople to the centre of Hungary, or from Scutari to the frontiers of Persia, requiring many weeks or months, was to perform a work of organization of the first order. In the long course of his reign and the many expeditions led by himself and his generals, the only failure to supply his armies in the field with food and munitions of war was in the attack on Vienna. Solyman had also unerring judgment and success in selecting his generals and other agents in his many campaigns. The same may be said of his naval campaigns, in which he took no personal part, and where success turned upon the selection of competent admirals to command his fleets. What a stroke of genius it was to go outside the professional men of his naval service, and to put at the head of his fleets and of his naval administration, such men as Barbarossa, Dragut, Piale, and others, who had gained experience and had made their reputation as freebooters and pirates! It was due mainly to this that the Ottomans acquired a virtual supremacy in the Mediterranean, that Algiers, Oran, and Tripoli were brought under the Empire, and that a fleet fitted out at Suez enabled the conquest of Aden and Yemen.

It was not, however, only in military and naval successes and in the additions to his Empire that Solyman showed his greatness. His firm and resolute, yet sympathetic, policy made its mark in every department of the State. He insisted on impartial justice to every class throughout his Empire. Governors of provinces, or other high officials, who erred in this respect, and who were guilty of injustice and cruelty, or who were corrupt and incompetent, were at once dismissed, and not unfrequently paid the penalty of death for their crimes. His very first act on becoming Sultan was to order the dismissal of a batch of unjust and corrupt officials. Von Hammer's pages are full of other instances of the same kind throughout Solyman's reign. He made no exception for favoured persons, however near to the throne. Ferhad Pasha, who was married to one of the Sultan's two daughters, was dismissed from the governorship of a province for gross acts of injustice, cruelty, and corruption. By the urgent entreaties of his wife, and of the Sultan's mother,

- 99 -

Ferhad obtained another appointment. But on the renewal of his misdeeds he was again dismissed, and, this time, was put to death by order of the Sultan.

The finance of the Empire under Solyman was most carefully husbanded. He fully recognized the strength given to his country by a well-filled treasury. In spite of his many wars, there were only two years in which he found it necessary to levy exceptional taxes. In other years the ordinary revenue sufficed. Taxation was comparatively light. His wars in part paid for themselves by levies and exactions on the invaded countries, and by the sale of captives. Janissaries and Spahis, numbering together about fifty thousand, formed the standing army, and were well paid. The holders of fiefs throughout the Empire were bound to military service in time of war, and to bring horses and arms. They numbered about eighty thousand, and received no pay. Neither did the horde of irregular cavalry, Tartars, and others who accompanied his armies, receive pay. They provided for themselves by ravaging the countries they passed through. Under these conditions, the wars of Solyman were not burdensome to the State.

Like so many of his predecessors, Solyman had a strong bent to literary studies and poetry. His poems have a reputation among his countrymen for dignity. He compiled a daily journal of his campaigns which is of historical value. He was a liberal patron of science and art. His reign was the Augustan age of Turkey. He was generous in his expenditure on mosques, colleges, hospitals, aqueducts, and bridges, not only in Constantinople, but in all the principal cities of his Empire.

It is to be noted that the sobriquet 'Magnificent' was given to Solyman by contemporaries in Europe. In Turkey, he was known as 'the Legislator.' His reign was conspicuous for great reforms in every branch of the law—all aimed at justice. The land laws were overhauled. The feudal system of fiefs, which had been partially adopted on the model of other countries in Europe, was simplified and improved. The position of the 'rayas,' was ameliorated. Something like fixity of tenure was secured to them. The condition of the peasantry in Turkey was distinctly better than that of the serfs in Hungary and Russia. The Greek population of the Morea preferred Turkish rule to that of the Venetians. A certain number of Hungarian peasants voluntarily left their country and settled under the more humane government of Turkey in Roumelia. A further proof of the general contentment of the people through the great expanse of the Turkish Empire was that during the forty-six years of Solyman's reign there was no outbreak among any one of the twenty different races which inhabited it—and this in spite of the fact that the country districts were denuded of troops for the many campaigns in Hungary and Persia. While giving Solyman full credit for all these great achievements of his reign, it is necessary to point out that impartial historians have detected defects in his system of government, which grew apace under his incompetent successors, and led inevitably to the decadence of the Ottoman Empire.

A Turkish historian, Kotchi Bey, who wrote on the decline of the Ottoman Empire in 1623, about sixty years after the death of Solyman, and who has been described by Von Hammer as the Turkish Montesquieu, attributed the decline in great part to the following causes:—

1. The cessation in Solyman's time of the regular attendance of the Sultan at the meetings of the Divan, or great Council of State. Solyman had a window constructed in an adjoining room opening into the council chamber, where, hidden behind a veil, he could listen to the discussions of the Divan without taking a part in them. His successors ceased even to listen from behind the veil. This absence of the Sultan from his Council added to his arbitrary power and belittled the influence of his ministers. So long as a very competent man like Solyman was on the throne, this new practice may not have produced the worst results, but in the case of his incompetent successors it led to immense evils. The Sultan was finally swayed in his decisions not by his responsible ministers or his Grand Council, but by the inmates of his harem or by other irresponsible and corrupt outsiders.

2. The habit introduced by Solyman of appointing men to high office who had not passed through the grades of lower offices. The first and most conspicuous case of this kind was the promotion of Ibrahim, the favourite companion of Solyman, from the post of Master of the Pages in the Sultan's household to that of Grand Vizier. Numerous other cases could be quoted of a less conspicuous character. Solyman, in fact, appointed outsiders to every kind of office, however important. Eunuchs and renegades of all kinds were elevated to the highest posts. Solyman himself appears to have been a very good judge of men, and rarely made mistakes in his appointments, but his successors had no such discernment, and appointments were conferred at the caprice, or under the influence of the harem or otherwise, on the most unfit persons.

3. The venality and corruption first practised by Roostem Pasha, who was Grand Vizier for fifteen years, and who was married to Solyman's daughter. The principal merit of Roostem in the eyes of his master was his skill in replenishing the treasury. Among the means he adopted of raising money was the exaction of large payments from persons on their appointment to civil offices in the State. These payments in Solyman's time were fixed in a definite proportion to the salaries. They were not adopted in the military and naval services. Under later Sultans they became arbitrary and exorbitant, and were extended to the army and navy. Practically appointments of all kinds were put up to auction and given to the highest bidder. In order to meet

these payments on appointment, governors of provinces and all officials, down to the lowest, were induced to adopt corrupt practices of all kinds and the sense of public duty was destroyed.

4. The evil practice introduced by Solyman of heaping favours on his favourite viziers, or of allowing them to amass wealth by selling their favours to those below them in the official hierarchy. Ibrahim, who was Grand Vizier for thirteen years, and Roostem for fifteen years, amassed enormous fortunes. They set up a standard of extravagant life, which was followed by other viziers and high officials. Roostem on his death was possessed of 815 farms in Anatolia and Roumelia, 476 watermills, 1,700 slaves, 2,900 coats of mail, 8,000 turbans, 760 sabres, 600 copies of the Koran, 5,000 books, and two millions of ducats. His example in gaining wealth was followed by others in a minor degree according to their opportunities. High office came to be regarded as a means and opportunity of acquiring great wealth, and this evil rapidly spread throughout the Empire and led to corruption and extortion.

There was a corrective, or perhaps it should be called a nemesis to this, in the fact that when an official was put to death, by order of the Sultan, his property was confiscated to the State. Ibrahim's immense wealth was thus dealt with, and even in Solyman's time, and much more so in those of his successors, the confiscated fortunes of viziers, governors, and other officials sentenced to death formed an important item in the annual income of the State. There can be little doubt that not a few pashas were put to death by the successors of Solyman in order that the State might benefit from the confiscation of their fortunes. It was perhaps thought that the mere fact of accumulation of wealth by an official was sufficient proof that it had been improperly acquired, and that the holder deserved to lose his life and fortune.

There may be added to these causes of ultimate decadence pointed out by the Turkish historian another which must occur to those who closely study the reign of Solyman—namely the growing influence in State affairs of the Sultan's harem. The fall and death of Ibrahim, the murder of Prince Mustapha, and the rebellion and consequent death of Prince Bayezid were mainly due to intrigues of the harem. Great as Solyman was, he fell under the evil influence of his favourite Sultana, the Russian Ghowrem, better known in history as Roxelana. Ghowrem was not only a most seductive concubine; she was a very clever and witty woman, with a great gift of conversation. She retained her influence over Solyman when age had reduced her personal charms. By the entreaties of the Sultan's mother, who perceived the malign influence of this woman over her son, she was for a time got rid of from the Seraglio. But Solyman could not forget her, and insisted on her recall. Ghowrem celebrated her triumph by getting the consent of the Sultan to many executions. Thenceforth till her death her influence was unbounded. "I live with the Sultan," she said, "and make him do what I wish."

Appointments to the highest offices were made at her instance and abuses of all kinds arose. But worst of all was the precedent that was set for the interference of the harem in matters of State.

With Solyman's successors the influence of the harem was continually a growing one, and was generally, though not always, as will be seen, a danger to the State. It became increasingly necessary for a minister who hoped to retain his post to secure personal support in the Sultan's harem. The harem itself became the centre of intrigue and corruption, with fatal effect on the interests of the State. But worst of all dangers to the Empire was the possibility—nay, the probability—that the succession of the great man at the helm of State able to restrain the lawlessness of the Janissaries, the fanaticism of the mullahs, and the corruption of pashas might not be maintained. Solyman never did a worse deed for the future of the Empire than when he put to death his eldest son, who had proved himself to be in every way fit to succeed him as Sultan, and when later, at the instance of Ghowrem, he secured the succession of his son Selim. He knew that Selim was a worthless and dissolute drunkard. He is said to have remonstrated with his son and endeavoured to induce him to reform his conduct. It will be seen that it was in vain. The succession of Selim was a nemesis for the murder of Mustapha. He was the first of a long line of degenerates, who ruined the great work of Solyman and his predecessors.

In spite of this crime and of the base murder of his most intimate friend and servant, Ibrahim, in spite of the inception of the grave abuses we have referred to, it must be admitted, on an impartial review of Solyman's reign, that Solyman was the greatest of the Othman race who created the Empire, and that in a generation of famous rulers in Europe, including Charles V, Francis I, Leo X, our own Henry VIII, Sigismund of Poland, and others, he excelled them all in the deeds and qualities which constitute the greatness and fame of a ruler. There is a Turkish proverb to the effect that "Happy is the man whose faults can be numbered, for then his merits cannot be counted."

XI

GRAND VIZIER SOKOLLI
1566-78

SOLYMAN was the last and greatest of the first ten Ottoman Sultans who, succeeding one another from father to son, in rather less than three hundred years, raised their Empire from nothing to one of the most extended in the world. They must have been a very virile race, for their reign averaged about twenty-eight years, far above the ordinary expectations of life. With one exception they were all able generals and habitually led their armies in the field. They were all statesmen, persistent in pursuing their ambitious aims. Many of them were addicted to literary pursuits, were students of history, and even had reputation as poets. In spite of these softening influences, there was in nearly all of them a fund of cruelty. It may be doubted whether, in the world's history, any other dynasty has produced so long a succession of men with such eminent and persistent qualities.

Solyman was succeeded by his third son, Selim, commonly called 'the Sot,' a sobriquet which sufficiently describes him. He was the only son spared from the bow-string. Selim was followed by twenty-four other Sultans of the Othman dynasty down to the present time. With the rarest exception, they were men wholly wanting in capacity to rule a great Empire. Only one of them was capable of leading his army in the field. The others had neither the will nor the capacity, nor even the personal courage to do so. They fell under the influence either of their viziers, or of the women or even of the eunuchs of their harems.

If the persistency of type and of the high qualities of the first ten Sultans was remarkable, no less so was the break which occurred after Solyman, and the almost total absence of these qualities in their successors down to the present time. One is tempted to question whether the true blood of the Othman race flowed in the veins of these twenty-five degenerates. Von Hammer refers to a common rumour at Constantinople, though he does not affirm his own belief in it, that Selim was not really the son of Solyman but of a Jew, and that this accounted for his infatuation for a favourite Jew adventurer, who obtained a potent influence over his weak mind. Such a break in true descent might well have been possible in the vicious atmosphere of the harem, in spite of the precaution that no men but those deprived of virility were to be allowed to enter it.

Whatever may be the explanation, there can be no doubt that the degeneracy of the Othman dynasty dates from the accession of Selim the Sot. But this did not necessarily involve the immediate decadence of the Empire. The Ottoman Empire could not have been built up by the energy and ability of a single autocrat in each generation. There must have been many capable men, statesmen, generals, and administrators, of all ranks, who contributed in each generation to the achievements of their rulers. Many such men survived for some years the death of Solyman, and preserved the Empire from the ruin which threatened it. The Empire, in fact, did not begin to shrink in extent till some years later, and for about twelve years, as if from the momentum given to it by the powerful Sultans of the past, it actually continued to expand. Selim was the first of the new type of Sultans. He took no interest or part in the affairs of State. He was a debauchee and a drunkard. He gave an evil example to all others, high and low. Judges, cadis, and ulemas took to drink. Poets wrote in raptures about wine. Hafiz, the most in esteem of them, wrote that wine was sweeter than the kisses of young girls. The attention of the Mufti was called to this, and he was asked to censor the poem as contrary to the injunctions of the Koran. But the Mufti replied that "when a Sultan took to drink it was permissible for all to do the same and for poets to celebrate it."

Selim fell completely under the influence of his Grand Vizier, who had held the post for two years under Solyman. Sokolli, who was a most capable man, was the virtual ruler of the Empire. He was a man of large views. He had two important and interesting schemes in his mind. The one to cut a canal across the Isthmus of Suez, so that the Turkish fleet might find its way into the Red Sea and Indian Ocean, the other to make a junction by a canal between the rivers Don and Volga. These two great rivers, which have their sources in Russia, run a parallel course for a long distance, and at one point approach one another within thirty miles. They then diverge again, the one flowing into the Sea of Azoff, the other into the Caspian Sea. By joining these two rivers by a canal at the point where the distance between them is the least, it would be possible for a Turkish flotilla to ascend the Don, and then, after passing through the canal, descend the Volga into the Caspian Sea, whence it would be able to attack the Persian province of Tabriz with great advantage. The commercial possibilities of this junction of the two great water highways were also obvious. The scheme, however, necessitated taking Astrakan and other territory from Russia—a country which had of late years largely extended its possessions and power.

In this view, Sokolli, in 1568, sent an army of twenty-five thousand Janissaries and Spahis by sea to Azoff. They were there joined by thirty thousand Tartars from the Crimea, and the combined force marched thence to Astrakan, at the mouth of the Volga. For the first time, therefore, the Ottomans came into direct conflict with the Russians. The expedition was a total failure. The Turks were unable to capture Astrakan, and a Russian army completely destroyed that of the Tartars. The main Turkish army was compelled to retreat to Azoff. Later, the greater part of it was lost in a great tempest in the Black Sea, and only seven thousand of its men returned to Constantinople. The project of a Don and Volga canal was consequently abandoned. That for a canal across the Isthmus of Suez was also indefinitely adjourned, owing to an outbreak of the Arabs in the province of Yemen, which necessitated sending an army there under Sinan Pasha. This was thoroughly successful, and Yemen and other parts of Arabia were completely and finally brought under the subjection of the Ottoman Empire.

After the reconquest of Yemen, Sokolli determined to attack Tunis, which since its capture by the Emperor Charles V had been in the occupation of the Spaniards. The fleet employed for this purpose was under the command of Ouloudj Pasha, a renegade Italian, who after a successful career as corsair and pirate was induced to take service under the Sultan. In 1568 he was appointed governor of Algiers, and in that capacity led the expedition against Tunis in the following year. He defeated the Spaniards and occupied the town. But the garrison retreated into the citadel, which they held till 1574.

In 1570 another expedition was decided on, this time for the purpose of capturing the island of Cyprus, which was then in possession of the Republic of Venice, with which the Porte was at peace. Sokolli, on this account, was at first opposed to the scheme. But on this occasion, for the first and, apparently, the only time, Sultan Selim overruled his minister. He loved the wine of Cyprus and wished to secure a certain supply of it. He had also, in a drunken orgy, promised to elevate his boon companion, the Jew, to the position of King of Cyprus. The Mufti, who had always hitherto given a full support to Sokolli, was consulted as to whether the treaty with Venice was binding on the Sultan so as to make an attack on Cyprus unlawful. He issued a *fetva* to the effect that, as Cyprus at some distant time had been under Moslem rule, as a dependency of Egypt, it was the duty of a Mussulman prince to avail himself of any favourable opportunity to restore to Islam territory which had been taken possession of by an infidel Power, and that, consequently, the treaty with Venice was not binding on the Sultan.

In accordance with this ruling of the Mufti, an expedition was fitted out in 1570 by the Ottoman government, consisting of a hundred thousand men, including irregulars, under command of Kara Mustapha, who was the rival of Sokolli, and a fleet under Piale. This force laid siege to Nicosia, the capital of Cyprus, a flourishing Christian city, where there were said to be as many churches as there are days in the year. After a siege of seven weeks the city was captured by assault, and was given up to sack by the Turkish soldiers. Thirty thousand of the inhabitants were massacred. Many women killed themselves and their children rather than give themselves up to the maddened soldiers. Two thousand of the better-looking children of both sexes were sold as slaves.

Mustapha Pasha then proceeded to invest Famagosta, the principal fortress in the island. It was heroically defended by a mixed force of Italians and Greeks, under command of Bragadino, a brave Venetian general. It successfully resisted attack throughout the winter of 1570. It was not till August in the following year (1571) that the garrison, reduced to less than four thousand men, was compelled by failure of food and munitions of war to surrender. Very favourable terms were promised to them by Mustapha. The lives of the garrison were to be respected, and the property and religion of the citizens were to be secured to them. The garrison were to be conveyed in Turkish galleys to Crete and there released. In pursuance of these terms the captives were embarked on board galleys ready to sail to Crete. At this stage an interview took place between Kara Mustapha and Bragadino and his suite of twenty officers, at which very hot words passed between them. The Turkish general complained that some of his men, taken prisoners during the siege, had been put to death. Bragadino denied this. His language was considered to be insolent by Kara Mustapha, who at once gave orders that all Bragadino's suite were to be strangled in his presence. Their leader was reserved for a more cruel fate. The men embarked on the galleys were landed again and were massacred. A week later, Bragadino, who had been treated in the interval with the greatest cruelty and the most barbarous indignities, was flayed alive. His skin, stuffed with hay, was exhibited to the scorn of the Turkish soldiers. The capture of Famagosta completed the conquest of Cyprus. It remained in the possession of the Ottomans till, as will be seen, it was handed over to the British Government, in 1878, in pursuance of a policy devised by Lord Beaconsfield. The Turks are said to have lost fifty thousand men in its capture. It was in revenge for this that Kara Mustapha resorted to the terrible deeds above described.

Meanwhile the Christian Powers had been greatly alarmed by the loss of Cyprus and the atrocities above described. At the instance mainly of the Pope, an alliance was formed in 1570 with Spain and Venice, with the object of opposing the growing strength of the Ottomans in the Mediterranean. A great fleet was fitted out by these Powers, and was placed under the command of Don John of Austria, the natural son of the late Emperor, Charles V, a young man of only twenty-four years, who had shown his capacity in the measures for the expulsion of the Moors from Spain, and was already reckoned one of the best generals of the time. The fleet consisted of two hundred galleys and six powerful galleasses with heavy armaments. It was manned by eighty thousand soldiers and rowers, one-half of whom were provided by Spain and one-third by Venice, the remainder, one-sixth, by the Pope. Don John was in supreme command. The Spanish division was commanded by the Prince of Parma, soon to become notorious in the Netherlands under Philip II, and who was later in command of the Armada fitted out in Spain for the invasion of England.

The fleet assembled at Messina on September 21, 1571, too late for the relief of Cyprus. The Turks collected in the Gulf of Lepanto a much greater fleet of two hundred and ninety galleys manned by a hundred and twenty thousand soldiers and rowers. But they had no large galleasses with powerful armaments to compare with those of the Spaniards. The fleet was commanded by the Capitan Pasha Ali, a young man without experience in naval war. The second in command was Ouloudj. Perted Pasha was in command of the troops. He and Ouloudj were opposed to an immediate battle with the allied fleet on the ground that their men were not as yet sufficiently trained. At a council of war heated discussion took place. The Capitan Pasha insisted on immediate attack. Ouloudj broke off the discussion, saying, "Silence. I am ready, because it is written that the youth of a Capitan Pasha has more weight than my forty-three years of fighting. But the Berbers have made sport of you, Pasha! Remember this when the peril draws near."

The rowers of both fleets were galley slaves chained to the oars. On the Turkish fleet they were Christians who had been made captives in war. On the Christian fleet they were the sweepings of the jails. In both cases the admirals promised liberty to them if they performed their duty in the coming battle.

The two fleets met near the entrance to the Gulf of Lepanto on October 7, 1571. The Christian fleet was ranged in a crescent with the Venetians on the left flank. The six powerful galleasses were posted like redoubts at intervals in front of the lines of galleys. Don John was at the centre of the crescent. The two fleets approached one another. The engagement soon became general. The Turkish galleys as their enemy neared them, were somewhat broken in line by the Spanish galleasses, which raked the Turkish galleys with their more powerful armaments. The Turkish admiral, in the *Sultana*, made a direct attack on Don John's ship, the *Real*, which was later supported by a second galley. The three were locked together, and the Spanish soldiers boarded the Turkish vessel. A desperate hand-to-hand combat took place, in which the Turkish admiral was killed. His head was cut off and, against the will of Don John, was stuck on the masthead of the Spanish vessel. This caused general discouragement in the Turkish fleet. All along the line the

Turkish vessels were worsted in the combats with their opponents. There resulted a complete defeat of their centre and left wing. Ouloudj, in command of the Turkish right wing, was more fortunate. He succeeded in outmanœuvring the Venetian vessels opposed to him. He made a violent attack on fifteen galleys which were detached from the main fleet of the allies and succeeded in sinking them. When he became aware that the main Ottoman fleet was completely defeated by the Spaniards, he made a dash with forty of his own galleys through the enemy's line and succeeded in escaping. With this exception, the whole of the Turkish vessels, two hundred and sixty-six in number, were captured or sunk. Fifty thousand Turks lost their lives in this great battle, and fifteen thousand Christian slaves were liberated.

It was an overwhelming defeat for the Ottomans. No such naval victory had occurred in the Mediterranean since that of Actium, very near to the same spot, where (B.C. 31) Marc Antony's fleet was destroyed by that of Octavius. Nor was there another such decisive naval encounter in those seas till that known as the Battle of the Nile, when Nelson captured or sank nearly the whole of the French fleet off the coast of Egypt.

It was to be expected that the allied Christian fleet would follow up its great victory by attack on some Turkish territory. No such project was entertained by its admirals and generals. The fleet dispersed after its victory. Each detachment of it returned to its own ports, there to receive ovations of triumph. Sculptors and painters celebrated the event by works of art in churches at Rome, Venice, Messina, and other cities. Never was so decisive a victory productive of so little further result.

The contrast between the action of the defeated Turks and that of the victors was most striking. Ouloudj, picking up forty stray galleys in the Ægean Sea, returned to Constantinople with eighty vessels. Piale joined him there with a few more. Sokolli and his colleagues in the Turkish Government made the most determined efforts to restore their fleet. Even Selim showed some spirit on this occasion. He contributed largely from his privy purse. He gave up part of the garden of his palace at Seraglio Point as a site for the construction of new vessels. One hundred and sixty galleys were at once commenced, together with eight galleasses of the largest size. By the spring of the next year they were completed. The losses at Lepanto were made good and the Ottoman fleet was as powerful as before the disaster. In the summer of 1572 the allied Christian fleet was again assembled on the eastern Mediterranean. It was still inferior in numbers of vessels to that of the Ottomans. The two fleets came in sight of one another twice in that season in the neighbourhood of the island of Cerigo and, later, off Cape Matapan, but no engagement took place. It may be concluded that Ouloudj, who was now Capitan Pasha of the Turkish navy with the honorary name of Killidj Ali, thought it the better policy not to risk his new fleet before the crews were thoroughly trained. He withdrew, and the sequel showed the wisdom of his action. The allied fleet was unable to do anything.

Later, in 1573, the Venetians found it expedient to negotiate terms for a separate peace with the Porte. Their envoy, who appears to have remained at Constantinople during the late war, interviewed Sokolli for this purpose. When he alluded to the losses which the two Powers had recently incurred, the one of the island of Cyprus, the other of its fleet, Sokolli proudly replied:—

You have doubtless observed our courage after the accident which happened to our fleet. There is this great difference between our loss and yours. In capturing a kingdom we have cut off one of your arms, while you, in destroying our fleet, have merely shorn our beard. A limb cut off cannot be replaced, but a beard when shorn will grow again in greater vigour than ever.

Terms of peace were concluded. Not only was the capture of Cyprus confirmed by a formal cession of the island, but the Republic agreed to pay to the Porte the cost incurred by its capture, estimated at 300,000 ducats. The tribute paid by Venice for the island of Zante of 500 ducats was increased to 1,500 ducats. The Republic was relieved of the annual tribute of 8,000 ducats in respect of Cyprus. The limits of the possessions of the two Powers in Dalmatia and Albania were restored to what they had been before the war. The terms were humiliating to Venice; they could not have been worse if the battle of Lepanto had never been fought.

The rapid restoration of its fleet by the Porte gave fresh evidence of its vital power and its unsurpassed resources. For a long time to come the Ottoman navy, supported by the piratical contingents from its Barbary dependents, held a virtual supremacy in the Mediterranean.

After the conclusion of peace between Venice and the Porte, Don John, in October 1573, commanded a Spanish fleet in an expedition against Tunis, which, as above stated, had been captured by Ouloudj on behalf of the Turks. The task of Don John was the more easy as the Turks had not succeeded in capturing the citadel, which was still in the possession of its Spanish garrison. He had no difficulty in defeating the few Turks who were in possession of the city of Tunis. He showed no disposition to restore to his throne the Sultan Hamid. This miserable creature appeared at Tunis and claimed to be reinstated there. But the Spaniards would have nothing to do with him. He was deported to Naples.

Don John, having effected his object, departed to Spain, leaving at Tunis a mixed garrison of eight thousand Italians and Spaniards. When news of this capture reached Constantinople, Sokolli and Ouloudj were greatly incensed. In 1574 a fleet of two hundred and sixty galleys and galleasses with forty thousand men was sent out, under command of Ouloudj, who made short work of the Spanish and Italian garrison at Tunis, and recaptured the province, and finally annexed it to the Turkish Empire. This probably could not have been effected if Venice had remained in alliance with Spain, but alone the latter was not able to meet the Ottoman fleet in the Mediterranean.

In 1574 Selim died under the influence of drink, and was succeeded by his son, Murad III, as much a nullity as regards public affairs as his father. Sokolli remained as Grand Vizier till his death, four years later, by the hands of an assassin, but with diminishing power, owing to the intrigues of the Sultan's harem, which eventually contrived his end.

In 1578, the last year of Sokolli's vizierate, war again broke out with Persia, and a great army was sent to Asia, under command of Mustapha, the conqueror of Cyprus. It began by invading Georgia, then under a native Christian prince in close alliance with, if not under the subjection of, Persia. Mustapha had no difficulty in conquering Georgia, and in occupying the adjacent Persian provinces of Azerbijan, Loristan, and Scherhezol. He penetrated to Dhagestan, on the Caspian. The war was continued under Sokolli's successors for some years with varying fortune. It was not till 1590 that a treaty of peace was concluded with Persia, under which these provinces were ceded to the Ottoman Empire.

It will be seen from this brief narrative that the acquisitions of the Ottoman Empire during the twelve years when the Grand Vizier Sokolli was virtually its ruler were very great and important. They included the island of Cyprus, the province of Tunis, the kingdom of Georgia, the provinces taken from Persia, and the Yemen, in Arabia. These, with one exception, were the last acquisitions of the Ottoman Empire. The exception was that of the island of Crete, which was not attacked by the Turks till sixty-seven years later, in 1645, and was not finally conquered till 1668. But by this time the Ottoman Empire had begun to shrink at the hands of its enemies in other directions. It may be concluded, therefore, that the last year of the vizierate of Sokolli, 1578, and not the last year of Solyman's reign, was the zenith of the Ottoman Empire.

The Empire was by this time extended from the centre of Hungary in the north to the Persian Gulf and the Soudan in the south, from the Caspian Sea and the borders of Persia in the east to the province of Oran in Africa in the west. It included nearly the whole of the southern shores of the Mediterranean, except that of Morocco, and all the shores of the Black Sea and the Red Sea. All the islands of the Ægean Sea except Crete belonged to it. These territories were inhabited by twenty different races. Their population has been variously estimated at thirty millions and upwards. Many of the Greek cities at that time existing in Asia Minor were still very populous, in spite of the massacres which had taken place when they were captured by the Turks. It is probable that the population of Asia Minor, of Syria, and of Mesopotamia was much larger than it is at the present time. That of Bulgaria, Greece, and Macedonia was also greater than it was in modern times before their emancipation from Turkish rule. After the death of Sokolli there ensued an era when misgovernment and corruption played havoc with the Empire, and a process of shrinkage began which extended over three centuries, the exact opposite to its growth in the previous three centuries.

It should here be noted that although the Sultans were autocrats in the full sense of the term, there existed in practice some ultimate check on their misdeeds. The Mufti, as the chief interpreter of the sacred law of Islam, had the right and power to declare whether any act of the Sultan, or any proposed act by any other person, was in accord with or opposed to such law. As the Mufti could be deposed by the Sultan and then be put to death, this power could be very rarely used by him. But when outbreaks occurred on the part of the Janissaries and reached a point when the deposition of the Sultan was demanded, the Mufti, as a rule, was asked for his opinion. It will be seen that of the twenty-five Sultans after Solyman eleven were deposed, and in almost every case the Mufti gave his legal sanction. The Janissaries may have been very lawless, but they were not the less a salutary check on the Sultans. With one possible exception the depositions were well deserved. It should be noted that there was also a check on the Sultans in the Divan, which was composed of the four viziers and many other functionaries, military, civil, legal, and religious. It met once or twice a week and discussed matters of State. Till the time of Solyman the Sultan presided, but he gave up this practice. In the absence of the Sultan the Grand Vizier presided. In the reign of the degenerate Sultans the Divan often played an important part.

London: T. Fisher Unwin. Ltd.   Stanford's Geog.¹ Estab.¹ London.

THE OTTOMAN EMPIRE
AT THE TIME OF
ITS GREATEST EXTENT.
Tributary and Vassal States are outlined with colour.

PART II

THE DECAY OF EMPIRE

XII

THE RULE OF SULTANAS
1578-1656

AFTER the death of Sokolli many years elapsed before another Grand Vizier was able to wield the power of the State, in place of the weak and incompetent Sultans who succeeded to the throne. The supreme power fell into the hands of women of the Sultan's harem. For a time the chief influence lay with the Sultana Baffo, a Venetian lady of the noble family of that name, who had been captured when young by a corsair and sold as a slave to the harem of Sultan Murad III. She was a very clever and ambitious, as well as a beautiful woman, and for a time Murad was devoted to her charms to the exclusion of other inmates of his harem. But his mother, the Sultana Valide, jealous of Baffo's exclusive influence in politics, contrived to draw Murad's affection from her by tempting him with two other very beautiful slaves. Later, the lady who presided over the harem and her assistant improved on this method by procuring for the Sultan a succession of beautiful slaves, in such numbers that the price of this ware rose enormously in the slave market.

Murad, under the influence of these attractions, devoted himself wholly to voluptuous life in his harem. He became the father of one hundred and three children, of whom forty-seven survived him. The Sultana Baffo, the mother of his eldest son, though she had lost her charm for him as a mistress, continued to influence him in public affairs by her wit and cleverness, sharing it, however, with the other ladies referred to. After the death of the Sultana Valide, the Sultana Baffo succeeded in regaining much of her earlier and exclusive influence. She retained the same authority over her son Mahomet III, who succeeded his father in 1595. It resulted, therefore, that this lady, for twenty-eight years, exercised the greatest power in the State. Mahomet was as much a nullity in public affairs as his father. He signalized his accession to the throne by putting to death his nineteen brothers. He thought apparently that this holocaust shed some lustre on these unfortunate princes, for he accorded to them a State funeral. They were followed to their graves by all the high dignitaries of the State, and were buried beside their father. Six favourite slaves of the eldest of these princes, who might be expected to give birth to future claimants to the throne, were sewn up in sacks and were flung into the Bosphorus.

Mahomet was the last Sultan who was allowed before his accession to have some experience in public affairs as governor of a province. Thenceforward it was the practice for reigning Sultans to immure their heirs in a building in the Seraglio, at Constantinople, known as the Cage, where they were allowed to have no intercourse with the outer world, and could have no experience, or even knowledge, of public affairs, and which they only left either to reign as Sultans or to be put to death. It has been suggested by some writers that this treatment of the heirs to the Ottoman throne was the main cause of the lamentable degeneracy of the Othman dynasty. It must undoubtedly have contributed to this, but it should be noticed that the three Sultans, Selim II, Murad III, and Mahomet III, who had not been subjected to this debasing treatment, and had been governors of provinces before their accession, were quite as worthless and incompetent as any of their successors.

Mahomet, after eight years of a vacuous reign, was succeeded by his son Achmet, who reigned for fourteen years. He was as incompetent to rule as his two predecessors. He fell under the influence of other ladies of his harem. The Sultana Baffo was ignored and lost her power. On the death of Achmet, in 1617, he was succeeded not by his eldest son but by his brother Mustapha, a lunatic. Achmet had spared his brother's life on account of his lunacy. Mustapha, therefore, by virtue of the law of succession, succeeded, but he was deposed after a few months, and was followed on the throne by Othman II, the son of Achmet, who showed some greater capacity. In his short reign, however, of four years he incurred the disfavour of the Janissaries, who insisted on his deposition and death. The lunatic Mustapha was then reinstated on the throne, and was again deposed, after a few months. He was succeeded by Murad IV, a lad under twelve years. Till he came to years of discretion his mother, the Sultana Validé, who was a clever woman, virtually ruled. It will be shown later that Murad was of very different type to his six predecessors. On coming of age he emancipated himself from the influence of the harem, and was the last of his dynasty who was a warrior and who personally led his army in the field. His rule lasted for only eight years. On his death, in 1640, he was succeeded by his brother Ibrahim II, a worthless voluptuary, during whose reign of another eight years the harem recovered its influence. He was followed by Mahomet IV, and for eight more years the rule of the harem was maintained. From this brief narrative it will appear that from the death of Sokolli in 1578 till 1656, a period of seventy-eight years, during which seven Sultans occupied the throne, the supreme power in the State was exercised by women of the harem, with the exception of the eight years of the reign of Sultan Murad IV. For twenty-eight of these years the Sultana Baffo, and later other ladies less known to fame, were virtually the rulers of the Empire. Grand Viziers were made and unmade at the will of these ladies, with occasional intervention of the Janissaries. They seldom held the office for more than a year. The Sultana Baffo was a grasping and avaricious woman. Under her evil influence, and later that of other ladies of the harem, the system of the sale of offices was greatly extended and became universal throughout the Empire for all appointments, high and low.

It has been shown that the Grand Vizier Roostem, in Solyman's reign, first introduced the system of requiring payments from persons appointed as governors of provinces and to other high civil posts; but the sums were fixed and definite, and were paid into the treasury of the State, and the system was not extended to the army. The payments now became arbitrary and universal, and were extended to appointments in the army. The Sultan himself was not above taking a part in this plunder, and the ladies of the harem had also their full share. Grand Viziers only succeeded in retaining their posts by large payments to the Sultan and his entourage, male and female.

Von Hammer, on the authority of the historian Ali, tells the story that a favourite of the Sultan, one Schemsi Pasha, who was descended from a family formerly reigning over a province of Asia Minor, on the borders of the Black Sea, which had been dispossessed by an early Ottoman Sultan, on coming from an interview with the Sultan, Murad III, exclaimed with a joyous air: "At last I have revenged myself on the House of Othman, for I have now persuaded it to prepare for its own downfall!" When asked how he had done that, he replied: "By persuading the Sultan to share in the sale of his own favours. It is true that I placed a tempting bait before him. Forty thousand ducats make no trifling sum. From this time forth the Sultan sets the example of corruption, and corruption will destroy the Empire."[21]

As a result of this evil practice of the sale of offices, the whole system of government throughout the Empire, from top to bottom, was infected with bribery and corruption. The judges, equally with other officers, were corrupt, and gave their judgments to the highest bidder. Criminals of the vilest kind who could bribe the judges were allowed to go free. All confidence in the administration of the law was destroyed. All officers in the State, from the highest to the lowest, held their posts at the will of those who appointed them, and were liable to be superseded at any moment. Having paid large sums for these posts, it was necessary for them to make hay while the sun shone, and to recoup themselves for their outlay by exactions on those below them, and by plundering the people in their districts.

The army being no longer exempt from this pernicious system, officers were appointed or promoted, not because they were efficient, but because they had the longest purses. The discipline of the army was therefore relaxed. There was also great dissatisfaction throughout the service because the soldiers were paid in debased coins. The garrisons of such frontier fortresses as Buda and Tabriz broke out in revolt. The Janissaries got out of hand. There were conflicts between them and the Spahis. The Janissaries frequently insisted on the dismissal, and even on the execution, of viziers and other ministers of State, and the craven Sultans and the ladies of their harems had to consent. There was rebellion in Transylvania, Moldavia, and Wallachia. The Christians of the Lebanon rose against their oppressors, the Turks. Brigandage increased to a lamentable extent in other parts of the Empire.

The ladies of the harem, it would seem, were not favourable to war. The Sultana Baffo, being a Venetian by birth, averted war with that Republic for many years. Peace was also made with Austria and was maintained for some years. But in 1593, when Transylvania and Wallachia were in rebellion, Austria and Hungary were induced by sympathy for their people to declare war against the Porte. Their army, under command of the Emperor Maximilian and Count Pfalfi, the Hungarian general, marched to the Danube, capturing on their way Gran, Pesth, Bucharest, and other strongholds of the Turks. They then crossed the Danube and marched to Varna.

There was the greatest consternation at Constantinople at the loss of so many strongholds and the defeat of the Turkish armies. There was a general demand that the Sultan himself, the incompetent Mahomet, should endeavour to restore confidence to the Turkish soldiers, by putting himself at the head of them, as his predecessors had done in past times. He was urged to unfurl the standard of the Prophet, and to appeal to the religious fervour and fanaticism of the army. Mahomet was most unwilling to adopt this course. He preferred to remain in the Seraglio at Constantinople. The Sultana Baffo, fearing that her influence might be lost if her son was out of her sight, backed his refusal to march. On the other hand, his preceptor, the historian Seadeddin, who had great influence over him, made every effort in the opposite direction. At last the Janissaries refused to go to the front unless their Padishah led them, and Mahomet, much against his will, was compelled to put himself at the head of his army. The sacred standard of the Prophet and his mantle, a most prized relic, were brought out for the occasion. With much pomp the Ottomans marched northwards to meet the invaders. The Austrians and Hungarians fell back at the approach of this great army of Turks. They abandoned all the fortresses they had captured in Bulgaria. They recrossed the Danube. The two armies at last came into conflict on the plain of Cerestes, in Hungary, on the 24th of October, 1596, where a memorable battle took place, extending over three days.

It does not appear that Mahomet took any part in the direction of his army. The Grand Vizier was virtually in command. The second in command was Cicala, an Italian by birth who had embraced Islam, a most brave and resolute soldier, greatly favoured by the ladies of the harem. The Sultan, however, was present in the field, surrounded by his bodyguard. The sacred banner of the Prophet was unfurled and roused, it was said, the fervour of the Turkish soldiers. On the first day the Turks met with a reverse, and a division of their army was defeated. A council of war was held, at which Mahomet expressed his wish to retreat and to avoid further battle. Seadeddin stoutly opposed this. "It has never been seen or heard of," he said, "that a Padishah of the Ottomans turned his back upon the enemy without the direst necessity." Mahomet then suggested that he himself should withdraw from the battle, and that the Grand Vizier, Hassan Pasha, should take command of the army. "This is no affair for pashas," said Seadeddin, "the presence of the Padishah is indispensably necessary." It was decided to continue the battle in the presence of the Sultan.

The second day was no better for the Ottomans than the first. On the third day, October 26th, the two main armies came into closer quarters. The Hungarians, under Count Pfalfi, attacked the Ottoman artillery in flank and captured all the guns. The battle seemed to be irretrievably lost. The Sultan, seated on a tall camel, surrounded by his bodyguard, watched the rout of his army. He wished to fly while there was time. He was dissuaded again by Seadeddin, who quoted a verse from the Koran: "It is patience which wins victory, and joy succeeds to sorrow." The Sultan, wrapping the Prophet's mantle round him, consented to remain on the field.

The Austrians now charged the Ottoman camp. The Imperial soldiers, breaking their ranks, devoted themselves to plunder. At this point Cicala, at the head of a large body of irregular cavalry, which had taken no part so far in the battle, charged with irresistible force the scattered host of the Christians. They carried everything before them. The Austrians, in their turn, were driven from the field. Maximilian and Sigismund were compelled to fly for their lives.

The Ottomans, as a result of this gallant charge, regained all that they had lost. Thirty thousand Austrians and Hungarians perished. Ninety-five of their guns were captured. The camp and the treasure of the Archduke were taken. Never was a more complete and unexpected victory. No thanks, however, were due to the Sultan. There can be no doubt that if he had acted on his own impulse and had fled, the battle would have been lost. He was a timid spectator of the conflict, and of much the same use as the sacred standard and the cloak of the Prophet. The victory was undoubtedly due to the courage of Cicala and the splendid charge of his cavalry, and to the determination of Seadeddin in compelling his master the Sultan, against his will, to remain on the field of battle.

No more important battle had taken place beyond the Danube since that of Mohacz in the time of Mahomet II. If the victory had resulted to the Christians, the whole of the Ottoman possessions north of the Danube would have been lost. The Christian army, under Maximilian, would again have crossed that river and have advanced into Bulgaria and Macedonia, and the dismemberment of the Ottoman Empire might have been precipitated by two or three centuries.

The craven Sultan returned to Constantinople immediately after the battle. He received there a great ovation for the victory due to Cicala. Never again did he lead an army on the field. He devoted himself thenceforth to a voluptuous life in his harem. The government of the Empire remained in the hands of the Sultana Validé.

Cicala, as a reward for his successful charge, was immediately promoted to be Grand Vizier. It was a most unfortunate selection. He treated with great severity the Ottoman troops who had misbehaved at the battle of Ceresties. He accused them of cowardice. He inflicted summary punishment on their leaders. Thirty thousand of the soldiers, mostly belonging to Asia Minor, dispersed and returned to their homes, spreading disaffection and rebellion in their several districts.

After this signal victory war of a desultory character was continued with Austria for some years, now one and now the other getting the better of it in the capture and recapture of fortresses. In 1606 peace was arrived at. A treaty was concluded between the two Powers at Silvatorok, which was, on the whole, unfavourable to the Ottomans. Transylvania was practically freed from their rule. They were confirmed in the possession of one-half of Hungary, but the other half was freed from tribute. The fortresses of Gran, Erlau, and Gradiscka were secured to Ottoman possession, Raab and Komorn to Austria. The annual payment of 30,000 ducats by Austria, which the Turks regarded as a tribute, was also to cease, but a lump sum of 200,000 ducats was to be paid to the Porte.

By the surrender of its claims on Transylvania the Ottoman Empire in Europe entered upon a course of shrinkage, which thenceforth, up to the present time, has been the normal course of events.

This decadence was soon to be illustrated in another direction. War had again broken out with Persia, and the Turks sustained a series of defeats. In 1618 peace was patched up for a time, by the terms of which all the provinces which had been captured under Murad III and Mahomet III were ceded again to Persia, and the boundaries between the two Empires were restored to what they had been under Selim II. Meanwhile, as a result of misgovernment, the Turkish Empire was going headlong to ruin. We have a very authoritative account of the deplorable condition into which it had fallen at this period in the reports of Sir Thomas Roe, who was sent as the first British Ambassador to the Porte by James I. Queen Elizabeth had already, a few years previously, entered into correspondence with the Porte, and had urged the Sultan to join in a naval alliance in the Mediterranean against Philip II, who was then threatening to invade England. The reply of the Porte was friendly, but nothing more.

In 1622 Sir Thomas Roe was sent on a mission, mainly for the purpose of protesting against the piratical destruction of British commerce by corsairs from Algiers and Tunis. He remained at Constantinople for five years, and succeeded in obtaining promises of redress from the Porte. The Pasha of Algiers was recalled and a successor was appointed. But apparently this had very little effect in abating piracy. The reports of Sir Thomas Roe are full of descriptions of the misery of the inhabitants of Turkey, of symptoms of decay, and of the falling grandeur of the Empire.

All the territory of the Grand Seignior [he says] is dispeopled for want of pasture and by reason of violent oppression—so much so that, in the best parts of Greece and Anatolia, a man may ride three or four, or sometimes six, days and not find a village to feed him or his horse, whereby the revenue is so lessened that there is not wherewithal to pay the soldiers and to maintain the Court. It may be patched up for a while out of the Treasury, and by exactions which are now onerous upon the merchants and labouring men to satisfy the harpies.[22]

I can say no more than that the disease works internally that must ruin this Empire; we daily expect more changes and effusion of blood. The wisest men refuse to sit at the helm, and fools will soon run themselves and others upon the rocks.

This State for sixteen months since the death of Othman hath been a stage of variety; the soldiers usurping all government, placing and displacing *more vulg.* as the wynd of humour or dissatisfaction moved them. In this kind I have seen three Emperors, seven Grand Viziers, two Capitan Pashas, five Agas of the Janissaries, and, in proportion, as many changes of governors in all the provinces, every new Vizier making use of his time displacing those in possession and selling their favours to others.[23]

In another passage he points out that the hope of booty was the main motive for war and invasion by the Turks:—

The Turkish soldier is not only apt but desirous to make invasion because all things are prey and all kinds of licence allowed to them; and his hope is more upon booty and prisoners than upon conquest. Every boy or girl is to them magazine and brings them the best of merchandise and worth 100 dollars, so that every village is to them a magazine and they return rich.... But I am persuaded versâ vice if they were invaded and the war were brought to their doors they would be found the weakest, unprovided and undisciplined enemy in the world.[24]

The pirates of Algiers have cast off all obedience to the Empire, not only upon the sea where they are masters, but presuming to do many insolences even upon the land and in the best parts of the Grand Seignior.[25]

There can be no doubt that at the beginning of the seventeenth century, when Sir Thomas Roe wrote these dispatches, the Ottoman Empire was in a condition of unparalleled disorganization, and its various races were in a state of untold misery, owing in part to the want of strong men at its head, and in greater part to the system of corruption which had infected every branch of its administration. If at this time any neighbouring Power had been in a position to attack it, the Empire would not have been able to offer resistance. But Spain, after the reign of Philip II, was almost as decadent as Turkey. Germany was distracted by internal religious wars and was unable to concentrate on external foes, while Russia had not as yet developed a position which made her formidable to the Turks.

It has already been stated that there was a break in the disastrous rule of the harem when Murad IV came of age and was able to take the reins of government from the hands of his mother. The Sultana Validé was a very clever woman, with excellent intentions, and practically ruled the State during his minority. But she was not equal to the task of coping with the grave difficulties of the time. The Empire was going to the bad in all directions. The Persians, taking advantage of the confusion in Turkey, declared war and successfully invaded the provinces of Erivan and Bagdad. The two Barbary provinces of Algiers and Tunis were asserting independence. They engaged in piratical attacks on the commerce of the allies of the Porte, and were negotiating separate treaties with them. The internal condition of the Empire became worse than ever. There were frequent outbreaks of Janissaries, who imposed their will on the Sultana.

In 1632, Murad, on reaching the age of twenty-one, took command of the State, and soon showed that he was of very different fibre from his six incapable predecessors. His first experience was an outbreak of the Janissaries, who demanded that the Grand Vizier and sixteen other prominent officials should be executed. Murad was compelled to yield. But he felt deeply the humiliation of his surrender and was determined to avenge it. He gathered round him a faithful band of Spahis, and suddenly, when it was least expected, dealt with the leaders of the Janissaries by putting them to death. This had the effect of cowing that mutinous body. He then devoted himself to the task of purging the State of corrupt and unjust officials of all ranks. He pursued this task with most ruthless energy. On the slightest suspicion officials in the highest positions were secretly put to death by his orders, and their bodies were flung into the Bosphorus. He became a terror to evildoers of all ranks. But he also became bloodthirsty and callous of life in the process. Brutal as were his deeds, they had the effect of restoring order in the State and discipline in the army. Throughout the length and breadth of the Empire his dominant will made itself felt, and his authority as Sultan was soon completely re-established.

Murad showed himself equally vigorous and competent as a general. His effective reign, after taking over the government from his mother, did not extend over more than eight years. During this time he personally led two expeditions against the Shah of Persia, each of them occupying two years. In the first of them he conquered Erivan. In the second he recaptured the city of Bagdad, after a most desperate resistance by the Persians. Of the garrison of twenty thousand men only six hundred survived. The Ottoman army was then allowed to sack the city, and thirty thousand of the inhabitants were massacred. The whole province was restored to the Ottoman rule. More than eighty years passed before another war took place with Persia.

In these campaigns Murad showed immense vigour. He marched at the head of his army and shared with the soldiers their hardships. His saddle was his pillow at night. There was no pitched battle with the Persians. The campaigns consisted of sieges and captures of fortresses. On his return to the capital after the second campaign, in 1639, Murad received a great popular ovation. He died soon after, in 1640, from fever, aggravated by intemperance, to which he was addicted. When he was on the point of death he gave orders for the execution of his brother, Ibrahim, the only surviving male of the descendants of Othman. Ibrahim had been immured in 'the Cage' during the lifetime of his brother. He was quite unfit to rule the Empire, and Murad must have well known this. It was surmised that Murad preferred to go down in history as the last Sultan of the Othman race rather than hand over the throne to such an incapable successor. Others thought that he intended his last and favourite Grand Vizier to be his successor. His mother, the Sultana Validé, with the object of saving the life of her second son, Ibrahim, feigned to carry out Murad's order. She sent a message to the dying Sultan that Ibrahim had been put to death in accordance with his instructions. Murad, it is said, when he heard of this "grinned a horrible and ghastly smile and then expired."

It may well have been that those who wished for the destruction of the Ottoman Empire regarded with complaisance the failure of Murad's intention of putting an end to the Othman dynasty. It was obviously impossible that Sultans of the type of those who had succeeded the great Solyman could for long hold the Empire intact. A new dynasty, founded by an ambitious vizier, or some other bold adventurer, might have invigorated the Empire and have long delayed its dismemberment. But *Dís aliter visum est.*

If Murad's intention to put his brother to death was prompted by the conviction that Ibrahim was unfit to rule the Empire, he was fully justified by subsequent events. In his short reign of eight years Ibrahim succeeded in undoing all the good which Murad had effected by his ruthless vigour. He proved to be a degenerate, whose original evil nature had been worsened by many years of immurement and constant dread of death at the hands of his brother. He was as bloodthirsty as Murad, without the same motive of restoring discipline in the army and order and justice throughout the Empire. He was also cowardly and mean. He wasted the resources of the State, which had been wisely accumulated by Murad, in self-indulgence and in gratifying the caprices of his harem. He was the most confirmed debauchee of the long line of the Ottoman Sultans. The Sultana Validé pandered to his passions by presenting to him every Friday a new female slave. By this means she obtained full influence over him and used it in every case to the great detriment of the State. Every abuse and evil which Murad had checked grew apace, and the Turkish Empire, so far as internal affairs were concerned, entered on a new course of decadence. The rule of the harem again prevailed, without any motive but that of gratifying the caprices of its inmates. Disaffection and rebellion spread among the Janissaries and Spahis, and also among the ulemas and all classes of people at Constantinople. A conspiracy was formed to get rid of Ibrahim. It was supported by the main body of ulemas. At a meeting of the conspirators the charge against Ibrahim was formulated as follows:—

The Padishah has ruined the Ottoman world by pillage and tyranny. Women wield the sovereignty. The treasury cannot satiate their expense. The subjects are ruined. The armies of the infidels are besieging towns on the frontiers. Their fleets blockade the Dardanelles.

It was determined to dethrone Ibrahim and to replace him by his son Mahomet, a lad of seven years of age. The Sultana Validé did her best to shield her son from the threatened blow, but she was ultimately induced to give her consent to his deposition. A large body of Janissaries then invaded the palace and insisted on Ibrahim appearing before them. They announced to him the decision to depose him. He was compelled to submit and was conducted to prison. The question was then submitted to the Mufti, "Is it lawful to dethrone and put to death a Padishah who confers all the posts of dignity in the Empire, not on those who are worthy of them, but on those who have bought them for money?" The Mufti replied by a *fetva* in the laconic word "Yes." There was a threat of an *émeute* among the Spahis in favour of Ibrahim. He was promptly put to death and his son Mahomet IV was installed as Sultan.

The eight years of Ibrahim's reign, however, were not without some importance as regards the external affairs of the Empire. They showed that there were still some capable men in the service of the Sultan. In 1641 an expedition was fitted out for the recapture of the important city of Azoff, which of late years had fallen into the hands of the Cossacks. It was a failure and met with a reverse. In the next year a much larger force was sent out, and was supported by a hundred thousand Tartars from the Crimea. It succeeded in its object. The Cossacks, before surrendering the city, destroyed all its fortifications and burnt the town. The Turks rebuilt it and left a garrison of twenty-six thousand in this important frontier fortress.

In 1644 another expedition was fitted out against the island of Crete, which then belonged to the Republic of Venice. It had been bought many years previously from the Marquis of Montserrat, to whom it had been allotted as his share in the spoil of the Greek Empire, after the capture of Constantinople by the Crusaders in 1204.

It appears that a fleet of merchant vessels, on their way from Constantinople to Egypt, was captured by corsairs from Malta, who sought shelter for a time for themselves and their prizes in one of the ports of Crete. The Sultan was greatly incensed at this, the more so as some of the captured vessels belonged to one of the eunuchs of his harem. His first design was to send a fleet to attack Malta, but he was dissuaded from this course. He decided, as an alternative, to attack Crete, although the Porte was at peace with Venice, and the Republic was willing to make amends for the violation of its neutrality by the Maltese corsairs.

A fleet was thereupon fitted out, in 1645, ostensibly to attack Malta, but with sealed orders to divert its course when at sea to Crete. It consisted of a hundred and four vessels carrying upwards of fifty thousand men. The fleet, under the above orders, steered for Crete, and made a sudden attack on Canea, one of the chief ports of the island. Having captured this city and also Retino, the army was landed. It overran the whole island and invested Candia, its chief fortress and capital. A memorable siege then commenced. It lasted for nearly twenty-five years. The Republic of Venice made desperate efforts to save the city. It was not supported by the native Greek population of the island, who hated their Venetian rulers, and were not unwilling to exchange them for Ottomans.

While the Porte was thus engaged in the endeavour to add to its domain at the expense of the Republic of Venice, it was incurring a very serious shrinkage of Empire in the Mediterranean, along the northern coast of Africa. Historians agree in assigning to the middle of the seventeenth century the virtual severance from Ottoman rule of the two Barbary States of Algiers and Tunis. It is not possible to fix a precise date in either case, for the process of amputation was slow and was spread over some years, and long after the Sultan had practically ceased to exercise any real power over these dependencies the semblance and form of suzerainty was maintained. The main cause for the loss of these provinces was the practice which had grown up, under the corrupt administration of the Porte, of selling the posts of governors of them to the highest bidders in money. In place of men of energy and of capacity, able to control the unruly elements of mutinous soldiers and disaffected Moors and Arabs, governors were appointed under a system of purchase who were quite incapable of performing the duties of their office, and who merely thought of filling their pockets and recouping themselves for their outlay. The practice then arose for the Janissaries and other Ottoman soldiers forming the garrisons of Algiers and Tunis to elect their own chiefs. The appointments of these men, Deys, as they were called, were for a time submitted to the Sultan for approval or veto, but later this form was discontinued, and the Deys elected by the soldiery became the real dominant authorities in these States, and eventually superseded in form, as well as in substance, the feeble pashas sent nominally as governors from Constantinople. Virtual independence was thus achieved. Both States provided themselves with fleets of powerful war vessels, which roamed over the Mediterranean and the Atlantic as far as the coasts of Ireland and Madeira, preying upon the commerce of all countries, irrespective of whether they were at war with the Porte or not. They were, in fact, pirates. The captured crews were employed as slaves in the bagnios of Algiers and Tunis. The best evidence of the actual, though not yet of the formal, independence of these Barbary States was that other Powers sent their fleets to attack and bombard them, and to destroy, if possible, their pirate craft, without declaring war against the suzerain power, the Porte. Thus, as early as 1617 a French fleet, under Admiral Beaulieu, made an attack on the Algerian fleet of forty vessels of from two hundred to four hundred tons, and destroyed many of them. In 1620 a British fleet, under Sir Richard Mansel, in retaliation for the capture of no less than four hundred British merchant ships in the previous five years, made a similar attack on Algiers, without, however, much result. In 1655, another British fleet, commanded by Admiral Blake, under orders from Protector Cromwell, bombarded Tunis, and destroyed a great part of its fleet, and having effected this proceeded to Algiers. There was much consternation there, and the captives of British birth were given up without a struggle. In both these cases there was no declaration of war against the Porte, and no offence was taken by the Sultan at the action of England.

In 1663 the British Government made a treaty with the Sultan empowering it to attack and punish the Algerines without being charged with a breach of amity with the Porte. It frequently availed itself of this, and many naval attacks were made on these nests of pirates, without, however, very effectual results. In some of its naval operations in the Ægean Sea the Porte received assistance from the fleets of these two Barbary States. But this was entirely at the discretion of their virtual rulers and was not considered obligatory on them. For our present purpose, it is sufficient to point out that the States became virtually independent of the Ottoman Empire about the year 1650. In the case of Algiers this independence continued till the State was conquered and annexed by France in 1830. In Tunis the same process took place, with the difference that an hereditary Beyship was eventually formed under a Greek adventurer whose descendants retained power there till 1881, when the French invaded the province and eventually annexed it to France.

Ibrahim was succeeded by his son, Mahomet IV. He reigned for thirty-nine years. During the first eight of these there was chaos in the Empire. The government remained in the hands of the harem. The position was aggravated by fierce dissension in that institution. There were two rival parties, the one led by the ex-Sultana Validé, the mother of the late Sultan, who was loath to part with the power she had acquired during her son's reign, the other by the mother of the new Sultan, Torchan by name. Both of them had their supporters among the Janissaries and Spahis, with the result that there were frequent disorders and encounters in the streets of the capital. Grand Viziers were made and deposed with startling rapidity, as one or other of these parties prevailed. Outbreaks occurred in many parts of the Empire and there was no one with sufficient authority to cope with them. The dispute between the two ladies was eventually settled by the murder of the elder one. Meanwhile it was fortunate for the Empire that Austria was so exhausted by thirty years of war in Germany that she was not able to avail herself of the opportunity afforded to invade the Ottoman Empire and recover Hungary and other provinces. But the war with Venice resulting from the unprovoked attack by Ibrahim on Crete was continued without intermission. A Venetian fleet under command of Admiral Macenigo defeated and destroyed an Ottoman fleet off the Dardanelles and took possession of the islands of Lemnos and Tenedos. It blockaded the Dardanelles. Strange to say, this did not put a stop to the siege of Candia by the Ottomans. This was maintained with pertinacity, but for a long time without success. Meanwhile anarchy prevailed in the Empire. Relief most unexpectedly came from the appointment of a Grand Vizier by Sultana Torchan, by which she made some amends for her previous misdeeds.

XIII

THE KIUPRILI VIZIERS
1656-1702

AT this stage, when the ruin of the Empire seemed to be imminent, owing to the failure of vigour and authority of so many Sultans, the general corruption of officials, and the lawlessness and mutinous conduct of the army, there rose to the front a man, or rather a succession of men of the same family, who were able to stem the evil tide and to restore, for a time, the credit and prestige of the Empire. In the following forty-six years four members of the Kiuprili family filled the post of Grand Vizier—not, however, without more than one unfortunate interregnum. They ruled the Empire in the name of the incompetent Mahomet and his successor. This advent of a family was the more notable as in Turkey there never was any trace of hereditary rank. While the throne had been filled without a break by members of the Othman family, who, in the first three hundred years, deservedly acquired prestige so great that it has survived a yet longer succession of degenerates, it has never been supported by an hereditary class of any kind. The structure of the political and social system of the Ottoman Turks has always been democratic. The highest posts in the State, equally with the lowest, were accessible to all, irrespective of merit, often by mere personal favour, or even, it would seem, by chance, without consideration of birth or wealth. The unique exception to this, where members of the same family rose to the highest position of the State under the Sultan, was that of the Kiuprili family.

Mahomet Kiuprili, the first of this remarkable stock, was of Albanian descent. His grandfather had migrated to Kiupril, a small town in Amasia, in Asia Minor, whence the family took their name. Their position must have been a very humble one, for Mahomet commenced his career as kitchen-boy in the palace of the Sultan. He rose to be chief cook and, later, steward and grand falconer, and thence by favour of the harem was appointed as governor successively of Damascus, Tripoli, and Jerusalem, acquiring in all of them the reputation of a just, firm, and humane ruler. At the full age of seventy, on the advice of the Sultana Validé, he was finally appointed Grand Vizier, in spite of the protests of all the pashas, ulemas, and other officials, who alleged that Kiuprili was in his dotage, that he could neither read nor write, and that he was quite incompetent for the post. Never were experts more mistaken. Kiuprili only consented to take the post upon the conditions, solemnly swore to by the Sultana Validé on behalf of her son, who was then only fifteen years of age, that all his acts as Grand Vizier would be ratified by the Sultan without examination or discussion, and that he would have a free hand in the

- 130 -

distribution of other offices and in the award of honours. He further fortified his position by getting from the Mufti a *fetva* sanctioning by anticipation all his measures.

Armed with this authority, Kiuprili entered upon the work of his high office, and at once proceeded to use his powers with inflexible firmness and with the utmost severity. He emulated Sultan Murad IV in his relentless war against wrongdoers of every class, high and low, throughout the Empire. There was not the same spirit of cruelty or bloodthirstiness as in Murad's case, but there was the deliberate policy to extirpate abuses by the forcible removal of those concerned in them. Corrupt officials, unjust judges, incompetent officers in the army, and mutinous soldiers were promptly put to death. The same fate befell those who were suspected of intriguing against the new Vizier. It was said that during his five years of office thirty-five thousand persons were executed by his orders. The number included a great many mutinous soldiers. The principal executioner at Constantinople admitted that he had strangled four thousand persons of some position during this period. Terrible as was this retribution on wrongdoers of all kinds, there cannot be a doubt that in the main it was salutary. The effect of Kiuprili's inflexible will and determination was speedily apparent throughout the Empire. Corruption and injustice were stayed. Disorders of all kinds were repressed. Discipline and subordination were restored in the army.

Kiuprili, by his vigorous action, was able to extinguish the revolts in Asia Minor and elsewhere. He reconstructed the Ottoman navy, with the result that naval supremacy was again asserted in the Ægean Sea and the war with Venice took a favourable turn. The islands of Lemnos and Tenedos were recovered by the Porte. The siege of Candia was again prosecuted with the utmost vigour.

Kiuprili practically ruled the Empire with unquestioned authority for five years, till his death in 1661. In prospect of that event he obtained from the Sultana Validé and the Sultan the reversion of the Grand Vizierate for his son, Ahmed Kiuprili. On his deathbed he is said to have given to the young Sultan the following heads of advice:—

Never to listen to the advice of women.

Never to allow a subject to become too rich.

To keep the treasury of the State well filled.

To be always on horseback and to keep the army on the move.

Ahmed Kiuprili, when he succeeded his father as Grand Vizier in 1661, was only twenty-six years of age. He has rightly been considered by Turkish historians as the most eminent in the long list of statesmen of the Ottoman

Empire, with the exception only of Sokolli. He had been given the best of education by his father, and had early experience in public affairs as governor of a province. He had all his father's inflexible will and firmness, without carrying them to excess by wholesale executions. For a year after his accession to power he continued his father's régime of severity, but when he felt assured of his position he relaxed it, and thenceforward his administration was humane and just. He had most engaging manners, dignified and modest. He spoke with reserve and without verbiage. He ruled the Empire for fifteen years, until his death in 1676. During this time he enjoyed the full confidence of Sultan Mahomet, who, though he had reached the age of twenty when Ahmed Kiuprili was appointed Grand Vizier, and might in due course have taken part in public affairs, devoted himself wholly to the pleasures of the chase and never interfered with the conduct of affairs by his great minister.

Ahmed was a most strict observer of the religious precepts of Islam. In spite of this, he was noted for his enlightened tolerance of other religions. He abolished the restrictions against the building of churches by the Christian subjects of the Porte. He did his best to improve the condition and lighten the burden of the rayas. His administration was free from abuses. He gave an example to all below him by refusing to take money for appointments to offices or for any administrative acts. He kept the treasury well filled, in spite of the many wars he was engaged in. It was, in fact, in the civil administration of the Empire that his ability and wisdom were chiefly conspicuous. His military career was chequered, for though he succeeded in adding to the Empire not a few important territories, he encountered for the first time in its history a great and historic defeat at the hands of the Austrians and a second serious defeat by the Poles.

In 1663 war broke out with Austria, and the Grand Vizier, in command of an army of a hundred and twenty thousand men with a hundred and twenty-three guns, crossed the Danube at Belgrade and marched northwards to Neuhausel, one of the three most important strongholds in the hands of the Austrians, which, after a siege of five weeks, was compelled to surrender. Meanwhile the Khan of the Crimea, at the head of a horde of irregular horsemen, overran Moravia, committing the most frightful devastation and carrying off eighty thousand Christians as captives for sale as slaves.

After the capture of Neuhausel, Ahmed Kiuprili took other minor strongholds in the neighbourhood, and then returned to Belgrade for winter quarters. In the following year he again issued from Belgrade with his army and marched to Neuhausel. He then crossed the River Mur and captured Serivar, and on July 26 he reached Komorn, on the River Raab, on the frontier of Hungary and Styria. The Austro-Hungarian army, under the command of the Comte Montecuculi, a general of great reputation—an

Italian by birth and the rival of Turenne—held a position on the River Raab not far from Komorn. It was greatly inferior in numbers to that of the Ottomans. But since the last great battle between the two Powers at Cerestes the Austrians had greatly improved in the quality of their generals and officers and in their armaments. The discipline of the Ottoman troops was no longer what it had been, and they had not kept pace in the improvement in guns.

On August 1, 1664, the two armies met near to the Convent of St. Gotthard, which gave its name to a memorable battle. In spite of their great numerical superiority, the Ottomans met with a severe defeat, largely due to the charge of heavy cavalry of the Austrians, under the command of Prince Charles of Lorraine, soon to become famous as a general. The Turks lost ten thousand men, many of whom were driven into the River Raab and were drowned. Thirty thousand of their cavalry, who were spectators of the battle from the other side of the River Raab, took to flight when they saw the issue of the battle and abandoned fifteen guns. The Grand Vizier was able to draw off the main body of his army without further loss. The Austrian losses were heavy, and they made no effort to follow up their victory. The battle, however, was of supreme importance, for it was the first great defeat of the Ottomans in the field by the Austrians. It broke the prestige of the former, which had been unquestioned since the battle of Mohacz in 1526.

In spite of their victory, the Austrians were willing to negotiate with the Grand Vizier for terms of peace, and ten days after the battle a treaty was signed at Vascar, where the Turks were encamped. It was, in the main, a renewal of the treaty of Silvatorok. So far as it differed, it was favourable to the Ottomans. It provided that Transylvania was to be evacuated by both Austrians and Turks. It recognized Apafy, whose claims had been maintained by the latter, as prince of that province, subject to payment of tribute to the Sultan. Serivar and Neuhausel were to remain in the hands of the Sultan. Of seven palatinates occupied by the Ottomans, four were to remain in their hands and three were to be restored to the Emperor. Ahmed Kiuprili had every reason to be satisfied with this treaty. Though defeated in a pitched battle, he had added to the Empire of the Sultan. He led his armies into winter quarters again at Belgrade at the end of October, and on his return to Constantinople received a popular ovation.

In 1667 Ahmed entered upon another campaign. He was determined to bring to a successful issue the siege of Candia, which for so many years had baffled all the efforts of his predecessors. He landed in the island of Crete with large reinforcements. The city of Candia was defended with the utmost tenacity and courage by the Venetians, under the command of Morosini, later famous for the conquest of the Morea. Ahmed spent nearly three years before the city. He urged on the siege with great engineering skill. The Venetians made every effort to retain possession of the city and of the island by offers of large sums of money. Ahmed Kiuprili proudly replied to these overtures: "We are not money-dealers. We make war to win Candia, and at no price will we abandon it."

In the course of 1669 the prospect of a successful defence of the city was increased by the arrival of a French fleet, commanded by the Duc de Noailles, and having on board the flower of the French nobility and six thousand soldiers. They were joined later by auxiliary squadrons of the Pope and the Knights of Malta. The combined fleet, consisting of seventy vessels, bombarded the Ottomans from the sea, while the besieged opened fire on their front. The allies hoped to place the Turks between two fires and to draw them from the trenches which invested the city by land. The attack, however, failed owing to the accidental blowing up of some of the attacking vessels. This brought confusion into the whole line. A sortie of the garrison was also unsuccessful. Later, a serious misunderstanding arose between Morosini and the Duc de Noailles, which led to the departure of the allied fleet and the abandonment of the city to its own resources. The garrison was now reduced to four thousand men capable of bearing arms. Defence against the overwhelming forces of the Turks was impossible. Terms of surrender were agreed to. The siege, which had lasted for nearly twenty-five years, was brought to an end. Favourable terms were accorded to Morosini and the garrison. The whole island fell into the hands of the Ottomans, and shortly after this a treaty of peace was effected with the Republic of Venice, which recognized the transfer of Crete, with the exception of three small ports on its coast, which were retained for commercial purposes.

A third war was undertaken in 1672 by Ahmed Kiuprili against Poland in support of the Cossacks of the Ukraine, who had risen against their oppressors, the Poles, and had appealed to the Porte for protection against the invasion of their country by Sobieski. It was decided by Ahmed to support these insurgents. An army of six thousand was sent there, in concert with a much larger force of Tartars from the Crimea. The Czar of Russia joined with the King of Poland in protesting against this intervention of the Porte. The proud answer of the Porte was:—

God be praised, such is the strength of Islam that the union of Russians and Poles matters not to us. Our Empire has increased in might since its origin; nor have all the Christian kings that have leagued against us been able to pluck a hair from our beard. With God's grace it shall ever be so, and our Empire shall endure to the Day of Judgment.

Ahmed Kiuprili himself, in a letter written in his own hand to the Polish envoy, defended his action in terms which might well have been quoted later when the Christian subjects of Turkey rose in arms against their oppressors and claimed the assistance of Russia.

The Cossacks [he said], a free people, placed themselves under the Poles, but being unable to endure Polish oppression any longer, they have sought protection elsewhere, and they are now under the Turkish banner. If the inhabitants of an oppressed country, in order to obtain deliverance, implore the aid of a mighty emperor, is it prudent to pursue them in such an asylum? When the most mighty and most glorious of all emperors is seen to deliver and succour from their enemies those who are oppressed, and who ask him for protection, a wise man will know on which side the blame of breaking peace ought to rest. If, in order to quench the fire of discord, negotiation is wished for, so let it be. But if the solution of differences is referred to that keen and decisive judge called 'the Sword,' the issue of the strife must be pronounced by God, by whose aid Islam has for a thousand years triumphed over its foes.[26]

In the campaign of 1672, the important city of Kaminiec, the capital of Podolia, was captured. The King of Poland then sued for peace, and the treaty of Bucsacs was agreed to, under which the province of Podolia was ceded to the Sultan. The treaty, however, was disavowed by Sobieski and the principal nobles of Poland. They renewed the war against the Turks. It lasted for four years. In 1673 the Turkish army, under Ahmed Kiuprili, met with a crushing defeat from the Poles, under Sobieski, near Choczim. His camp was surprised. The Wallachians and Moldavians deserted him on the field and went over to the enemy. There was great slaughter of the Turks. In the following year the Turks returned to the charge, but were again worsted. In 1675 Sobieski, aided by the Russians, gained another great victory over the Turks at Lemberg. But in the following year the Turks, under the command of Ibrahim Pasha, turned the tables on the Poles. The superior resources of the Turks, under the able administration of Kiuprili, told at last in their favour. Sobieski, who had become King of Poland, was defeated. The whole of Podolia fell into the hands of the Ottomans. Sobieski was now willing to come to terms. Under the treaty of Zurawna (October 27, 1676) terms rather more favourable than those under the repudiated treaty of Bucsacs were conceded to the Ottomans. Podolia was ceded to them.

Ahmed Kiuprili died a few days after the signature of this treaty from the effect of drink. Though he had incurred severe defeats at the hands of the Austrians and Poles, he had retrieved them by his persistence and by the effective use of the resources of the Empire, which he enlarged by the province of Podolia, the island of Crete, and the district of Neuhausel and Serinvar, in Hungary. These entitle him to be ranked among the makers of the Empire so far as Europe was concerned. His enlightened administration, his humane and just bearing, his insistence on equal justice for all, irrespective of religious creeds, his strict observance of his plighted faith in public and private affairs, in matters great and small, his patronage of science and literature, earned for him a place in the first rank of Turkish statesmen.

It was hoped in many quarters that the Sultan would appoint as successor to Ahmed Kiuprili his brother, Zadé Mustapha Kiuprili, who had shown as governor of provinces that he had many of Ahmed's high qualities. In an evil moment Mahomet conferred the post of Grand Vizier on his son-in-law, a favourite companion in the chase, Kara Mustapha—the black Mustapha—who was notorious for his bloodthirsty disposition and his avidity and corruption. This seems to have been one of the few acts of the Sultan Mahomet IV where he exercised his royal prerogative, for as a rule he left everything to his Vizier, when appointed, and cared for nothing but the pleasures of the chase. A more unfortunate appointment could not have been made. Thirteen years elapsed before Zadé Kiuprili was at last invested with the office. They were years fraught with disaster to the Empire.

The first military effort of the new Grand Vizier was to lead an army in 1678 across the Danube into the Ukraine. He came into conflict there with the Russians as well as the Poles, and met with a severe defeat. The war, however, simmered on with varying results till 1681. Peace was then concluded with Russia, and the Turks gave up the disputed country.

In 1682 the population in that part of Hungary which was under the rule of the Emperor Leopold revolted against his bigoted tyranny. Kara Mustapha thought that this afforded an opportunity for attacking Austria. He seems also to have been inflated with ambition to create a kingdom for himself. He collected an enormous army at Adrianople, and in the spring of the following year, 1683, he crossed the Danube at the head of two hundred and seventy-five thousand men, without counting a horde of irregular Tartars and camp followers. He met with little resistance in his march northwards till he reached the walls of Vienna at the head of two hundred thousand men. The Emperor, on his part, was very ill-provided with troops to meet this enormous host of invaders. He had no more than thirty-five thousand men under arms. Of these, eleven thousand were left to garrison Vienna, and the main body was quite insufficient to meet the Turks in the field. In his peril the Emperor appealed for aid to Sobieski, the King of Poland. The Poles had very recently concluded peace with the Turks. But this made no difficulty. Sobieski undertook by treaty to send an army of fifty thousand men in support of the Emperor. There was a clause in the treaty of a significant character. It was not to be annulled by any future dispensation of the Pope. The Polish army, however, was at some distance and could not reach Vienna in less than eight weeks. There can be little doubt that if Kara Mustapha had pressed the siege with vigour Vienna must have fallen before the arrival of the Polish army.

This second great siege of Vienna began on July 15, 1683. The Emperor and his family fled to Bavaria. The fortifications of Vienna had been much neglected and offered no serious obstacle. But the city was heroically and obstinately defended by its commander, Count von Stahremberg, who emulated Count Salms of the first siege. Twenty thousand of its citizens enrolled in its defence. The Turkish batteries shattered the walls. There were frequent sorties without avail. It was said that the Ottoman army, with its enormous superiority in numbers, might easily have carried the city by storm, but that Kara Mustapha hoped to gain it by capitulation, in which case the wealth of the city would be at his own disposal as representative of the Sultan, whereas, if it were taken by assault, the great booty would fall mainly to the soldiers. He delayed, therefore, the final attack. Meanwhile Sobieski had time to bring up his army from Poland and to join Prince Charles of Lorraine, who was in command of the Imperial troops, making a total force of eighty thousand. They crossed the Danube at Tulm by a bridge of boats, and then made a detour through a most difficult country behind the Kalemberg, so as to attack the Turkish army before the city from the rear. Kara Mustapha was guilty of incredible neglect in not offering resistance to the crossing of the Danube by the Christian force, or to their passage through the difficult country behind the Kalemberg. On September 6th rockets from the Kalemberg announced to the garrison of the city that the relieving army had occupied these heights behind the Turkish camp.

When Sobieski saw the great array of the Turkish camp exposed to attack, he felt very confident of success. He contemptuously said of the Grand Vizier: "This man is badly encamped. He knows nothing of war. We shall certainly beat him." In an address to his troops he said:—

Warriors and friends, yonder on the plains are our enemies, in numbers greater indeed than at Choczim, where we trod them underfoot. We have to fight them on a foreign soil, but we fight for our own country, and under the walls of Vienna we are defending those of Warsaw and Cracow. We have to save to-day not a single city but the whole of Christendom, of which the city of Vienna is the bulwark. The war is a holy one. There is a blessing on our arms and a crown of glory for him who falls.... The infidels see you now above their heads, and with hopes blasted and courage depressed are escaping among the valleys destined to be their graves. I have but one command to give—Follow me! The time is come for the young to win their spurs.[27]

Kara Mustapha, when he saw the Christian army on the heights above him, made immediate preparations for battle. He gave orders for the massacre of thirty thousand Christian captives, mostly women and children, taken prisoners on the route to Vienna and destined to be sold as slaves. Leaving the best of his men, the Janissaries, in the trenches before the city, he concentrated the main part of his army to meet the attack of the Poles from the rear. Sobieski ranged his army in a great semicircle and made a general advance against the Turks. The Tartar irregulars fled and carried confusion to the rest of the army. Sobieski then led his best troops direct against the centre of the Turks. The mass of the Ottoman army was broken and routed. Terrible slaughter followed, and the whole of the Turkish camp, with immense booty, fell into the hands of the Christians. The Janissaries in the trenches before the city were then attacked on two sides, by the victorious Poles from the rear and by the Viennese garrison on the front. They were cut to pieces and annihilated. The victory of Sobieski was complete and final. Three hundred guns, nine thousand ammunition wagons, and twenty-five thousand tents were captured.

The Turkish army was driven from the field and, panic-stricken, took to flight. Untold thousands of them were killed, together with great numbers of pashas and generals. Kara Mustapha escaped with the mob of fugitives, carrying with him the sacred banner of the Prophet. The débris of the army found its way to Raab, and thence to Buda, where the Grand Vizier ordered the execution of some of the best officers of the army, whom he falsely accused of being responsible for the disaster. He himself then made his way to Belgrade, where, in his turn, he was put to death, with much more justification, by order of the Sultan. His immense and ill-gotten wealth was confiscated by the State. He had lived in unprecedented splendour. In his harem were fifteen hundred concubines, attended each by a servant, and seven hundred eunuchs to guard them. His own personal servants and horses were counted by thousands.

The second siege of Vienna, thus brought to so glorious an end by its brave garrison and by Sobieski, differed essentially from that undertaken by Sultan Solyman in 1529. Solyman was compelled to raise the siege and to retreat by the failure of food and munitions. He met with no reverse in the field, and he was able to withdraw his army intact. Mustapha fought a pitched battle against a very inferior army coming in relief of the city, and was defeated, and his army was routed and broken up. There never was a greater disaster to an army or to a general. It brought most serious results to the Ottoman Empire. It broke once for all the prestige of the Turks as a conquering nation. It removed the fear of an Ottoman invasion which for two centuries had been a nightmare to the Central States of Europe.

The attack on Vienna was practically the last effort of the Ottomans to extend their Empire into an enemy's country. Henceforth they were almost always on the defensive. It will be seen that the defeat of the huge army by

Sobieski resulted in the loss to the Turks of the greater part of their conquests in Hungary, and that, in a few years, it led to their being driven across the Danube.

Sobieski and Lorraine, after their great victory in front of Vienna, followed it up with vigour. At Paskenay they fell into an ambuscade prepared for them by the retreating Turks and lost two thousand men, but two days later they attacked the enemy and defeated them with great slaughter. The bridge of boats across the Danube by which the Turks retreated was broken by the rush of fugitives and seven thousand were killed or drowned. The Christian army then pressed on to Gran and invested and captured that important fortress. It had been in possession of the Turks for many years. Henceforth it was a rampart of Austria and Hungary against them. This concluded the year's campaign. The Austrians and Poles went into winter quarters.

Meanwhile the effect of the great victory at Vienna was to stimulate other Powers to join the combination against the Turks. The Pope preached another crusade against them—the fourteenth. The Republic of Venice fitted out a fleet, which was joined by galleys of the Pope, the Knights of Malta, and the Grand Duke of Tuscany. In the following year this fleet attacked and captured the island of Santa Maura and the city of Prevesa, at the entrance to the Gulf of Arta. A Venetian army also invaded Bosnia and Albania.

In this year also (1684) the Austrians, under Lorraine, issuing from Gran, crossed the Danube and attacked and defeated the Turks at Warzen, and again in another battle before Buda, and then besieged that fortress. But after some weeks they were compelled by the rainy season and disease in the army to raise the siege and retreat. Meanwhile another Austrian army advanced into Croatia and fought and defeated the Turks. As a result of this the province of Croatia, which had been for one hundred and fifty-one years under Turkish rule, was freed from it, and was thenceforward an Austro-Hungarian possession.

In the following year, 1685, the Austrians made further progress. The important stronghold of Neuhausel, which twenty-two years previously had been captured by the Turks, was now recaptured after a desperate resistance. Of its garrison of three thousand men only two hundred survived. The women and children of the Turks were sold to landowners in the Austrian Empire. The capture of this city was the cause of great rejoicing throughout Europe. In 1686 the siege of Buda was renewed. The Imperial army consisted of ninety thousand men—Germans, Hungarians, and Croats. It was under the command of the Prince of Lorraine. The siege was commenced on June 18th. Three attempts to relieve it under Grand Vizier Solyman failed. After six weeks of siege the Austrians assaulted and captured the city. Its brave defender, Abdi Pasha, and its garrison perished, and the city was given up to ruthless sack. The city had been in possession of the Turks for a hundred and forty-five years, and during this time had resisted successfully six sieges. It now passed finally into the hands of the Hungarians.

The campaign of the following year, 1687, was opened on the Drave. The Grand Vizier led an army of fifty thousand men and sixty-six guns. It met the Austrians at Mohacz on the very field where, a hundred and sixty years previously, the Hungarians had been defeated in the battle which gave one-half of their country to the Turks. The Ottomans were now in their turn defeated and routed. Twenty thousand of them were killed, while the loss of the successful army was only a thousand. Slavonia was in the same year cleared of all Turkish forces, and was permanently restored to Austria, while in Transylvania the Voivode Apafy, who owed his position to the Turks, now turned against them.

Meanwhile the Venetians had been equally successful during the past three years. Their army, under Morosini, invaded the Morea in 1686, captured all its strongholds, and drove the Turks from the country. They also successfully invaded Dalmatia. In 1687 they attacked and captured the Piræus and Athens. It was on this occasion that the Parthenon, which, in spite of many centuries of war and dangers of all kinds, still existed in all its original grandeur and beauty, was irreparably ruined. The Turks had made use of it as a powder magazine, thinking probably that it was safe from attack. A bomb from the Venetian batteries exploded there, whether purposely or not, and converted the temple into a ruin as we now see it. The whole of Greece was now practically in the hands of the Venetians. The Greek population had given no aid to the Turks in resisting the new invaders. They had soon to learn that there was little to choose between their old and their new masters. If anything, the Venetians proved to be the more tyrannical and rapacious.

On the conclusion of the campaign of 1687 in Hungary the Turkish army, as a result of its long series of defeats, was seething with discontent, and was almost in a state of mutiny. Its leading officers met and petitioned the Sultan, demanding the dismissal and execution of its general, the Grand Vizier Solyman. They elected Siawousch Pasha as their general. The army then retreated across the Danube to Philippopolis, and thence to Adrianople, from whence it sent a deputation to the Sultan to enforce its views. The Sultan summoned a great Council of State, at which it was decided to accede to the demands of the army. Siawousch Pasha was appointed Grand Vizier in place of Solyman, who was soon after put to death by order of the Sultan. It was hoped by this concession to appease the army, and to prevent its march to Constantinople. The army, however, persisted in its threatening attitude and renewed its march to the capital. It now increased its demands. It insisted on the deposition of the Sultan. There was general concurrence in this among officials at Constantinople. Mustapha Kiuprili, the brother of the late Ahmed Kiuprili, who was Kaimachan, and performed the duties of Grand Vizier in his absence from the capital, called an assembly of ulemas at St. Sophia. He addressed them in these words:—

Since the Padishah thinks only of diverting himself in the chase, and at the time when the Empire is assaulted from all quarters we have seen him dismiss all men capable of repairing our misfortunes, can you doubt any longer that the dethronement of a Padishah who thus conducts the affairs of the State is legally permitted?

The ulemas unanimously concurred. They decided on the dethronement of Sultan Mahomet and his replacement on the throne, not by his son, but by his legal heir, his next brother, Solyman. They then betook themselves to the abode in the Seraglio where that prince was secluded, called him forth, and announced to him their decision, citing in favour of it a verse from the Koran: "We have named you to be Khaliff of the country."

There was no opposition to this. Solyman, who had spent his life in seclusion, in constant fear of being murdered by his brother, and who was only saved by the brave efforts of the Sultana Validé, his mother, came out of what was virtually a prison to be invested with the insignia of Sultan. Mahomet, who had reigned as Sultan for thirty-nine years, which he had devoted wholly to the chase, to the neglect of every duty of his great office, retired to the secluded building which his brother had occupied so long. He died there a few years later, regretted by no one.

Von Hammer gives a detailed account of one of Sultan Mahomet's organized expeditions in pursuit of game, which may be worth quoting as an illustration of his pursuits and character. The scene of it was between Adrianople and Tirnova, and it occurred in 1683, the year in which his army was engaged in the invasion of Austria and on the siege of Vienna. Thirty thousand peasants were brought from all parts for the purpose of beating the woods and putting up the game. For their subsistence a levy was made on the district of 150,000 marks. This battue cost the lives of a great number of beaters, who succumbed to the fatigue of the operations. Many rayas were brought from as far as Belgrade for the occasion. The Sultan, on seeing the bodies of those who had perished, said to his followers: "These men would doubtless have rebelled against me. They have received their punishment in anticipation of this."

Mahomet, it would seem, owed his deposition not so much to his own callous neglect of his duties as Sultan as to the arrogant incapacity of Kara Mustapha in his campaign against Vienna and the imbecility of the two succeeding Grand Viziers, Ibrahim and Solyman.

Solyman, who thus mounted the throne in 1687, at the age of forty-one, showed greater capacity than was to be expected after his long seclusion in 'the Cage,' but he was quite unequal to the task of controlling the mutinous Janissaries. They filled Constantinople with riot and slaughter. They pillaged the palaces of the viziers and others. They attacked the harem of the Grand Vizier Siawousch, whom they had so recently elevated to the post. He was killed in bravely defending his harem. His favourite wife and sister were dragged naked through the streets after being cruelly mutilated. The disorder of the capital became so unendurable that the population rose in arms and assisted the authorities in resisting the Janissaries. Their Agha and principal officers were put to death, and order was at last restored.

In the spring of the next year, 1688, a well equipped army was sent to the Hungarian frontier, in the hope of retrieving the defeats of the past five years. The Austrians, however, had made good use of the interval. They had now three armies in the field, under the command of Prince Charles of Lorraine, Prince Louis of Baden, and Prince Eugène of Savoy—all three generals of exceptional ability. They invested the fortress of Erlau and captured it. The road to Belgrade now lay open to them. This supremely important city, the bulwark to the Balkans and the gateway to Hungary, was treacherously surrendered by its garrison in August 1688 after a bombardment of only twenty-one days. Prince Louis of Baden about the same time invaded Bosnia and occupied a great part of it. Dalmatia revolted and threw over Turkish rule. Nisch was later occupied by the Austrians, and Widdin, on the Danube, fell into their hands. By 1689 the only fortresses in Hungary remaining to the Turks were Temesvar and Waraidin.

Farther eastward the Turks had been more fortunate. An army of Tartars from the Crimea overran Poland in 1688 and defeated a Polish army on the Sereth. In the following year, when Russia joined in the combination against the Ottomans and sent an army into the Crimea, it met with a severe defeat. These were the only rays of light to the Turks. Elsewhere they met with a succession of disasters. The Balkan provinces, for the first time since the days of Hunyadi, were threatened by the Austrians. Parts of Bosnia and Serbia were in their hands. The whole of Greece and Albania had been conquered by the Venetians, under Morosini, and the Turkish fleets had been swept off the Mediterranean by the combined fleets of Venice, the Pope, the Knights of Malta, and the Duke of Tuscany. On the Ottoman side no single general of any capacity had appeared.

It was under these conditions that a general council of the Empire was summoned at Adrianople at the end of 1689. After a long discussion, it advised the Sultan to appoint as Grand Vizier Zadé Kiuprili, who had been passed over by Sultan Mahomet IV in favour of the corrupt and incompetent Kara Mustapha after the death of Ahmed Kiuprili. After thirteen years of misgovernment and calamity this third member of the Kiuprili family was called to power. He showed at once great vigour and capacity. Addressing the chief dignitaries of the Empire, he described the perilous condition of affairs: "If we go on as we have been in the past, another campaign will see the enemy encamped before Constantinople." He took immediate steps to restore the financial position.

Zadé Kiuprili repleted the treasury by heavy contributions on the officials, who had enriched themselves at the expense of the public. He filled the ranks of the army by calling out veterans. He revived the Ottoman navy. He fitted out a flotilla of vessels for service on the Danube. He replaced a number of incompetent and corrupt governors by honest men on whom he could rely. He endeavoured to win the support of the Christian rayas throughout the Empire. He issued imperative orders to all governors and pashas that no one should be allowed to oppress the rayas. No taxes were to be levied on them except the capitation tax. He allowed the Christians everywhere to build churches, though he himself was a most strict Mussulman. He freed trade from many unwise and unnecessary restrictions. He was personally austere and simple in his habits, very reserved in his utterances. It was said of him that he never committed a crime and never used a superfluous word. He was commonly called 'Kiuprili the Virtuous.' Unfortunately for his country, he held the post of Grand Vizier for less than two years, for it will be seen that he was killed in battle in 1691.

At the time when he assumed the Grand Vizierate the Austrians had crossed the Danube and had advanced far into Macedonia. Kiuprili sent an army against them and defeated them in two engagements. As a result, nearly all the important posts south of the Danube were recovered and the pressure on the Empire in this quarter was removed. Zadé Kiuprili now took command of the army in person, and in August, 1690, advanced through Bulgaria, drove the Austrians from their position between Sofia and Nisch, and besieged and captured the latter place. He then attacked and captured in succession Semendria, Widdin, and Belgrade. Another Ottoman army under Tekeli Pasha invaded Transylvania and drove the Austrians from it. Kiuprili returned to Constantinople covered with glory.

About this time Sultan Solyman died and was succeeded by his brother, Achmet II, who, like himself, had been brought up in the seclusion of the Seraglio, and was quite incompetent to rule the Empire or to lead its armies. Fortunately he left matters in the hands of his Grand Vizier. Kiuprili again led the army in the field and, advancing from Belgrade in May, 1696, marched northwards on the right bank of the Danube to meet the Austrians under Prince Louis of Baden, who were advancing from Peterwardein. The two armies met at Salankemen. Their flotillas engaged on the Danube and the Turks were there the victors. But on land the battle ended in great disaster to them. Against the advice of the most experienced of his generals, Zadé Kiuprili insisted on fighting, without waiting for reinforcements that were on their way. A most desperate battle took place in which the Turks were completely defeated. The Grand Vizier, in the hope of restoring the fortunes of the day, rushed into the mêlée, sword in hand, and was killed while hewing his way through the Austrian ranks. The Turkish troops were dispirited by the death of their general and gave way. Panic and rout followed. The Turkish camp and a hundred and twenty guns fell into the hands of the Austrians. About the same time Tekeli Pasha was also defeated by the Austrians and was driven out of Transylvania. The Ottoman Empire was again at a very low ebb after these disasters. Sultan Achmet died heartbroken by the burden of shame and grief, and was succeeded by his nephew, Mustapha II, the son of Mahomet IV.

The new Sultan was not wanting in the will to relieve the plight of his country, but it will be seen that he had not the capacity or the persistency required in such an emergency. He fully recognized that the main causes of disaster were the dissolute habits and incapacity of his predecessors. Immediately after his accession to the throne he issued a Hatti-Scheriff in which he announced his intention of restoring ancient usages and leading his armies in person. In the course of this notable document he said:—

Under monarchs who are the slaves of pleasure or who resign themselves to indolent slumber, never do the servants of God enjoy peace or repose. Henceforth voluptuousness, idle pastime, and sloth are banished from this Court. While the Padishahs who have ruled since the death of our sublime father Mahomet have heeded naught but their fondness for pleasure and for ease, the unbelievers, the unclean beings, have invaded with their armies the four frontiers of Islam. They have subdued our provinces. They have pillaged the goods of the people of Mahomet. They have dragged away into slavery the faithful with their wives and little ones. This is known to all, as it is known to me. I therefore have resolved, with the help of the Lord, to take a signal revenge upon the unbelievers, that brood of hell; and I will myself begin the holy war against them.... Do thou, my Grand Vizier, and ye others, my viziers, my ulemas, my lieutenants and agas of my armies, do ye all of you assemble round my person and meditate well on this my imperial Hatti-Scheriff. Take counsel and inform me if I ought to open hostilities in person against the Emperor or remain at Adrianople. Of these two measures choose that which will be most profitable to the Faith to the Empire and to the servants of God.[28]

In response to this, the Divan met and discussed for three days whether the new Sultan should command in person the army about to be sent against the Austrians. They came to an adverse decision. They thought that it would not only expose the sacred person of the Sultan to too much risk, but would also involve excessive expense. They probably thought also, but scarcely dared to express it, that the Sultan, being quite inexperienced in military matters, would be an encumbrance to the army. They advised the Sultan that he ought not to commit his imperial person to the chances of a campaign, but would do better to leave the conduct of the war to the Grand Vizier. The Sultan replied in the laconic words, "I persist in marching." In accordance with this decision, Mustapha in person, in spite of his inexperience, led a well appointed army in the summer of 1696 from Belgrade to Temesvar, capturing on the way various minor fortified places. His first encounter with the enemy near Temesvar was successful. The Austrians were defeated with heavy loss and Temesvar was relieved. Mustapha, however, did not pursue his success further. He returned to Constantinople and there received an ovation.

In the following year, 1697, Mustapha again marched with his army from Belgrade into Hungary, without any definite plans as to what he proposed to do. After many councils of war and much irresolution, it was decided to advance northwards to the River Theiss. The Austrian army was now under command of Prince Eugène of Savoy, who, we have seen, made his début at the siege of Vienna. He was the ablest general of his time. The two armies met at Zenta on the River Theiss, about sixty miles above its junction with the Danube. The Turks had erected a bridge over the river at this point. The Sultan and his cavalry, and a great part of the artillery, had already crossed the bridge. The infantry were still on the other side. Prince Eugène with his army, coming suddenly upon them, caught the Turkish army *in flagrante delicto*, divided by the river. Advancing in a wide crescent, he attacked the whole line of the Ottoman infantry who had not crossed the river. There was great confusion in the ranks of the Ottomans and discord among the leading officers and a want of direction. A large body of Janissaries mutinied on the field of battle and began to massacre their officers. There ensued an overwhelming defeat of the Ottomans. Twenty-six thousand Turks were slain on the battlefield and ten thousand were drowned in their attempt to cross the river.

The Grand Vizier, four other viziers, and a great number of pashas and thirty aghas of Janissaries were killed; four hundred and twenty standards were captured. The Sultan, who had witnessed the battle from the other side of the river in comparative safety, was able to escape with some of his cavalry to Temesvar, and thence he returned to Belgrade and Constantinople. This experience satisfied his military ardour, and he never again appeared at the head of his army. An immense booty fell into the hands of the Austrians. All the Turkish guns were captured. What remained of the army defeated at Zenta found its way to Belgrade, and thence returned to Adrianople, while Prince Eugène crossed the Danube into Bosnia and made himself master of the greater part of that province. This great victory of the Austrians, after fourteen years of almost uninterrupted success, decided not only the campaign but the war in their favour, and marked irrevocably the decadence of the military power of the Ottoman Empire.

Six days after the battle the Sultan, in his peril, turned once more to the Kiuprili family for help. In place of the Grand Vizier, who had been killed at Zenta, he appointed Hussein Kiuprili, a son of the elder brother of Mahomet Kiuprili, and therefore a cousin of Ahmed. Until the siege of Vienna he had given himself up to a life of pleasure, but after that grave defeat of the Turks he filled with great distinction many high posts in the government. He was the fourth member of his family to hold the position of Grand Vizier, and showed himself fully capable of bearing the burden.

In the course of the following winter of 1697-8, many efforts were made to bring about peace. Lord Paget, the British Ambassador, offered the mediation of Great Britain and Holland on the principle of *Uti possidetis*— that each of the Powers concerned, Austria, Venice, and Poland, were to retain what they had wrested from Turkey. Hussein Kiuprili summoned a great Council of State to consider this. He had personally fought at St. Gotthard and other battles, and fully recognized the superiority of the Austrian army. The Ottomans, since the siege of Vienna, had been defeated by them in nine great battles, and had lost by siege nine fortresses of the first rank. He felt that if the war were prolonged there would be further reverses of the same kind. At his instance, it was decided by the Council to accept the mediation of Great Britain and Holland. The other Powers, with the exception of Russia, were equally willing. The Czar, Peter the Great, alone objected, and warned the other Powers not to trust in Great Britain and Holland, who, he said, were only thinking of their own commercial interests. In spite of his efforts, it was decided to hold a Peace Congress, at which all these Powers, including Russia, eventually were represented. It was held at Carlowitz, not far from Peterwardein, on the Danube, and after seventy-two days' discussion and negotiation it resulted in peace on the basis suggested by Lord Paget. Austria, it was finally agreed, was to retain possession of Transylvania and Sclavonia and of all Hungary north of the River Marosch and west of the River Theiss. This left to the Ottomans only about one-third of their previous dominions in Hungary. The Emperor also was relieved from payment of tribute in respect of Hungary and Transylvania. The Republic of Venice was to retain the Morea and Albania, but was to give up its conquests north of the Isthmus of Corinth—the only departure from the principle of *Uti possidetis*. The Republic was also relieved from payment of tribute to the Porte in respect of the island of Zante. Poland was to retain Podolia. Russia was to have Azoff and the districts north of the Sea of Azoff which were actually in her occupation. The Czar Peter was dissatisfied with this and refused to enter into a treaty upon these terms. He would only agree to an armistice for two years on this basis. The other three Powers concerned entered into treaties of peace for twenty-five years.

This treaty of Carlowitz was of supreme importance in the international relations of Europe. It recognized for first time that the status of the Ottoman Empire was a matter for the concern of all the Powers of Europe, and not only of those at war with it. It established the principle of equality of the Powers concerned, and rejected finally the pretensions of the Ottoman Empire, founded on its long career of conquest. Thenceforth there was no longer any fear of the invasion of Central Europe by the Turks. The settlement was not so ignominious to them as the later treaties of Passarowitch, Kainardji, Adrianople, and Berlin, but not the less it was a great triumph for the Christian Powers of Europe. In view of the long series of defeats of the Ottoman army and the exhausted state of the Empire, Hussein Kiuprili acted the part of a wise statesman in assenting to the treaty. If his advice and that of other members of his family had been followed, and the Christian subjects of the Empire had been treated with justice, later humiliations might have been avoided, and the Empire might have survived intact to a much later date.

Hussein Kiuprili retained the post of Grand Vizier for three years after the treaty of Carlowitz. During this time he showed that he had most of the qualities of his more distinguished relative, Ahmed Kiuprili. He was a man of high culture and public spirit. He did his best by wise and salutary reforms to stem the growing evils of the State. He aimed at curbing the mutinous power of the Janissaries. He endeavoured in many ways to improve the deplorable condition of the rayas. His reforms met with violent opposition from reactionaries. His health broke down under the stress and he was compelled to resign his post. He died within a few weeks, in 1702. His reforms did not survive him. His successor, Daltaban Pasha, was a man of a totally different type, a savage Serbian, who could neither read nor write, and who had acquired a reputation for gross cruelty which he fully justified in his more exalted position.

Once again, in 1710, another member of the Kiuprili family, Nououman Kiuprili, was appointed Grand Vizier, but though he had many of the virtues of his race he did not prove to be equal to the post. He insisted on attempting to do too much. He interfered with every detail of the State and accumulated the hostility of all his subordinates. The affairs of the government fell into confusion and he was in consequence deposed after a very few months. The names of five other members of the same family appear in the history of the next few years as generals and governors of provinces.

It may be doubted whether in the annals of any country a single family has produced so many distinguished men, owing their position, not to personal favour, but to their own merits and to the exigencies of the State. The case is unique in the history of Turkey, where it would be difficult to find another instance where two members of any family rose to distinction.

XIV

TO THE TREATY OF PASSAROWITCH
1702-18

MUSTAPHA did not long survive as Sultan the death of his great Vizier, Hussein, the fourth of the Kiuprilis. He had not fulfilled the early expectation of his reign, when, against the advice of the Divan, he took command of his army in the field. Disappointed and discouraged by his failure, he fell back on a life of indolence and debauchery. After the death of Hussein Kiuprili there was widespread discontent throughout the Empire, and in most parts imminent danger of rebellion. Mustapha had not the courage to cope with it. He abdicated the throne and retired voluntarily to the Cage. He was succeeded by his brother, Achmet III, at the age of thirty, who reigned for twenty-seven years till he was deposed at the instigation of the Janissaries.

Achmet had not been subjected by his uncle to the customary seclusion. He came to the throne, therefore, with greater knowledge of the world. He was not a warrior. He did not attempt to lead his armies in the field. But he did not allow the affairs of State to fall into the hands of women of his harem. Neither did he permit ambitious Viziers to monopolize power. He changed them so often that this was impossible. During the first fifteen years of his reign there were twelve Grand Viziers. It was imputed to him that these frequent changes were due to his want of money and the extravagances of his harem. It was the custom for Grand Viziers, on their appointment, to make very large presents in money to the Sultan, and Achmet looked on this as a source of income. But during their short tenures of office he interfered very little with them. He was, however, personally in favour of a policy of peace, and supported his Viziers in its maintenance. The first six years and the last twelve years of his reign were periods of almost unbroken peace to the Empire. In the other nine years there were many important events bearing on the extension or reduction of his Empire. Territory formerly in the possession of the Ottomans was reconquered, and provinces long held by them were lost. The city of Azoff and its adjoining territory—important for the protection of the Crimea—were recovered from Russia. The Morea and Albania were reconquered from the Republic of Venice. By agreement with Russia a partition was made of important provinces belonging to Persia, some of which had formerly been in the possession of the Porte. On the other hand, as the result of war with Austria, the remaining part of Hungary, not included in the cession made by the treaty of Carlowitz, and considerable parts of Serbia and Wallachia were lost to the Empire. The gains in territory exceeded in area the losses. But there can be little doubt that the loss of prestige by the Ottomans from the defeats of their armies by the Austrians

- 149 -

under Prince Eugène was not compensated for by victories over the Venetians and Persians, or over the very inferior army of Peter the Great.

The first of the wars thus referred to was that with Russia, then under the rule of Peter the Great. He was ambitious of extending his Empire by the acquisition of the Crimea, and of thus getting access to the Black Sea. It was only after the defeat of Charles XII, the King of Sweden, at the battle of Pultowa in 1709, and the consequent conquest of Livonia, that his hands were free for aggression elsewhere. Russia was already in possession of the important fortress of Azoff, on the north-east shore of the sea of that name. The Czar had also fortified Taganrog and other places threatening the Crimea. The Porte was alarmed by these manifest preparations for war. The relations of the two Governments were also embittered by the fact that the Swedish King, Charles XII, after his defeat at Pultowa, sought refuge in Turkey, and that the Sultan accorded a generous hospitality to him, and with great magnanimity refused the demand of Peter for his extradition. It followed that, in 1711, the Porte anticipated the undoubted hostile intention of the Czar, and declared war against Russia. An army was sent by the Sultan across the River Pruth into Moldavia, under command of Grand Vizier Baltadji. This pasha had risen to his post from the humble position of woodcutter at the palace, through the intrigues of his wife, who had been a slave in the Sultan's harem. The Czar, on his part, had collected his forces in the south of Poland and marched into Moldavia. The two armies met on the River Pruth. The Russian army, already greatly reduced in number by want of food and disease, numbered no more than twenty-four thousand men. The Ottomans, who had been reinforced by a large body of Tartars, under the Khan of the Crimea, were at least five times more numerous. The Czar Peter, unaware that the Ottomans had crossed the Danube, advanced rashly on the right bank of the Pruth, and was posted between that river and an extensive marsh not far from Zurawna. The position was dominated by hills, which the Grand Vizier occupied in force, and his numerous and powerful guns swept the position of the Russians, cut off their access to the river, and completely hemmed them in. Their plight is best described in a letter which the Czar wrote to the Russian Senate at Moscow from his camp at this point:—

I announce to you that, deceived by false intelligence and without blame on my part, I find myself shut up in my camp by a Turkish army. Our supplies are cut off, and we momentarily expect to be destroyed or taken prisoners, unless Heaven should come to our aid in some unexpected manner. Should it happen to me to be taken prisoner by the Turks you will no longer consider me as your Czar and Sovereign, nor will you pay any attention to any orders that may be brought to you from me, not even if you recognize my handwriting; but you will wait for my coming in person. If I am to perish here, and you receive well confirmed intelligence of my death, you will then proceed to choose as my successor him who is most worthy among you.

There can be no doubt that the Russian army was completely at the mercy of the Ottomans, and might have been entirely destroyed or captured. It was saved from either fate by the Czar's wife, Catherine. She was the daughter of a peasant, married in the first instance to a dragoon in the Russian army, and later the mistress of Prince Menschikoff. Peter, smitten by her beauty and wit had recently married her, and she was with him on this campaign. This lady, with great presence of mind, collected what money she could, to the value of a few thousand roubles, and sent it and her jewellery with a letter to the Kiaya of the Grand Vizier, suggesting a suspension of hostilities with a view to terms of agreement. In this way relations were established between the two generals, and a treaty of peace was agreed to. Its terms were very humiliating to Russia. Azoff and its surrounding district were to be surrendered to the Porte. Taganrog and some other fortresses were to be dismantled. The Russian army was to withdraw from Poland. The King of Sweden was to be allowed safe conduct through Russia to his own country. There was to be no Russian ambassador in the future at Constantinople. In return for these great concessions the Russian army was to be permitted to retreat without molestation.

The preamble to the treaty contained the following remarkable admission of the predicament in which the Czar and his army were placed:—

By the grace of God, the victorious Mussulman army has closely hemmed the Czar of Muscovy with all his troops in the neighbourhood of the River Pruth, and the Czar has asked for peace, and it is at his request that the following articles are drawn up and granted.

It was also declared in the treaty by the Grand Vizier "that he made the peace by virtue of full powers vested in him, and that he entreated the Sultan to ratify the treaty, and overlook the previous evil conduct of the Czar."

The signing of the treaty of the Pruth was vehemently opposed by the King of Sweden, who was in the Ottoman camp, and by the Khan of the Crimea. They doubtless had good reasons of their own for wishing the war with Russia to be prolonged. It was due to their intrigues at Constantinople that violent opposition was roused to the ratification of the treaty. Baltadji found on his return that, instead of being received with acclamation for having recovered Azoff and other territory, of which the Porte had been deprived a few years previously, he was dismissed from his office with disgrace. The Kiaya Osman and the Reis Effendi Omer, who were believed to be largely responsible for the treaty, were put to death by order of the Sultan.

The Porte refused to ratify the treaty, and preparations were made for a renewal of the war with Russia. But wiser counsels ultimately prevailed, largely through the advice of the British Ambassador, Sir R. Sutton; and two years later, after long negotiation, another treaty was concluded with the Czar, which embodied all the terms of that effected by Baltadji which had been so much objected to.

Many historians have found fault with Baltadji for having neglected the opportunity of destroying or capturing the Russian army and the Czar Peter himself, and for having allowed them to escape by concluding the treaty. It has been suggested that he was bribed by the Empress Catherine. It is, however, inconceivable that one in the high position of Grand Vizier, where there were such immense opportunities for enrichment, could have sold himself and his country for so small a price. It is more probable that the presents of the Empress were made to the subordinate of the Grand Vizier for the purpose of opening negotiations with him. It is also more reasonable to conclude that Baltadji was convinced that no better terms could be obtained by a prolongation of the war. The destruction of the Russian army or its capture, together with the Czar, would have roused the Russian people to a great effort to avenge such a disaster. It is significant that the Sultan, while putting to death the Kiaya and Reis Effendi, spared the life of Baltadji, who was mainly responsible, and simply dismissed him from the office of Grand Vizier. This seems to indicate that the Sultan had given authority in advance to Baltadji, as stated in the treaty, to agree to terms such as were actually obtained. It seems to be unlikely that Sultan Achmet desired to extend his Empire beyond the territory of Azoff into the heart of Russia. What better terms, then, could have been obtained by prolonging the war?

It has also been contended by some historians that it was unwise policy to impose such a humiliation on the Czar as that embodied in the treaty; that it was certain to lead to a renewal of the war for the purpose of avenging it. But the Czar himself did not apparently take this view of the case. After the escape of his army from disaster he showed no inclination to renew the war. He was willing, two years later, to re-enact the treaty, in spite of its humiliating terms. He did not break peace with the Turks in the remaining ten years of his reign. He did not bear a grudge against them and after a few years he entered into an arrangement with the Sultan for the partition of a large part of Persia.

On a review of the whole transaction, we must conclude that the Grand Vizier Baltadji was fully justified in effecting the treaty of the Pruth, and that it was no small achievement, by the skilful manœuvring of his army and without the loss of a single life, to impose terms on the Czar, under which the Ottoman Empire recovered Azoff and its district, the key to the Crimea, and obtained the other valuable concessions embodied in the treaty.

In 1715 the Porte embarked on another war, this time against the Republic of Venice, with the object of recovering the Morea, which sixteen years previously had been conquered by the Republic, when in alliance with Austria, and the possession of which had been confirmed to the Republic by the treaty of Carlowitz. Morosini, the Venetian general by whom this conquest had been achieved, was now dead. It was thought that Austria would not intervene. A pretext for the war was found in the assistance which the Republic rendered to the Montenegrins in an insurrection against the Porte. The army, which had been equipped for war with Russia, was now available for other purposes. The Grand Vizier Damad, who was also otherwise known as Coumourgi, son-in-law of the Sultan, took command of an army of a hundred thousand men. A fleet of one hundred sail co-operated by sea. The Sultan himself accompanied the army as far as Larissa, in Thessaly, but no farther. He left the direction of it wholly in the hands of Damad, who showed great ability in the conduct of the war. It commenced with the siege of Corinth, which, after a brave defence of three weeks, capitulated on July 7, 1715, on favourable terms. But a powder magazine blew up during the evacuation of the fortress, killing six or seven hundred of the Turkish soldiers. This afforded an excuse for breaking the agreement, and for a general massacre of Venetians and Greeks, whether of the garrison or inhabitants—much to the disapproval of Damad. This siege of Corinth formed the subject of Lord Byron's well-known poem, in which Damad is referred to under the name of Coumourgi:—

Coumourgi—can his glory cease,

That latest conqueror of Greece,

Till Christian hands to Greece restore

The freedom Venice gave of yore?

A hundred years have rolled away

Since he refixed the Moslem sway.

With poetic licence Byron attributes to the Venetian governor of Corinth the setting fire to the powder magazine and the fearful destruction of life which it caused:—

When old Minotti's hand

Touched with the torch the train—

'Tis fired.

There seems to have been no more justification in fact for this than for the statement that the Venetians gave liberty to the Greeks. Nothing is more certain than that the Greeks hated the rule of Venice as more oppressive than that of the Turks.

After the capture of Corinth the Ottoman army, in two divisions, invaded the Morea, and had no difficulty in capturing all the Venetian fortresses there, such as Modon, Coron, and Navarino. The Greek inhabitants gave no assistance to their Venetian masters. They welcomed the Turks as their deliverers from an odious tyranny.

The reconquest of the Morea occupied Damad and his army for only a hundred and one days. There was no pitched battle with the Venetians. The campaign consisted of a succession of sieges of fortresses. It was the intention of the Ottomans to complete the expulsion of the Venetians by the capture of Corfu and the other Ionian islands, but at this stage the Emperor of Austria, Charles VI, intervened, and entered into a defensive alliance with the Republic of Venice. It was too late, however, to save the Morea. There was much difference of opinion at the Court of the Sultan whether the action of Austria should be treated as a *casus belli*. The Grand Vizier Damad vehemently contended that it was a breach of the treaty of Carlowitz. He was a man of great force of character and very eloquent. But there was strong opposition to him. The debates in the Divan, in presence of the Sultan, have been recorded and are interesting reading. The Mufti, when consulted on the subject, gave his judgment in favour of Damad. This decided the Council. War was declared against Austria, and in 1716 an army of a hundred and fifty thousand was sent, under command of Damad, to attack the Austrians. It reached Belgrade in September. A council of war was then held to decide whether to advance towards Temesvar or Peterwardein. There was again difference on the subject. Damad ultimately gave his decision in favour of the latter project.

The Turks crossed the River Saave by a bridge of boats, and then marched along the bank of the Danube towards Peterwardein. Their van came in contact with that of the Austrians at the village of Carlowitz, where, sixteen years before, the last treaty had been signed. From Carlowitz to Peterwardein the distance is only two leagues. The Austrian army, greatly inferior in numbers to that of the Turks, was posted in front of the great fortress, behind entrenchments which had been made by Siawousch Pasha in the last war. It was again commanded by Prince Eugène of Savoy, who, in the interval, had gathered fresh laurels in many hard-fought battles for Austria, and who was second to no living general, save only the Duke of Marlborough, by whose side he fought so many battles. The two armies came to issue on August 10, 1716. At first the battle went in favour of the Ottomans. Their redoubtable Janissaries broke the line of the Austrian infantry opposed to them. Prince Eugène then brought up his reserve of cavalry. They charged the Janissaries with irresistible force, and retrieved the fortunes of the day. Damad Pasha, when he saw that the tide of battle was turning against him, put himself at the head of a band of officers and galloped into the thick of the battle, in the hope of infusing fresh courage in his army. He was struck down and was carried from the field to Carlowitz, where he died.

As so often happened to the Turks, the loss of their leader caused a panic in their ranks and completed their discomfiture. Their left wing retreated in the direction of Belgrade, and was followed by the débris of the rest of the army. One hundred and forty of their guns were captured. Their camp and an immense booty fell into the hands of the enemy. The battle, however, was not very costly in men to either side. The Austrians lost three thousand men and the Turks about double the number. Eugène followed up his success by the siege of Temesvar, the last great stronghold of the Ottomans in Hungary. He appeared before it twenty days after the battle of Peterwardein. Its garrison of eighteen thousand men capitulated, after a siege of five weeks, on November 25th. This completed the campaign of 1716. The Turks had not been more successful in other directions. They were compelled to raise the siege of Corfu. Their fleet often met that of the Venetians and had rather the worst of it, though there was no decisive battle.

In the year following, 1717, another large army was sent from Constantinople to the Danube, under Grand Vizier Khalil, who had succeeded Damad after the battle of Peterwardein. It consisted of a hundred and fifty thousand men, of whom eighty thousand were Janissaries and Spahis. It was no more fortunate than that under Damad in the previous year. Prince Eugène, still in command of the Austrians, had opened the campaign by marching to Belgrade with a force of not more than seventy thousand men. He besieged the city and fortress, which was garrisoned by thirty thousand Ottomans. When, after three weeks of siege, the Ottoman army came in sight, so vastly superior in numbers, the position of Eugène was most critical. The garrison of Belgrade was in front of him and Khalil's army, double in number of his own, threatened his rear.

It is highly probable that if the Ottoman general had attacked the Austrians without delay he would have been successful. He hesitated and delayed. He ended by an effort to besiege the besiegers. He entrenched his army in the rear of that of Eugène. The two armies then fired their heavy guns on one another without much result. The Turks were greatly superior in this respect. They were provided with a hundred and forty guns and thirty-five mortars. Failure of food would have compelled the Turks to an issue. But Prince Eugène anticipated this by making an attack himself on the Ottoman lines. Never was a bolder course attempted by a general, and never was there a more brilliant success. With greatly inferior force, the Austrians stormed the Turkish lines on August 16, 1717, little more than a year from the day on which the battle of Peterwardein had been fought. The Ottomans gave way along their whole line. Twenty thousand of them were killed or wounded, while the loss of the Austrians in killed was no more than two thousand. Prince Eugène himself was wounded for the thirteenth time in his great career. The Turks retreated in disorder. They lost a hundred and thirty-one guns and thirty-five mortars and a vast supply of munitions. On the following day Belgrade and its garrison of thirty thousand men surrendered.

After the battle before Belgrade and the capture of that fortress, the Austrians advanced and occupied a great part of Serbia and Western Wallachia. They appealed to the Serbian people to rise against their Ottoman masters, but not more than twelve hundred answered the appeal and joined the Austrian army. There was no desire on the part of the Serbians to exchange Turkish for Austrian rule. The occupation by the Austrians of territory south of the Danube proved to be temporary. Twenty-two years later the Ottomans recaptured Belgrade and drove the Austrians from Serbia.

Meanwhile the Grand Vizier Khalil was dismissed from office by the Sultan for the incapacity which he had shown in the campaign and in the battle of Belgrade. After a time he was succeeded by Damad Ibrahim, a son-in-law and lifelong favourite of the Sultan, who held the post for twelve years, till the deposition of Achmet in 1730. He proved himself in every way worthy of his high office. There was a desire in many quarters to embark on another campaign for the recovery of Hungary. But in the winter of 1717-18 the British Ambassador again proposed mediation, on behalf of England and Holland, on the principle of *Uti possidetis*. This was accepted by both Austria and the Porte. The Emperor was willing to content himself with what he had already achieved, the more so as there was danger of war in other directions. There was more difficulty on the part of the Ottomans. But the Sultan and the Grand Vizier ultimately gave their decision in favour of peace.

The precedent of the Congress of Carlowitz was closely followed. A congress was held at Passarowitch, a small town in Serbia. England and Holland again acted as mediators. After long discussion, agreement was arrived at, and was embodied in a treaty known as that of Passarowitch, on July 21, 1718. By its terms the whole of what remained of Hungary to the Ottoman Empire after the treaty of Carlowitz, a large part of Wallachia, bounded by the River Aluta, and the greater part of Serbia, and a portion of Bosnia bounded by the Rivers Morava, Drina, and Unna, together with the fortresses of Belgrade and Semendria, were ceded to the Emperor.

The Republic of Venice, on whose behalf Austria had embarked on the war, fared badly by the treaty. It had to give up to Ottoman rule the whole of the Morea which had been reconquered by Damad, but received some concessions in Dalmatia. It was, however, arranged by the Congress that the

Porte should have an access to the Adriatic, so as to protect the Republic of Ragusa from Venice. There remained to Venice of its possessions in this quarter only the island of Corfu, the other Ionian islands, and a few ports on the Albanian and Dalmatian coasts. The Porte engaged by the treaty to put a stop to the piracy of Algiers, Tunis, Tripoli, and Ragusa, and to prohibit the residence of the Hungarian rebels in the vicinity of the new Austrian frontier.

The treaty of Passarowitch, following on the great defeats of the Ottomans at the battles of Peterwardein and Belgrade, was almost as important as that of Carlowitz. It determined finally the release of the whole of Hungary from the Ottomans. Their rule there had never been more than a military occupation. There was no real incorporation of the country in the Ottoman Empire. There had been no attempt to settle Turks there, or to impose the Moslem religion on its population. After the expulsion of the garrisons from the various fortresses, all vestiges of the Ottomans disappeared, and no trace of them remained as evidence that they had ever been masters there.[29] It was a great achievement of the Austrians, for which Prince Eugène was mainly responsible. It should be added, however, that there does not appear to have been any popular rising of the people of Hungary, whether Magyars or Sclavs, either in these last two years of war or in the previous war of 1698-9, against their Ottoman rulers. It has been shown that the earlier war had its commencement in an insurrection against the Austrians in that part of Hungary subject to their rule. The Turks hoped to take advantage of this. They appear to have been in close relation with these insurgents throughout these two wars. The Austrians defeated the Turks and drove them out of the country, but their bigoted tyranny was not more acceptable to the inhabitants than that of the Turks. Many years were to elapse before the Magyars of Hungary secured for themselves the benefits of self-government.

The war with Austria, which resulted in the treaty of Passarowitch, did something more than free Hungary from Ottoman rule. It completed the destruction of the prestige of the Turkish armies which had so long weighed on the mind of Europe. The great battles of Peterwardein and Belgrade, in which the Turks were defeated by Austrian armies of very inferior numbers, following as they did a long succession of similar defeats from the battle of St. Gotthard downwards, showed conclusively that the Ottoman armies were no match for the well-disciplined forces of Austria when led by competent generals. The Ottomans seem to have been completely cowed by the succession of defeats. Thenceforth they were always on the defensive in Europe, and never willingly acted the part of aggressors. It became the settled conviction of Europe not only that there was no longer any reason to fear invasion from the Turks, but that it was only a question of time when they would be driven back into Asia.

XV

TO THE TREATY OF BELGRADE
1718-39

THE remainder of Sultan Achmet's reign, till his deposition in 1730, was a period of uninterrupted peace, so far as Europe was concerned. Damad Ibrahim retained his post as Grand Vizier for twelve years, during which he had the absolute confidence of the Sultan and practically ruled the Empire. His policy was distinctly favourable to peace. The only disturbance to it was on the frontier of Persia. That kingdom was in a state of commotion. Its feeble and incompetent ruler, Shah Hussein, was subverted by an Afghan adventurer, Mahmoud. Hussein's son, Tahmasp, appealed to the Czar of Russia and to the Sultan of Turkey for aid to recover his kingdom. Peter the Great offered his support in return for the cession of provinces in the Caspian and Black Sea, and sent an army to take possession of them. This greatly alarmed the Porte, and it threatened war with Russia. Eventually, however, war was avoided. An agreement was arrived at, in 1723, between the two Powers for the partition between them of the greater part of North Persia. The Porte was to have as its share the provinces of Georgia, Erivan, Tabriz, and Baku. Russia was to have Schirvan and the other provinces already promised to it by Tahmasp. Russia was practically already in possession of its share. The Porte had to send an army to conquer the provinces which were to be its portion. It met with some opposition, but the cities of Erivan and Tabriz were captured. This brought the Porte into conflict with Tahmasp, but eventually an agreement was arrived at. Tahmasp was thrown over, and Mahmoud recognized the sovereignty of the Porte over the provinces referred to. It is not worth while entering further into details of these transactions, for it will be seen that in a few years Persia, under Nadir Khan, acting on behalf of Tahmasp, recovered these provinces.

After a reign of twenty-seven years a mutiny broke out against Achmet among the turbulent Janissaries, headed by Patrona, an Albanian soldier in their ranks. It speedily spread among the whole body of soldiers, and was supported by the dregs of the population of the city and by a band of criminals whom they had released from prison. It was probably promoted by enemies of the Grand Vizier. There was much want of vigour in dealing with the outbreak at its early stage. Subsequent events under Achmet's successor showed that it was not really of a formidable character and that it might easily have been put down at its inception by strong measures against its ringleaders. It was allowed, however, to gather head and to spread. It was said that the mutiny was due to the unpopularity of the Sultan, his profuse expenditure, and the great pomp he maintained. This scarcely seems to afford a sufficient explanation. It has also been suggested that among other causes was the discontent of the soldiers on account of the long peace and the lack of opportunity for loot, and perhaps also the expectation of the customary large presents on the accession of a new Sultan. When the rebels got the upper hand they made no substantial proposals for a new policy.

The Sultan, at an early stage, consulted his sister, the Sultana Khadidjé, who advised him to keep his ministers close at hand, so that he might save his own life at their expense, if the rebels would be satisfied by a concession of this kind. He appears to have followed this advice. He lost his head in the crisis, and quailed before the mutineers. He entered into parleys with them. They demanded the surrender to them of three of the principal ministers. Achmet asked whether they wished these ministers to be handed to them alive or dead. They unanimously agreed that they wished to have the dead bodies. The Sultan thereupon had the base and incredible meanness to order that his Grand Vizier—his lifelong friend, married to his daughter—the Capitan Pasha, and the Kiaya were to be strangled and their bodies given up to the mutineers. This did not content the Janissaries. They demanded the deposition of the Sultan. Achmet then offered to abdicate the throne on condition that his life and those of his children should be spared. They agreed to this. Achmet thereupon summoned before him his nephew, Mahmoud, whom he acclaimed as Padishah in place of himself and made obeisance. He then retired to the Cage from which Mahmoud had emerged, and there spent the remainder of his life in seclusion.

Mahmoud, the son of Mustapha II, succeeded at the age of thirty-four. Achmet had not treated him with the same generosity that he had himself experienced from Mustapha II, but had insisted on his seclusion in the Cage. After spending so many of his best years in this way, Mahmoud was unfitted for active duties as head of the State. He had a turn for literature, and was a generous patron of public libraries and schools; but as regards the direction of affairs of the Empire he was wholly incompetent. He fell completely under the influence of the Kislaraga, the chief eunuch of his harem, Bashir by name, who acted as his secretary. Bashir had been an Abyssinian slave, and was bought for the Sultan's harem for 30 piastres. Little is known of the personality of this man, save that, from behind the curtain of the harem, he practically exercised supreme power for nearly thirty years, and died at a very advanced age, leaving a fortune of more than thirty millions of piastres and immense quantities of valuables. These included more than eight hundred watches, set with precious stones, which, it must be presumed, were the gifts of applicants for appointments. Bashir made and unmade Grand Viziers at his will, and if any one of them complained of Bashir's interference with his duties, that was the more reason for his instant dismissal. In Mahmoud's reign of twenty-four years there were sixteen Grand Viziers. In any case, it must be admitted that the success of Mahmoud's reign, such as it was, and the continuity of policy, were mainly due to this aged eunuch.

In the first few weeks of the new Sultan's reign the supreme power of the State was practically in the hands of the rebel Janissaries, under the leadership of Patrona and Massuli, who were soldiers in their ranks. These men soon made themselves intolerable by their insolence and bravado. Patrona installed his concubine in one of the Sultan's palaces, and when she gave birth to a child there, insisted on the Sultana Validé treating her with all the courtesies due to royalty. He insisted also on the appointment as Hospodar of Moldavia of his personal friend, a Greek butcher named Yanaki, who had lent him money. The bolder men about the Sultan determined to get rid of these men. The Janissaries and other soldiers who had joined in the deposition of Achmet were brought to a better frame of mind by large distributions of money. They promised to obey their officers, on condition that no punishment should be awarded to them for their part in the rebellion. Patrona and Massuli and twenty-one of their leading adherents were then summoned to a meeting of ministers at the palace, and were massacred there in presence of the Sultan himself. Within three days seven thousand of the rebellious Janissaries were put to death.

Pacification having thus been effected at the capital, attention was turned to Persia, where, as has been pointed out, a partition treaty with Russia had assigned a large part of that kingdom to the Porte, but the possession of which had not yet been obtained. In the meantime a brigand chief, Nadir, later to become world-famous as the invader of India, had taken service under Tahmasp, the son of the dethroned Hussein. Nadir succeeded in driving the Afghans out of Persia and reinstating Tahmasp as Shah. He proceeded, however, to usurp the power of that feeble monarch, and eventually got himself accepted as Shah in place of Tahmasp. He declared war against the Turks in 1733-5 and, after defeating them in several engagements, compelled them to sue for terms of peace. The Porte was the more ready to accede to terms as war with Russia was imminent. A treaty of peace was therefore agreed to with Nadir in 1735, under which all the provinces which were the subject of the partition treaty with Russia were restored to Persia. Russia also, in prospect of war with Turkey, came to terms with Nadir, and surrendered nearly all the territory which had been acquired under the partition treaty with Turkey.

Peter the Great had died in 1727, and in 1730 was succeeded by the Empress Anne, a clever and ambitious woman. She was incited to war with Turkey by Marshal Munnich, the ablest general whom Russia so far had produced. He promised to drive the Turks out of Europe. At Constantinople the eunuch Bashir was in favour of a policy of peace. He was over seventy years of age and wished to end his days in repose. He resisted as far as he could every attempt to draw the Sultan into war. The French Ambassador, under instructions from his Government, was most anxious to embroil Turkey with Austria. The two maritime Powers, however—Great Britain and Holland—pulled in the opposite direction, and peace was maintained as long as possible. But when, in 1735, the Russians, though nominally at peace with Turkey, captured two fortresses in the neighbourhood of Azoff and threatened that most important outpost of the Empire, the Porte declared war. A Russian army of fifty-four thousand men, under command of Marshal Munnich, then invaded the Crimea. They stormed and broke through the fortified lines of Perekop at the isthmus of that name, joining the Crimea to the mainland, hitherto thought to be impregnable. They captured the city of Perekop, and then overran the whole of the Crimea, devastating it and massacring its inhabitants by thousands. The Russian army, however, suffered greatly from exhaustion and disease in the campaign, and it eventually withdrew from the Crimea before the winter. Another Russian force, under General Leontiew, captured Kilburn, and a third, under General Lascy, an Irishman by birth, attacked and captured the city of Azoff.

Meanwhile the Russian diplomatists discovered that the Emperor of Austria, Charles VI, was quite as anxious as the Czarina Anne to possess himself of Turkish provinces, and was ready to enter into a coalition for the purpose. In the winter of 1736-7 a secret treaty for this purpose was entered into between the two potentates. But as it was not thought expedient by the Austrians to commence their attack until all their preparations for it were completed, a pretence was made of negotiations with the Porte, who had made overtures of peace to the Russians. For this purpose a Congress was held at Nimirof early in 1737. Later it became known that the negotiations on the part of the two allied Empires were illusory, and that there never was any intention to come to terms. The Porte, on its part, was extremely anxious for peace, and was ready to make large concessions, but the terms suggested on behalf of Russia were so extortionate that it was quite impossible for the Sultan and his ministers to entertain them. The Russians demanded the cession of the Crimea, the independence of Wallachia and Moldavia under a native prince, subject to the supremacy of Russia, the opening of the Black Sea and access to it through the Bosphorus and the Dardanelles to Russian vessels of war, and the payment of fourteen millions of roubles. Austria, on its part, demanded the cession of the whole of Bosnia and Serbia. Such terms could only be assented to by the Porte after complete and disastrous defeat. They were indignantly rejected, and, much against the wish of the Porte, the Congress came to an end, and the Sultan was forced to take up arms in defence of his Empire.

A Russian army of seventy thousand men, under Marshal Munnich, opened the campaign of 1737 by an attack on Oczakoff, the most important of the

Ottoman fortresses on the northern shores of the Black Sea, and General Lascy, with forty thousand men, again invaded the Crimea. Oczakoff was vigorously defended by twenty thousand Turks. After some days of siege the principal powder magazine in the fortress blew up, causing enormous destruction and loss of life. The Turkish general, dismayed by this, capitulated on favourable terms. But this did not prevent the massacre of the greater part of the garrison, and only three thousand of them survived. The losses of the Russians, chiefly by disease, were also very great, and nothing more was done by Munnich in this year's campaign. Meanwhile Lascy in the Crimea had repeated the operation of Munnich of the previous year, and eventually retreated from it.

The Austrians, on their part, invaded Bosnia and Serbia with two armies. The principal one, under General Seckendorf, attacked and captured Nisch and, later, Widdin. But this exhausted their efforts for the year, and most of their army perished from disease in the marshes of the Danube.

The campaign of 1738 was little more decisive. The Ottomans, with revived courage, took the offensive, and, advancing into Hungary, under Grand Vizier Yegen Mahomet, captured Semendria and Orsova. The Austrians fell back on Belgrade. General Lascy again, for a third time, invaded the Crimea, but the country had been so devastated by the two previous invasions that he could find no means there of feeding his army, and he was soon compelled to withdraw. In the winter great efforts were made by the Porte to arrive at terms of peace, and it was willing to make great sacrifices. But Marshal Munnich vehemently opposed all peace proposals at the Russian Court. He was still inflamed with the desire to invade Turkey and to capture Constantinople. At his instance emissaries were sent into the European provinces of the Ottoman Empire to incite the Christian rayas to rise in arms against their masters and oppressors—the first instance of the kind.

On the opening of the campaign of 1739 Munnich led his army through Podolia, a province then belonging to Poland, whose neutrality he violated. He spread desolation along his march, as though he were passing through an enemy's country. He crossed the frontier of Moldavia and defeated a Turkish army at Khoczim, and then advanced to Jassy, the capital of the province, and captured it.

Meanwhile the Austrians renewed their attack on Serbia and Bosnia under two new generals, Wallis and Niepperg. An army of fifty-six thousand Austrians issued from Peterwardein and marched southwards, apparently in total ignorance of the strength of the Turkish army which was advancing to meet them. By great efforts the Porte had raised and equipped an army of two hundred thousand men, under the Grand Vizier Elhadji Mahomet. It met the Austrian army at Krotzka, half-way between Semendria and

- 162 -

Peterwardein. The Austrians were defeated, as was to be expected, in view of the enormous disparity of the two armies. They fell back again on Belgrade. The Ottomans followed up their victory and commenced a bombardment of Belgrade.

Nothing could exceed the imbecility and infatuation of the Austrian generals, Wallis and Niepperg. They were now as anxious to make peace as they had been boastful and bellicose at the commencement of the campaign. The French Ambassador, Villeneuve, was with the Turkish army. His mediation was accepted by the Austrians, and terms of peace were agreed to, without consultation with the Russian generals. Belgrade and all the parts of Serbia and Bosnia which had been ceded to Austria by the treaty of Passarowitch and a great part of Wallachia were restored to the Ottoman Empire. The victory of the Ottomans at Krotzka and, still more, the treaty of Belgrade which followed, caused dismay and indignation to the victorious Russians in Moldavia. It was obviously impossible for their army at Jassy to make any further advance into Turkey, or even to hold its own in Moldavia, when an Ottoman army of two hundred thousand, fresh from victory over the Austrians, was on their flank on the Danube. Munnich's grandiose scheme for the capture of Constantinople was extinguished. It became necessary for the Czarina to follow the example of the Austrians and to make peace with the Turks. Terms were ultimately agreed to, under which the Russian conquests in Moldavia and the Crimea and the city of Oczakoff were given up. Russia retained only a narrow strip of land on the shores of the Black Sea. The city of Azoff was to be demolished and its territory was to form a belt of borderland, uncultivated and desert, between the two Empires. The Russians were prohibited from maintaining a fleet either in the Black Sea or the Sea of Azoff.

The two treaties, as a result of the campaign of 1739, were a triumph for Turkey. They were more due to the imbecility and incapacity of the Austrian generals than to the valour of the Ottomans, for it was no great feat of arms for two hundred thousand Turks to defeat fifty-seven thousand Austrians at the battle of Krotzka. But the strategy of the Porte in concentrating their main force against the Austrians on the Danube, while making little resistance to the Russians in Moldavia, was fully justified.

XVI

TO THE TREATY OF KAINARDJI
1739-74

THE campaign, and the resulting treaty of Belgrade, saved the Ottoman Empire from further shrinkage for many years. There followed a long period of peace. This was due not merely to the fact that the Porte pursued a policy of peace, but because the two great Powers in Europe, Russia and Austria, who were bent on the dismemberment of Turkey, were not in a condition to prosecute their aims, and were not able to enter into any combination for the purpose. In 1740 the Emperor Charles VI died. This event led to a scramble among the neighbouring Powers for his inheritance, and to the war known as that of the Austrian Succession, which was brought to an end by the Treaty of Aix-la-Chapelle in 1748. This was followed later again by another war, known as the Seven Years War, which was concluded in 1763. In neither of these great wars did the Porte take any part, and it is to its credit that it did not take advantage of them to attempt the recovery from Austria of any of its lost dominions in Hungary. Till war broke out with Russia in 1768 there was profound peace.

Sultan Mahmoud died in 1754 and was succeeded by his brother, Othman II, who reigned for three years only. He was deformed—a hunchback. He does not appear to have made any change in the foreign policy of his government. In his three years of reign there were six Grand Viziers, and it seems probable that the real power of the State was exercised by the successor to the Kislaraga Bashir, from behind the curtain of the harem.

Mustapha III succeeded his brother at the age of fifty. He had spent his life up to this time in seclusion, in the Cage of the Seraglio, cut off from all contact with, or even knowledge of, public affairs. For the first six years of his reign he left matters very much in the hands of his Grand Vizier, Raghab Pasha, the last of the many who had filled this post under Mahmoud. Raghab proved to be a most wise and competent statesman, not far behind Sokolli and the Kiuprilis, and, like them, devoted to a policy of peace.

After the death of Raghab in 1763 Mustapha gradually took into his own hands the reins of government. Though well-intentioned and with a sense of public duty, he was feeble, hasty, and impatient, and was wanting in the most essential faculty of a ruler, that of selecting competent men as generals and administrators. He abandoned the policy of peace and allowed himself to be drawn into war, with the most unfortunate results to his Empire. It was his misfortune that his reign coincided with those of two such able and unscrupulous neighbouring potentates as Catherine II of Russia and Frederick the Great of Prussia.

The Empress Catherine was invested with supreme power in Russia in the year 1762, in place of her worthless husband, after a military revolt. At her instance, Russia embarked on a policy of aggrandizement against both Poland and Turkey. Frederick the Great also, who had very recently favoured an alliance with the Porte with the object of checking the advance of Russia, now reversed his policy. In 1764 he made a treaty with the Russian Empress reciprocally guaranteeing their possessions, and promising assistance to one another, if the territories of either of them were invaded. But if France were to attack Prussia, or Turkey to attack Russia, assistance was to be given in money. Very soon after this an agreement was arrived at between these two Powers for the dismemberment of Poland and the partition between them of part of its territory. The Empress of Austria, Maria Theresa, also, though most unwillingly, became a partner in this scheme. The Porte was much opposed to this Polish policy of the three conspirators. It protested strongly but in vain against the occupation of Poland by Russian and Prussian troops and against all the infamous proceedings which led to the first partition of Poland. The Russian Government made no effort to avert war. On the contrary, it showed by many actions a deliberate intention to drive the Turks into war. It fomented and encouraged rebellion against the Sultan in the Crimea, the Morea, Montenegro, and Georgia. It violated the neutrality of Turkey by pursuing Polish refugees across the frontier of Bessarabia into territory belonging to the Khan of the Crimea, a vassal of the Sultan, and destroying there the town of Balta.

At a Divan held at Constantinople in October 1768 it was decided that Russia, by its proceedings against Poland, had broken the treaty of Belgrade, and that war against her would be just and necessary. The only opposition to this came from the Grand Vizier, Mouhsinzade Pasha. He did not, indeed, object in principle, but he maintained that it was most unwise to declare war until full preparations had been made for it. He pointed out that the frontier fortresses were in a most unprepared state, and that as military operations could only be commenced by the Turks in the next spring, Russia would be placed in an advantageous position by an immediate declaration of war. For this advice, which the sequel fully justified, the Grand Vizier was dismissed from his office. In his place Emen Mahomed was appointed—a most incompetent man, knowing nothing about military matters, by his own admission. As a result of this premature declaration of war, Russia had full notice, and entered on the campaign of 1769 in Moldavia before the Porte was ready to send an army to defend that province. The Empress put into the field three armies. The principal one, under command of Prince Galitzin, invaded Moldavia and laid siege to Khoczim. It was not till May 1769 that the Grand Vizier was in a position to issue from his camp at Babatagli and march to Isakdji, near Ismail. He there summoned his generals to a council of war and opened the proceedings by an astounding admission of incompetence. Asking for their opinion as to what direction his army should be led, he said, "I have no experience of war. It is for you to determine what operation shall be undertaken and what are the most favourable chances for the army and the Sublime Porte. Speak without hesitation and enlighten me by your counsel."

The generals were struck dumb with astonishment at this confession of ignorance and impotence. Eventually a discussion arose. There was great difference of opinion. As a result, the only decision arrived at was to cross the Danube into Moldavia, and then proceed as circumstances might suggest. In fact, there was no definite plan of campaign. The army, in accordance with this, crossed the Danube. It was then decided to march to the River Pruth. It reached a point about half-way between Khoczim and Jassy. But already it suffered greatly from want of food, for which no preparations had been made. The soldiers also were harassed by swarms of mosquitoes in the marshes of the Danube and the Pruth. It was unable to prevent the capture of Khoczim by the Russians. It was ultimately forced to retreat before coming into serious contact with the enemy, and it found its way back to the Danube; and thus concluded the campaign of 1769.

The Russians did little in the early part of 1770. Prince Galitzin was almost as imbecile and incompetent as the Grand Vizier. The Empress recalled him and appointed in his place General Romanzoff, a most able and determined soldier. The Sultan, on his part, recalled Emen Pasha and gave orders for his execution.

Meanwhile, the Empress Catherine was engaged in carrying out another part of her 'Oriental project,' as it was called. She had sent numerous emissaries disguised as priests to various parts of Greece with the object of stirring up rebellion against the Sultan. Under the belief that a general rising would take place, she sent a great fleet from the Baltic to the Mediterranean for the purpose of giving support to the insurgents. It consisted of twelve ships of the line, twelve frigates, and numerous transports conveying a military force. The expedition was under the supreme command of Alexis Orloff, the brother of her then lover, who had led the military revolt which placed her on the throne. He had expectations that a throne would be found for himself at the expense of the Turks. The fleet was under virtual, though not nominal, command of an Englishman, Admiral Elphinstone, who was supported by numerous other British officers. It was said that every vessel in the fleet had one of these officers on board. This must have been with the cognizance and approval of the British Government, which at that time favoured the aggrandizement of Russia. This fleet left Cronstadt at the end of 1769, and arrived off the coast of the Morea in February 1770. It was welcomed by a large body of insurgent Greeks (Mairotes) and a Russian force was landed. The insurgents perpetrated the most atrocious acts of cruelty on the comparatively few Turks resident in the district.

The ex-Grand Vizier, Mouhsinzade Pasha, now Governor of the Morea, showed great vigour. Collecting a force of Albanians, he succeeded in defeating the insurgent Greeks, fifteen thousand in number, and their Russian allies. The Russians were compelled to re-embark in their fleet. The Greeks who remained on shore were subjected to ruthless slaughter, as were also the inhabitants of the district. The whole countryside was devastated by the Albanians. The Russian fleet, after ineffectual attempts to capture Modon and Coron, sailed away. It came in contact, off the island of Scios, with the Ottoman fleet, not very unequal in number and size of vessels. A naval battle took place on July 7, 1770, in which the Turks were worsted. The defeat would have been the more serious if it had not been for the extraordinary bravery of one of their captains, Hassan of Algiers, who had gained experience as a corsair. Laying his vessel alongside of that of the Russian admiral, he fought with the utmost desperation till both vessels were blown up.

The defeated fleet sought refuge in the small harbour of Tchesmé, where it was blockaded by Admiral Elphinstone. The British officers devised a scheme for destroying the Turkish fleet. Lieutenant Dugdale volunteered to pilot a fire-ship against them. Before coming to close quarters the Russian sailors deserted the vessel, and Dugdale alone remained on board. He steered the vessel against a Turkish ship and set fire to it. The fire spread to the other vessels, closely packed in the harbour, and the whole of the Ottoman fleet was burnt and destroyed with the exception of a single frigate. A more gallant and successful attack has never been recorded in the annals of naval warfare.

Elphinstone, who had fortunately escaped death—as did also Hassan the Algerian, when their warships were blown up in the recent naval battle—then advised that the Russian fleet should sail without delay to the Dardanelles and force its way through the Straits to the Sea of Marmora and Constantinople. But Orloff hesitated and delayed, with the result that the Turks, getting wind of the intention, hastily erected four batteries at the Dardanelles, two on either side of it, crossing their fire. These were sufficient to make it impossible for the Russian fleet to force its way through the Straits.

Orloff and the Russian fleet then proceeded to the island of Lemnos, where it landed troops and besieged the chief fortress. It was evidently hoped to secure a base for the fleet in the Ægean Sea. After sixty days of siege the garrison gave in, and terms of capitulation were agreed upon with Orloff. In the meantime, however, Hassan had persuaded the Porte to allow him to make a desperate effort to save Lemnos. He enlisted four thousand ruffians at Constantinople for this purpose. When it was pointed out what a hazardous enterprise it was, the reply was that it mattered little whether it was successful or not. If successful, Lemnos would be saved; if unsuccessful, Constantinople would be rid for ever of four thousand of its greatest blackguards. Hassan landed unexpectedly in Lemnos, and, declining to recognize the capitulation, attacked the Russians and defeated them, and compelled them to take to their ships again.

Hassan, after this successful exploit, was made Capitan Pasha of the Ottoman navy. He managed to collect together another fleet, and engaged the Russian fleet again off Mondreso. Both fleets claimed victory, but it would seem that the Russians had the worst of it, for they sheered off and left these waters. When next heard of, the Russian fleet was engaged in giving support to Ali Bey, the head of the Mamelukes of Egypt, who had risen in rebellion against the Turkish pasha there, and who was now invading Syria. Orloff landed four hundred soldiers in Syria in support of this rebel. But Ali Bey soon found himself in difficulties. An outbreak took place in his own army against him, fomented by his brother-in-law. Ali Bey was defeated and put to death, and the four hundred Russians were slain in battle. The Porte for a time recovered its hold on Egypt.

The story of Orloff's expedition has been told as it is a good illustration of the use of a naval force which can command the sea in a war of this kind, and of its inability to undertake operations on land, or to force its way against land batteries, unless supported by an adequate army. Orloff's fleet remained in the east of the Mediterranean till the close of the war in 1773, but it did not effect anything of importance.

Reverting to the military operations on the Danube, the autumn campaign of 1770 was very unfavourable to the Ottoman cause. Khalil Pasha, who was now in command, proved himself to be no more competent than his predecessor. Romanzoff, in command of the Russian army, overran the whole of Moldavia. Khalil led thirty thousand efficient soldiers and a host of Tartar irregulars against him. The two armies came in contact at Karkal, where Khalil entrenched himself in front of the Russians, while his Tartars ravaged the country behind them and threatened their communications. Romanzoff then stormed the Turkish line. The Turks fled in panic. Their camp and guns and immense stores fell into the hands of the Russians. The surviving Turks recrossed the Danube. At the close of the campaign of 1770 all the Turkish fortresses north of the Danube were in the hands of the Russians. The Grand Vizier's army was practically destroyed. Only two thousand men were left to him under arms.

In the following year, 1771, still greater disasters attended the Turks. Prince Dolgorouki, at the head of eighty thousand Russians and sixty thousand irregular Tartars, invaded the Crimea after storming successfully the lines of Perekop. The whole province was overrun. Kertch and Yenikale were captured. Wallachia and Moldavia successively fell into the hands of the Russians. Khoczim and Jassy were captured. The only gleams of success to the Turks in this campaign were the recovery of Giurgevo on the Danube and the successful defence of Oczakoff and Kilburn on the shores of the Black Sea. In the Caucasus the Russians were also successful and drove the Turks from Georgia and Mingrelia.

These repeated successes of the Russians began to cause alarm to Austria and Prussia, who by no means wished for the undue aggrandizement of their neighbour. They therefore attempted negotiations with Russia for mediation on behalf of the Ottoman Empire. But the Empress Catherine obstinately resisted anything in the way of interference by other Powers, and made it known to the Sultan that terms of peace must be settled with herself alone. In his desperation the Sultan proposed to Austria a joint partition of Poland as a bribe for assistance against Russia, oblivious of the fact that he had entered upon war with Russia on behalf of Poland. The offer was declined by the Emperor, not because he had any objection to a scheme of plunder, but because he did not consider the Porte to be in a position to become an effective partner in such a scheme. As a matter of fact, Austria, Russia, and Prussia were continually negotiating schemes for the dismemberment either of Poland or Turkey, as might be most convenient to them.

At the end of the campaign of 1771 an armistice was agreed to between Russia and the Porte, and the greater part of the following year was occupied in discussing terms of peace at a conference or congress at Bucharest. An ultimatum was eventually presented by Russia, embodying terms of what might seem to be a very moderate character, in view of the great success of her armies and the extent of territories which they had practically conquered. The Sultan himself and his Grand Vizier and principal ministers and generals were in favour of accepting the terms as offered, but the Mufti and the whole body of the ulemas were vehemently opposed to them. The Divan therefore rejected them and war was renewed. As these terms did not substantially differ from those which were accepted two years later, it is not worth while at this stage to explain them.

Meanwhile there had been for more than a year a suspension of hostilities, and a breathing time had been afforded to the Porte, during which strenuous efforts were made for another campaign. At the end of 1772, Mouhsinzade Pasha, who had so distinguished himself in the defence of the Morea, was again appointed Grand Vizier. He infused new vigour into the army. In the spring of 1773, when the negotiations at Bucharest were brought to a conclusion, hostilities were recommenced. The campaign in Europe, in this year, was confined within the quadrilateral formed by the fortresses in Silistria and Rustchuk on the Danube, the city of Varna on the Black Sea, and the great fortress of Schumla to the north of the Balkan range. There were several engagements between divisions of the two armies in this district, in which the Turks were generally worsted, but these victories were not of much avail to the Russians so long as the three great fortresses of Silistria, Varna, and Schumla remained in the hands of the Turks.

The two main features of the campaign were the successful defences by the Turks of Silistria and Varna against overwhelming forces of Russians. General Romanzoff crossed the Danube early in the year near Silistria. He defeated a Turkish division and compelled it to retreat to that fortress, where it added to its garrison. Romanzoff then laid siege to it. His army stormed the outer defences with the utmost vigour and succeeded in forcing them. But their difficulties only then commenced. The Turks, under command of Osman Pasha, maintained an heroic resistance. The whole male population turned out in aid of the army. They fought the advance of the Russians street by street. In the end the Russians were compelled to retreat, after the loss of eight thousand men. Later, Romanzoff inflicted a severe defeat on the Turks at Korason. This opened the way to Varna. But here again a successful defence was offered by the Turkish garrison, supported by the seamen of the Ottoman fleet in the Black Sea. This was the closing scene of the campaign of 1773. Sultan Mustapha died towards the close of this year, and was succeeded by his brother, Abdul Hamid, who had been secluded in the Cage for forty-eight years. As was to be expected, he showed no capacity for the position to which he was now at last called. He was, however, favourable to peace, as was also Mouhsinzade, who was maintained as Grand Vizier.

At the commencement of the campaign of 1774 the Grand Vizier issued from his camp at Schumla with twenty-five thousand men, with the intention of taking the offensive and attacking the Russians at Hirsova, on the Danube. The Russian forces in that district were under command of Suvorov, who now and later was to show himself the greatest general Russia had as yet produced. He did not wait to be attacked by the Turks. He advanced from Hirsova and met the Grand Vizier's army at Kostlidji, where he gained an overwhelming victory. The Turkish camp and all its guns and stores were captured. The defeated army dispersed, and the Grand Vizier found himself with only eight thousand men to defend Schumla. The Russians manœuvred so as to cut off the communications of Schumla with the capital. Mouhsinzade thereupon asked for an armistice. This was refused by the Russians, but they were willing to discuss terms of peace. The assent of the Porte was obtained by the Grand Vizier, and on July 16, 1774, after seven hours only of discussion between plenipotentiaries at the village of Kainardji, a treaty of peace was agreed to.

The terms were almost identical with those which had been rejected by the Porte two years before, after the conference at Bucharest. In view of the fact that the Ottoman armies had been everywhere defeated during the war, and that the Russians had obtained actual possession of the Crimea, Wallachia, Moldavia, and Bessarabia in Europe, and of Georgia and Mingrelia in the Caucasus, the terms were distinctly moderate. The Empress must have been very desirous of peace. There was a serious rebellion of her southern provinces. Affairs in Poland were causing her great anxiety. Her losses in the war with Turkey had been very great, though her victories were many. It was all-important to her that her hands should be free. These were doubtless adequate reasons for moderation in her terms to Turkey.

Under this treaty Russia gave up nearly all the Turkish territory occupied by her armies. The Crimea was not, indeed, restored to the Turks. The independence of the Tartars there and in Bessarabia up to the frontier of Poland was recognized under a native prince, in whose election Russia and Turkey were forbidden to interfere. Neither Power was thenceforth to "intervene in the domestic, political, civil, and internal affairs of this new State." There was, however, a grave reservation pregnant of future aggrandizement to Russia. She was to retain the fortresses of Kertch, Yenikale, and the cities of Azoff and Kilburn. These would necessarily give access to and virtual command over the Crimea to Russia at any future time. For the present, however, the Crimea, though lost to the Turks, was not acquired by Russia. It is probable that the ulemas would not have assented to the transfer of a Moslem province to a Christian Power, and that the war would have been continued if Russia had insisted on this. Oczakoff, on the opposite side of the Dnieper to Kilburn, was retained by the Porte. But the two Karbartas on the shores of the Euxine, though inhabited by Moslems, were retained by Russia. With these exceptions, all the Ottoman territories in the hands of Russia as a result of the war—Wallachia, Moldavia, Bessarabia, Georgia, and Mingrelia—were restored to the Sultan. In the case of Wallachia and Moldavia, this retrocession was subject to the condition that free exercise of the Christian religion was to be secured to their population, and that there was to be humane and generous government there for the future. The right of remonstrance in these respects was secured to the ministers of Russia at Constantinople on behalf of these provinces.

Another most important clause, full of danger for the future to the Ottoman Empire, related to its Christian subjects. "The Sublime Porte," it ran, "promises to protect constantly the Christian religion and churches and allow the ministers of Russia at Constantinople to make representation on their behalf."

This most important provision gave to Russia a preferential right of protection of the Christian rayas not conceded to any other Christian Power. Provision also was made for the full access of Russian subjects to the holy city of Jerusalem. Free navigation was provided for Russian ships on the Black Sea and the Mediterranean, but nothing was said as to a right of access through the Dardanelles and Bosphorus. There was no mention of Poland in the treaty, though it had been the original cause of the war. Two secret clauses provided for the payment by the Porte of four millions of roubles within three years and for the withdrawal of the Russian fleet from the Archipelago.

The importance of this treaty, moderate though it was in many of its terms, has always been recognized by historians as the starting-point for further and greater dismemberments of the Turkish Empire. The treaty of Carlowitz had secured the deliverance of the Christian population of Hungary from Ottoman rule. But this treaty now, for the first time, tore from the Empire a Moslem province and gave to Russia a right of intervention on behalf of all the Christian population—an immense innovation, humiliating to the Turks, and fraught with the gravest peril to their Empire in the future.

There can be no doubt that the Grand Vizier was fully authorized by the Porte to agree to the terms of this treaty. He was, however, recalled and deposed immediately after its signature, and he died from the effects of poison on his way to Constantinople. It was probably thought by the ministers of the Sultan that Mouhsinzade, if called to account for concluding so humiliating a treaty, would be able to show their full responsibility for it. It remains only to state that the Russian plenipotentiaries at Kainardji delayed the signature of the treaty for four days in order that it might synchronize with the anniversary of the treaty of the Pruth, which had been the cause of so much humiliation to Russia.

XVII

TO THE TREATY OF JASSY
1774-92

EIGHTEEN years elapsed between the peace of Kainardji, 1774, and the treaty of Jassy, 1792, the next conspicuous event in the downward course of the Ottoman Empire. The first thirteen of these years were a period of external peace to the Empire under the rule of Abdul Hamid I. The country had been completely exhausted by the late war with Russia, and the Sultan— or, rather, his ministers, for he appears to have been little competent himself to carry on the government—were strongly in favour of maintaining peace, and did so in spite of great provocation from the Empress Catherine. That able and unscrupulous woman pursued her designs for the complete subjection of the Crimea with relentless resolution and activity. It was an essential condition of the peace of Kainardji that the Crimea was to be an independent State under the rule of a native Tartar prince. The breach of it, by the assumption of sovereignty, direct or indirect, on the part of Russia, would undoubtedly be a just cause of war to the Turks. The Porte, however, was not in a position to take up a challenge of the Empress. The knowledge of this was doubtless the main motive for her proceedings during the next few years.

The steps by which Catherine attained her object bore a striking resemblance to those by which other annexations were carried into effect by Russia, and might well have been predicted. A member of the princely Tartar family of Gherai, Dewlet, was elected by the Tartars of the Crimea as their Khan. The agents of Russia thereupon supported the claims of a rival Gherai, Schahin. They fomented disaffection and revolt against Dewlet. While sedulously disclaiming any project of annexation, Catherine then sent an army into the peninsula with the ostensible purpose of restoring order. It compelled the abdication of Dewlet and the election of her nominee, Schahin. This prince, raised to the throne by Russian arms, found it necessary to follow the advice of the Russian agent, and soon made himself most unpopular with his subjects. A revolt took place against him. He appealed to the Empress for assistance. A Russian army again appeared in the guise of pacificator. The Tartars who opposed were slaughtered or driven from the country. Schahin was compelled to resign his throne, and the Empress thereupon proclaimed the annexation of the Crimea, with professions of acting only for the benefit of its people and to save them from misgovernment. The wretched tool Schahin was imprisoned for a time in Russia, and later was expelled the country into Turkey, where he was speedily put to death. The Porte was unable to undertake a war on behalf of the independence of the Tartars, and

- 173 -

in 1784 a new treaty was made between the two Powers, recognizing the sovereignty of Russia over the Crimea and a district along the north of the Euxine inhabited by Tartars.

Later, there were many indications of the intention of Catherine to exploit her wider project of driving the Turks from Europe. In 1779, when a second grandson was born to her, the name of Constantine was given to him. Greek women were provided for him as nurses, and he was taught the Greek language. Everything was done to stimulate the hope that there would be a revival of a Greek Empire at Constantinople, in substitution for that of the Ottomans.

Meanwhile there was a succession of grave internal troubles in Turkey, fomented in part by emissaries from Russia. The brave old Hassan of Algiers, now Capitan Pasha, who had the complete confidence of the Sultan, was continually being called upon to put down revolts. Thus in 1776 he defeated the Sheik Jahir, who had revolted in Syria. In 1778 he was engaged in expelling from the Morea the rebellious Albanians, who had been employed against Orloff in his invasion of that province, and who, after his defeat, had remained in the Morea, establishing themselves in a lawless ascendancy there, oppressing, plundering, and slaughtering Turks and Greeks alike without discrimination. Hassan succeeded in defeating and expelling these wild ruffians. Later, Hassan was employed in putting down a rebellion of the Mamelukes in Egypt. He led an army there, and succeeded in restoring the authority of the Sultan. In 1787 he was again recalled to Constantinople, on the imminence of war with Russia, and at the age of seventy-five was employed for a time in command of the Turkish fleet in the Black Sea and later as commander-in-chief of the army. It will be seen that for the first time in his life his good fortune deserted him and that he met with serious defeats.

It has already been shown that the Empress Catherine was very provocative in her policy and action to Turkey. In 1787 an agreement was arrived at between Catherine and Joseph II, Emperor of Austria, for common action against the Turks, and with the deliberate intention of driving them from Europe. A partition was to be made of their European provinces between the two Powers and a Greek Empire was to be set up at Constantinople.

The Empress made a triumphal progress through the Crimea, under the auspices of her favourite and paramour, Prince Potemkin, to whose efforts its annexation had been mainly due. The Emperor Joseph met her on the way there at Kherson, and hatched with her a scheme of war with Turkey. A triumphal arch was erected, with the inscription, "This is the way to Byzantium." Emissaries were sent to stir up rebellion in Wallachia and Moldavia. Claims were raised officially against Turkey for the province of Bessarabia and the fortress of Oczakoff, on the ground that they had formerly been part of the domains of the Khans of the Crimea. These claims greatly irritated the Turks. The few years of peace had renovated them. They were now ambitious of recovering the city of Kilburn, and even had hopes of regaining the Crimea. Popular feeling was aroused, and at the instance of the Divan, and without waiting to make preparations for the defence of the frontier fortresses, the Sultan declared war against Russia on August 15, 1787.

A large force was then sent by the Porte to Oczakoff, the fortress on the embouchure of the Dniester, with the intention of attacking Kilburn on the opposite side. A fleet was sent, under Hassan, to co-operate with it, and to convey the army across the river to Kilburn. Unfortunately for the Turks, the Russian force at Kilburn was under the command of Suvorov, a military genius of the first rank. He allowed the larger half of the Turkish army to be conveyed across the river and then attacked it by land, while a flotilla of gunboats from Nicholaif engaged the Turkish fleet. This strategy was completely successful. The Ottoman force of eight thousand men landed on the Kilburn side was overwhelmed and slaughtered. Nearly the whole of Hassan's fleet was destroyed. The attack on Kilburn was completely defeated.

Nothing more was effected by either of the two combatants in 1787. At the beginning of the next year, 1788, the Emperor of Austria, on February 10th, declared war against Turkey without any provocation. He had been delayed fulfilling his agreement with Catherine by disturbances in his own dominions. He was now free to carry out his undertaking. The Turks, therefore, found themselves confronted by two formidable enemies. Fortunately for them, Russia was prevented putting forth its full strength in the south, in consequence of war having broken out with Sweden. The Empress was unable on this account to carry out her engagement with the Emperor to send an army into Moldavia in support of that of the Austrians. Nor was she able to send a fleet into the Ægean Sea, as had been promised. But Joseph took command himself of an army of two hundred thousand men with which to attack the Turks. He soon proved himself to be the most incompetent of generals. The only defeat he was able to inflict was upon his own soldiers, under circumstances unprecedented in war.

The Turks, when they found that there was no danger of any advance on the part of the Russians, sent a great army across the Danube, which encountered and defeated an Austrian army, under Wartersleben, at Mendia. Joseph then marched to relieve this defeated force and to protect Hungary. He took up a position with eighty thousand men at Slatina, within easy reach of the Grand Vizier's army. At the last moment, when all the preparations had been made to attack the Ottomans, the Emperor took alarm. He abandoned his project of attack, and retreated in the direction of Temesvar. The retreat was begun at midnight. Great confusion took place. An alarm was spread that the Turks were close at hand and were about to attack. The wildest panic occurred. The Austrian artillery was driven at full speed in retreat. The infantry mistook them for the enemy. They formed themselves into small squares for defence, and began to fire wildly in all directions. In the early morning, when the sun rose, it was discovered that these squares had been firing into one another, with the result that ten thousand men were *hors de combat*. The Turks now came up and made a real attack. They defeated the Austrians and captured a great part of their artillery and baggage. No other engagement took place in this direction in the course of this year. The Emperor lost thirty thousand men in his attempted manœuvre and forty thousand by disease. He never again ventured to command an army.

Little was attempted in 1788 by the Russians till August, when Potemkin found himself in a position to invest Oczakoff. The siege was protracted till December, when Suvorov was called in to assist. Under his spirited advice, an assault was made on the fortress, and, in spite of enormous losses, the Russians overcame all opposition and entered the city. A frightful scene of carnage then occurred. The city was given over to the Russian soldiers. Of a population of forty thousand only a few hundreds escaped death, and twenty thousand of the garrison were slaughtered. In spite of this great loss, the campaign of 1788 had not been altogether to the detriment of the Turks. Though they lost Oczakoff, and all hopes of recovering Kilburn and the Crimea had vanished, they had successfully resisted Austria. Joseph's attack had ignominiously failed.

The campaign of the following year was far more disastrous to the Turks. Early in 1789 Sultan Abdul Hamid died, and was succeeded by his nephew, Selim III, a young man of twenty-seven, of vigour and public spirit. He had not been subjected by his uncle, Abdul Hamid, to the debasing seclusion which had for so long been the fate of heirs to the throne. He had been allowed much freedom. His father, Mustapha, had left him a memoir, pointing out the dangers of the State, and advising extensive reforms, and the young man had deeply studied this. He was fully conscious of the necessity for radical changes, and though he very wisely did not attempt to lead his troops in the field, he spared no effort to improve the condition of the army and to stimulate the warlike zeal of his subjects. He sent the immense accumulation of plate in his palace to the Mint, and he persuaded the ladies of the harem to give up their jewellery in aid of the treasury. He was ardently in favour of reforms in all directions. He deserved a better fate than was in store for him. It will be seen that his reign was one of most bitter reverses.

Unfortunately for the Turks, ill-health prevented the Emperor Joseph from again taking the field in command of the Austrian army. He was replaced by Marshal Loudon—a veteran of the Seven Years War, a Scotsman by race, who had risen from the ranks and had deservedly won great reputation. It was said of him that he "made war like a gentleman." He was noted for his quick decision on the field of battle, and though over seventy-five was still in full vigour. A new spirit was infused into the Austrian army. A part of it under Marshal Loudon invaded Bosnia and Serbia, where it met with brilliant success. In Bosnia it was stoutly resisted by the Moslem population. In Serbia it met with cordial co-operation of the rayas, who detested their Moslem oppressors. The greater part of these two provinces was occupied. Another Austrian army, under the Prince of Coburg, was directed to Moldavia to act in concert with the Russian army, under Suvorov. The Sultan, on his part, appointed Hassan as Grand Vizier and commander-in-chief of the army. Hassan was not equal to the task of confronting such a general as Suvorov. He advanced with a large army against Coburg, who was stationed at Fokshani, on the frontier of Moldavia. Coburg would have been overwhelmed by the superior force of the Turks had it not been for the wonderful activity of Suvorov, who marched sixty miles through a difficult and mountainous country in thirty-six hours to relieve the Austrians. Suvorov, immediately on arrival, late in the afternoon, made preparations for attacking the Ottoman army. Two hours before daylight the next day he assaulted the fortified camp of the Turks. Never was a bold course more completely justified. The camp was carried by the Russians with the bayonet. The Turks lost all their artillery and immense stores. Another great army was sent by Selim and was also utterly defeated by Suvorov on the River Rimnik in September of the same year.

These two serious defeats caused panic at Constantinople. To allay this the Sultan, to his infinite discredit, gave orders for the execution of the brave old Hassan—the victor in so many battles, whose advice for the better training of the Janissaries had been cruelly neglected. But it was the habit of the Turks to attribute every defeat to the treason of the general and to put him to death, just as the Convention at Paris, during the revolutionary wars, sent to the guillotine the generals who failed—not, it must be admitted, without some result in stimulating others to better efforts.

Farther to the west, Belgrade and Semendria were captured by the Austrians in this campaign of 1789. In the following year the tide of victory on the part of the Russians and Austrians was stayed by two events. The one was that the Emperor Joseph found it necessary, in consequence of outbreaks in almost every part of his own dominions, caused by his hasty and ill-considered measures of centralization, in defiance of all local customs, to hold his hand against the Turks, and withdraw his conquering armies in order to employ them in putting down revolution at home. His death occurred early in 1790. Leopold, who succeeded, a wise and sagacious ruler, the very opposite to Joseph, reversed the policy of his brother. He did not favour a Russian alliance against Turkey.

Another cause of Austria withdrawing from the war was the entry into the field of politics in the east of Europe of England, Prussia, and Holland. These Powers had formed a close defensive alliance, and had already exercised great influence by joint action. They had extinguished French influence in Holland. They had intervened with good effect between Russia and Sweden and had brought about peace between them. They now proposed mediation between Austria and Turkey, not without threats of stronger action. An armistice was agreed to between these Powers. The death of Joseph greatly facilitated an arrangement. Terms were agreed upon with the Turks, and were ultimately embodied in the treaty of Sistova, on the principle of the *status quo* before the war, under which all the territory which Austria had occupied in Bosnia, Serbia, and Wallachia, including the fortresses of Belgrade and Semendria, were given back to Turkey, with the exception of a small strip of land in Croatia and the town of Old Orsova. The acquisitions by Austria were of very small importance and made but a poor return for the great effort put forth in the war. But the new Emperor, Leopold, did not think that Austria had anything to gain by the dismemberment of either Turkey or Poland. Had he lived, subsequent events might have turned out differently, and Poland, in all probability, would not have been victimized.

The defection of Austria from the alliance with Russia against the Turks was a very serious matter for the Empress Catherine. It was balanced, however, in part, by peace with Sweden, which enabled her to use her whole force on land and sea against her remaining enemy. She still adhered to the project of driving the Turks from Europe, and reconstituting a Greek Empire at Constantinople. She sent numerous emissaries to Greece to persuade its people "to take up arms and co-operate with her in expelling the enemies of Christianity from the countries they had usurped, and in regaining for the Greeks their ancient liberty and independence."

Early in 1790 she received a deputation at St. Petersburg from some leading Greeks. They presented a petition to her.

We have never [it said] asked for your treasure; we do not ask for it now; we only ask for powder and shot, which we cannot purchase, and to be led to battle.... It is under your auspices that we hope to deliver from the hands of barbaric Moslems an Empire which they have usurped, to free the descendants of Athens and Lacedæmon from the tyrannous yoke of ignorant savages—a nation whose genius is not extinguished, which glows with the love of liberty, which the iron yoke of barbarism has not destroyed.

The Empress, in reply, promised to give the assistance they asked for. They were then presented to the young Prince Constantine, who replied to them in the Greek language: "Go, and let everything be done according to your wishes."

The wealthier Greeks in the Levant had already fitted out a squadron of thirteen frigates in support of their cause. These were now, by order of the Empress, supplied with guns at Trieste and were put under command of a brave Greek admiral, Lambro Caviziani. This squadron, when fitted out, made its way to the Ægean Sea, where it made its base in the Isle of Scios. The Turkish fleet in those waters was at a low ebb. The best of the Turkish vessels were being employed in the Black Sea. But seven Algerine corsairs came to the assistance of the Porte, and, in concert with some Turkish ships, fought a naval battle with the Greek squadron and sank the whole of its vessels.

The Russian army on land was more fortunate. Their chief operation in 1790 was the capture of Ismail, a most important fortress on the northern affluent of the Danube, about forty miles from the Black Sea. So long as this city was in the hands of the Turks an advance of an invading army from Bessarabia into Bulgaria was hardly possible. The fortress was defended by a very large garrison. Suvorov was again put at the head of a *corps d'armée* by Potemkin, the commander-in-chief, with the laconic order, "You will capture Ismail, whatever may be the cost." Six days after his arrival before the fortress, Suvorov ordered his troops to assault it. Speaking to them in his usual jocular manner, he said: "My brothers, no quarter; provisions are scarce." At a terrible cost of life the city was taken by storm. A scene of savage carnage ensued, unprecedented even in the experience of Suvorov. Thirty-four thousand Turks perished. Suvorov admitted to a friend that he was moved to tears when the scene was over. But he was accustomed to shed these crocodile tears after horrors of this kind, when he had made no effort to mitigate them. When news of the achievement arrived at St. Petersburg, the Empress, at her levée, addressing the British Ambassador, Sir C. Whitworth, said, with an ironic smile: "I hope that those who wish to drive me out of St. Petersburg will allow me to retire to Constantinople."

Meanwhile the allied maritime Powers—England, Prussia, and Holland—having succeeded in their mediation between Austria and Turkey, and in restoring peace between them, on the basis of the *status quo*, were now engaged in efforts of the same kind as between Russia and Turkey. They offered mediation to the Empress Catherine in the course of 1790. In a reply to the Prussian King, she indignantly rejected intervention. "The Empress," she said, "makes war and makes peace when she pleases. She will not permit any interference whatever in the management or government of her affairs." It was understood, however, that she was not disinclined to peace upon the terms that Oczakoff and the district between the Rivers Dniester and Bug, which were in her full possession, were to be retained by her, and that all other of her conquests were to be restored to Turkey. The allied Powers were unwilling to assent to this, and made preparations for an armed mediation to compel Russia to restore Oczakoff to Turkey.

In the case of Great Britain, the proposed intervention on behalf of the Turks in support of their Empire was a new departure in policy. Its Government had been closely allied with that of Russia during the greater part of the eighteenth century. Its policy had been mainly determined by jealousy of France. It looked upon Russia as a counterpoise to that State. It had never raised any objection to the ambitious projects of Russia against Turkey. Lord Chatham, whose foreign policy had prevailed till now, had always held that it was not the interest of England to enter into a connection with the Turks. England had looked on with indifference in 1784, when the Empress Catherine had taken possession of the Crimea. Charles Fox was at that time Minister of Foreign Affairs in England, and he showed himself as much in favour of Russia as Chatham had been. "My system of foreign politics," he wrote, "is deeply rooted. Alliance with the northern Powers (including Russia) ever has been and ever will be the system of every enlightened Englishman." It was an entirely new departure when the younger Pitt, in 1790, entered the lists in alliance with Prussia against Russia in order to restore and maintain the balance of power in the south-east of Europe in favour of Turkey.

The British Government renewed its offer of mediation. Its Ambassador at St. Petersburg was instructed to inform the Empress that if she would accept a peace on the basis of the *status quo*, England would use her influence to obtain from the Turks a formal renunciation of their claims to the Crimea under the guarantee of the allies. The Empress, in her reply through her minister, expressed her indignation at the unparalleled conduct of the allies in attempting to dictate in so arbitrary a manner to a sovereign perfectly independent, and in want of no assistance to procure the conditions which seemed to her best suited to satisfy her honour. Rather than diminish the glory of a long and illustrious reign, the Empress was ready to encounter any risk, and she would only accept the good offices of the King of England "inasmuch as they may lead to preserve for her the indemnification she requires of Oczakoff and its district."[30]

The reply was important, for it showed that Russia was, at all events, willing to bring the war to an end and to forgo its intention of driving the Turks out of Europe. The fact was that, in spite of repeated victories, the Russian losses in killed and wounded, and still more by disease, were very serious. The Empress also had other troubles on her hands. The Polish question, in which she was more interested than in that of Turkey, was imminent. The Second Partition was decided on. It was necessary for her to have a free hand. In spite of this, she was determined not to yield possession of Oczakoff.

Meanwhile the British and Prussian Governments were in consultation. They were agreed that they were bound to insist upon the surrender of Oczakoff and its district, and upon a peace based on the *status quo* before the war. It was contended that, as Austria and Sweden had both made peace on such terms, the allies could not with honour demand less for the Turks, and that Turkey would consider itself betrayed if the allies were willing to give up those districts.

It was decided, therefore, by the allies to enforce by arms their mediation on the basis of the *status quo*. The British Government engaged to send a fleet of thirty-five vessels of the line into the Baltic, and Prussia to march an army into Livonia. It was agreed that neither Power would look for any territorial acquisition, but would only insist on greater security for the Porte in the Black Sea.

In this view Mr. Pitt, on March 28, 1791, presented to the House of Commons a message from the King asking for the supply of means to augment the forces of the Crown. He based his justification, says Mr. Lecky, who has given a summary of Pitt's speech, mainly on the interests of Prussia and the obligation of Great Britain to defend her.

Prussia [Pitt said], of all European Powers, is the one who would be the most useful ally of England, and the events that were taking place were very dangerous to her. The Turkish Empire is of great weight in the general scale of European Powers, and if that Empire is diminished or destroyed, or even rendered unstable or precarious, the situation of Prussia would be seriously affected.... Could any one imagine that the aggrandizement of Russia would not materially affect the disposition of other Powers—that it might not produce an alteration in Poland highly dangerous to Prussia?... If a powerful and ambitious neighbour were suffered to establish herself upon the very frontier of Prussia, what safety was there for Denmark, or what for Sweden when Prussia shall no longer be in a position to help them? The safety of all Europe might afterwards be endangered. Whatever might be the result of the war in which the Turks were now unhappily engaged, if its results were to increase the power of Russia the effect would not be confined to the two Powers alone; it would be felt by the rest of Europe.

He asked for the means to equip a great fleet to be sent to the Baltic and a smaller one for the Black Sea.

The proposal of Pitt for giving effect to this policy was violently opposed by Charles Fox in a speech which produced a very great effect in the House of Commons and on the country.

The insistence [he said] on the surrender by Russia of Oczakoff and its district was in the highest degree unjust and impolitic. It was unjust because Russia had not been the aggressor in the war and because, in spite of her great successes, she had consented to concessions which displayed her signal moderation. It was impolitic, for the only result of an expensive and dangerous war would be to alienate, perhaps for ever, a most valuable ally, without obtaining any object in which England had a real interest.... Russia was the natural ally of England. What had England to gain by this policy? In what way could English interests or English power be affected by the acquisition by Russia of a fortress on the Dniester and a strip of barren land along the northern shore of the Black Sea?... The assertion that England was bound by the spirit of its defensive alliance with Prussia was in the highest degree dangerous and absurd. If defensive alliances were construed in such a way they would have all the evils of offensive alliances, and they would involve us in every quarrel in Europe. We bound ourselves only to furnish assistance to Prussia if she were attacked. She had not been attacked. She was at perfect peace. She was absolutely unmenaced. It was doubtful whether the new acquisition of Russia would under any circumstances be injurious to Prussia, and it was preposterous to maintain that it was the duty of England to prevent any other nations from acquiring any territory which might possibly in some future war be made use of against Prussia.

Fox was supported by Burke in a powerful speech, in spite of their growing differences on the subject of the Revolution in France.

Considering the Turkish Empire [he said] as any part of the balance of power in Europe was new. The Turks were essentially Asiatic people, who completely isolated themselves from European affairs. The minister and the policy which should give them any weight in Europe would deserve all the ban and curses of posterity. For his part, he confessed that he had seen with horror the beautiful countries that bordered on the Danube given back by the Emperor of Austria to devastation. Are we now going to vote the blood and treasure of our countrymen to enforce similar cruel and inhuman policy?... That so wise a man as Pitt should endeavour, on such slight and frivolous grounds, to commit this country to a policy of unlimited adventure, sacrificing the friendship of one of our oldest allies and casting to the winds the foreign policy of his own father, was the most extraordinary event that had taken place in Parliament since he had sat within its walls.

Pitt's motion was carried, but by many votes short of his usual party majority. Two other debates took place on the subject. Though Pitt maintained his majority, it was evident that the opinion of the House of Commons, and still more of the country, was opposed to going to war with Russia on behalf of

Turkey. Pitt very wisely decided to abandon his policy of war. He withdrew his proposal in the House of Commons. The Foreign Minister, the Duke of Leeds, who was personally committed to it, resigned his office. Another messenger was sent to the British Ambassador at St. Petersburg with instructions not to present the menacing despatch to the Czar, and, fortunately, arrived in time to prevent it.

Sir E. Creasy describes the action of Charles Fox in thus defeating the policy of Pitt as due to violent and unscrupulous party motives, and Mr. Lecky, while agreeing in substance with the arguments of Fox, and condemning Pitt's policy, does not acquit the former of political partisanship. He never loses an opportunity of impeaching the conduct of Charles Fox, on account of his action in the war with the American colonies and in the revolutionary war with France. It may be permitted to us to say, in spite of these high authorities, that seldom has a greater service been done to the country than in the defeat of Pitt's proposal to go to war with Russia on this occasion. It was a unique case in our constitutional history when the House of Commons by its debates, and not by its votes, defeated a proposal for war made to it by a Prime Minister, with all the authority of the Crown and the Government. The merit of this was mainly due to Fox.

In the meantime the Turks were incurring further defeats on the Danube. They made desperate efforts to replenish their armies, but the men were ill-trained and were unable to meet the veteran troops of Russia. Kutusoff, at the head of a Russian army, routed a great Ottoman army at Babatagh in January 1791, and in July of the same year Prince Repnin, with forty thousand Russians, defeated and dispersed seventy thousand Turks at Maksyu, on the southern bank of the Danube. The Turks were equally unfortunate on the east of the Black Sea. A Russian army invaded the province of Kuban and defeated a Turkish army there, and occupied the whole of the province.

As a result of all these reverses the Divan was dispirited. There was no prospect of assistance to Turkey from any quarter. They were willing to come to terms. The Empress, on her part, was equally willing. She wanted her army to march into Poland to put down an outbreak of the Poles, under Kosciuszko. In spite of her recent victories, which had secured to her the occupation of Bessarabia, Moldavia, Wallachia, and the Kuban, she was ready to give up all with the exception of the fortress of Oczakoff and the country between the Rivers Dniester and Bug. Terms on this basis, and without any mediation or interference of other Powers, were agreed on between Russia and Turkey in August, 1791, and were embodied in the treaty of Jassy in January of the following year. Under this treaty the River Dniester was the new boundary of the Russian Empire, and all conquests west of it were restored to the Turks. Russia also gave back the province of Kuban, but the treaty recognized the Empress as the protector of the petty independent principalities in that region.

The project of carving for Potemkin a kingdom out of the Danubian principalities was abandoned, and that of a Greek Empire at Constantinople was indefinitely adjourned. Potemkin, who was a Pole by birth and had been raised from the position of a sergeant in the Russian army to princely rank with a fortune estimated at seven millions of our money, died a few days after the treaty.

In the next four years the Empress achieved the final partition of Poland, and obtained for Russia the lion's share. Had she lived, she would probably have used her acquisitions there as a vantage-ground for new aggressions on the Ottoman Empire. Meanwhile Greece was abandoned to the tender mercies of its oppressors.

XVIII

TO THE TREATY OF BUCHAREST
1792-1812

TWENTY years after the treaty of Jassy, another slice of the Ottoman territory was ceded to Russia in 1812 by the treaty of Bucharest. The history of Turkey during the interval is full of interest in its relation to the Napoleonic wars, but much of it has little bearing on the shrinkage of the Empire.

After the conclusion of the war with Russia in 1792, Sultan Selim was most anxious to maintain peace and to keep out of the complications arising from the French Revolution. He was fully conscious of the necessity for reforms in every branch of the administration of his country, and especially in the constitution and training of the army. He regarded the Janissaries as a grave danger to the State. He initiated many great schemes of reform. But in 1798 these were nipped in the bud by a fresh outbreak of hostilities. War was forced upon him most unexpectedly, and without just cause or even pretext, by the Revolutionary Government of France, a country whose traditional policy had been to support the Ottoman Empire against that of Austria. France had recently become a near neighbour to Turkey. Under the treaty of Campo-Formio in 1797, after the great victories of General Bonaparte in Italy, the Republic of Venice ceased to exist. Venice itself, and much of its Italian territories, were subjected to the rule of Austria, and its possessions in the Adriatic, the Ionian Islands, and the cities on the mainland, such as Prevesa and Parga, were ceded to France. This change of masters was welcomed by the inhabitants of the islands, who were weary of the tyranny of the Venetians.

The Directory, which then ruled in France, was filled with ambition for further extensions in the East. It was under the impression that the Ottoman Empire was on the point of complete dissolution. There was much, at the time, to justify this view. The central power of the State was almost paralysed. The pashas of many provinces, such as Ali of Janina, Passhwan Oghlou of Widdin, and Djezzar of Acre, had made themselves all but independent of the Sultan. Egypt was virtually ruled by the Mamelukes. Its pasha, appointed by the Porte, was without any authority. Serbia and Greece were seething with rebellion. Bonaparte, while commanding the army in Italy, sent emissaries to several of these provinces, and especially to Greece, holding out hopes of support in the event of open rebellion. It seemed at first as though his ambition was for extension of French dominion in Greece and other European provinces of the Porte. An army of forty thousand men, including the best of the veterans who had fought in Italy, was mobilized at

- 185 -

Toulon. Two hundred transports were prepared to convey them to some unknown destination, and a powerful fleet of fifteen battleships and fifteen frigates was ordered to act as convoy. At the last moment the Directory, at the instance of Bonaparte, decided on the invasion of Egypt. A blow was to be struck there, not against the Porte, but against England, with whom France was at war. There were vague intentions or dreams, after the conquest of Egypt, of invading India and founding a great Eastern Empire for France on the ruins of the British Empire. It was pretended that the attack on Egypt was not an act of hostility to the Porte. Egypt, it was said, was to be delivered from the cruel and corrupt government of the Mamelukes. There was no declaration of war against the Sultan. It was expected that he would acquiesce in the suppression of the Mamelukes.

The utmost secrecy was maintained as to the destination of the expedition. It left Toulon on May 19, 1798, under the command of Bonaparte. He took with him many of the ablest generals who had served under him in Italy and a large party of 'savants,' who were to explore the monuments of Egypt. The orders from the Directory to Bonaparte, drawn up doubtless by himself, were

to clear the English from all their Oriental possessions which he will be able to reach, and notably to destroy all their stations in the Red Sea; to cut through the Isthmus of Suez and to take the necessary measures to assure the free and exclusive possession of that sea to the French Republic.

The destination of this great fleet and army was unknown to the British Government. But there was a strong British fleet at the entrance of the Mediterranean, under Lord St. Vincent, who detached a large part of it, under command of Nelson, to watch the issue of the French fleet from Toulon. It was composed of an equal number of battleships to that of the French fleet, but of inferior size, and with fewer guns. It was very deficient in frigates.

On June 10th, three weeks after escaping from Toulon, the French fleet arrived at Malta. The Knights of St. John, who had made so valiant and successful a defence of the island against the Ottomans in 1565, now offered a very feeble resistance to the French. The knightly monks had become licentious and corrupt. They very soon capitulated. Bonaparte annexed the island to France, and the ancient Order came to an ignominious end.

Leaving four thousand men at Malta, the fleet sailed for the island of Crete, and hearing there that Nelson was in pursuit, Bonaparte at once decided to sail to Alexandria. He then for the first time announced to the army its destination.

Soldiers [he said in a proclamation], you go to undertake a conquest of which the effects upon the civilization and the commerce of the world will be incalculable. You will strike at England the most certain and the most acute blow, while waiting to give her the death-blow.... The Mamelukes, who favour exclusively English commerce, some days after your arrival will exist no more.

Nelson meanwhile, when he discovered the departure of the French fleet from Toulon, shrewdly guessed that it was bound to Egypt, and bent his course there, hoping to find the enemy's ships at Alexandria. He arrived there on June 28th, before the French fleet, and, hearing nothing of it, he doubled back to Sicily. The two fleets crossed one another not far from Crete, and within sight of one another if the weather had been bright; but a dense haze and the want of frigates to act as scouts prevented Nelson discovering the proximity of his enemy. But for this it is certain that the French fleet, encumbered as it was with two hundred transports, would have been totally destroyed and the whole armada would have met with unparalleled disaster. It is interesting matter for speculation what effect this would have had on the career of the Corsican general and on the history of Europe. As it was, the French fleet and army, favoured by their extraordinary good luck, arrived safely at Alexandria on July 1st. The army disembarked there. The battleships, not being able to get into the harbour, were anchored in Aboukir Bay. Alexandria was captured, after a slight resistance by its small garrison— though Bonaparte himself was slightly wounded in the attack. A week later the army commenced its march to Cairo.

Bonaparte issued one of his bombastic and mendacious proclamations to the Egyptian people, explaining that he was making war against the Mamelukes, and not against them or the Sultan.

For a long time [it said] the crowd of slaves bought in Georgia and the Caucasus have tyrannized the most beautiful place in the world; but God, on whom all depends, has ordained that their empire is finished. People of Egypt, they have told you that I have come to destroy your religion. Do not believe them. Answer that I am come to restore your rights, to punish the usurpers, and that I respect more than the Mamelukes, God, his Prophet, and the Koran.... Thrice happy are those who will be on our side. They will prosper in their fortune and their rank.... But woe threefold to those who arm themselves for the Mamelukes and fight against us.... Each man will thank God for the destruction of the Mamelukes and will cry "Glory to the Sultan! Glory to the French army, his friend! Malediction to the Mamelukes and good luck to the people of Egypt."

The army suffered greatly on its march to Cairo from the heat and the sand. The soldiers murmured and asked for what purpose they were brought to such a country, where they saw no evidence of wealth, and where there was nothing to loot. But they fought two battles on the way against the Mamelukes and easily defeated them. The armies against them on both occasions consisted of no more than twelve thousand men, of whom only five thousand were Mamelukes and the others ill-trained fellaheen. These were of no avail against thirty thousand veterans of the French. The city of Cairo, on the approach of Bonaparte, was sacked by the retreating Egyptians. He presented himself rather as the saviour of life and property. He had no difficulty in restoring order there.

Meanwhile Nelson, on the arrival of his fleet at Naples, heard definite accounts of the destination of the French armada. He retraced his course to Egypt. On the memorable 1st of August, 1798, he came in sight of the enemy's fleet, anchored in Aboukir Bay. The oft-told story of the decisive and glorious battle need not be repeated. The French fleet, under Admiral Brueys, was annihilated by the British fleet, much inferior in number of men and guns. The admiral was killed. His flagship was blown up. Only two of his ships escaped for a time, and later were captured before reaching France. As a result, the communications of the French army with France were thenceforth completely severed. It was hopelessly stranded in Egypt. Bonaparte did not hear of the disaster till August 19th, on his return from an expedition, in which he defeated and chased from the country a force of Mamelukes, under Ibrahim Pasha. His sole remark was: "Eh bien! It will be necessary to remain in these countries or to make a grand exit like the ancients. The English will compel us to do greater things than we intended."

The signal victory of the British fleet had far-reaching results. The Sultan of Turkey, who had hitherto been undecided as to his policy, now felt that he might safely take up arms against the French and reassert his sovereignty in Egypt. He well knew that Bonaparte could receive no reinforcements from France and that the invading army must gradually melt away. He declared war against France, and entered into alliances, offensive and defensive, with Russia and England. His alliance with the former led to strange results. A combined fleet of Russia and Turkey, hitherto the most deadly foes to one another, issued from the Dardanelles, and attacked and drove the French from the Ionian Islands, so recently acquired by them, and from their fortresses on the mainland.

The Porte also collected two armies for the reconquest of Egypt, the one in Syria, the other in the island of Rhodes. Bonaparte decided to anticipate attack by the invasion of Syria. He spent at Cairo the winter of 1798-9, the least reputable period of his amazing career. His private life there was most scandalous, far more so than that, bad enough, of his wife, Josephine, whom he had left at Paris. His public life was little better. In the hopes of conciliating the Egyptian people and facilitating the further conquests in the East, of which he dreamt, he professed unbounded admiration for the Moslem religion. He feigned to be a convert to that faith. His vaunting proclamations were headed: "In the name of Allah. There is no God but

God. He has no son and reigns without a partner." He did his best to induce his soldiers to become Moslems, but in vain. No one was taken in by these fooleries. He gained no respect from Egyptians of any creed. There were many outbreaks in different parts of the country, and a most serious one in Cairo. They were put down with ruthless severity. He followed the Turkish practice of decapitating the prisoners and great numbers of suspects, and exhibiting their bleeding heads in public places as a warning to others.

Bonaparte left Egypt in January, 1799, with an army of twenty-five thousand, made up in part by sailors of his sunken fleet, and in part by recruits from the Mamelukes. He crossed the Isthmus of Suez, and reached Gaza on February 25th and Jaffa on March 7th. This last city was held by five thousand Turks. After a brave defence they capitulated on terms that they should be treated as prisoners of war. In disregard of this they were marched down to the beach and, by order of Bonaparte, were slaughtered in cold blood because it was inconvenient to encumber his army with prisoners. No worse deed of Turkish atrocity has been recorded in these pages. Leaving Jaffa, his army arrived before Acre in a few days. "When I have captured Acre," he said to his generals, "I shall arm the tribes. I shall be in a position to threaten Constantinople. I shall turn the British Empire upside down."

But he reached at Acre the end of his tether in the East. He had sent his heavy guns by sea to meet him there. They were captured on the way by the British fleet, and were now mounted on the mud ramparts of the fortress and used against him. A British fleet, under command of Sir Sidney Smith, was lying in the roadstead and kept the communications open with Constantinople. The admiral and his sailors assisted in the defence of the city, the garrison of which consisted of only three thousand men. Its weak fortifications had been strengthened by Colonel Philippeaux, a distinguished French royalist. Against these defences Bonaparte hurled his army in vain. In the sixty days of siege there were forty assaults and twenty sorties of the garrison. "In that miserable fort," said Bonaparte, "lay the fate of the East."

On May 7th large reinforcements arrived from the Turkish army at Rhodes. A last and desperate assault, led by General Kléber, was unsuccessful. Bonaparte was compelled to admit his failure. His dream of an Eastern Empire was dissipated for ever. On May 20th he commenced a retreat, after a loss by death of four thousand men and eight generals. The army suffered most severely in passing through the desert.

Shortly after the return of the French troops to Egypt on July 14th, an army of fifteen thousand Turks, convoyed by the British fleet, was landed at Aboukir. Bonaparte attacked on the 25th and utterly defeated it. Thousands of the Turks were driven into the sea and drowned. This victory of the veterans of the French army over the ill-trained Turkish levies, without guns or cavalry, was a godsend to Bonaparte. It shed a gleam of glory over the terrible failure of the whole expedition. His dispatches made the most of it. At this stage news from France showed the necessity for his return there. He decided to abandon the army to its fate. With the utmost secrecy arrangements were made for the embarkation of the general and his staff on board two frigates. They rode down to the shore and got into boats, leaving their horses behind them. The return of the riderless horses was the first intimation to those left behind that they were abandoned by their general. The two frigates left Egypt on August 22nd and, by hugging the African coast, they escaped the British cruisers, and after a most hazardous voyage of six weeks they landed their passengers in France, where Bonaparte posed as a conqueror. Nor did his failure in Egypt interfere with his subsequent triumphant career.

Early in March 1801 a British army of fifteen thousand men, under Sir Ralph Abercromby, landed in Egypt, and later another contingent, under General Baird, coming from India, also arrived there. The French army of occupation was badly handled. It was divided between Cairo and Alexandria. It was defeated in detail and ultimately surrendered. It was then said to number twenty-four thousand men and three hundred and twelve guns. On hearing of this disaster Bonaparte is said to have felt great anguish. "We have lost Egypt," he said. "My projects have been destroyed by the British." Egypt was restored to the Sultan, freed not only from the French but also from the Mamelukes, and for a time Turkish pashas, appointed by the Porte, ruled the country. There can be no doubt that the Sultan owed this wholly and solely to the British Government. It will be seen that he showed little gratitude, for in a very few years' time he took the part of the French in the great war.

Meanwhile, in 1802, a peace was patched up for a time between England and France at Amiens. Concurrently with this terms of peace were agreed upon between France and the Porte, under which the sovereignty of the Sultan over Egypt was recognized. When, two years later, war again broke out between France and England and other Powers, Bonaparte, then First Consul, reversed his action as regards the Ottoman Empire, and made an alliance with it a cardinal point of his new policy.

After the conclusion of peace with France in 1802, Sultan Selim had a respite for a very few years before he was again involved in war. He directed his attention to serious internal reforms of his Empire. He fully recognized that the first and foremost of these must be the reorganization, if not the suppression, of the corps of Janissaries. Not only had the experience of late wars shown that they had become a most incompetent military force, quite unable to meet on equal terms the well-trained soldiers of Russia and France, but in every part of his Empire they were a danger to the State, endeavouring to monopolize power and to oust that of the pashas appointed by himself.

They were also the main oppressors of the rayas. The task of suppressing them and of creating an army on the model of those of European Powers was a most difficult and dangerous one, for the Janissaries were, or pretended to be, the most devout of Moslems, and were supported by the fanatical part of the population. They had strong supporters in the Divan. The ulemas were almost unanimously in their favour. The Divan was divided into two parties, those who favoured reform and who gave support to the Sultan, and the reactionary party, who were opposed to all reform and championed the Janissaries. There was another serious division of the Divan—namely those who espoused the cause of Russia, not infrequently in the pay of that Power, and those who favoured France. After the conclusion of peace, France was represented at the Court of the Sultan by very able ministers, who soon regained the influence for that country which it had formerly enjoyed.

Nowhere throughout the Empire were the Janissaries more turbulent and dangerous or more oppressive to the rayas than in Serbia. They aimed at governing the province in the same way as the Mamelukes in Egypt and the military Begs in Algiers and Tunis, and if they had been allowed to have their way, Serbia would have achieved a virtual independence of the Porte, under a military and fanatical Moslem despotism. The Janissaries there were almost as hostile to the Spahis inhabiting the provinces as to the rayas. They aimed at ousting the Spahis from their feudal rights in the country districts and at an assumption of ownership of land, more oppressive to the peasant Christian cultivators of the soil than that of the Spahis. Both Spahis and rayas appealed to the Porte for protection against these ruffians. The rayas in their petition to the Sultan said that—

not only were they reduced to abject poverty by the Dahis (the leaders of the Janissaries), but they were attacked in their religion, their morality, and their honour. No husband was secure as to his wife, no father as to his daughter, no brother as to his sister. The Church, the cloister, the monks, the priests, all were violated. Art thou still our Czar? then come and free us from these evildoers, and if thou wilt not save us, at least tell us that we may decide whether to flee to the mountains and forests, or to seek in the rivers a termination of our miserable existence.[31]

The Sultan was willing to listen to these grave complaints, and to put down the turbulent Dahis and their attendant Janissaries, not so much out of sympathy for the rayas as in order to restore his own authority in the province and as a first step towards the reformation or suppression of the Janissaries elsewhere throughout his Empire. He began by threatening the Dahis. If they did not mend their ways, he would send an army against them. These ruffians, knowing that the Sultan could not venture to employ a Moslem force against them, came to the conclusion that he meant to arm the rayas of the province. They determined to anticipate this by a general massacre. If no resistance had been offered to this, the whole Christian population of Serbia would have been exterminated. The rayas, however, were no longer the submissive and patient people they had been reduced to by servitude for two hundred and fifty years under the Turks, during which no one of them had been allowed to carry about him a weapon of defence. As has been already stated, they had been invited to rebel by the Austrians in their last war with the Turks, had been armed by them, and had given valuable assistance. Great numbers of them had been trained as soldiers, and retained their arms when the Austrians retired from the country, after the peace of Sistova, which provided no adequate security for these unfortunate people.

They now, in 1807, rose in arms against their oppressors, who were bent on exterminating them. They elected as their leader George Petrowitsch (Kara George, as he is known in history), a peasant like themselves, a most brave man, who had served in the Austrian army, and who soon showed great qualities as a general. Under his leadership the rayas succeeded in driving the Dahis and Janissaries out of the country districts.

The Sultan at the commencement of this servile war lent his assistance to the rayas. The Pasha of Bosnia was instructed to support them with an armed force. The local Spahis also, who were still in the country and had not been driven away by the Dahis, lent assistance. On the other hand, the Dahis received assistance from the fanatical part of the Moslems in the towns. They had also the sympathy and aid of Passhwan Oghlou, the mutinous Pasha of Widdin. It was, however, almost wholly due to the efforts of the Serbian rayas that the Dahis were completely defeated. Most of them were slaughtered, and the world was well rid of them. When this was achieved, the whole of Serbia was practically in the hands of the Christian rayas, with the exception of Belgrade and a few fortresses, which were garrisoned by the Sultan's troops.

At this stage the Sultan, when all that he really aimed at was achieved—namely the suppression of the local Janissaries—summoned the insurgent rayas to lay down their arms and to resume their position as subjects of the Porte and as rayas under the yoke of the local Spahis as of yore. The war, however, had evoked a national spirit among the Christian population, which would not be content with the old condition of servitude. They sent a petition to the Russian Government claiming assistance on the ground that they were members of the Greek Church. The Czar, in reply, advised them to present their claims at Constantinople, and promised to give his support to them at the Porte. They then sent a deputation to the Sultan, and boldly claimed that Belgrade and the other fortresses should be given up to them, and asked that arrears of taxes and tribute should be remitted. The first of these was the most important, for it virtually meant a claim for autonomy under the suzerainty only of the Sultan.

These demands caused the greatest indignation among the Moslems of the capital, and the Sultan forthwith rejected them. He ordered the members of the deputation to be imprisoned. He directed the Pasha of Nisch to invade Serbia and reduce the contumacious rayas to their former condition. He threatened them with death or slavery. Kara George met this force on the frontier of Serbia and defeated it. He also defeated two other armies which the Sultan sent against him, and he was able, unaided by any external force, to capture Belgrade and the other fortresses and expel the Turkish garrisons. Thus it happened that the native Christians of Serbia, by their own heroic efforts, without any foreign assistance, achieved a virtual independence of Ottoman rule, an event of supreme importance in its effect on other Christian communities under servitude to the Turks.

Meanwhile important events were developing at Constantinople. It was the scene of a violent diplomatic struggle between Russia and England on the one hand, and France on the other, for the support of the Porte in the war then raging in Europe. The Emperor Napoleon sent as ambassador there General Sebastiani, formerly a priest, now a soldier and able diplomat. His demands were supported by the great victory of the French over the Austrians at Ulm. The recent acquisition by France of Dalmatia and a part of Croatia brought that Power into close relation with Turkey. Sebastiani pressed for the support of Turkey with great insistence.

On the other hand, Russia was equally cogent in its demands, and even more threatening. It insisted on an alliance, offensive and defensive. It demanded that the Sultan should recognize the Czar as the protector of all the Christians in Turkey professing the Greek religion, and that the Russian Ambassador should have the right of intervention on their behalf. The Sultan, conscious of the inferiority of his military force, could only temporize.

Moslem pride and fanaticism was greatly excited by the demands of Russia. Sebastiani, working on this, persuaded the Sultan, by way of retort to Russia, to depose the Hospodars of Moldavia and Wallachia, on the ground that they were suspected of being pensioners of Russia. The Czar treated this as a gross breach of the engagement entered into by the Porte, in 1802, under which the Hospodars of the two principalities were only to be removed from their posts with the consent of Russia. He thereupon ordered an army of thirty-five thousand men, under General Michelsen, to invade Moldavia. The army entered Jassy and, a little later, Bucharest before the Porte was able to make any resistance.

The British Government at the same time gave full support to Russia. Its Ambassador, Mr. Arbuthnot, insisted on the Porte joining the alliance of England and Russia against France. The Sultan refused to do so. Mr. Arbuthnot thereupon sailed away in a frigate and joined the British fleet lying off the island of Tenedos, under the command of Admiral Duckworth, which consisted of seven battleships and two frigates. This fleet, favoured by a fair wind, then forced the Dardanelles against the Turkish batteries on February 19, 1807, with little damage, and made its appearance in the Sea of Marmora. It there destroyed a Turkish battleship and four corvettes.

The fleet anchored off the Prince's Islands, within a few miles of Constantinople, which was exposed to bombardment from the sea. The admiral presented a demand to the Porte for the surrender of the Ottoman fleet lying at Constantinople and for compliance with the demands of Mr. Arbuthnot. He threatened to bombard the city if his ultimatum was rejected. If any serious effect could have been given to this menace, immediate action should have been taken. The Ambassador and the admiral allowed themselves to be drawn into a negotiation spread over ten days, during which the Sultan and the whole male population of his capital were engaged, with feverish haste, in strengthening the defences of the city. A thousand guns and a hundred mortars were mounted on its batteries. The Turkish fleet, consisting of twelve battleships, was removed to a point in the harbour beyond the reach of the guns of a bombarding fleet. The defences of the Dardanelles were also greatly strengthened. Admiral Duckworth was compelled at last to the conclusion that a bombardment would be attended with very serious risk to his own fleet. If it were damaged, the Turkish fleet, coming out of the Bosphorus, might assail it with advantage. It might also be impossible for it to repass the Dardanelles. He decided to withdraw. On March 1st he weighed anchor, and on the 3rd he repassed the Dardanelles, this time with considerable damage to his ships and loss of life. Some of the ships were struck by the enormous stone balls fired from the Turkish batteries. Two corvettes were sunk and six hundred men were killed. The fleet narrowly escaped destruction. The whole adventure redounded little to the credit either of the diplomacy or strategy of the British Government.

Not content with this futile demonstration against Constantinople, the British Government attempted another expedition, even more futile and senseless, this time against Egypt, in the hope, it may be supposed, of bringing pressure to bear on the Sultan. A force of five thousand soldiers was sent from Sicily, then in British occupation, and was landed on the Egyptian coast near Alexandria on March 18th. It marched on that city, which, garrisoned by only four hundred and fifty Turks, surrendered. This was its first and last success. A few days later fifteen hundred men were sent to attack Rosetta, at the mouth of the Nile, and were repulsed. Another expedition was even more unsuccessful. Of two thousand men sent out, one thousand were killed and wounded. There seems to have been expectation that the Mamelukes would assist the British against the Turkish troops. This was not realized. The remains of the small army under General Fraser were cooped up in Alexandria until September, when, owing to the serious disaffection of the inhabitants of the city and the approach of a large body of Turks from Cairo, it was recognized that its position was untenable. A flag of truce was sent to the advancing Turks with the offer to evacuate Egypt if the British prisoners in their hands were given up to them. This was accepted, and on September 25th the little army embarked again on its transports and returned to Sicily.

These two senseless expeditions had an effect the very reverse of which was intended. They exasperated Turkish opinion and drove the Porte into closer alliance with the French. In the meantime, and since the failure of the demonstration by Duckworth's fleet, momentous events occurred in Constantinople. The Sultan took advantage of the departure of the main body of Janissaries with the army sent to the Danube to extend his scheme for raising a military force, clothed and drilled and paid on the European system. He issued an edict that the youngest and best of the Janissaries were to be enrolled in this new corps. This caused the gravest discontent among the Janissaries still in garrison at Constantinople, to the reactionary party in the Divan, and to the ulemas. The Janissaries broke out in mutiny at the end of May 1807. They put this question to the Mufti: "What punishment is deserved by one who has established the new military force?" The Mufti replied: "Death, and that according to the Koran, since the Divan had introduced among Mussulmans the manners of infidels and manifested an intention to suppress the Janissaries, who were the true defenders of the law and the prophets."

Fortified by this *fetva*, the Janissaries then passed a resolution that Selim must be deposed. They sent a deputation to the Sultan to insist on his abdication. Selim, however, had already heard of their intention. He had no force at hand sufficient to overcome the mutinous Janissaries. He anticipated their demands by himself going to the Cage, where his cousin Mustapha, the next heir to the throne, was immured, making obeisance to him as Sultan, advising him not to listen to those who desired great changes, and wishing him a happier reign than his own. He then attempted to commit suicide by taking poison, but Mustapha dashed the cup containing it from his hands and swore that his life should be saved. On the arrival of the deputation of Janissaries at the palace they found that a new Sultan was already installed there. Selim retired with dignity to the apartments in the Cage vacated by Mustapha.

The new Sultan, Mustapha III, was a very weak and incompetent man. He was aged thirty, of imperfect education and poor intellect. He filled the throne for a few months only, during which there was practically no government. Though Selim himself was reconciled to the loss of his throne, he had powerful friends who resented his fall. Bairactar, the Pasha of

Rustchuck, who owed his post to Selim, marched upon Constantinople with forty thousand Bosnians and Albanians. They overawed the Janissaries and invaded the palace. They knocked at its gates and demanded that Selim should be brought out to them. Mustapha, however, on their approach, had already given orders that Selim and Mahmoud, the only survivors of the Othman race besides himself, were to be put to death, in the hope that this might save his own life. The mutes were able to strangle Selim, not without a desperate struggle, which, if prolonged for a few minutes, would have saved him, for Bairactar was already storming at the gate of the palace. Mahmoud could not be found. Selim's body was then cast out to Bairactar and his men. "Here is he you seek!" it was called out. On entering the palace Bairactar found Mustapha seated on his throne. He was dragged from it and was sent to prison. Mahmoud, who had been hidden in the furnace of a bath, was found and was installed as Sultan.

Bairactar, having succeeded in deposing Mustapha and installing Mahmoud, most unwisely allowed the Bosnian and Albanian troops to return to their homes. There remained only four thousand men as a bodyguard on whom the new Sultan could rely. They were not sufficient to withstand the Janissaries. These turbulent men broke out in another rebellion. They attacked Bairactar in his palace. He took refuge in a tower used as a powder magazine. He was there blown up, whether by accident or wilfully is not known. There ensued a few days of civil war. The artillery on whom the Sultan relied went over to the Janissaries. A counter-revolution was effected. Mustapha would have been restored to the throne if he had not been put to death in the interval. Mahmoud owed his life to the fact that he was the last surviving male of the Othman race. He was compelled to yield to the menaces of the Janissaries, who were now masters of the city. An edict was issued in his name which repealed all the reforms effected by Selim. The old system was restored, with all its abuses. In the next three or four years the Janissaries were virtually the rulers of the Empire. Grand Viziers were appointed and dismissed at their dictation. Mahmoud was greatly humiliated. But he bided his time, and it will be seen that before long he inflicted a most bloody revenge on the Janissaries and extinguished their corps for ever.

Meanwhile affairs on the Danube fared badly with the Turks, as might be expected. The Russians gained complete possession of Moldavia and Wallachia. Their armies crossed the Danube and laid siege to fortresses on the right bank. In 1807 Russia and France came to terms. The treaty of Tilsit provided that hostilities were to cease between Russia and Turkey, and that the Russian troops were to be withdrawn from Moldavia and Wallachia, till a definitive agreement had been come to between these two Powers. But a secret article, which was not made public till some time later, provided that all the European provinces of Turkey, except Roumelia and Constantinople, were to be taken from the Sultan. We now know that there were long discussions between Napoleon and the Czar, on the River Niemen, as to the future disposal of these and other provinces. Napoleon was ready to concede to Russia the Danubian principalities and Bulgaria. He claimed for France Egypt, Syria, Greece, all the islands of the Archipelago, and Crete. Austria was to be propitiated by the cession of Bosnia and Serbia. The question remained what was to be done with Constantinople. Napoleon would not concede it to Russia. The Czar insisted upon this. The agreement broke down on this point. But it is certain that Napoleon was willing enough to throw over his recent allies, the Turks, and to join with their hereditary foe in dismembering their Empire. A more perfidious transaction is not to be found in history.

In compliance with the treaty of Tilsit, Russia suspended hostilities with the Porte. But the Russian army remained in occupation of Wallachia and Moldavia, and showed no intention to evacuate them. War was renewed in 1809. Prince Bagration, at the head of a Russian army, crossed the Danube and captured several Turkish fortresses on its right bank. In the following year, 1810, the Russians captured the important stronghold Silistria, but failed with very heavy loss in an assault on Rustchuck. Later in the year they inflicted a severe defeat on the army of the Grand Vizier at Baltin. They then succeeded in a second attack on Rustchuck, and captured Sistova. But they failed to take the fortified camp at Schumla, and were unable therefore to cross the Balkan range.

In 1811 war was again imminent between Russia and France, and the Russian generals on the Danube received orders to stand on the defensive. The Turks took advantage of this, and sent a large army across the Danube. It was eventually defeated and compelled to surrender. In spite of their successes, the Russians were willing to come to terms. They had hitherto insisted on the retention of Wallachia and Moldavia. They were now ready to make concessions. The invasion of Russia by Napoleon was imminent. It was necessary for the Czar to concentrate all his forces in defence of his own Empire. Negotiations were commenced in 1811, and they resulted in the treaty of Bucharest of May 28, 1812. It was agreed that the River Pruth was to be the new boundary between the two Empires. The whole of Wallachia and a great part of Moldavia were restored to Turkey. Bessarabia and a part of Moldavia were ceded to Russia.

The treatment of Serbia in the treaty was ungenerous on the part of Russia. An amnesty was to be granted to its people. They were to be secured in future the regulation of their internal affairs. But the supremacy of the Sultan was to be maintained, and Belgrade and other fortresses which had been captured by the Serbians were again to be garrisoned by Turkish troops. This last was the cause of great troubles in the future. But for the impending invasion of Russia by Napoleon the terms would undoubtedly have been far less favourable to the Porte.

XIX

MAHMOUD II
1808-39

THE first four years of Mahmoud's long reign of thirty-one years were fraught with bitter humiliation to him at the hands of the Janissaries. There was no indication of his subsequent career, when he proved himself to be the most able and resolute of Sultans since Solyman the Magnificent. But he was also the most unfortunate, for he was unable to prevent a greater reduction of the Turkish Empire than had been incurred by any one of the long line of degenerate Sultans. It may well be, however, that but for his action still greater losses would have resulted, for on his advent to the throne the Empire seemed to be on the brink of ruin. In every part of it turbulent and rebellious pashas were asserting independence. In Epirus the celebrated Ali Pasha of Janina had cast off allegiance, and was threatening to extend his rule over Greece, Thessaly, and the Ionian Islands. At Widdin on the Danube, at Bagdad on the Tigris, at Acre in Syria, the same process was being pursued by other pashas. In Egypt, Mehemet Ali had assumed the position of Governor and was creating an army and a navy independent of the Porte. In Arabia, the sect of Wahabees had attained a virtual independence, and had obtained possession of the holy cities. Other provinces, such as Serbia, Wallachia, Moldavia, and Greece, were seething with disaffection caused by long and intolerable misgovernment. The difficulty of holding together the distracted Empire was greatly increased by the want of an effective army under the full control of the central Government, so as to enable it to cope with the centrifugal forces which threatened disruption. The Janissaries, who had contributed so largely to the growth of the Empire, were now a standing danger to it. They were able to overawe the Sultan, and to dictate to him the appointment and dismissal of Viziers. But successive campaigns on the Danube, and conflicts with rebellious pashas, had given abundant proof of their inefficiency as a military force. Compared with the armies of European Powers they were an ill-disciplined and badly armed mob. They arrogantly refused to be armed, clothed, and drilled after the fashion of European armies. While useless for war, they were formidable for other purposes. They were under no control. They terrorized the capital, and in the provinces they were at the disposal of any adventurous pasha who suborned them to support his ambitious and rebellious projects. Mahmoud from the earliest years of his reign fully recognized, as many of his predecessors had done, how urgent the necessity was to put an end to this turbulent force, and to create a new army which would obey and support him as Sultan, and be of value against external enemies. It is his principal claim in the history of

Turkey that he was able to effect this. Eighteen years, however, elapsed before he felt strong enough to grapple with these foes of his dynasty and State.

Apart from this great achievement, he showed inflexible firmness and courage in the great difficulties which confronted him, and almost alone he bore the burden of the State for thirty-one years of unparalleled peril, and often of most serious disaster. It will be seen that, in spite of these high qualities, and in spite of the reform of his army, the losses of territory to his Empire were very serious. In Greece, the Morea, and the provinces north of the Gulf of Corinth up to the frontier of Thessaly, acquired complete independence under the guarantee of the three Great Powers of Europe. Egypt, Moldavia and Wallachia, and Serbia attained almost similar independence, subject only to the nominal suzerainty of the Sultan of Turkey and the payment of fixed tributes. They no longer added to the real strength of the Empire. On the other hand, he completely destroyed the power of the rebellious Pashas of Janina, Widdin, Bagdad, and Acre, and through Mehemet Ali, the Pasha of Egypt, he subdued the Wahabees and recovered the holy cities of Mecca and Medina.

It should be added that Mahmoud, unlike so many of his predecessors, devoted his life to affairs of his State rather than to his harem. He committed at times acts of great cruelty. He put to death his brother Mustapha and Mustapha's only son, and caused to be drowned in the Bosphorus four ladies of Mustapha's harem who were enceinte. He had no scruple in directing the secret assassination of any persons whom he suspected of harbouring schemes in opposition to his own. He authorized the perpetration of ruthless massacres of Greeks in all parts of his Empire at the inception of the revolution in Greece. But these were acts of policy in accord with the traditions of his family, approved by public opinion of the Turks, by whom terrorism and massacre were recognized as justifiable methods of government. The murder of his relatives left him the sole survivor of the Othman race, a position which secured him from intrigues against his throne by the Janissaries.

The most serious of the losses to the Empire in Mahmoud's reign was that of Egypt, for it was a Moslem country, and though for many years previously the hold on it by the Ottoman Porte had been slender, and the Mamelukes had been able, as a rule, to impose their will and to govern the province, yet the Porte could in the main rely on it for support to the Empire in times of emergency. It will be well, therefore, to explain the changes effected in Egypt, for it will be seen that they had a great bearing on events in other parts of the Ottoman Empire.

Mehemet Ali, who effected the virtual independence of Egypt, subject to the nominal suzerainty of the Sultan, was the most remarkable man that the Mahommedan world had produced in modern times. The son of an Albanian Moslem fisherman and small landowner at Kavala, on the borders of Thrace and Macedonia, he was left a penniless orphan, and was brought up as a dependent in the household of the chief magistrate of the district, who was a distant relative. He never learnt to read or write. He said of himself in later years that the only books he ever read were men's faces, and that he seldom made a mistake in them. When the French invaded Egypt under General Bonaparte, Mehemet Ali was sent in defence of it with a band of three hundred Albanians, as one of their junior officers, and before long, on the return home of the commanding officer, contrived to step into his place. When the Turkish army was driven into the sea at Aboukir in 1794 by Napoleon, he was saved from drowning by a boat from the British admiral's ship. Later he was put in command of all the Albanians employed in Egypt, and was attached for a time to the British army.

After the departure of the British from Egypt, conflict arose between the Turks and the Mamelukes for the control of the government. Mehemet at first sided with the Mamelukes, but later he threw them over in favour of the Albanians in the service of the Turks. When the British Government sent its futile expedition to Egypt in 1808, Mehemet was chiefly concerned in opposing it. He was in command at Rosetta when a great number of British soldiers were slain, and a few days later he entered Cairo in triumph through an avenue of British heads stuck on pikes. Thenceforth he rapidly rose in influence and position, and at the age of thirty-five was the most powerful man in Egypt, and was able to instal himself as Pasha. He was harassed and opposed by the Mamelukes. He determined to get rid of them. He invited about five hundred of their leading men to a friendly conference at the citadel of Cairo. After entertaining them at a sumptuous repast, he ordered the gates to be shut, and had them all shot down in the narrow street of the citadel. A single man only of them survived by leaping his horse from the wall of the citadel, a height of 30 feet. This was followed by a slaughter of nearly all the Mamelukes in the country. Mehemet in this set the example which was followed a few years later by Sultan Mahmoud in suppressing the Janissaries.

Thenceforward Mehemet was undisputed ruler of Egypt. He had a genius for organization and government. Though cruel and vindictive, and even bloodthirsty, as regards his enemies and against evildoers of all kinds, he had a keen sense of justice, and a determination to mete it out equally, and without favour, to the people of all sects and races. He brought about peace and order and prosperity such as Egypt had never of late years enjoyed. He was ambitious to extend his rule. He organized for this purpose, and for asserting himself against the Porte, an army of a hundred thousand men raised by conscription and armed and drilled on the model of European armies, with the aid of French and Italian officers who had served under Napoleon. He also built a powerful fleet with the help of French naval constructors. He soon proved the value of his new army by putting down a revolt in Arabia of the Wahabees. He did this, on behalf of, and in the name of the Sultan. He also conquered the oasis of Senaar and extended the rule of Egypt into the Sudan. It will be seen that later, in 1825 and 1826, he sent his army and navy in support of the Sultan to the Morea for the purpose of putting an end to the revolution in Greece, which the Sultan had been unable to cope with. Before dealing with this, however, it will be well to revert to Mahmoud and explain the course of events which compelled him to call in aid Mehemet Ali's army.

One of the earliest matters which Mahmoud had to deal with was that of Serbia. The treaty of Bucharest had left that province in a very unsettled and ambiguous position. The Turks, under its terms, were permitted to garrison Belgrade and other fortresses, and were to concede to the Serbians self-government, but there was no adequate guarantee for this. The Serbians, who were in possession of the fortresses, refused to give them up to the Turks until a scheme of self-government was arranged. The Porte insisted on immediate surrender. Subsequent proceedings showed that there was no intention to give effective self-government to the Serbians. The Sultan in 1813 sent an army to enforce his claims. Kara George, in most strange contrast to his previous heroic action, lost courage on this occasion. After burying the treasure which he had amassed as virtual ruler of Serbia, he fled the country and sought refuge with the Austrians. In so doing he passed out of the history of his country, save that when, some years later, he thought he might safely return to Serbia, he was arrested and shot as a traitor.

After this defection Serbia seemed to be at the mercy of the Turks, and the greater part of it was occupied by them. But at the moment of its great peril another national patriot and hero rose to the front in the person of Milosch Obrenowitch, who, much as Kara George had done a few years previously, took the lead in rousing the Christian population to resistance, and in leading them to victory. He succeeded in driving the Turks from all the country districts and shutting them up in the fortresses. Mahmoud then sent another army with the object of relieving the Turks in the Serbian fortresses and subduing the rebels. The army, however, halted on the frontier, and negotiations ensued which lasted for some years without any result. The Sultan, it seems, was unwilling, in view of the numerous other difficulties pending in his Empire, to risk the loss of an army in a guerrilla war in the mountains of Serbia.

The most serious of Mahmoud's other difficulties at this period was the insurrection of the Greeks in 1821. Never was rebellion of a subject race more justifiable. Nowhere throughout the Ottoman Empire were the results of its rule more degrading and intolerable than in Greece. It served none of the purposes for which governments exist. Life and property and honour were without security, and justice had degenerated into the practice of selling injustice to the highest bidder.

The condition of the Greek population was infinitely worse than that of their compatriots in most other parts of the Empire. In Constantinople the Greeks were a wealthy community. They had a large share in the administration of the Empire. The Porte, in fact, could not do without them. Their religion was under the special protection accorded to it by Mahomet the Conqueror. The trade of the Empire was largely in their hands. At Smyrna, Salonika, and many other cities, there were large numbers of Greeks who had enjoyed facilities of trade and had accumulated wealth. Mahmoud, like many of his predecessors, recognized that, by largely contributing to taxes, these people were a source of wealth to his Government, and was not disposed to adopt any measure proposed by the more fanatical of Moslems to extirpate them or to drive them into rebellion. Not a few of the islands of the archipelago, such as Scios and Psara, were practically allowed to govern themselves, and life there was as well-ordered as in any part of Europe.

It was very different with Greece on the mainland. It seems to have been the policy of the Porte to prevent its becoming a populous and wealthy country, with a view to keeping it under close subjection. Much of its land was in the ownership of Moslems, a majority of whom were Greeks by race, who had adopted Islam in order to save their property. They were a fanatical class who were quite as oppressive to the rayas, the cultivators of the soil, as were those of pure Turkish descent. The Ottoman Government presented itself to the Greeks only as an engine to extract taxes, and the pashas who were sent to govern them thought only how best and most quickly to fill their pockets, knowing that their tenure of office would be very short. The people there compared their condition with that of the self-governing communities of Scio and other islands. Education had spread to some extent in spite of the neglect of the Government. Wealthy Greeks from other districts had endowed some schools and colleges. With education came the study of the past history of Greece and the ambition to renew its nationality and greatness. For some time past secret societies such as the Hetairia, promoted in the first instance by the Greeks of Odessa, had been spreading their influence in Greece, and had laid the seeds of revolution.

The insurrection in Greece was not only based on political and racial ideals, it was also an agrarian war, the revolt of cultivators of the soil against their feudal oppressors. This gave to the outbreak in rural districts its intensely persistent, passionate, and cruel attributes.

The revolution broke out in the Morea at the beginning of April 1821, and soon spread over the whole of its country districts. It was estimated that at that time there were twenty thousand Moslems thinly spread in the country districts, most of them of Greek race, feudal lords of the soil and oppressors of the rayas. Nearly the whole of these Moslems were now brutally murdered, without distinction of age or sex. The survivors fled into the fortresses, which were garrisoned by Turks. These fortresses were speedily invested by the Greeks, and within three months nearly all of them were compelled to surrender. In most cases capitulations were agreed to on the terms that lives would be respected, but in no case were these terms adhered to. The garrisons and the Turkish inhabitants and the refugees from the country districts who had gathered there were brutally murdered.

The first encounter between the Turkish soldiers and the Greeks that could be called a battle was at Valtetsi, in the neighbourhood of Tripolitza, the capital of the Morea. Three thousand Greek peasants there defeated five thousand Turks, with a loss of four hundred Turks and a hundred and fifty Greeks. The battle destroyed the prestige of the Turks. It showed that they were no match for the insurgent Greek peasants.

As a result of this victory, Navarino and Tripolitza fell into the hands of the Greek insurgents after short sieges. In both cases the garrisons capitulated on favourable terms for themselves and the inhabitants of the towns. In neither case were the terms observed. All the Moslem troops and inhabitants were ruthlessly massacred. At Tripolitza these numbered eight thousand, including women and children. "Greek historians," says Finlay in his *History of Greece*, "have recoiled from telling of these barbarities, while they have been loud in denouncing those of the Turks."

When news of the massacres in the Morea arrived at Constantinople the greatest alarm and indignation arose. Bloody and ruthless reprisals ensued against the Greeks residing there. The Sultan set the example. He directed that many of the leading Greeks were to be immediately executed. The Greek Patriarch was hanged by his order at the gate of the episcopal residence. The *fetva* authorizing this was pinned to his body. There was no reason to believe that the Patriarch was implicated in the outbreak in Greece. Four other bishops met the same fate. Thousands of Greeks of inferior position fell victims to the fury of the people at the capital and at many other cities, such as Smyrna and Salonika, and in Cyprus. The Sultan took no steps to restrain these horrors. Women and children equally with men were murdered. Their houses were burnt, their property was pillaged. It was estimated that the number of Greeks thus massacred was not short of the number of Moslems slaughtered in Greece at the outbreak of the revolution. Thenceforth Greeks and Turks emulated one another in their acts of barbarity. The Turks had always been bloodthirsty when their passions and fears were roused, and they now had terrible wrongs to avenge. The Greeks had been degraded by long oppression, and were little better than Turks. Both people evidently thought that the results of their cruelties were proof of the wisdom of inflicting them. The Greeks, by extirpating the Moslems in the Morea, cleared the country, once for all, of their oppressors and effected that separation of the two races which, it will be seen later, the Great Powers of Europe thought desirable, though they hoped to attain it by peaceful expropriation and indemnity. The Turks claimed that their severities checked the spread of the revolution, and compelled one half of the Greek people living within their midst to submit to Ottoman rule.

It has been shown that the revolution broke out in the Morea. Within a few months the whole of that country was cleared of Ottoman troops and of Moslem inhabitants. The outbreak extended to most of the islands of the archipelago, where the Greeks predominated, where there was less admixture of Slav blood than on the mainland, and where the traditions of a long-past national existence and of high civilization survived in a stronger form. In spite of their greater prosperity, due to milder treatment at the hands of the Turks, they were ardently in favour of independence. It was in the islands that the majority of Greek merchant vessels were owned. They numbered between four and five hundred, and were manned by twelve thousand Greek sailors. An active war fleet was formed out of these vessels and sailors. They frequently met and defeated the Turkish fleet. They made special use of fire ships, and blew up or burnt many of the Turkish vessels and caused the greatest alarm to the Turkish sailors.

In the course of the four years 1821-4, the Turks were generally worsted by the Greek insurgents on land and sea. Not only the Morea, but the parts of Greece north of the Gulf of Corinth up to the frontier of Thessaly, including Athens—then reduced to a squalid, third-rate town—and the islands of the archipelago, achieved a practical independence. A national government and a representative assembly were constituted. The outbreak in Greece roused the sympathies of great numbers of persons in Western Europe, especially in England and France. In spite of this, the Governments of these countries for long held aloof and discouraged the rebellion, not wishing to see Turkey weakened as against Russia. Lord Byron was an enthusiast for the Greeks, and in 1824 landed at Missolonghi and joined their army. But it cannot be said that he effected much during the short time he survived there. He was evidently disillusioned, like so many other Philhellenes who joined the Greeks, by the discords, intrigues, and corruption of their leaders. But he never lost faith in their future. He confidently predicted that the Greek nation would prove itself worthy of freedom. He gave his life to the cause. He died of malarial fever within a few weeks of landing at this unhealthy spot. This did much to arouse the interest of Europe and to promote its intervention on behalf of the Greeks.

After four years of futile efforts to stamp out the Greek revolution, it became clear to Sultan Mahmoud that his army, as then constituted, was unequal to the task. He was much impressed by the success of Mehemet Ali in Egypt in creating an army armed and drilled in the manner of European armies. In 1824, he called on this great vassal to aid in the reconquest of Greece by sending his new army and fleet there. Mehemet consented to do so, but only on the promise of the Sultan that Syria, Damascus, and Crete, would be added to his Pashalic. He sent his fleet to co-operate with that of the Sultan on the coast of the Morea. It sailed from Alexandria on July 25, 1824, with an army of ten thousand infantry and a thousand cavalry, under command of Ibrahim Pasha, the son of Mehemet Ali. They were landed at Modon and marched thence to Navarino. That fortress was garrisoned by sixteen hundred Greeks. The flower of the Greek army of seven thousand men advanced to relieve the fortress. Ibrahim with three thousand men attacked and utterly defeated them. The Greeks fled in wild confusion. This battle was proof that the best Greek troops were unable to encounter the well-disciplined Egyptians in a pitched battle.

After the capture of Navarino, Ibrahim continued his reconquest of Greece with uniform success. The Greeks were exhausted by their long struggle against the Turks. They could offer but a very feeble resistance to this new and far more effective enemy. In April, 1826, the Egyptian army captured Missolonghi, causing a loss to the Greeks of four thousand men. Thence he gradually subdued the whole of the Morea. Later the cities of Corinth and Athens fell into the hands of the Turks, and on May 6, 1827, at a battle at Phalerum, in the neighbourhood of this last city, Reschid Pasha, in command of an Albanian army, defeated and dispersed the last army of the Greeks then in the field. The Greek Government was forced to remove from the mainland to the island of Poros. The whole of Greece then fell into anarchy. Though the Greek fleet continued to make a gallant stand against the combined Turkish and Egyptian fleets, it was not strong enough to maintain a mastery at sea and to cut off the communication between Ibrahim's army and its base in Egypt. It is certain that if the Great Powers of Europe had not intervened, Greece would have been completely subdued, and Turkish rule would have been reinstated there. Ibrahim threatened to remove the whole Greek population and sell them into slavery, and to replace them by Egyptians and Arabs.

Meanwhile the success of Ibrahim's army, armed and disciplined on the model of European armies, as compared with the failure in previous campaigns in Greece of the ill-disciplined and badly armed troops of Turkey, produced a great impression at Constantinople. Mahmoud now found that his long-cherished project for the reform of the army was supported almost unanimously by the Divan and by the whole of the ulemas. He determined, therefore, to carry it into effect, and to suppress his mortal foes, the Janissaries. He had been long engaged in making preparations for a decisive issue with these turbulent troops. He had formed a body of fourteen thousand artillerymen, drilled and armed on the new model, and on whom he could thoroughly rely for support. His predecessor, Selim, had enlisted a small body of infantry on the same model. The Agha of the Janissaries, Hussein Pasha, was devoted to him, as was also the Mufti. The Sultan thereupon, in May 1826, gave orders to the Janissaries that one-fourth of them were to be incorporated in the new corps of infantry. The Janissaries refused. They marched in a body, on June 14th, to the palace, intent on overawing the Sultan, as they had so often done in the past. They met their master on this occasion. The Sultan summoned the artillery to his support. He unfolded the sacred banner and directed their action. They pounded the Janissaries with cannon shot in the streets leading to the palace and drove them back to their barracks with heavy loss. The guns were then concentrated on the barracks and set fire to them. No quarter was given. The Janissaries perished either by gun fire or in the burning barracks. Four thousand of them were disposed of in this holocaust. The Sultan ruthlessly followed up his victory. Many more thousands of the Janissaries were put to death in Constantinople and in other cities of the Empire. The force was entirely destroyed. Its very name was erased from official records. Mahmoud had obtained an overwhelming victory. His new army was at once increased to forty-five thousand men, exclusive of his artillery, with the intention of gradually raising it to two hundred thousand. It was recruited, however, wholly from the Moslem population. The Christians were excluded from its ranks as rigidly as under the old régime. There can be no doubt that if time had been allowed to Mahmoud to complete the number and efficiency of this new army, the Ottoman Empire would again have become a most formidable military Power. The Sultan did much more to centralize power in himself. He abolished the military feudal system, which had become a gross abuse. The beys were everywhere suppressed, or were allowed to draw their incomes only for the term of their lives. The rents hitherto paid to these persons were in the future to be paid directly to the State.

Mahmoud also effected many other important reforms. He abolished the Court of Confiscations, which had provided a revenue to the State out of property of persons condemned to death or exile, and which had become a great abuse. He deprived pashas of their power to put people to death at their will without trial. He enacted that no one should in future be so dealt with without formal trial and the right of appeal. He put the vast Vacouf property (dedicated to Islam) under State management. He prohibited the wearing of turbans and made the use of the fez universal in his Empire. He set the example of clothing himself after the European fashion. He entertained ambassadors and their wives and others at his palace as other sovereigns did. He contemplated great reforms in favour of his Christian subjects, but it will be seen that the task was left incomplete for his successors.

At this point of his career Mahmoud had attained unqualified success. He had succeeded in putting down all the rebellious pashas, such as Ali of Janina and others. Mehemet Ali of Egypt had recognized the supremacy of the Sultan by sending his army and navy to suppress the Greek rebellion. Greece had been practically reconquered. The Greeks in other parts of the Empire had been terrorized into submission. Insurrection in Moldavia and Wallachia had been suppressed. The Serbian fortresses were in his hands. Above all, the Janissaries, who had proved to be so useless as a military force and who had murdered two of his predecessors and deposed many others, were suppressed. He had carried out great reforms in his Empire. Mahmoud had effected all this by his own inflexible firmness and by statesmanship of a high order, not unmixed with cruelty and cunning.

Two events now occurred which materially affected the position of Turkey, and deprived Mahmoud of the fruits of his ably devised policy. The one was the death of Alexander, the Emperor of Russia, the other the decision of the British Government to intervene on behalf of Greece. Alexander for some years past had been on the horns of a dilemma. He had a deep sympathy for the subjects of the Ottoman Empire who were members of the Greek Church, and a great aversion to Turkish rule. But he also hated and feared revolution. He believed in the divine right of rulers, however bad, and would take no step to support the revolt of their subjects, however oppressive their government. He feared that a dangerous precedent might be extended to his own Empire. This conflict of views paralysed his action. He gave no assistance to the Greek insurgents. So long as he lived there was little hope that Greece would recover its independence. He died late in 1825, and was succeeded by his brother, Nicholas, a much younger and more vigorous man, and a truer exponent of Russian ideals. The new Czar had no objection to insurrection if it was not directed against his own government. He hated the Turks and wished to drive them out of Europe much more than he sympathized with the Greeks. He had many other grounds of complaint against the Porte. It has also been suggested that he wished to come to conclusions with it before time had been given for perfecting his new army.

As regards Great Britain, its Government had not originally sympathized with the Greek revolution, but the reverse. But public opinion, outraged by the barbarities which had been committed, had produced an influence on it, and Mr. Canning, the Foreign Secretary, was personally very favourable to the cause of Greece. The Government as a whole held the view that the continuance of disorder in Greece was a menace to the peace of Europe.

They had no wish for the extension of Russia at the expense of Turkey. They thought that if Greece were not pacified Russia would intervene, and would not confine its claim to the settlement of the Greek claims, but would aim at other conquests. They decided, therefore, to make an effort to settle the Greek question on the basis of autonomy, subject to the suzerainty of the Sultan. In this view the Cabinet sent the Duke of Wellington to St. Petersburg in 1826 to negotiate with the Czar. He effected an arrangement which was later embodied in the treaty of London of July 6, 1827, between the three Powers, Great Britain, Russia, and France, for the pacification of Greece. Under the terms of this treaty it was agreed, with a view to bringing about a reconciliation between the Ottoman Porte and the Greeks, to offer mediation, and to demand an immediate armistice as a preliminary to the opening of a negotiation.

Under the arrangement to be proposed to the Ottoman Porte, Greece was to be granted complete autonomy, under the suzerainty of the Sultan, and was to pay a fixed annual tribute. It was to be governed by authorities whom its people were to nominate. In order to bring about a complete separation between the individuals of the two nations and to prevent the collisions resulting from a long struggle, the Greeks were to enter upon possession of all Turkish property, either on the continent or in the isles of Greece, on condition of indemnifying the former proprietors by the payment of an annual sum to be added to the tribute. By an additional secret article it was provided that "if, within one month, the Ottoman Porte did not agree to accept the mediation of the three Powers and consent to an armistice, the signatories of the treaty would find the necessity for an approximation with the Greeks by entering into relations with them, and would employ all their means for the accomplishment of the objects of the treaty without, however, taking any part in the hostilities between the two contending parties."

In accordance with this treaty, a demand was made on the Porte, by the ambassadors of the three Powers, for an armistice, and for a pacification of Greece on the basis above described. The Porte indignantly refused to entertain the proposed mediation. It denied the right of the Powers to intervene as regards its Greek subjects. In a manifesto to its own people, the Porte justified its refusal to mediate on the proposed basis. It denied that the Greeks had any cause for complaint against the Ottoman rule. "It is notorious," it said, "that these Greeks have been treated like Mussulmans in every respect and as to everything which regards their property, their personal security, and the defence of their homes, and that they have been loaded with benefits by the present Sultan."

The negotiations between the Porte and the ambassadors were protracted by the former, in order that an Egyptian fleet, bringing large reinforcements to Ibrahim in Greece, might arrive at Navarino before the conclusion of them.

After the final rejection of the proposals of the ambassadors, instructions were given to the combined fleet of the three Powers to effect a blockade of the Greek ports, and to prevent the entrance or departure of any Turkish or Egyptian vessels of war.

The combined fleet, under command of the British admiral, Sir Edward Codrington, thereupon took up a position outside the bay of Navarino. The admiral then entered into negotiations with the Turkish admiral and concluded an armistice on behalf of the Greeks. In spite of this, the Egyptian troops, under Ibrahim Pasha, continued to ravage the Morea in the most cruel manner, devastating property, murdering the men, and carrying off the young women for sale as slaves in Egypt. As the winter was approaching, the British admiral thought it would be difficult to maintain his position outside the bay. He determined, therefore, to enter the bay with his fleet. The combined fleet consisted of ten vessels of the line, ten frigates and smaller vessels, with about twelve hundred guns. The Turko-Egyptian fleet consisted of five ships of the line, fifteen frigates, and sixty-two smaller vessels, armed with two thousand guns. It was anchored in a crescent facing the entrance of the bay. There were also batteries on shore commanding the entrance of the bay. The allied fleet entered the bay without opposition from these batteries and anchored in a line alongside of the Turkish and Egyptian vessels.

It was obvious that the position was a most critical one, almost certain to lead to an armed conflict. The Turks fired the first gun and broke the armistice, whether intentionally, or not, is not quite clear. The challenge was taken up. There followed a fierce battle between the two fleets. In a few hours of this 20th of October, 1827, the Turko-Egyptian fleet was completely destroyed. With the exception of some of the smaller craft, all the vessels were sunk or burnt. Their crews had fought valiantly, but they were no match for those of the allied fleet. But their guns caused much loss of life and did much damage, and the British battleships, after the battle, were compelled to return to England for repairs. The batteries on shore did not begin to fire until the allied fleet had taken position. They might have effected much more damage if they had fired on the fleet when entering the bay. A more complete destruction of a fleet had never occurred.

This great victory gave no satisfaction to the British Government. The spirit of Canning no longer inspired it. He had died since the initiation of the policy which inevitably led to this naval battle. On the meeting of the British Parliament, early in 1828, the Speech from the Throne referred to the battle in the following terms: "His Majesty deeply laments that this conflict should have occurred with the naval force of our ancient ally. He still entertains a confident hope that this untoward event will not be followed by further hostilities." The Duke of Wellington, who was now Prime Minister, when challenged in the House of Lords as to the expression 'untoward event,' said:—

The Ottoman Empire was an essential part of the balance of power in Europe. Its preservation had been for many years an object to the whole of Europe. While he acquitted the British admiral of all blame, he pointed out that, under the treaty of London, one of the stipulations was that the operation was not to lead to hostilities. When, therefore, the operation under the treaty did lead to hostilities, it certainly was an untoward event.

It is difficult, however, to conceive how the Duke, who had negotiated the treaty with the Czar of Russia, could have supposed that, in the event of the Sultan not agreeing to the terms of mediation, the use of force against him could be avoided.

However that might have been, the destruction of the Ottoman fleet at Navarino was of momentous importance. It cut off the communication between Ibrahim Pasha and Egypt. It restored to Greece command of the sea in the archipelago. It assured the supremacy of the Russian fleet in the Black Sea. This last was of enormous value to the Russians in the war which soon broke out with Turkey. It facilitated the capture of Varna, and enabled the Russian army to advance across the Balkans and to threaten Constantinople.

Ibrahim Pasha, finding his position in the Morea untenable, entered into a convention with the British admiral under which he was permitted to withdraw the Egyptian army from Greece and embark it for Alexandria without molestation from the allied fleet. There remained in the Morea only the Turkish troops. They held most of the fortresses there. Later, a French army, under General Maison, was, by agreement with the allies, sent to the Morea. It soon cleared the whole country of the Turkish troops.

Meanwhile, the Sultan at Constantinople, in spite of the destruction of his fleet at Navarino, still maintained an obstinate refusal to accede to the terms of the treaty of London. The ambassadors of England and France thereupon left the city. Differences then began to arise between the three allied Powers. The Emperor of Russia proposed to employ coercive measures against Turkey, and for this purpose to occupy Moldavia and Wallachia. England and France rejected the proposal. They wished to preserve the Ottoman Empire as well as to secure the independence of Greece. But the Greek question was only one of the complaints of Russia against Turkey. It had also grave reasons to complain that the treaty of Bucharest and the later treaty of Akermann of 1826, confirming and extending it, were disregarded by the Porte, which still occupied Moldavia, Wallachia, and Serbia by its armies. The Sultan, in a manifesto to his own people, had publicly announced that he had entered into the treaty of Akermann with the full intention of not being bound by its terms, and that he regarded Russia as his hereditary foe.

On April 26, 1828, Russia declared war against Turkey. England and France found themselves in a position when they could not object, for the Porte still refused their demands as regards Greece. They had joined with Russia in destroying the Turkish fleet. They were now compelled to stand by while the Russians invaded Turkey. The position, and still more the results of the war, showed what a grave error Mahmoud committed when he refused to agree to the scheme of the allied Powers for granting autonomy to Greece under the suzerainty of Turkey. If he had accepted, his fleet would have been intact. England and France would have been in a position to object to Russia's schemes. As it was, Greece secured an absolute independence, and Wallachia, Moldavia, and Serbia were soon, by the victories of Russia, to secure the status of complete autonomy which the Sultan had refused to Greece.

The Emperor Nicholas, in nominal command of his army, crossed the Pruth on May 7, 1828. His force consisted of not more than sixty-five thousand men, a surprisingly small number for the greatest military Power in Europe to put into the field. It was necessary, however, to keep a large army in Poland, where an outbreak was expected. Another army was stationed in the Ukraine to watch Austria, who regarded the Russian attack on Turkey with suspicion and malevolence; and a fourth army of thirty thousand men, under General Paskiewich, invaded Asia Minor from the Caucasus. With the main army it was hoped to cross the Balkans and to menace Constantinople. The Turks offered no resistance in Moldavia and Wallachia. But it was not till June 8th that the Russians were able to effect a crossing over the Danube. The Sultan, on his part, commenced the campaign under great disadvantages. His old army of Janissaries had recently been destroyed. The new army, equipped and drilled in the fashion of European armies, was very raw and ill-trained. It consisted of very young men, who were recruited with difficulty, often by compulsion, for the new service was very unpopular, and the older men could not be induced to join. It did not count more than forty-five thousand men, exclusive of the artillery. It was supplemented by irregulars from Asia, and the total force under arms was estimated at one hundred and eighty thousand men, of whom, after providing for the defence of Constantinople and the Dardanelles, for a reserve at Adrianople and for other demands on the Empire in Europe and Asia, there remained only fifty thousand men to oppose the Russians in Bulgaria, and to provide garrisons for the fortresses on the Danube and for Schumla and Varna. These garrisons, however, were supported by the armed Turkish inhabitants of the towns, who could be relied on for a vigorous resistance. The Turks were under the further disadvantage that the greater part of their fleet had been destroyed at Navarino. The Russians were, in consequence, completely masters in the Black Sea. They were able to send to the Ægean archipelago another fleet, which blockaded the Dardanelles.

In spite of these difficulties, the Turks made an unexpectedly vigorous defence against the Russian invasion in Europe. The campaign of 1828 was mainly one of sieges, where the Turkish soldiers, supported by Moslems of the fortified towns, fought to the best advantage behind walls and earthworks. They could make but a poor stand in the open against their better trained enemy.

The Russians, after crossing the Danube, laid siege to Ibrail, the most important fortress on the lower stretch of the river, and which it was essentially necessary to capture before making an advance to Schumla. The garrison and inhabitants made a gallant resistance, and it was only after five weeks that it was compelled to surrender, on June 17th. The Russian army was then divided into three parts—the one to attack Silistria, the capture of which was almost as necessary as that of Ibrail; the second to besiege Varna; the third and most important, under the Emperor, to march to Schumla. The attack on Silistria failed, and after some weeks the force employed against it marched in the direction of Schumla to support the Czar's army. Even with this addition it was found impossible to invest the fortified camp of the Turks behind Schumla, and, after a demonstration, it was compelled to hold a defensive position, in front of Schumla, while the Czar and a part of the army marched in support of the division before Varna.

On August 18th the Czar arrived there with a reinforcement of nine thousand men, and the siege then commenced, while the Russian Black Sea fleet of eight ships of the line and three frigates, under command of Admiral Greig, joined in the attack from the sea. The Turks again made a desperate and prolonged defence, which might have been successful if it had not been that Jussuf Pasha, in command of the garrison, with five thousand of his men, traitorously deserted the city, on October 14th, and threw themselves on the mercy of the Czar. The remainder of the garrison, under the Capitan Pasha, refused to be a party to the surrender. It was said that the cause of this extraordinary act of treachery was that the Sultan, in pursuance of his policy of concentrating all power and authority in himself, had been persuaded by an intrigue to confiscate the property of Jussuf, who was one of the few large landowners in Turkey, while the owner was gallantly fighting the enemy at Varna. However that may be, the remaining garrison was soon compelled to capitulate, and this most important stronghold fell into the hands of the Russians. Without it no advance could possibly have been made across the Balkans.

The campaign of 1828 came to an end with the surrender of Varna. Though the Russians had been able to capture two of the four fortresses which barred their way to the Balkans, the campaign had not been without success to the Turks. They had shown unexpected powers of resistance, and had prevented for a year the achievement of the main object of the Russians—their advance to Constantinople. The losses of the Russians had been very great, not only in the sieges, but by disease, which dogged their armies as usual.

Baron von Moltke, the German general, who, at the invitation of the Sultan, was with the Turkish headquarters during this war, writes of the Russian and Turkish troops in his remarkable history of it:—

The faults of the Russian Staff were atoned for by the innate excellence of the Russian troops. The self-sacrificing obedience of the commanders, the steadiness of the common soldiers, their power of endurance and unshaken bravery in times of danger, were the qualities that enabled them to avert the dangers of their position before Schumla and to hold the Turks in check, and to make up for all deficiencies and overcome all resistance at Varna.[32]

Of the Turks he adds:—

We cannot say much for the skill of the Turkish commanders, but the conduct of the Turks, from the highest officers to the last soldier at the storming of Ibrail, their courage and steadiness in the mines and trenches before Varna, were far above all praise.

In Asia the Turks had not done so well. General Paskiewich was able to defeat the army in front of him and to capture the important stronghold of Kars and its adjoining district.

The campaign of 1829 began late. It was not till the middle of May that the Russian army again took the field, not on this occasion under the Czar, but under General Diebitsch, who proved to be a most able general and diplomatist. The army was again most inadequate for the campaign which was in contemplation—namely, the crossing of the Balkans and an advance to Constantinople. It consisted of no more than sixty-eight thousand men, a force which, in these days, eighty-eight years later, would count for little or nothing. It was thought necessary, as a condition precedent to any advance, to capture Silistria. The siege was commenced on May 17, 1829. The Russian force detailed for this was not more than fourteen thousand men. The Turks who defended it were twenty-one thousand in number, including eight thousand armed inhabitants. In spite of this disparity of numbers, the town was captured after a siege of forty-four days, on July 26th, at a loss to the Russians of two thousand five hundred men.

In the meantime Diebitsch had advanced with the main army in the direction of Schumla. Reschid Pasha, who had replaced Hussein Pasha as Grand Vizier and Seraskier, issued from Schumla with forty thousand men, and on June 18th a great battle took place at Kulewtska. The Turks were utterly defeated by a very inferior force of Russians. They had begun the battle with an impetuous charge, but they could not sustain it against the serried ranks of the Russian veterans. Some ammunition wagons exploded and, as often happened with the Turks, a wild panic ensued. They fled from the field of battle and dispersed in all directions. All their artillery fell into the hands of the Russians. Reschid escaped at the head of six hundred men and found his way to Schumla, where there were ten thousand Turks, and where a large number of fugitives from the battle eventually found refuge. This victory at Kulewtska had far-reaching effects. It was the first great battle in which the new troops of Mahmoud were tested. It showed that the Russian soldiers had an overwhelming superiority.

Silistria fell on July 13th. The Russians who had been engaged in the siege then joined Diebitsch before Schumla. The general thereupon decided on the bold and even perilous course of crossing the Balkans, without previously capturing Schumla and its army. Leaving ten thousand men to mask that fortress, where a much greater force of Turks was now assembled, consisting largely of men demoralized by the recent defeat, Diebitsch commenced his march with such secrecy that for some days the Turks were not aware of it. Reschid Pasha, expecting an attack on Schumla, and thinking his force insufficient for its defence, had called in the various corps who were posted for the defence of the mountain passes. Diebitsch therefore met with no opposition. He crossed the mountains in nine days of forced marches fraught with great hardship to his troops. When south of the mountain range, he deflected his route to the Black Sea and got into communication with the Russian fleet, under Admiral Greig, which assisted in the capture of Bourgas and other ports along the coast, and afforded supplies to Diebitsch's army.

Three battles were fought south of the mountains, at Aidos, Karnabad and Slivno, where small divisions of Turks were defeated and dispersed. After three weeks from crossing the Balkans, Diebitsch arrived in front of Adrianople, a city of eighty thousand inhabitants, with a garrison of ten thousand men. His army was by this time reduced to less than twenty thousand men. Its appearance before Adrianople caused wild panic. Never before had a hostile army crossed the southern range of the Balkans. It was thought to be impossible. It was confidently believed that the Russian army numbered over one hundred thousand men. The city and its garrison surrendered without making a show of fight. Everywhere on its route through Bulgaria the Christian raya population had received the invaders with acclamation and the Turks had thrown away their arms and fled. The campaign of 1829 in Asia had been almost equally disastrous to the Turks. Paskiewich had defeated them in a pitched battle and had captured Erzerum. He was now approaching Trebizond, after dispersing an army on the way.

When news reached Constantinople of the crossing of the Balkans and the capture of Adrianople, there was consternation and dismay among Turks of all classes. The Sultan almost alone maintained his presence of mind. He issued a proclamation calling on all the Turks in the city to join in its defence. He announced his intention to take command in person. The sacred banner of the Prophet was unfurled. But when, at the first review of the forces, the Sultan appeared in a carriage and not on horseback, this "unheard of and indecorous innovation" chilled the enthusiasm of the volunteers, and undid the good which was expected from his action.

There was no great zeal for the defence of the capital. The chief ministers of the Porte were unanimous in advising the Sultan to sue for terms of peace. They were quite ignorant of the weakness of the Russian army. They believed the stories that more than a hundred thousand men were advancing on the capital. There were no troops at Constantinople, they said, able to meet this army. The ambassadors of England and France, who had recently returned to Constantinople, at the invitation of the Sultan, backed up the ministers, and urgently advised him to come to terms with the enemy. We now know that all this advice and these alarms were founded on false information and that there was no real justification for them. In fact, the real position of the Russian army was one of extreme danger. It had suffered great losses on the battlefields and from the hardships of the forced marches, and was also being decimated by disease. There was no possibility of its being reinforced. Retreat across the Balkans was almost impossible. The Turkish army at Schumla was now reinforced. On its flank there was an army of twenty thousand Albanians, under the rebellious Pasha of Scotra, who had refused aid to the Porte in the earlier part of the campaign, but who, now that the existence of the Empire was threatened, might confidently be expected to come to its aid. Advance to Constantinople might also be dangerous, if not impossible. It was distant one hundred and forty miles. Its garrison of thirty thousand men, supplemented by fresh volunteers, might be relied on to meet the Russians, now reduced to much less than twenty thousand. These difficulties of the Russian army, however, were not known to the Porte.

In view of the strong pressure brought to bear upon him, the Sultan, for once in his life, gave way, and agreed to send plenipotentiaries to Adrianople to discuss terms of peace. Diebitsch well knew the danger of his position, and was anxious to make peace, but he maintained an attitude of firmness and confidence. He was ready, he said, to discuss terms, but he was equally willing to advance with his army against the capital. Already a part of his army was pressed forward. It occupied a line from the Black Sea at Kilia to Enos in the archipelago—a distance of over one hundred miles, much too long for his weak force. It is recognized by Moltke and all military authorities that if the Porte had stood firm and had refused to agree to terms, Diebitsch could not have made good his threatened attack on the capital. In the history of war there has never been a more successful case of 'bluff.' The Porte gave in to unreasoning and ill-informed fear, and on September 19th peace was concluded between the two Powers and the treaty of Adrianople was signed.

It is certain [said Moltke] that this treaty released Diebitsch from a position as perilous as could well be conceived, and which, if prolonged for a few more days, might have caused him to be hurled down from the summit of victory to the lowest depth of ruin and destruction.[33]

The terms of peace agreed to were moderate, so far as Russia itself was concerned, though very serious in their effect on the Ottoman Empire. The Czar had proclaimed at the outset of the war that he had no desire for territorial aggrandizement. He fully adhered to this promise. With two comparatively small exceptions, Russia gave up all the territory which it had conquered in the war, both in Europe and Asia. It retained only a small part of Moldavia which gave access to the Sulina mouth of the Danube, a position of great importance to it in the future. In Asia, Kars and Erzerum were given back to Turkey. In Europe, the Pruth continued to be the boundary of the two States. But Moldavia and Wallachia, though nominally restored to the Ottoman Empire, were practically freed from it. They were to enjoy complete autonomy. The Hospodars, in future, were to be appointed for life. The two States were to be allowed to raise armies independent of the Porte. The tribute payable in future was to be fixed, and could not be increased. Religious and commercial freedom were to be secured to them. The Sultan was to be their suzerain and nothing more. This meant practical independence. The same privileges were secured for Serbia, with the exception that the Porte was to be permitted to garrison the fortresses of Belgrade and Orsova. The Turks were required to depart from all other parts of the country. Silistria was to be returned to Turkey, but other fortresses on the Danube were to be razed. That river, therefore, ceased to be the first defence of the Turkish Empire to the north. An indemnity of eleven and a half million ducats, equal to five millions sterling, was to be paid by Turkey for the expenses of Russia in the war. The payment was to be spread over ten years, and the territory occupied by Russia was not to be wholly surrendered till this was effected.

As regards Greece, the treaty embodied and made obligatory on the Sultan the provisions of the treaty of London of July, 1827, between the three Powers, and the further protocol between them of March 1829, which defined the future limits of Greece. Under the protocol, the boundary line was to run from the Gulf of Volo to the Gulf of Arta, so as to include the greater part of Thessaly. The country south of this was to be subject to a monarchical government, hereditary in a Christian prince to be chosen by the three Powers, with the consent of the Porte and under the suzerainty of the Sultan, and with an administration best calculated to ensure its religious and commercial liberty. This proposal had been submitted to the Sultan by the ambassadors of England and France on March 22, 1829. He had then obstinately refused to have anything to say to it. When the Russians had crossed the Balkans, the Sultan, in the hope of propitiating England and France, offered to the ambassadors to agree to an autonomous Greece under a Hospodar, limited, however, to the Morea. This the ambassadors refused. The Porte, under the treaty with Russia, now agreed to their full demand.

The Governments of England and France appear to have taken umbrage at the action of Russia in dealing with the subject of Greece in a separate treaty with the Porte. It was thought that the Czar wished to get all the credit of liberating Greece from Turkish rule. They therefore informed the Russian Government that the execution of the treaty of London of 1827 did not belong to the Czar alone, but was to be the work of the three Governments. In consequence of this a further conference took place in London, at which it was decided that the suzerainty of the Sultan over Greece was to be abolished, and complete independence was to be secured to the Greeks. They also came to the unfortunate decision that the line of boundary of the new kingdom was to be greatly restricted, and instead of running from the Gulf of Volo to the Gulf of Arta, was to be drawn from the mouth of the Archilous to the mouth of the Sperkius, thus excluding from the new kingdom the whole of Acarnania and the greater part of Thessaly, where the population was almost wholly Greek. They also decided that Crete was not to be included, but was to be restored to Turkish rule. Mr. Finlay says of this: "Diplomatic ignorance could not have traced a more unsuitable boundary."[34]

The Sultan agreed to this new project. He probably preferred a smaller Greece with complete independence to a larger one with full autonomy, subject to his suzerainty. Greece was accordingly recalled into national existence with a greatly reduced area, leaving outside large districts with completely homogeneous Greek populations. This was fraught with grave difficulties in the future. One effect of it was that Prince Leopold of Saxe-Coburg, who, later, as King of the Belgians, proved to be one of the most able rulers of his day, refused to accept the throne of Greece on the ground that its area was too restricted, and Otho, a son of the King of Bavaria, was selected by the Powers for the post, and proved to be a most incompetent and reactionary ruler. It would seem that Lord Aberdeen, who was Minister of Foreign Affairs in England at the time, and who was mainly responsible for these changes, was anxious to restrict the kingdom of Greece to the smallest possible area.

Reverting to the treaty of Adrianople, it is to be observed that while Russia acquired a very insignificant extension of territory, and was content with the prestige of having dictated its terms, and with having acquired a position such that it might insist on its behests to the Porte, as regards its Christian subjects, being obeyed in the future, Turkey lost very greatly. It was said that the Sultan, after signing the treaty, shut himself up in his palace at Therapia for weeks in gloomy despair. There was much cause for this. The treaty was a complete surrender of all that he had been contending for since his accession to the throne. It was humiliating to himself and his Turkish subjects. It was the inevitable precursor of much that was to occur to other parts of his Empire. His grief and indignation must have been greatly aggravated when he came to know the real condition of the Russian army at Adrianople and to appreciate that, if he had stood firm in resisting the advice of his ministers and of the ambassadors, the Russian army would have been quite unable to make an advance against Constantinople. This, however, should not lead us to forget the supreme error which Mahmoud committed in refusing to come to terms with the three Powers as regards Greece after the treaty of London. If in 1827, the Sultan had been willing to make concessions in the direction of autonomy to Greece, it is nearly certain that there would have been no declaration of war on the part of Russia, and in the event of war he would not have been wanting in allies. His fleet would not have been destroyed at Navarino, and time would have been afforded to him to reorganize his army and to make it effective against those of the Christian Powers. As it was, not only did he lose all real hold over Moldavia, Wallachia, and Serbia, not only did Greece gain its independence, but he was soon to lose all real authority in Egypt, a Moslem country, except the barren right of suzerainty of the Sultan and a fixed tribute in money.

It has already been stated that when, in 1824, the Sultan invited the aid of the Pasha of Egypt to crush rebellion in Greece, Mehemet Ali only consented to lend his army and fleet on the express promise that the Pashalics of Syria, Damascus, Tripoli (in Asia), and Crete would be given to him, in addition to that of Egypt. But when in 1827, after the destruction of the Turko-Egyptian fleet at Navarino and the expulsion of the Egyptian army from the Morea, Mehemet Ali pressed for the performance of this promise, he met with a blank refusal, except as regards the island of Crete, the Pashalic of which alone was conferred on him. Mehemet was very indignant at this breach of promise, and determined to seize by force the provinces which he coveted. He set to work with great resolution to build another fleet, in place of that which had been burnt or sunk, and to improve and strengthen his army.

By 1832 he completed these preparations for war. He then picked a quarrel with the Pasha of Syria and, pretending to make war against him and not against the Sultan, sent an army, under Ibrahim, across the desert into Syria. It captured Gaza and Jerusalem without difficulty, and then marched to Acre, where the Egyptian fleet met it and co-operated in a successful attack on that fortress. After this success Ibrahim marched with his army to Aleppo and

Damascus, defeating two Turkish armies. He then crossed the mountains into Asia Minor, and fought another great battle at Konia on October 27, 1832, and defeated a large Turkish army. He then marched to Brusa.

These disasters caused the greatest alarm at Constantinople. There was no other Turkish army in the field capable of resisting the march of Ibrahim's army to the Bosphorus. In his peril the Sultan appealed to the British Government for aid against the Egyptians, offering a close alliance for the future. He met with a refusal, at the instance of Lord Palmerston, who did not then appear to value a Turkish alliance, though the British Ambassador at Constantinople, Sir Stratford Canning, strongly advised it. Mahmoud then appealed for aid to the Emperor of Russia, who gladly availed himself of the opportunity of increasing his influence in Turkey and of effecting a virtual protectorate over it. For a second time, within recent years, a close alliance was formed between the Czar and the Sultan, and in February, 1833, a Russian fleet issuing from Sebastopol conveyed an army to the Bosphorus for the defence of Constantinople.

For a time the influence of Russia became predominant. None but Russians had access to the Sultan. Russian troops and sailors were seen everywhere, and Russian officers were employed to drill and command the Turkish battalions. This state of things caused great alarm to the British and French Governments. They were both concerned in preventing Russia obtaining possession or control of Constantinople. They felt it was necessary to stay the advance of Ibrahim's victorious army, which was the excuse for the presence of the Russians at Constantinople. They offered, therefore, to the Sultan that if he would insist on the withdrawal of the Russian army from his capital, they would guarantee him against the further invasion of Mehemet Ali's army. France, though always very friendly to Mehemet Ali, and in favour of his independence as against the Sultan, had no wish to see Constantinople in the hands of Russia.

By dint of great diplomatic pressure, in which Lord Palmerston took the leading part with the greatest ability, a double arrangement was effected. On the one hand, Mehemet Ali, perceiving that he would be powerless to attack Constantinople against the opposition of Russia, England, and France, was induced to come to terms with the Sultan. A convention was signed between them in 1833, and a firman was issued by the Porte under which Mehemet was confirmed as the Pasha, not only of Egypt, but of Syria, Damascus, Adana, Tripoli, and Crete, an immense accession of dignity and power to him. The Sultan was to be suzerain and the Pashalics were conferred on Mehemet Ali only for his life, and there was no promise that they would be continued to his son Ibrahim or other descendants. The concession, however, as it stood, was most humiliating to the Sultan. On the other hand, Russia agreed with the Porte to withdraw its troops from Constantinople and the Bosphorus, but only on the promise, embodied in the treaty of Hunkar Iskelesi, that Russian ships of war should have the privilege of passing through the Bosphorus and Dardanelles, at any time, without obtaining the consent of the Porte, a privilege which was to be denied to the ships of other Powers, unless with the previous consent of Russia. It also secured to Russia the right to send an army to the Bosphorus and land it there whenever the exigencies of the Turkish Empire made it expedient to do so. The firman to Mehemet Ali was dated May 5, 1833, and the treaty of Hunkar Iskelesi was agreed to with Russia on July 8th of the same year. By these two measures, the result of a great diplomatic struggle, the menace of Mehemet Ali against Constantinople, which at one time seemed likely to involve all the Powers in Europe in war, was brought to an end. The Egyptian army was withdrawn into the provinces added to the Pashalic of Mehemet Ali, and the Russian troops were recalled by the Czar from Constantinople.

After this settlement, very favourable both to Russia and Egypt, but humiliating to Turkey, a period of a few years' repose was accorded to the Sultan, so far as his relations with the Emperor Nicholas and Mehemet Ali were concerned. But there were frequent internal troubles and outbreaks, which were put down by Mahmoud, not without some difficulty. Both Mahmoud and Mehemet Ali spent the interval in making preparations for another encounter. Mahmoud could not acquiesce in the virtual independence of so large a part of his Empire under Mehemet Ali. The latter was determined to convert his Pashalic into an hereditary one and to attain virtual independence of the Porte. He had ambitions also to supplant Mahmoud as the head of the Ottoman Empire. The Sultan, during this time, employed a large number of Prussian officers, under Colonel von Moltke— later to become so famous in the Franco-German War of 1870 in command of the German army—to train his army, while Mehemet Ali again employed French officers for the same purpose. Five years elapsed before war again broke out between them.

In 1838 Mehemet Ali, having completed all his arrangements for war with his suzerain, announced his intention to pay no more tribute in the future to the Porte. This amounted to a declaration of independence and a renunciation of allegiance. Mahmoud, on his part, was determined to crush his rebellious vassal, and collected an army on the Euphrates for the invasion of Syria. The opportunity seemed to be a favourable one, as the population of Syria was in revolt against Mehemet Ali, whose government had proved to be almost as oppressive and tyrannical as that of the Sultan. Early in 1839 Mahmoud declared war and gave directions to his army to invade Syria. He also fitted out a fleet, consisting of nine ships of the line and twenty-four smaller vessels, and directed it to proceed to Syria and to co-operate with his army advancing from the Euphrates.

Both these expeditions of the Porte came to grief. The army which invaded Syria met the Egyptians, again under command of Ibrahim, at Nazeb on June 25, 1839. The two armies were about equal in number, each of them about forty thousand. The Turks were completely defeated. Many of their battalions deserted on the field of battle and went over to the enemy; the remainder were routed and dispersed. Six thousand of them were killed and wounded; ten thousand were taken prisoners. One hundred guns and great masses of stores fell into the hands of the Egyptians. The Turkish army in these parts ceased to exist.

The great Turkish fleet had sailed from the Bosphorus on July 6th amid many popular demonstrations. It was under the command of the Capitan Pasha, Achmet, who proved to be a traitor. After passing through the Dardanelles, instead of following his instructions by making his course to the coast of Syria, Achmet sailed direct to Egypt, and there entered the port of Alexandria with flying colours and handed over the fleet to the enemy of the Sultan, the rebellious Pasha Mehemet Ali, a proceeding without precedent in history. It was only accomplished, we may presume, by profuse bribery on the part of the crafty Pasha.

Mahmoud was spared the knowledge of these two signal disasters to his Empire. He died on July 1, 1839, some writers allege from the effect of alcohol, though this is doubtful. Creasy and many other historians are unstinting in praise of Mahmoud. They assign to him a very high position in the list of Sultans. They bear testimony to his high civic courage, and to the firm resolution with which he confronted the many crises of his reign. We must fully admit these qualities. Few sovereigns in history have had to deal with such a succession of grave difficulties. Almost alone he bore the weight of Empire. We must not, however, lose sight of the fact that his administration and diplomacy were fraught with failure, that his Empire incurred greater losses than under any previous Sultan, that his armies met with invariable defeat, not only on the part of numerically weaker armies of Russia, but also from insurgent Greeks and Serbians, and even from Egyptians, whose fighting qualities were much inferior to those of the Turks. His firmness and resolution were very great, but they failed him at the supreme crisis of his career, when the Russian army, with quite inadequate numbers, after serious losses in battle and by disease, threatened Constantinople from Adrianople, and when it is now quite certain that, if Mahmoud had stood firm and had refused to come to terms, overwhelming disaster must have befallen the Russians. At another crisis also his firmness amounted to most unwise obstinacy when he refused, in 1827, to concede autonomy to Greece at the instance of the Great Powers—a supreme error from which all his subsequent misfortunes logically followed. Mahmoud seems also to have been wanting in magnetism to inspire his generals and soldiers with his own courage and resolution. He does not compare in this respect with his contemporary and rival, Mehemet Ali. He had little of the martial vigour and of the craft of that great vassal. If the Great Powers had not intervened, it was highly probable, if not certain, that Ibrahim's army would, either in 1833 or in 1839, have marched to Constantinople, have effected a revolution there, and have put an end to the Othman dynasty. It might have given new life to the decadent Turkish Empire. In any case, there was no reason why Mahmoud, if he had been endowed with Mehemet Ali's genius and administrative capacity, should not have created an army superior in force and discipline to that of the Egyptian Pasha, and equal to the task of preventing the Russians from crossing the Balkans.

XX

THE RULE OF ELCHIS
1839-76

MAHMOUD was succeeded by his son, Abdul Mehzid, a youth of sixteen years, who proved to be of very different stamp from his father. He was of mild and gentle nature, without physical or mental vigour, and wanting in force of character. He was enfeebled early in his reign by excessive indulgence in his harem. Later he was addicted to alcohol, like many of his predecessors. His father had monopolized power, and had frequently changed his ministers, with the result that he left no statesman behind him who could impose his will on the young Sultan and govern in his name. Nor was any lady of the harem ambitious and competent to guide or misguide the ship of State, as had not infrequently been the case in the past, when the reigning Sultan was unequal to the task. The main power during this reign as regards foreign affairs, and to some extent even as regards internal affairs, seems to have been vested in the ambassadors of the Great Powers. This power was exercised collectively by them on the rare occasions when they were unanimously agreed, but at other times by one or other of them, and chiefly, as will be seen, by the British Ambassador, Sir Stratford Canning, later Lord Stratford de Redcliffe, who, by his force of character and commanding presence, obtained immense personal influence over the feeble mind of Abdul Mehzid, and exercised an almost undisputed sway from 1842 to 1858, with the exception of brief intervals when he was in England on leave, and when the Russian Ambassador succeeded in obtaining exclusive influence.

The new Sultan was fortunate, as compared with his father, that in the thirty-one years of his reign his Empire experienced no serious loss of territory. It is necessary, however, to advert to the two main events of it—the one, the suppression of Mehemet Ali's ambitious projects and the restriction of his hereditary Pashalic to Egypt; the other, the Crimean War, as it is known in history—the war with Russia, the effect of which was to stave off for nearly twenty years the dismemberment of the Turkish Empire in Europe.

As regards the first of these events, it has been shown that, in the last year of Mahmoud's reign, Mehemet Ali was in a position of great strength, which might have enabled him to overthrow the Othman dynasty. He had destroyed the main Turkish army in Asia, at Nazeb, on the frontier of Syria, and by the infamous treachery of Achmet Pasha he had obtained possession of the Turkish fleet. He comported himself, however, with moderation at this stage. He informed the Porte that he was willing to come to terms if they would recognize the Pashalics of Egypt, Syria, Tripoli (in Asia Minor), Adana, and Crete as hereditary in his family. He had no intention, he said, to use the Turkish fleet against his suzerain, the Sultan. He would give it back to the Porte, if his terms were agreed to. If Sultan Mahmoud had been alive, it may be confidently assumed that he would have rejected these terms with contumely, and would have fought it out with his rebellious vassal. But Abdul Mehzid was wanting in courage to meet the crisis. The two disasters caused the greatest alarm at Constantinople. The majority of the Divan were ready to concede the demands of Mehemet Ali. They were prevented from doing so by an unprecedented occurrence. The ambassadors of the five Great Powers—England, France, Russia, Austria, and Prussia—met in conclave and came to the conclusion that it was contrary to the interests of their respective Governments that Mehemet Ali's demands should be acceded to. They informed the Porte that their Governments desired to discuss the questions raised by Mehemet Ali, and invited the Sultan to suspend a definitive arrangement with him. This was agreed to by the Divan. The settlement of the relation of the rebellious pasha to the Sultan fell into the hands of the ambassadors, and a kind of tutelage was established over the Turkish Empire.

The conduct of the Emperor Nicholas on this occasion was most conciliatory to the other Powers. He intimated to them that, if they were united on a scheme to settle the Egyptian question, he would not insist on the special right which he had acquired under the treaties of Bucharest and of Akermann to exclude the ships of war of other Powers from the Dardanelles, and that he would withdraw his few remaining troops from Constantinople and the Bosphorus. Lord Palmerston, on behalf of Great Britain, expressed his admiration of this attitude of the Russian Emperor. As a result, a conference took place in London between the representatives of the Great Powers, at which Lord Palmerston, on behalf of England, and Baron Brunnow, on behalf of Russia, took the leading part. Grave difference soon arose at the conference on the part of France. Its Government, though strongly opposed to Russia obtaining possession of Constantinople, had always been favourable to the claim of Mehemet Ali to an hereditary Pashalic in Egypt and Syria, and had secretly encouraged him to make himself independent of the Porte. It now supported him against the veto of the other Powers. Eventually England, Russia, and Austria, finding that they could not come to agreement with France, decided to act without its concurrence, and to compel Mehemet Ali to evacuate Syria and to restore to the Porte the Turkish fleet. After long discussion between these three Powers, a convention was agreed to on July 15, 1840. They presented an ultimatum to Mehemet Ali, calling upon him to submit himself to the Porte. They promised that if, within ten days of the receipt of the ultimatum, he would give orders for the withdrawal of his army from Syria, and would give up the Turkish fleet to the Porte, he would be recognized as hereditary Pasha of Egypt and as Pasha of Syria for his own life; but, if not, the offer of the life Pashalic of Syria and the hereditary Pashalic of Egypt would be withdrawn, and he would have to content himself with the Pashalic for life of Egypt. It was also intimated to him that if there was refusal or delay the fleets of the three Powers would at once institute a blockade of Egypt and Syria. This ultimatum of the three Powers, when it became known in France, caused the most profound indignation; the more so when, on the refusal of Mehemet Ali to accede to the ultimatum, the British fleet, supported by war vessels of the two other Powers, made its appearance on the coast of Syria. This was thought to be an insult to France. War between that country and England was imminent. There were violent scenes in the French Chambers, and most bitterly hostile articles in the French papers. There were threats of war on the part of the Government of France. But prudent counsels ultimately prevailed, when it was discovered that France was not prepared for a naval war, and that its fleet could not hope to contend with the British fleet in the Mediterranean or to land an army in Syria.

The three Powers, on their part, mainly at the instance of Lord Palmerston, declined to submit their policy to the threats of France, and persisted in their demonstration of force against Mehemet Ali. War was averted between England and France, and Louis Philippe (then King of the French) contented himself with the cynical observation that there was all the difference in the world between threatening war and actually going to war.

Meanwhile the British fleet, under Admirals Stopford and Napier, appeared before Beyrout and bombarded and destroyed its forts. Two thousand men were landed, under Napier, and defeated the Egyptian forces. The same operation was repeated a few days later at Acre. The powerful defences of this fortress were demolished by the guns of the British fleet, and six thousand men were landed, under Napier, and defeated Ibrahim's army. It was in these attacks on Beyrout and Acre that steamships made their first appearance in maritime war. The allies were greatly assisted by the revolt of the people of Syria against Mehemet Ali's oppressive government. Desertion also was very rife in the Egyptian force, and Ibrahim's army, which had originally consisted of seventy-five thousand men, had dwindled down to twenty-five thousand.

After these operations on the coast of Syria, Napier and his squadron appeared before Alexandria and threatened bombardment. But Mehemet Ali, by this time, had realized that he could not hope to make war successfully against the three Great Powers as well as the Sultan. He entered into negotiations with Admiral Napier. He agreed to evacuate Syria and to give up the Turkish fleet to the Porte, provided that the Sultan would recognize him as hereditary Pasha of Egypt. In the meantime the Sultan of Turkey had issued a firman deposing Mehemet Ali from all his Pashalics. This did not necessarily mean much, for the Porte on four previous occasions had publicly deposed the rebellious pasha, but without any result. Eventually, on September 20, 1841, agreement was arrived at between Mehemet Ali and the three Powers. In spite of his deposition by the Sultan, Mehemet Ali was confirmed in the position of hereditary Pasha of Egypt, but was deprived of all his other governments. He was to pay tribute to the Porte equal to one-fourth of the revenue of Egypt—later fixed at an annual sum of £400,000. He was to withdraw his army from Syria and to maintain no larger force in Egypt than eighteen thousand men.

The intervention of the three Great Powers, taking the matter out of the hands of the Sultan, brought about an arrangement much more favourable to him than the Divan were willing to agree to. Syria was relieved of the government of Mehemet Ali and was placed again under the control of the Porte. Egypt, on the other hand, was made practically independent, subject only to a fixed tribute in recognition of the nominal suzerainty of the Sultan. This result was achieved not by the force of arms of the Sultan, but by the action of the three Great Powers, directed chiefly by the able diplomacy of Lord Palmerston, who steered this concert through all its difficulties and against the violent opposition of France. The final settlement thus imposed on Mehemet Ali, which extinguished his ambitious projects and reduced his rule to Egypt alone, is said to have broken the heart of the old man. He lived on for eight more years, but they were spent in gloom and depression, aggravated by the death of his able and distinguished son Ibrahim. It should be added here that in 1841, as a sequel to the arrangement about Egypt, a convention was agreed to between the Great Powers, including Russia, and Turkey by which the vessels of war of all countries except Turkey were forbidden to pass through the Straits to and from the Black Sea.

The settlement of these grave questions, in 1841, was followed by twelve years of comparative repose in Turkey, broken only by occasional revolts of pashas, or of subject races driven to desperation by chronic misgovernment. These were put down by the Seraskier, Omar Pasha, who proved to be a very competent general for this purpose. It was during this period that Sir Stratford Canning, as British Ambassador to the Porte, attained a personal influence over the Sultan, Abdul Mehzid, of an unprecedented character, such that he may be said to have virtually ruled the State.

Canning on three previous occasions had represented the British Government at Constantinople during the reign of Mahmoud. In 1812 as Minister Plenipotentiary, when quite a young man, he had gained immense credit by inducing the Sultan to come to terms with Russia, by the treaty of

- 227 -

Bucharest. The effect of this was to free the hands of the Czar and to enable him to withdraw his army from the Danube and to use it on the flank of Napoleon's army in the celebrated Moscow campaign. This largely contributed to the defeat of the invasion of Russia.

Later he had been engaged in the delimitation of Greece, after the recognition of its independence, and had shown himself a Philhellene. In 1842 Lord Aberdeen, then Foreign Minister of England, sent him again as ambassador to the Porte at the age of fifty-seven. He remained there, with two short intervals, till 1858. He acquired, during these sixteen years, the title of "The Great Elchi," the ambassador *par éminence*. By the Christian rayas of the Ottoman Empire he was known as the Padishah of the Padishahs. He was the most distinguished envoy ever employed in the British Diplomatic Service. He belonged to an old school of diplomats, when communications with the Home Government were long in reaching their destination, and when ambassadors necessarily took much responsibility upon themselves, and dictated rather than followed the policy of their Governments. He held himself to represent his sovereign rather than the transient ministers of the day. His mien was such as greatly to impress the Turks. It was stately and dignified. His countenance was noble and spirituelle. His eyes seemed to penetrate the minds of those with whom he transacted business, and made it difficult for them to conceal their intentions. His own methods were always honourable and straightforward. Though he was well versed in the arts of diplomacy and could meet mine by countermine, he never resorted to trickery. The Turks learned that his word was implicitly to be trusted, and that he wished well to their country. He treated the Turkish ministers with the utmost hauteur. With some of them, whose hands were known to be stained with blood, he refused to have any communication. If his demands were refused at the Porte, he went direct to the Sultan and fairly bullied that weak, gentle, and well-intentioned sovereign into acquiescence. He entered on his work in this embassy with two main convictions, one might almost say obsessions—the one that it was the interest of England, and therefore his own duty, to oppose the schemes of Russia at every turn; the other that it was his duty to urge, and even to compel, the Porte to carry out internal reforms, and to come into line with other civilized countries in Europe, in default of which he fully recognized that the Ottoman Empire could not be maintained. He had a firm belief that this was possible, and that he was himself the appointed man to effect it. For this purpose he freely made use of threats of force from England if his behests were refused, and of promises of protection against Russia if they were agreed to. An envoy of this character, great as were his qualities and personal merits, was a cause of embarrassment to British policy, for the Government could not control him. One might say of him, in the words of Shakespeare:—

If great men could thunder as Jove himself does,

Jove would ne'er be quiet.

Canning used the thunder of his country freely in pursuance of his own policy. He was undoubtedly the main cause of the war which soon ensued between Great Britain and Russia.

Meanwhile the reform of its administration and its laws had long been recognized by the very few honest and capable statesmen of Turkey as indispensable to the maintenance of its Empire. Mahmoud himself, in the latter part of his life, had appreciated this necessity, and had given his sanction to a scheme of reform. But death came to him before it was issued. He must have instructed his son as to this policy, for one of the first acts of Abdul Mehzid, by the advice of his Grand Vizier, Reschid Pasha, was to issue the important declaration of reform which had been prepared by Mahmoud, and was known as the Hatti-Scheriff of Ghulkané. It promised equally to all his subjects, without distinction of creed or race, security of life, of honour, and of property, the equitable distribution of taxes, the public trial of all prisoners, the right of all to hold and devise property, and the systematic recruiting of the army. It appointed a council to elaborate the details of administrative reform to give effect to these principles. But this great charter of reform lacked the will of a Mahmoud to enforce it. There ensued a dangerous reaction. Reschid Pasha was compelled to resign. Riza Pasha, who succeeded him, and his colleagues, were reactionary, fanatical, and anti-Christian. The Hatti-Scheriff, like almost every other promise of reform in Turkey, became a dead letter. Riza was also corrupt and venal, and robbed the treasury of untold sums. It became the principal object of Canning to obtain the dismissal of this man and of the gang of peculators who worked with him, and the reinstatement of Reschid. Proposals for reform in favour of the rayas were impossible with ministers who carried their hatred of Christianity to the length of excluding from the public service every Turk who could speak a Christian language.

By dint of long and patient efforts Canning obtained such a mastery over Abdul Mehzid that he was able to bring about a change of ministers, and to reinstate Reschid Pasha as the only statesman in Turkey who was capable of carrying out reforms, and who was willing to be guided by himself as to their main principles.

In 1852 a serious diplomatic dispute broke out at Constantinople, between the representatives of France and Russia, as to the guardianship of the Holy Sepulchre at Jerusalem and many trumpery details connected with it. Early in 1853 there were strong indications that the Emperor Nicholas intended to take the opportunity of this dispute to raise a much more serious question against the Porte. He evidently desired to disarm the opposition of England to his schemes. In a private conversation at St. Petersburg with Sir Hamilton Seymour, the British Ambassador at his Court, he opened his mind:—

The affairs of Turkey are in a very disorganized condition. The country itself seems to be falling to pieces. The fall will be a great misfortune, and it is very important that England and Russia should come to a perfectly good understanding upon these affairs, and that neither should take any decisive step of which the other is not apprised.... We have on our hands a sick man— a very sick man. It will, I tell you frankly, be a great misfortune if one of these days he should slip away from us before all necessary arrangements were made.

With this intimation the conversation appears to have dropped. A few days later it was renewed at a private entertainment.

You know [the Emperor said] the dreams and plans in which the Empress Catherine was in the habit of indulging; these were handed down to our time; but while I inherited immense territorial possessions, I did not inherit these visions—those intentions, if you like to call them so. On the contrary, my country is so vast, so happily circumstanced in everything, that it would be unreasonable in me to desire more territory or more power than I possess; on the contrary, I am the first to tell you that our great, perhaps our only, danger is that which arises from an extension given to an Empire already too large.

Close to us lies Turkey, and in our present condition nothing better for our interests can be desired. The time has gone by when we had anything to fear from the fanatical spirit or the military enterprise of the Turks, and yet the country is strong enough, or has hitherto been strong enough, to preserve its independence, and to insure respectful treatment from other countries.

In that Empire there are several millions of Christians whose interests I am called to watch over, while the right of doing so is secured to me by treaty. I may truly say that I make a moderate and sparing use of my right, and I will freely confess that it is one which is attended with obligations occasionally very inconvenient; but I cannot recede from the discharge of a distinct duty....

Now, Turkey has by degrees fallen into such a state of decrepitude that, eager as we all are for the prolonged existence of his life, he may suddenly die on our hands; we cannot resuscitate what is dead. If the Turkish Empire falls it falls to rise no more, and I put it to you, therefore, whether it is not better to be provided beforehand for a contingency than to incur the chaos, confusion, and the certainty of a European war, all of which must attend the catastrophe, if it should occur unexpectedly and before some ulterior system has been sketched. That is the part to which I am desiring you should call the attention of your Government.

Now, I desire to speak to you as a friend, and as a gentleman. If England and I arrive at an understanding in this matter, as regards the rest it little matters to me. It is indifferent to me what others do or think. Frankly, then, I tell you plainly that, if England thinks of establishing herself one of these days at Constantinople, I will not allow it. For my part, I am equally disposed to take the engagement not to establish myself there—as proprietor, that is to say— for as occupier I do not say; it might happen that circumstances, if no previous provisions were made, if everything should be left to chance, might place me in the position of occupying Constantinople.

On the 20th February, in a further conversation, the Emperor said:—

If your Government has been led to believe that Turkey retains any element of existence, your Government must have received incorrect information. I repeat to you, the sick man is dying, and we can never allow such an event to take us by surprise. We must come to some understanding.

The next day he added:—

The principalities are, in fact, an independent State under my protection. This might so continue. Serbia might receive the same form of government. So again with Bulgaria; there seems to be no reason why these provinces should not form one independent State. As to Egypt, I quite understand the importance to England of that territory. I can thus only say that if, in the event of a destruction of the Ottoman succession upon the fall of the Empire, you should take possession of Egypt, I shall have no objection to offer. I could say the same thing of Candia. That island might suit you, and I do not see why it should not become an English possession.

Sir Hamilton Seymour, in reply to the Emperor, said to his Government:—

I simply observed that I had always understood that the English views upon Egypt did not go beyond the part of securing a safe and ready communication between British India and the Mother Country.

"Well," said the Emperor, "induce your Government to write again upon this subject—to write more fully and do so without hesitation. I have confidence in the British Government. It is not an engagement or convention which I ask of them; it is a free interchange of ideas in case of need—the word of a gentleman—that is enough between us."

In reporting these conversations to the Foreign Secretary, Sir Hamilton Seymour expressed his own opinion as follows:—

It can hardly be otherwise but that the Sovereign who insists with such pertinacity upon the impending fall of a neighbouring State must have settled in his own mind that the hour, if not *of* the dissolution, at all events *for* the dissolution, must be at hand.

In answer to these overtures the British Government, through Lord John Russell, the Foreign Secretary, disclaimed all intention of aiming at the acquisition either of Constantinople or any other of the Sultan's possessions, and accepted the assurances of the like effect which were given by the Czar. It combated the opinion that the extinction of the Ottoman Empire was near at hand and deprecated a discussion based on this supposition as leading directly to produce the very result against which it was hoped to provide. Finally, the British Government, with abundance of courtesy, but in terms very stringent and clear, peremptorily refused to enter into any kind of secret engagement with Russia for the settlement of the Eastern question.

Lord Clarendon, who succeeded Lord John Russell as Foreign Minister in the course of these proceedings, in a final despatch to Sir Hamilton Seymour (March 23, 1853), expressed the following opinion:—

Turkey only requires forbearance on the part of its allies, and a determination not to press their claims in a manner humiliating to the dignity and independence of the Sultan—that friendly support, in short, which among States as well as individuals the weak are entitled to expect from the strong— in order not only to prolong its existence but to remove all cause for alarm respecting its dissolution.

It will be seen that the British Government took much too sanguine a view of the prospects of reformed Government in Turkey, and that the Emperor of Russia was much nearer the mark.

We have quoted these conversations at length because of their extreme importance when read by the light of subsequent events. They produced a bad impression at the time on the British Government, and still more so on public opinion in England, when later they were made public.[35] It was thought that they indicated a deliberate intention on the part of the Emperor of Russia to force the Eastern question to the front, and to dismember the Ottoman Empire by a partition of the same kind as that to which Poland had been treated, a few years back, and in which Russia would have the lion's share.

A more reasonable view may now be taken of the policy of the Emperor Nicholas. Subsequent events have conclusively shown that he was fully justified in describing the Turkish Empire as sick, almost to death, for since then it has lost almost the whole of its dominions in Europe. Russia also has acquired but a very small share of the vast territories that have been taken from it. It is also subject to the reflection that, although the British Government in 1852 disclaimed any wish or intention to join in a scheme of partition of the Ottoman Empire, it has since acquired a considerable part of it, approximating to the offer of the Czar—namely Egypt, the Sudan, and the island of Cyprus.

Early in 1853 the Czar sent as a special envoy to the Porte Prince Menschikof, a rude and bluff soldier. He was instructed to insist on Russia's claim to the guardianship of the Holy Sepulchre, in opposition to that of France, and with a further demand, of a more serious kind, for a protectorate in matters of religion over members of the Greek Church throughout the Ottoman Empire.

It was no doubt in consequence of the conversations of the Czar with Sir Hamilton Seymour and of this special mission of Prince Menschikof that Canning, who had, in 1852, resigned the embassy at Constantinople, and had been created a peer, with the title of Lord Stratford de Redcliffe, was again sent as ambassador to the Porte by Lord Clarendon, who was now Foreign Minister in England. Lord Stratford himself appears to have drawn up the instructions of the Foreign Office. He was directed to neutralize, by England's moral influence, the alarming position opened up by the demands, as regards the Holy Places and other matters, of Russia and France, and the dictatorial, if not hostile, attitude they had assumed. He was left unfettered for the settlement of the Holy Places. His own judgment and discretion might be trusted to guide him. The Porte was to be told that it had to thank its own maladministration and the accumulated grievances of foreign nations for the menacing tone now adopted towards it by certain Powers; that a general revolt of its Christian subjects might ensue; that the crisis was one which required the utmost prudence on the part of the Porte, and confidence in the sincerity and soundness of the advice it would receive from him, to resolve it favourably for its future peace and independence. He was to counsel reform in the administration of Turkey, by which alone the sympathy of the British nation could be preserved.

In the event of imminent danger to the existence of the Turkish Government, the ambassador was authorized to request the admiral in command of the British fleet at Malta to hold himself in readiness, but he was not to direct the approach of the fleet to the Dardanelles without positive instructions from her Majesty's Government.

Lord Stratford, on arrival at Constantinople, found that his protégé, Reschid Pasha, had been dismissed from the post of Grand Vizier, at the instance of the new envoy of Russia, and replaced by a pasha favourable to that Power. Prince Menschikof, by the use of menaces, and probably with the aid of bribes, had obtained a commanding influence over the Sultan's Government. He insisted that his demands on the Porte should be kept secret, and threatened to leave Constantinople if they were divulged to the British

Ambassador. Lord Stratford, however, found no difficulty in obtaining full information as to the Russian demands. He showed very great diplomatic skill in separating the question of the Holy Places from the more serious one of the protectorate over the Greek Church. He contrived to settle between Russia, France, and the Porte the dispute as to the Holy Sepulchre. There remained, however, the more serious one of the protectorate. This was aggravated by personal rivalry and hate between the Czar Nicholas and Lord Stratford. The real question in dispute became largely whether Russian or British influence was to predominate in Turkey, and whether reforms, so essential for the security and well-being of its Christian population, were to be carried out under a protectorate by Russia or by England. It is impossible to read the able biography of Lord Stratford by Mr. Lane Poole, or Mr. Kinglake's well-known chapters on the causes which led to the Crimean War, without concluding that the policy of England at this crisis was virtually directed, not by the British Cabinet in London, but by Lord Stratford at the Embassy at Constantinople. Prince Menschikof, in the struggle which ensued at the Porte, was little competent to contend against so practised and wary a diplomat as Stratford, and was completely worsted in the attempt.

Early in May, after the arrival of Stratford, a reconstruction of the Turkish ministry was effected at his instance. The nominee of Russia was dismissed. Ref'at Pasha took his place as Grand Vizier, and Reschid, Lord Stratford's main ally, was reinstated in office as Minister of Foreign Affairs.

By Stratford's advice the Porte determined to resist the Russian demands. The claim to protect the members of the Greek Church was pronounced to be inadmissible. Prince Menschikof was informed to this effect, and on May 21st he broke off diplomatic relations with the Porte, and left Constantinople in high dudgeon. This was followed, on May 31st, by an arrogant despatch to the Porte from the Russian Government, insisting on the acceptance of the Menschikof demands. At the instance of Stratford, the Porte again refused, and thereupon a Russian army crossed the Pruth, on July 3rd, and occupied Moldavia and Wallachia. In a manifesto, issued a few days later, the Czar disclaimed any intention of conquest, and justified his occupation of the provinces as a material guarantee for the fulfilment of his demands on behalf of the Christian population of Turkey.

That there was ample cause for the complaints of the Russian Government of the maltreatment of the Christian population in Turkey cannot be disputed. On July 22, 1853, Lord Stratford himself, in a formal communication to the Porte, forwarded reports from the British Consuls at Scutari, Monastir, and Prevesa, which detailed "acts of disorder, injustice, and corruption of a very atrocious kind, which he had frequently brought to the notice of the Ottoman Porte." He complained that the assurances given by the late Grand Vizier of remedies for such evils had not been carried out, and he observed, with extreme disappointment and pain, the continuance of evils which affected so deeply the welfare of the Empire.

Again, on July 4th of the same year, in a further communication to the Porte, Lord Stratford wrote:—

The character of disorderly and brutal outrages may be said with truth to be in general that of Mussulman fanaticism, excited by cupidity and hatred against the Sultan's Christian vassals.

Unless some powerful means be applied without further delay, it is to be feared that the authority of the central Government will be completely overpowered and that the people, despairing of protection, will augment the disorder by resorting to lawless means of self-preservation.

Lord Clarendon, the Foreign Minister, also, in a communication to the British Ambassador, showed that he was fully alive to the serious character of the disorders in the Turkish Empire. He wrote:—

It is impossible to suppose that any true sympathy for their rulers will be felt by the Christian subjects of the Porte, so long as they are made to experience in all their daily transactions the inferiority of their position as compared with that of their Mussulman fellow-subjects; so long as they are aware that they will seek in vain for justice for wrongs done either to their persons or their properties, because they are deemed a degraded race, unworthy to be put into comparison with the followers of Mahomet. Your Excellency will plainly and authoritatively state to the Porte that this state of things cannot be longer tolerated by Christian Powers. The Porte must decide between the maintenance of an erroneous principle and the loss of sympathy and support of its allies.

In spite, however, of the experience of the futility of all past promises to carry out the most elementary reforms in favour of the Christian subjects of the Porte, both Lord Stratford and Lord Clarendon appear to have based their policy largely on the belief that the Porte would be more amenable in the future.

The occupation of the Danubian principalities by a Russian army did not of itself necessarily involve war with Turkey. Though the Sultan was suzerain of these provinces, they enjoyed complete autonomy under the protection of Russia. Under certain conditions that Power was entitled to send its army there. But the continued occupation of them was clearly antagonistic to the sovereign rights of the Sultan and would ultimately lead to war.

With a view to avoid war, a conference was held by the representatives of all the Powers except Russia at Vienna, and an agreement was arrived at for the settlement of the question between Russia and Turkey by England, France, Austria, and Prussia. This was agreed to by Russia. It was commended to the Porte by the Powers, and Lord Stratford was instructed by Lord Clarendon to use all his efforts to obtain its consent.

Officially, Lord Stratford performed his task in due accord with the instructions of Lord Clarendon. But his biographer and, still more, Mr. Kinglake admit that the rejection of the Vienna demand was mainly due to the British Ambassador. After quoting the words of Lord Stratford, in which he described his efforts to induce the Porte to accede to it, Kinglake writes:—

These were dutiful words. But it is not to be believed that, even if he strove to do so, Lord Stratford could hide his real thoughts from the Turkish ministers. There was that in his very presence which disclosed his volition; for if the thin, disciplined lips moved in obedience to constituted authorities, men who knew how to read the meaning of his brow, and the light which kindled beneath, could gather that the ambassador's thoughts concerning the Home Governments of the four Great Powers of Europe were little else than an angry *quos ego*; the sagacious Turks would look more to the great signs than to the terms of formal advice sent out from London, and if they saw that Lord Stratford was, in his heart, against the opinion of Europe, they could easily resolve to follow his known desire and to disobey his mere words. The result was that without any sign of painful doubt the Turkish Government determined to stand firm.

This is the view of a panegyrist of Lord Stratford. We have quoted it for the purpose of showing that it was practically Lord Stratford who guided the Turkish Government in this matter.

After the failure of the settlement prepared at the Vienna Conference, the Porte, on October 1st, by the advice of Lord Stratford, made a formal demand on Russia for the evacuation of the Danubian principalities, and in default of this, a fortnight later it declared war. The Turks then boldly took the initiative. Their army, under Omar Pasha, crossed the Danube in November, 1853, and fought two battles successfully against the Russians at Oltenitza and Citale in Wallachia.

Meanwhile, on October 22nd, when Russia and Turkey were already at war, the fleets of England and France entered the Dardanelles. Though this was not an infraction of the treaty of 1841, it was a distinctly hostile act on the part of these Powers against Russia. But negotiations still continued. Whatever hopes, however, there were of a favourable issue were destroyed when, on November 30th, a Russian fleet of six battleships, issuing from Sebastopol, attacked and completely destroyed a Turkish squadron of eleven cruisers and smaller vessels lying at anchor in the port of Sinope, on the coast of Asia Minor. Four thousand Turkish sailors perished in this engagement. This was an act of war, as legitimate as the attack by the Ottoman army on the Russian force north of the Danube, the more so as the Turkish vessels were believed to be carrying munitions of war to arm the Circassians against Russia. It caused, however, an immense sensation in England and France. It was denounced as an act of treachery and as a massacre rather than a legitimate naval action. The fleets of the two Powers then lying in the Bosphorus were at once instructed to enter the Black Sea and to invite any Russian ships of war they might meet there to return to their ports. They were to prevent any further attack on Turkey. This made war inevitable. But negotiations were still for a time continued, and it was not till March 28, 1854, that war was actually declared against Russia by England and France. Armies were then sent by these Powers to Constantinople, and thence to Varna, in the Black Sea, with the object of protecting Turkey against the attack of a Russian army and of assisting the former in compelling the evacuation by the Russians of the two Danubian provinces.

Meanwhile, early in the spring of this year (1854), a Russian army had crossed the Danube and had invested Silistria, the great fortress which barred the way to the Balkans and Constantinople. It was defended with the utmost bravery and tenacity by a Turkish army under Moussa Pasha, assisted by two British engineer officers, Butler and Nasmyth. On June 25th the Russians recognized that they could not capture the fortress. They raised the siege and retreated across the Danube, after incurring immense loss of life and material.

All danger of an advance by the Russians across the Danube and the Balkans was now at an end. The Turks unaided had effectually prevented any such project. The Russian army thereupon retreated from the Danubian principalities. Their place there was taken by an Austrian army, with the consent of both Russia and the two Western Powers. No reason existed, therefore, why the war should be continued, so far as England and France were concerned. There was no longer any necessity for their armies to defend the frontiers of Turkey. But a war spirit had been roused in the two countries and was not to be allayed without much shedding of blood. The two Powers decided to use their armies which had been collected at Varna for the invasion of the Crimea and the destruction of the naval arsenal at Sebastopol, which was regarded as a permanent menace to Turkey.

Thenceforth, the part of the Turks in the war became subordinate and even insignificant. The war was fought *à outrance* between the two allied Powers and Russia. The successful landing of the two armies at Eupatoria, in the Crimea, their splendid victory over the Russian army at the Alma, their flank march to the south of Sebastopol, the commencement of the long siege of that fortress, the famous battles of Balaklava and Inkerman and the terrible sufferings of the British army in the winter of 1854-5, the memorable defence of Sebastopol under General Todleben, the capture of the Malakoff by the French on September 8th, 1855, and the consequent evacuation of the city and forts of Sebastopol, on the southern side of its great harbour, are events of the deepest interest in the histories of the allied Powers and Russia, but have comparatively little bearing on our present theme. Very little use was, in fact, made of the Turkish army by the Allies in the course of the war. A division of seven thousand men was sent to the Crimea in the autumn of 1854, and was employed for the defence of Balaklava. It was led by most incompetent officers, and when attacked by the Russians on the morning of the Battle of Balaklava, the men precipitately fled. This exposed the flank of the allied army to great danger. Later, another Turkish force under Omar Pasha was sent to Eupatoria. It was attacked there by a much superior Russian army, early in 1855, and fighting behind earthworks it made a very effective resistance and completely repulsed the Russians. It was said that the humiliation of this defeat of his troops by the despised Turks was the immediate cause of the death of the Emperor Nicholas.

In Asia Minor another Russian army invaded Turkish territory and laid siege to the fortress of Kars. There followed the memorable defence of this stronghold by the Turks, assisted, if not commanded, by General Williams, later Sir Fenwick Williams, and Colonel Teesdale. It was ultimately, after a four months' siege, compelled by want of food and munitions to capitulate. The failure to relieve it was due to the grossest and most culpable negligence of the Turkish Government. In this siege and in that of Silistria and the defence of Eupatoria, the Turkish soldiers gave ample proof that when well led they had lost none of their pristine valour in defence of earthworks. The allied Powers, however, seem to have been quite ignorant or unmindful of the military value of the Turkish soldiers and made little or no practical use of them. An army of fifty thousand Turks led by English or French officers would have been of the utmost value in the earlier part of the war. It was only towards the close of it that twenty thousand Turks were enrolled under British officers. But this action was too late, and they took no part in the war.

The writer, as a young man, spent a month in the Crimea in 1855, and was present as a spectator on Cathcart's Hill on the eventful day when the Malakoff was captured by the French, and the British were repulsed in their attack on the Redan. He well recollects the prevalent opinion among British officers, whom he met, that the Turkish army was a negligible force and of no military value in the field. This opinion was abundantly shown in the attitude of British and French soldiers to the Turkish soldiers whenever they met, and must have been very galling to the pride and self-respect of the latter.

The capture of the Malakoff, a great feat of arms on the part of the French army, was the last important event in the campaign of 1855. Early in 1856 there were strong indications that the Emperor of the French was weary of the war. Public opinion in France declared itself unmistakably against its continuance. France had nothing to gain by its prolongation. Its military pride had been satisfied by success in the capture of Sebastopol and the destruction of the Russian fleet. Its army in the Crimea was suffering severely from disease. With the British it was otherwise. Their army before the enemy was in greater force than at any previous period of the war. It was eager to retrieve its prestige, which had been somewhat impaired by the failure at the Redan. The British Government was as anxious for another campaign as was the army. But without their French ally they could obviously do nothing. The French Emperor entered into secret negotiations with the Emperor Alexander, who had succeeded Nicholas. The success of the Russian army in the capture of Kars and the valour it had shown in defence of Sebastopol made it easy to negotiate peace without slur on its military fame. It is impossible for us, who now look back on these times, to perceive what possible object could have been gained by England in prolonging the war. The projects of completing the conquest of the Crimea, and of sending an army to the Caucasus in aid of the Circassians, and another army to the Baltic to free Finland from Russia, were fantastic and perilous. England was saved from these adventures by the wiser policy of the French. The British Government against its will was compelled to enter into a negotiation for peace. This was effected through the mediation of Austria. Terms were provisionally agreed to, and a Congress of the Great Powers was held in Paris in 1856, at which a treaty of peace was finally concluded.

Under the terms of this treaty all the territories conquered by Russia in Asia or by the allied Powers in Europe were restored to their former owners. The small part of Bessarabia conceded to Russia by the treaty of Bucharest and giving access to the Danube was reannexed to Moldavia. The exclusive protectorate of Russia over the two Danubian principalities was abolished, and they were placed under the joint protection of all the Great Powers. The suzerainty of the Sultan over them was recognized. But the Porte engaged to preserve for them an independent and national administration, with full liberty of worship, of legislation, and of commerce. They were to be permitted to organize national armed forces. Serbia was accorded the same treatment, except as regards a national army, but the armed intervention of the Porte was to be permitted only with the consent of the Powers who were signatories to the treaty. The Black Sea was neutralized. It was thrown open to the mercantile marine of all nations, but was interdicted to the war vessels of either Russia or Turkey, and these two Powers engaged not to establish or maintain any military maritime arsenals on its coasts.

As regards the internal administration of Turkey and the treatment of its Christian population, the treaty contained the following clause:—

The Sultan, having by his constant solicitude for the welfare of his subjects issued a firman (the Hatti-Humayun), which, while ameliorating their condition without distinction of religion or race, records his generous intentions towards the Christian population of his Empire, and wishing to give a further proof of his sentiments in that direction, has resolved to communicate to the contracting Powers the said firman emanating spontaneously from his sovereign will. The contracting Powers recognize the high value of this communication. It is clearly understood that it cannot give to the said Powers the right to interfere either collectively or individually in the relations of H.M. the Sultan with his subjects or in the internal administration of his Empire.

The latter part of the clause, it will be seen, completely nullified and destroyed the effect of the earlier part of it, and practically gave full licence to the Sultan to continue his misgovernment of his Empire and to refuse the just demands of his Christian subjects—a very lame and impotent conclusion to the war.

In explanation of this clause, it should be stated that Lord Stratford, shortly before the meeting of the Congress, had succeeded, after long efforts, in extracting from the Porte another charter of reform in favour of its Christian subjects, known as the Hatti-Humayun. This was referred to in the treaty, not as an act binding on the Porte, but merely as an indication of the Sultan's good intentions, and with the express condition that neither the Great Powers signatories to the treaty nor any one of them were to be entitled to call him to account in the event of his pious intentions not being carried into effect. Lord Stratford, when he heard at Constantinople of the intentions of the Congress, but before a final conclusion was arrived at, wrote to Lord Clarendon the following strong protest:—

There are many able and experienced men in this country who view with alarm the supposed intention of the Conference at Paris to record the Sultan's late Firman of Privileges (the Hatti-Humayun) in the treaty of peace, and at the same time to declare that the Powers of Europe disclaim all right of interference between the Sultan and his subjects. They argue thus: The Imperial firman places the Christians and the Mussulmans on an equal footing as to civil rights. It is believed that the Porte will never of its own accord carry the provisions of the firman seriously into effect. The treaty, in its supposed form, would therefore confirm the right and extinguish the hope of the Christians. Despair on their side and fear on that of the Turks would, in that case, engender the bitterest animosity between them, and not improbably bring on a deadly struggle before long.[36]

- 240 -

This protest, which doubtless represented Lord Stratford's own convictions, was of no avail. Lord Clarendon was powerless at the Congress. He met with no support from the French representatives. They cared nothing for reforms in Turkey. The Russians, in view of the origin of the war and the refusal of the other Powers to recognize their claim to intervention on behalf of the Christians in Turkey, were naturally indisposed to concede it to others, either individually or collectively. The nullifying provision was inserted in the treaty. It abrogated whatever effect the recognition of the firman might have had. The Hatti-Humayun became, *ipso facto*, a dead letter. Lord Stratford was bitterly disappointed. "He felt very keenly," says his biographer, "the pusillanimity of his own Government, who had made him a victim to their deference to France." In a letter to his brother after the conclusion of the treaty, Lord Stratford wrote: "To be the victim of so much trickery and dupery and charlatanism is no small trial. But I have faith in principles as working out their own justification, and fix my thoughts steadily on that coming day when the peace of Paris will be felt and its miserable consequences."

Lord Clarendon, in a letter to the ambassador, thus described his own views of the treaty:—

I think as you do about the terms of peace, but I am not the least sorry that peace is made, because, notwithstanding our means of carrying on the war, I believe we should have run risks by so doing for which no possible success would have compensated. We should have been alone.... If you could have seen all that was passing when I got to Paris—the bitterness of feeling against us, the kindly (I might almost say the enthusiastic) feeling towards Russia, and the determination, if necessary, to throw over the Vienna conditions in order to prevent the resumption of hostilities (money matters and Bourse speculations being the main cause), you would have felt as I did, that our position was not agreeable, and that Brunnow was justified in saying that they did not come to make or negotiate peace, but to accept the peace which was to be crammed down their throats.... Unluckily, too, just as negotiations began the French army fell ill, and the Emperor himself admitted to me that, with twenty-two thousand men in hospital and likely to be more, peace had almost become a military as well as a financial and political necessity for him.[37]

Lord Stratford's words on hearing that the treaty was signed were, "I would rather have cut off my right hand than have signed that treaty."

The writer paid a second visit to Constantinople in 1857. He rode there from Belgrade, passing through Bulgaria on the way, and was witness of the miserable condition to which this province had been reduced by Ottoman rule. He spent a few weeks at Therapia, where the Ambassador was residing, and was favoured by many conversations with him. Lord Stratford was always most kind and communicative to young men. He made no secret of his bitter disappointment. The treaty of Paris, he alleged, was a death-blow to the cause of reform in Turkey. If the Christian population were not protected from misgovernment, the Empire was doomed. He was under no illusion as to the misgovernment of the country. He knew that if left to themselves the Turks would do nothing, and that all the reforms promised by the Hatti-Humayun which he had obtained with so much labour and difficulty before the conclusion of the Crimean War would remain unexecuted and would be a dead letter. He considered that England had been betrayed at the Congress of Paris, that the clause in the treaty which embodied the Hatti-Humayun was nullified by the provision that its recognition did not entitle the Great Powers either collectively or separately to interfere in the internal affairs of Turkey. He held that this was fatal to the enforcement of the new reforms. He maintained that the only way to induce the Turks to act in accordance with them was through threats and fear, and that some external Power should bring such pressure to bear on them. This might be done by England alone, or by England in alliance with France, or by the Great Powers collectively. He preferred the first of these; he had little hope of the last; but the treaty had extinguished all methods equally.[38] It was the last year of the Great Elchi's reign at Constantinople. He retired from his post and from the public service in the following year at the age of seventy-one.

He was succeeded by Sir Henry Bulwer, later Lord Dalling, an ambassador of a very different type. Though an able diplomat, he cared nothing for reform in Turkey. He allowed himself to be placed under personal obligation to the Sultan, which destroyed his influence. He made no effort to induce, still less to compel, the Porte to give effect to the Hatti-Humayun which his predecessor had obtained with so much labour.

The cause of reform in Turkey [says Mr. Lane Poole], for which Lord Stratford had striven for so many years, began its downward course when the Turks understood the altered character of the British Embassy under Sir Henry Bulwer. Lord Stratford's farewell to Constantinople was the occasion for a stately ceremony, in which the Sultan and all his ministers and the whole population joined in paying a last tribute to the departing Elchi.... He knew, however, that he was assisting in the obsequies of his hopes. His long struggle for reform of the Ottoman Empire was at an end, and in the character of his successor he could trace the antithesis of all he had striven for, the abandonment of all he had won.[39]

Lord Stratford lived on in retirement to the age of ninety-three, long enough to see the verification of all his fears as to the effect of the unfortunate clause in the treaty of Paris in nullifying the promises of reforms in Turkey and of all his predictions as to the result of this in the revolt in 1874 of the Christian populations of Bosnia, Herzegovina, and Bulgaria under the stress of appalling misgovernment and tyranny, and in their final liberation from Turkish rule by the armies of Russia. On this occasion the revolt of these subjects of the Porte had his full sympathy, and he admitted that Russia was fully justified in its intervention.[40]

Mr. Gladstone in 1876 dedicated to Lord Stratford his pamphlet on Bulgarian atrocities, which had such a powerful effect in preventing England from taking up arms again in support of Turkey.[41]

Looking back at the Crimean War, it is now possible for us to perceive and admit that its main, if not its only, result was to postpone for a few years the break up of the Turkish Empire in Europe. It negatived for a time the claim of Russia to an exclusive protectorate over the Christian populations of the Balkans which would secure to them the benefit of good government. Lord Stratford's hopes of a reformed Turkish Empire, more or less under the ægis of England, were frustrated by the treaty of Paris. As a result, no reforms were effected in Turkey. Its downward course was retarded, but not averted. When, in 1876, the accumulated grievances of the Christian population compelled an outbreak, it will be seen that the intervention of Russia on their behalf was practically admitted by England and the other Great Powers.

Abdul Mehzid died in 1861. He had not realized even the small promise of his youth. He had many instincts that were sound and good. He was the most humane of the long list of Sultans. He fully recognized the urgent necessity for reforms in his State, in order to bring it into line with other civilized States in Europe. But he had not the energy or the will to carry them into effect, and the programme of reform conceded to Lord Stratford remained a dead letter. He was prematurely aged by debauchery. He was the first Sultan to fall into the hands of moneylenders of Western Europe. Great sums were borrowed ostensibly for the war with Russia. But the larger part of them was expended by Abdul Mehzid in wild extravagance, in gratifying the caprices of the multitude of women in his harem, in building palaces, and in satisfying the demands of corrupt ministers. On the occasion of the marriage of one of his daughters with the son of a Grand Vizier he spent forty millions of francs on her trousseau and in fêtes. Meanwhile the services of the State were neglected, nothing was done to relieve Kars, and corruption spread in all directions.

Abdul Aziz, who succeeded his brother and reigned for fifteen years, was physically one of the finest of his race. He was majestic in appearance. His mien was gracious. He was every inch a Sultan. But this was about all that could be said for him. His mind was vacuous. His education had been neglected. He had spent many years in forced seclusion, but had secretly intrigued with the more fanatical party in the State against his brother, and had raised hopes that on coming to the throne he would reverse the measures of reform, such as they were, which his two predecessors had initiated. But he belied these expectations for a time. On his accession he issued a proclamation announcing his intention to follow his two predecessors in the path of reform. He promised to economize the resources of the State and to reduce the vast expenditure of the palace. He pensioned off the multitudes of concubines of his brother, and gave out that he meant to content himself with the most modest harem. But these proved to be no more than good intentions, which only paved the way to very opposite measures. Before long his own retinue of women was increased to nine hundred, and the number of eunuchs in his palace to three thousand. His extravagance soon emulated that of his brother. His reign was one of external peace, which afforded full opportunity for giving effect to the reforms promised by his brother and registered by the treaty of Paris. Nothing was ever done. The firman proved to be a dead letter. His ministers cared no more than himself for reforms. Successive British Ambassadors made no serious efforts in this direction. Indeed, they were precluded by the treaty of Paris from any exclusive pressure on the Porte, without the support of all the other Powers.

The reign was chiefly conspicuous for the enormous borrowings of money in London and Paris by the Porte, following on the bad example set by Abdul Mehzid. The debt was rapidly increased by Abdul Aziz till it reached a total of nearly two hundred millions sterling. It does not appear that the accruing interest on this great debt was ever paid out of the revenues of the Empire. Fresh loans were continually raised, out of which the accumulated interest on previous loans was provided. Huge commissions to financiers who brought out the loans, and bribes to pashas for consenting to their issue, accounted for another large part of the borrowed money. What remained was mainly devoted by the Sultan to new palaces and to extravagances of his harem. This merry game went on as long as credulous people in Western Europe could be induced to continue lending. But the credit of the Turkish Empire was exhausted in 1874. A repudiation of half of the interest was then announced, and in the following year the remaining half was repudiated. This did much to weaken the interest of Western Europe in the Turkish cause. Eventually a composition was arrived at with the creditors of the State. An International Commission was appointed, in whom certain revenues of the State were vested, out of which the interest of a greatly reduced total of the original debt was to be paid. The principle of foreign control over the finance of the Empire was thus introduced.

The Russian Government during this reign, by its skilful diplomacy, backed by threats of force, recovered much of its old influence at the Porte, and its ambassador, General Ignatief, began to dominate its councils and to nominate its Grand Viziers. Three events during the period showed the gradual downward course of the Empire. In 1867 the two Danubian principalities succeeded in accomplishing their long-desired object of uniting together in a single State, thenceforth known as Roumania; and in 1868 Prince Charles of Hohenzollern was elected, and was invested by the Sultan as the hereditary ruler of this new State. The union of the two provinces into a single State practically secured independence to it, while the connection of its ruler with the reigning family of Prussia marked the advent of that Power into the political system of the Christian States founded on the débris of the Turkish Empire in Europe, and was the first of many important alliances of which we now see the intent and result. Serbia also made an important advance to independence. In 1867 the Turkish garrison in Belgrade, the occupation of which had been confirmed by the treaty of Paris, was withdrawn by the Porte. These two events were the result of pressure of the ambassadors of the Great Powers, who were anxious to minimize the causes of friction to the Porte, which did not add to its real strength.

Another important event was the repudiation by Russia on October 31, 1870, during the Franco-German War, of the clause in the treaty of Paris of 1856 which interdicted the Black Sea to Russian and Turkish vessels of war, and forbade to both Powers the creation or maintenance of naval arsenals on the coasts of that sea. We now know that Prince Bismarck, on behalf of Prussia, secured the neutrality of Russia in the war with France, in 1870, by promising to support this repudiation by the Czar of his treaty obligation. Complaint has not unfrequently been made of the refusal or neglect of the British Government, of which Mr. Gladstone was then the head, to insist on the maintenance of this treaty by Russia, even at the risk of war. But the Porte, in whose interest the provision had been framed by the Congress of Paris, and which was primarily concerned in its maintenance, showed no desire or intention to make its breach by Russia a *casus belli*, and it would have been sheer madness for England, either with or without Turkey, to have taken up the challenge of the Czar. A humiliating restriction such as this on the sovereign rights of a great country was obviously of a temporary character, and could not, in the nature of things, be a permanent arrangement. It had served its purpose by giving to the Porte a respite of fourteen years from naval attack by Russia. Lord Palmerston, who was Prime Minister in England when the treaty was made, had himself put on record the opinion that the enforced neutrality of the Black Sea might be expected to last for fifteen years. It is to be noted that some years would necessarily elapse after the repudiation of the treaty before a Russian fleet could be created in the Black Sea and before Sebastopol could be restored as a naval base. In point of fact, in the war, which was soon to break out between Russia and Turkey, in 1877, the latter Power had virtual command of the Black Sea, and the Russian army which crossed the Balkans and advanced to the vicinity of Constantinople did so without the support of a naval force in the Black Sea, as had been the case in 1829.

Another event also occurred in 1870, the significance of which was not fully appreciated at the time. Previous to that year the Christian Slav populations of the Balkans, such as the Bulgarians, Bosnians, and others, were under the spiritual jurisdiction of the Greek Ecumenical Patriarch and were regarded as Greeks. The ancient history of Bulgaria and its claims to a distinct nationality appear to have been forgotten or ignored by politicians interested in the Eastern question. On March 10, 1870, Abdul Aziz, under pressure from Russia, backed by its able ambassador, General Ignatief, issued a firman recognizing the separate existence of Bulgaria, and creating for it a national Church independent of the Greek Church, though differing in no important respect in point of doctrine or ritual. This laid the foundation for a new nationality in the Balkans. Bulgaria, long forgotten, emerged from obscurity and came to the front as a competitor of the Greeks. The importance of this will be appreciated later, when we come to the rivalry of these races for the débris of the Ottoman Empire in Europe.

In 1876 a bloodless revolution took place in Constantinople. A new ministry was forced upon Abdul Aziz, of which Midhat Pasha—one of the few genuine and convinced reformers among the leading Turks—was a member. They decided to depose the Sultan. They obtained a *fetva* from the Mufti justifying this on the ground of his incapacity and extravagance. No single hand was raised in his favour. After a vain protest, he submitted to his fate, and was removed from his palace to another building destined to be his prison. Four days later he was found dead there, and nineteen physicians of the city, including men of all nationalities, testified that Abdul Aziz died by his own hand.

XXI

ABDUL HAMID II
1876-1909

ON the deposition of Abdul Aziz, his nephew, the eldest son of Abdul Mehzid, much against his will, was proclaimed as Sultan, under the title of Murad V. His feeble mind, reduced to a nullity by long seclusion in the Cage, and by the habit of intemperance, was completely unhinged by this unexpected elevation, and after a few weeks—on August 31, 1876—it became necessary for the committee of ministers who had set him on the throne to depose him in favour of the next heir. His brother, Abdul Hamid II, held the Sultanate for thirty-three years, and is still alive, in the custody of another brother, the present Sultan, after being deposed, in his turn, in 1909.

Abdul Hamid proved to be the most mean, cunning, untrustworthy, and cruel intriguer of the long dynasty of Othman. His mother was an Armenian. He was destitute of physical courage. He lived in constant fear of plots and assassination, and in suspicion of every one about him. He trusted no one, least of all his ministers. He allowed no consultations between them. If he heard that two of them had met in private, his suspicions were aroused and they were called to account. He employed a huge army of spies, who reported to him directly and daily as to the doings of his ministers, of the ambassadors, and of any one else of importance. They fed him with reports, often false, on which he founded his actions. Plots were invented in order to induce him to consent to measures which otherwise he would not have sanctioned. He claimed and exercised the right of secret assassination of his foes or suspected foes. No natives of Turkey were safe. They might disappear at any moment, as so many thousands had done by the order of the Sultan, through some secret agent, either to death or exile. This was not so much from pure wickedness of heart as from fear of being assassinated himself, and the belief that his safety lay in exterminating his enemies before they had the chance of maturing their plans against himself. The ambassadors of foreign Powers had little influence with him, except so far as they were able to threaten the use of armed force, when, sooner than risk war, he gave way. He showed great cunning in playing off one ambassador against another, and was an adept in all the meanest intrigues of diplomacy.

Abdul Hamid's life was one of incessant labour. He devoted himself most assiduously to the work of his great office. Whatever his demerits, he was absolute master of his ministers and of his State. There never was a more centralized and meticulous despotism. As he trusted no one, he was overwhelmed by most trivial details and graver questions were neglected. He could not, indeed, administer the vast affairs of his Empire without information or advice from others, but no one knew from day to day who was the person on whose advice the Sultan overruled his ostensible ministers, whether a favourite lady of his harem, or a eunuch, or some fanatical dervish, or an astrologer, or a spy. There was constant confusion in the State, arising from antagonism between the officials of the Porte and the minions of the palace.

Outwardly, Abdul Hamid had the manners of a gentleman, but inwardly he was as mean a villain as could be found in the purlieus of his capital. He was avaricious to an extreme, and though his expenditure was most lavish and his charities wide, he amassed immense wealth, which he invested secretly through German bankers against the rainy day which he expected. When it came and he was deposed, amid universal execration and loathing, his life was spared in the hope mainly of extracting from him these secret investments. He was not above receiving bribes himself, on a great scale, from financiers in search of concessions. He did nothing to check the chief evil of Turkish rule—the sale of offices and the necessity for officials to recoup themselves for their outlay by local exactions. Though he was not without some instincts for good government, and was free from any fanaticism, his system was such that everything went to the bad in his reign, and that many years of peace, after the treaty of Berlin, were attended by no improvement in the condition of his people, but the reverse. The result of his policy was that his Empire suffered a greater dismemberment than had been the bad fortune of any of his predecessors, and as he monopolized power, he must be held mainly responsible for its evil results.

At the very outset of his reign Abdul Hamid was confronted with most serious questions affecting the integrity of his Empire. In 1875 an outbreak had occurred in Bosnia and Herzegovina, the result not merely of misgovernment by the Turkish pashas and officials, their rapacity and exactions, and of the system of farming the taxes, but of a vicious agrarian system. The great majority of landowners, though of the same Slav race as the rayas, the cultivators of the soil, were Moslems by religion. Their forbears had become so when the Ottomans conquered their State in order to save their property. They were as rapacious and fanatical as any landowners of Turkish race in any part of the Empire. No Christians were employed in the administration of these provinces. The evidence of the Christian rayas was not admitted in the courts of law. Justice or injustice could only be obtained by bribes. The police and other officials lived by extorting money from those whom it was their duty to defend.

The bad harvest of 1874 was the immediate cause of the outbreak, for the farmers of the taxes refused to make any concessions. It was, in the first instance, directed rather against the Moslem landowners and the local

Turkish officials than against the Sultan, but it rapidly developed into a general insurrection against the Sultan's government. Every effort was made by Austria and Russia to localize it and to induce the Porte to make concessions. Count Andrassy, the Austro-Hungarian Foreign Minister, drew up a scheme for the pacification of the two provinces. It proposed that the system of farming the taxes should be abolished, that the taxes raised in the provinces should be expended locally for their benefit, that complete religious equality should be established, and that a mixed commission should be appointed to supervise the carrying out of these reforms. The scheme was agreed to by Russia, Great Britain, and the other Powers, and was presented to the Sultan, who acquiesced in it. But it proved, like other promises of reform in Turkey, to be a dead letter. Not a single step was taken to give effect to any part of it. The rebellion in the two provinces continued. The insurgents increased their demands. They insisted that one-third of the land should be given up to the rayas. The movement soon extended to Bulgaria, which was seething with disaffection.

On April 21, 1876, an outbreak of Bulgarians occurred on the southern slopes of the Rhodope Mountains, of which Batak was the centre. It was put down without difficulty by a small Turkish force sent from Constantinople, under Achmet Agha, with little loss of life to the troops engaged, but with relentless cruelty, not only to the actual insurgents who surrendered on promise of life, but to the whole population of the district. Bands of Bashi-Bazouks, consisting of Tartars from the Crimea who had been planted in Bulgaria, were let loose on them. Indiscriminate murders, rapes, and rapine took place. Sixty villages were burnt. Twelve hundred persons, mostly women and children, took refuge in a church at Batak and were there burnt alive. In all about twelve thousand persons perished in these brutal reprisals. Achmet Agha received a high decoration from the Sultan for this performance. There was nothing new in this method of dealing with an outbreak by the Porte. It was in accord with its traditional system and policy to wreak vengeance on those revolting by orgies of cruelty, which would strike terror among subject races and act as a warning to them in the future.

What was new in the case of the Bulgarians in 1876, and was fraught with misfortune to the Turkish cause, was that full and graphic accounts of the horrors committed at Batak, written by Mr. Edwin Pears (now Sir Edwin), the correspondent at Constantinople of the *Daily News*, appeared in the columns of that paper. They produced a profound impression on public opinion in England. Discredit was thrown on the story in the House of Commons by Mr. Disraeli, the Prime Minister, but it was fully confirmed by Mr. MacGahan, another correspondent of the same paper, who visited the district, and later by Mr. Walter Baring, a member of the British Embassy at Constantinople, who, by the direction of the Government, made full personal inquiries on the spot. He described what had taken place as "perhaps the most heinous crime that has stained the history of the present century."

It was also unfortunate for the Turks that Mr. Gladstone, the only survivor in the House of Commons of the British statesmen responsible for the Crimean War, who had recently retired from the leadership of the Liberal party, was fired by the description of these horrors in Bulgaria to emerge from his retirement and to take up the cause of the Christian population of European Turkey, for which he held that the treaty of Paris had made his country responsible.

Meanwhile the horrors at Batak had also aroused the indignation of Russia and the fears of Austria. A fanatical outbreak of Moslems at Salonika resulted in the murder of the Consuls of France and Germany. Serbia and Montenegro, impelled by sympathy for their fellow Slavs in Bosnia, declared war against Turkey. A Turkish force defeated the Serbians, who appealed to Russia for assistance. At this stage another effort was made by Russia and Austria, supported by Germany, to avert a general conflagration, and a scheme was embodied in what was known as the Berlin Memorandum for compelling the Porte to carry out the reforms which it had admitted to be necessary. The British Government, however, very curtly refused to be a party to the scheme, on the ground that they had not been consulted in framing it and did not believe in its success. About this time also the British fleet in the Mediterranean was ordered to Besika Bay, a step taken avowedly for the purpose of protecting British subjects in the turmoil which had arisen, but which seemed to the Porte to indicate an intention to support them against the demands of the other Powers.

Mr. Gladstone, fearing that these actions indicated the intention of the British Government to withdraw from the concert of Europe and to renew the separate policy which had led to the Crimean War, made a vehement attack on it in the House of Commons for refusing to agree to the Berlin Memorandum. Later, in September 1876, he published his well-known pamphlet on "the Bulgarian Horrors," in which, with passionate language, he dwelt at length on the massacres at Batak and denounced the Turkish Government. He protested that he could no longer bear his share of responsibility for the Crimean War. Otherwise he might be accused of "moral complicity in the basest and blackest outrages upon record in that century."

Those [he wrote] who opposed the Crimean War are especially bound to remember that the treaty of Paris made Europe as a whole, and not Russia alone, responsible for the integrity and independence of the Ottoman Empire, which had given this licence to Turkish officers to rob, murder, and

- 250 -

ravish in Bulgaria.... As an old servant of the Crown and State, I entreat my countrymen, upon whom far more than perhaps any other people of Europe it depends, to require and insist that our Government, which has been working in one direction, shall work in the other, and shall apply all its vigour, in common with the other States of Europe, in obtaining the extinction of the Turkish executive power in Bulgaria. Let the Turks now carry away their abuses in the only possible manner, namely, by carrying off themselves. Their zapties and their mudirs, their bimbashis and their yuzbashis, their kaimakans and their pashas, one and all, bag and baggage, shall, I hope, clear out from the province they have desolated and profaned.[42]

The pamphlet produced an immediate and profound effect on public opinion in Great Britain. It was followed up by speeches of the same force and eloquence on the part of the veteran statesman. Meetings took place in every part of the country, at which sympathy was expressed for the Christian populations of Turkey. The Turks were denounced for their cruelties and bad government. Resolutions were unanimously passed in accord with the policy recommended by Mr. Gladstone. Lord Stratford himself expressed sympathy with the movement, differing only in this from Mr. Gladstone, that England, in his view, should exert its influence not only for the Bulgarians, but for all the oppressed subject races in Turkey. Many of the most cultivated men in England joined in the movement quite irrespective of party politics.

Mr. Disraeli, who was created Earl of Beaconsfield in the course of these events, on his retirement from the House of Commons, showed great courage and persistence in resisting the movement. His sympathies lay wholly in the opposite direction. His Eastern policy was in accord with that of the previous generation of statesmen, such as Palmerston, and, indeed, Gladstone himself in his earlier stage of opinion, who believed that the maintenance of the Turkish Empire was essential to the integrity of the British Empire. He saw no reason for change. He dreaded the further advance of Russia. He did not believe in the honesty of the professions of its Emperor. He enforced his views at a public meeting at Aylesbury on September 20th, and endeavoured to stem the movement. He scoffed at the Bulgarian horrors. He declared the perpetrators of them were not so bad as those who made them the subject of agitation for their political purposes. He was evidently prepared to support the Turks against any invasion of their country by Russia, and to renew the policy of the Crimean War. But it was in vain.

Though the agitation promoted by Mr. Gladstone did not result in inducing the Government to join the other Powers in compelling the Turkish Government to concede autonomy to its Christian provinces, or to carry out reforms, it had two effects of great historical importance, which must be our justification for referring to the subject. It made impossible the renewal of the policy of the Crimean War—the armed support by Great Britain to the Turks against an invasion by Russia on behalf of the Christian population of the Balkans. It paralysed the hands of those, like Lord Beaconsfield, who desired to support the Turks and the *status quo*. On the other hand, it doubtless stimulated Russia to armed intervention, by making it clear that there would be no resistance on the part of Great Britain. Lord Beaconsfield's Cabinet was divided on the subject. A majority of its members evidently concurred with Lord Derby, the Foreign Secretary, in opposition to war with Russia on behalf of Turkey.

On September 21st, the day after Lord Beaconsfield had delivered his fiery pro-Turkish speech at Aylesbury, Lord Derby, on behalf of the Government, in a despatch to the Ambassador at Constantinople, directed him to inform the Porte that the atrocious crimes of the Turkish authorities and troops in Bulgaria had aroused the righteous indignation of the British people, and that Great Britain, as signatory to the treaty of Paris, could not be indifferent to them. He demanded that examples should be made of the perpetrators of these crimes.

On October 30th Lord Derby further informed the Russian Government, through the ambassador at St. Petersburg, that, however strong the feeling in England against the Turkish cruelties, it would be superseded by a very different sentiment if it were believed that Constantinople was threatened, or that British interests in the Suez Canal were in any danger. This message to the Emperor could only be interpreted as meaning that the British Government would not interfere with any action that Russia might take against Turkey, provided it did not involve the conquest of Constantinople or endanger British interests in Egypt. It was evidently so understood by the Emperor, for immediately on receipt of the above despatch, on November 2nd, he gave his word of honour to the British Ambassador that he had no designs on Constantinople and no intentions whatever to annex Bulgaria.

In spite of this explicit announcement on the part of the Emperor, in response to the despatch from the British Foreign Minister, Lord Beaconsfield, a few days later, on November 9th, at the annual civic banquet at the Guildhall of London, delivered himself of a most bellicose speech on behalf of Turkey, practically threatening war with Russia, without any reference to the pacific assurance of the Czar, which, as we now know, was in his hands at the time when he made this speech. There could not well be a clearer intimation on the part of the British Premier that he had no belief in the good faith of the Emperor.

This menacing speech of the British Prime Minister was telegraphed to Russia, with the result that the Czar was greatly incensed, and on the next day, November 10th, he made a public pronouncement at Moscow to his people of the gravest importance, to the effect that, if he could not obtain adequate guarantees from the Porte for the protection of its Christian subjects, he would act independently of other Powers, relying on the loyalty of his people to support him.

In the meantime, through Lord Derby's efforts, it had been arranged with Russia and the other Great Powers that a Conference should be held at Constantinople of representatives of all the Powers, for the purpose of deciding what administrative changes should be proposed to the Sultan, with a view to the common purpose—namely the better protection of his Christian subjects in Europe.

Lord Salisbury, as a member of the British Cabinet and Secretary of State for India, represented England at this Conference. It met at Constantinople on December 23, 1876. On the day before the meeting of the Conference at Constantinople a firman was published by the Sultan, at the instance of Midhat Pasha, promulgating a scheme of constitutional reform, which had been agreed to by the ministers of the Porte in the short reign of Murad, but which Abdul Hamid on his accession had refused to sanction. A National Assembly was convoked, to be elected by universal suffrage, without distinction of race or religion, throughout the Empire. It was hoped to anticipate the demands of the Conference by a scheme of reform wider than they were likely to advise. This was effected with perfect good faith by Midhat, who was earnestly in favour of reform. But subsequent events showed that the Sultan adopted this course for the purpose only of throwing dust in the eyes of the Conference, and with the full intention of setting aside the Constitution as soon as the Conference had broken up. The Conference might perhaps have acted more wisely in treating this act of the Sultan as an honest proposal, and in making it the basis of a wide reform of the Ottoman Empire. They held it to be a sham. They proceeded with their discussions as if it had not been issued. They preferred an alternative scheme of providing autonomous institutions for the Christian provinces of Turkey, and for the appointment of governors subject to the approval of the Great Powers. There was practically no difference of opinion at the Conference between the British and Russian delegates, Lord Salisbury and General Ignatief. The Conference, at their instance, reduced its demands on the Porte to the most moderate minimum.

The Sultan refused point-blank to entertain the proposals of the Conference, on the ground that they interfered with his sovereign powers. He pleaded the new Constitution which he had just accorded to the Empire. There never was any intention on his part to make any concessions. He was under the belief that if war resulted with Russia from his refusal to agree to reforms his country would not stand alone. He took the policy of England from the speech of Lord Beaconsfield at the Guildhall; and not from Lord Derby or

Lord Salisbury. Lord Beaconsfield had, in fact, thrown over his colleague, Lord Salisbury, in that unfortunate utterance and had insured the failure of the Conference at Constantinople.

A few days after the break-up of the Conference, Midhat Pasha was ignominiously dismissed from office. The new Constitution did not long survive its author. In May, 1877, Abdul Hamid suspended it and dismissed the National Assembly which had been convoked. During the two months of its existence its members had shown a determination to expose the scandalous abuses of the Hamidian system. Later Abdul Hamid trumped up a charge against Midhat of having been responsible for the murder of Sultan Aziz. Two men employed by that Sultan, a wrestler and a gardener, were suborned to confess that they strangled Aziz at the instance of Midhat. Midhat was tried by corrupt judges and was not allowed to cross-examine these men. He was found guilty and condemned to death. At the instance mainly of the British Government the sentence was commuted to banishment to Arabia. Midhat was there strangled by order of Abdul Hamid in 1882, and his embalmed head was sent to Constantinople, in order that the Sultan might be assured of his death. The two men who had confessed to the murder of Aziz were released and were pensioned by the Sultan. Sir Henry Elliot, who was British Ambassador at Constantinople at the time of the death of Sultan Aziz, put on record his conviction that it was a case of suicide, that the charge against Midhat was trumped up, and that the whole proceedings are an indelible stain on Abdul Hamid.

Meanwhile, in 1877, another attempt was made by the Great Powers to effect a settlement of the Eastern question. Count Schouvaloff was sent to London by the Emperor of Russia on a special mission for the purpose. Agreement was arrived at between the Powers. It was embodied in a protocol, and was presented to the Porte. It was promptly rejected on April 10th by the Sultan as inconsistent with the treaty of Paris by interfering with the independence of the Ottoman Empire. Russia thereupon declared war against Turkey, justifying it in a dignified manifesto, on the ground that the Sultan, by rejecting the protocol, had defied Europe. Russia, therefore, held the strong position of acting on behalf of Europe. England was the only Power to take exception to this. Lord Derby, in a despatch to the Russian Government, said that he and his colleagues regarded the action of Russia as an obstacle to reform in Turkey, and held that the plight of the Christian population could not be improved by war—a most unfortunate prediction, as the result proved. More fortunate was the prediction of Mr. Gladstone at the close of a speech which he made in the House of Commons, on April 24, 1877, immediately after the declaration of war by Russia, when moving a resolution intended to prevent the Government from taking up a hostile attitude to Russia in the coming war.

I believe, for one [he said], that the knell of Turkish tyranny in these provinces (the Balkan provinces) has sounded. So far as human eyes can judge, it is about to be destroyed. The destruction may not come in the way or by the means that we should choose; but come from what hands it may, I am persuaded that it will be accepted as a boon by Christendom and the world.[43]

The answer of the Government to Mr. Gladstone was given in the debate by the Home Secretary, Sir Richard Cross, later Lord Cross. It showed that the policy of Lord Derby, and not that of Lord Beaconsfield, had prevailed in the Cabinet. The Government, he said, regretted the war which had been declared by Russia, and did not believe that it would do any good, but it would not give support to either side, unless the Suez Canal or Egypt or Constantinople were threatened.

It followed from this decision of the British Cabinet that the hopes which the Sultan had formed from the speeches of Lord Beaconsfield were not realized. He was left alone to fight against Russia in another attack on his Empire. Immediately after the declaration of war, on April 24, 1877, two Russian armies invaded Turkey—the one in Europe, of two hundred and fifty thousand men, under the nominal command of the Grand Duke Nicholas, the other in Asia, of a hundred and fifty thousand men from the Caucasus, under that of the Grand Duke Michael. The former crossed the Pruth into Roumania, which was still nominally a part of the Ottoman Empire. But on April 15th the Roumanian Chamber had given its assent to a convention with Russia providing for the passage of the Russian troops through the principality and otherwise giving promise of friendly support. The Porte, as was to be expected, treated this as a hostile act, and directed the bombardment of Calafat, a Roumanian fortress on the Danube. The Roumanians thereupon, on May 21st, declared war against Turkey. They gave most effective support to the Russians throughout the campaign. Indeed, it may be fairly said from the course of the campaign that the invasion of Bulgaria would not have been successful without the help of the Roumanians.

The Emperor of Russia had further prepared the way for the invasion of Turkey by securing the neutrality of Austria-Hungary. At a personal meeting in the previous year at Reichstadt, he had assured the Emperor of Austria that he had no intention of taking possession of Constantinople. He further promised that Bosnia and Herzegovina would be handed over for occupation by Austria-Hungary as a reward for neutrality in the event of success in his war against the Turks.

Owing to unprecedented inundations in the valley of the Danube, it was not till two months after the commencement of the campaign that the Russian army was able to cross that river. It did so at two points, the one in the Dobrudscha, the other at Hirsova. In neither case did it meet with serious opposition. The Turkish army of defence was little inferior in numbers to that of the Russians, but its general, Abdul Kerim, proved to be quite incompetent. He spread his forces in detachments over a front of five hundred miles, and was too late in concentrating them. The Russians, after capturing Nicopolis, the Turkish stronghold on the Danube, advanced into Bulgaria and captured Tirnovo, its ancient capital. Everywhere they were received by the Bulgarians with rapturous demonstrations of delight at the prospect of deliverance from Ottoman rule.

General Gourko, with a flying corps, then made a very hazardous but successful march across the Balkans by the Hainköi Pass, and advanced into Bulgaria along the Trudja Valley as far as Eski Zagra. Thence, turning back, he attacked the more important Shipka Pass from the south, and defeated a Turkish force in occupation of it. Meanwhile, early in July, the main Russian army from Tirnovo came in contact at Plevna, twenty miles south of the Danube, with a Turkish army of fifty thousand men under Osman Pasha, who had been sent in relief of Nicopolis, but was too late for the purpose.

Plevna was not a fortress. It was a strong natural position, where the Turks entrenched their army behind earthworks and redoubts with great engineering skill, and where they maintained an obstinate and memorable defence for nearly five months, the most striking incident of the campaign of 1877. Three unsuccessful assaults were made by the Russians, assisted by a Roumanian army, in which great losses were incurred. Thereupon, by the advice of General Todleben, the hero of the defence of Sebastopol in the Crimean War, the attempt to take these works at Plevna by assault was given up, and it was subjected to a close investment. The occupation of the Shipka Pass by Gourko prevented the advance of a Turkish army in relief of Plevna, in spite of successive attacks by the Turkish army under Suleiman Pasha. As a result, after five months of heroic resistance, Osman Pasha found himself in great straits for want of food for his army. He determined to make a great effort to break through the lines of the investing army. The sortie failed, and Osman and his whole remaining army of thirty-two thousand men were compelled to surrender on January 9, 1878. This had the effect of releasing the Russian army in front of Plevna. General Gourko and the main part of the Russian army thereupon marched to Sofia. General Skobeleff, in command of another army, determined to force his way across the Balkan range. An army of ninety thousand Turks under another Pasha was stationed at the southern end of the Shipka Pass and barred his way. Directing a part of his army to make a feint attack along the Shipka Pass, Skobeleff led the remainder by two sheep tracks distant about six miles from the pass, and crossing the mountains, was able to attack the enemy on the flank at Shenova. The Turks were defeated and their whole army was compelled to surrender. By this brilliant manœuvre of Skobeleff, the Grand Duke Nicholas, in nominal command of the whole Russian army, was able to advance without further opposition to Adrianople. He took possession of it on January 28th. Meanwhile the Turks met with further defeats from the Serbians and Montenegrins. The former captured the important town of Nisch. The latter captured Spizza, in the bay of Antivari, and Dulcigno, in the Adriatic.

In Asia the Turks were no more fortunate than in Europe. Their army under Muktar Pasha was little inferior in numbers to that of the Russians, but it was divided between Kars, Ardahan, and Erzerum. The Russians in the course of the campaign of 1877 succeeded in successively capturing these important fortresses and in getting possession of nearly the whole of the districts inhabited by Armenians.

By the middle of January 1878 the resistance of the Turks was practically at an end in both continents. They were compelled to sue for peace and to appeal for the mediation of the other Powers of Europe. On January 31st an armistice was agreed on.

The capture of Adrianople and the fact that there was no Turkish army capable of resisting the further advance of the Russians to Constantinople caused great alarm to the British Government. Opinion in England, which had not supported Lord Beaconsfield in his desire to renew the policy of the Crimean War, and to assist the Turks against the invasion of Bulgaria by the Russians, now veered round, at least among the wealthier and a large section of the middle class, and declared itself vehemently opposed to the occupation of Constantinople, which appeared to be imminent, even if it should be only of a temporary character.

The British fleet at Besika Bay was ordered to enter the Dardanelles. The House of Commons was asked to vote six millions for war purposes. Every preparation was made for war. Russia replied to these demonstrations by advancing its army nearer to Constantinople. The headquarters of the Grand Duke Nicholas were established at San Stefano, a village on the shore of the Marmora, within sight of Constantinople. A portion of the British fleet then took up a position near to Prince's Island, also within sight of the capital. The position between the two countries, England and Russia, was therefore most critical.

Meanwhile negotiations took place directly between Russia and the Porte. Terms of peace were offered and agreed to, and on March 3, 1878, a treaty was signed between the two Powers at San Stefano. It was in accord with the promises which had been made to the British Government by the Czar.

Constantinople, the province of Thrace, and Adrianople were left in possession of the Turks, and the capital was not even to be temporarily occupied by the Russian army. Bulgaria was not to become a Russian province or even an independent State. But a great Bulgaria from the Danube southward, with frontiers on the Black Sea and the Ægean Sea, and including the greater part of Thrace, was constituted as an autonomous State, subject to the nominal suzerainty of the Sultan, under a prince to be elected by its people and approved by Russia. As thus constituted, it would cut off the Porte from direct junction and communication by land with its remaining possessions in the Balkan peninsula, such as Macedonia, Epirus, and Albania. Serbia and Montenegro were to be greatly enlarged and both were to be independent States. Bosnia and Herzegovina were to be endowed with autonomous institutions while remaining subject to the Porte. Reformed administration was to be secured for the remaining Balkan provinces. No extension was conceded to Greece, but Thessaly, Epirus, and Crete were included in the provision of reformed administration. The Roumanians were very shabbily treated after the valuable assistance they had rendered to the Russian army. The part of Bessarabia, inhabited largely by Roumanians, which had been taken from Russia by the treaty of Paris and added to Moldavia, was to be restored to the Czar, together with a small strip which brought Russia up to the Danube as a riverain State. In exchange, Roumania was to be content with the barren Dobrudscha, sparsely inhabited by Bulgarians and Turks. Roumania was to be an independent State. In Asia, Kars, Ardahan, Bayezid, and Batoum, and their districts were to be ceded to Russia. Erzerum was to be restored to Turkey. An indemnity for the war of twelve millions sterling was to be paid by Turkey.

The publication of these terms did not allay the apprehensions of the British Government. They were regarded, in the first instance, as meaning the complete dismemberment of Turkey in Europe. Lord Beaconsfield and the Turkophil members of the Government believed that a great Bulgaria would be completely under the influence of Russia, and would be used as a stepping-stone for the ultimate acquisition of Constantinople by that Power. They could not understand, what was often insisted upon by Mr. Gladstone in his speeches, that the best barrier against the advance of Russia, in the Balkan peninsula, would be a self-governing, contented, and prosperous State, and that the larger it was the better it would serve that purpose. The Government, under these misapprehensions, determined to resist the creation of a big Bulgaria, even at the risk of war with Russia. They maintained that the treaty of San Stefano was completely at variance with the treaty of Paris of 1856, and must be revised by a new Congress of the great Powers of Europe.

The Russian Government would not agree to submit the whole treaty to a Congress, but only some parts of it. A collision between Russia and England seemed to be imminent. War preparations were continued by the latter, and Indian troops were sent to Malta. Lord Derby, the Foreign Minister, and Lord Carnarvon, the Colonial Secretary, who were opposed to war, resigned, and the war party in the Cabinet prevailed. But the Czar was very averse to war, whatever might be the wishes of his generals at the front before Constantinople. At the last moment terms of reference to a Congress were agreed upon between the two Governments, and war was averted. By an agreement which was intended to be secret, but which was divulged to the Press in England by an unscrupulous employé at the Foreign Office, the British Government promised to support, at the Congress, the main clauses of the treaty of San Stefano, subject to a concession, on the part of Russia, as to Bulgaria. Under this agreement, the intended big Bulgaria was divided into three parts. That between the Danube and the Balkan range was to be dealt with as proposed in the San Stefano treaty. It was to be an autonomous State under the suzerainty of the Sultan, with a prince elected by its people. A second part of it, immediately south of the Balkan range, to be called Eastern Roumelia, was to be an autonomous province more directly under the control of the Porte. A third, the part bordering on the Ægean Sea and containing a mixed population of Bulgarians, Serbians, Greeks, and (in parts) Moslems, was to be restored to the Porte subject to conditions for better administration equally with other Turkish provinces in Europe. This part has since been generally spoken of as Macedonia.

The Congress of the Powers met at Berlin on June 13, 1878, under the presidency of Prince Bismarck. It was the most important gathering of the kind since the Congress of Vienna in 1815. The Great Powers were represented by their leading statesmen. England, by Lord Beaconsfield and Lord Salisbury; Russia, by Prince Gortchakoff and Count Schouvaloff; France, by its Prime Minister, Waddington; Italy, by Count Corti, its Foreign Minister; Austria, by Count Andrassy. The Porte, apparently, was unable to find a competent Turk for the purpose. It was represented by Karatheodori, a Greek, and by Mehemet Ali, a renegade German. Germany, it need not be said, was represented by Bismarck, who acted as the 'honest broker.' Although apparently invested with unlimited authority to deal with all questions arising out of the treaty of San Stefano, the Congress found that its hands were practically tied behind its back by the agreement between England and Russia. It had no other option than to cut down the big Bulgaria under the tripartite scheme already described, which was the essence of the Anglo-Russian agreement. As regards the artificially created province of Eastern Roumelia, Lord Beaconsfield, who throughout the proceedings of the Congress championed the Turkish cause, insisted that the Porte was to have the right to maintain garrisons in its frontier fortresses. He threatened to break up the Congress if this was not conceded. Russia, though strongly opposed to this, ultimately gave way. This was a triumph for Beaconsfield, the value of which we can now appreciate, with the knowledge that no advantage was ever taken by the Porte of this permission to garrison Eastern Roumelia.

The most important point on which the Congress effected a change in the treaty of San Stefano was in respect of Bosnia and Herzegovina. At the instance of Bismarck, these two provinces, instead of being endowed with autonomous government, were handed over to Austria for occupation and administration, while remaining nominally a part of the Turkish Empire. Montenegro was to lose half of the territory conceded to it at San Stefano.[44] The claims of Greece for a definite extension of its territory were championed by the representative of France, but were opposed by Lord Beaconsfield. The Congress contented itself with a recommendation to the Sultan that the boundaries of Greece should be extended so as to include Thessaly and a part of Epirus. Organic reforms of administration and law were to be carried out by the Porte in the European provinces of the Empire on the recommendation of a Commission to be appointed by the Great Powers.

The Congress confirmed to Russia the acquisition of the provinces in Asia above referred to, and the restoration of Erzerum and Bayezid to the Porte. The Armenians were guaranteed good government and protection from the raids of Kurds and Circassians. Some other amendments of the San Stefano treaty of no great importance were decided upon, and on July 13, 1878, the treaty of Berlin was signed by the representatives of all the Powers, after exactly a month of discussion.

After his success at the Congress in respect of the Roumelian garrisons, obtained by the threat of war, Beaconsfield was able to return to England with a flourish of trumpets, boasting that he had succeeded in obtaining 'peace with honour.' Though the treaty of Berlin nullified that of San Stefano as regards the big Bulgaria, it did, in fact, ratify the virtual dismemberment of the Ottoman Empire in respect of four-fifths of its territory in Europe and freed about eight millions of people from its rule. This great achievement was due to Russia alone, and the gains to that Power in Bessarabia and Armenia were in comparison small and unimportant. The splitting up of Bulgaria, which constituted the main difference between the two treaties, was due to British diplomacy, backed by threats of war. But the result obtained did not stand the test of even a short experience. Two of the Bulgarian provinces thus torn asunder were reunited seven years later. More recently, the parts of Macedonia and Thrace restored to full Turkish rule by the treaty of Berlin have, within the present century, again been freed from it, and have been annexed to Serbia and Greece in about equal portion.

It will be seen from this brief statement that by the treaty of Berlin Great Britain obtained nothing for itself, unless it were that the division of Bulgaria was of permanent value to it in strengthening the hold of the Turks on Constantinople, a contention which has not been confirmed by subsequent events. It did, however, succeed in getting something out of the general scramble for territory. By another secret treaty which, to the amazement of the members of the Congress at Berlin, was made public during their sittings, the Porte agreed to hand over to the occupation of England the island of Cyprus, on terms very similar to those under which Bosnia and Herzegovina were placed under the charge of Austria. The occupation of the island was limited to the time during which Kars and Ardahan should be in possession of Russia. As a condition of this occupation, Great Britain guaranteed to the Porte its Asiatic possessions. But this guarantee was conditional on good government being secured to the Armenian population in the east of Asia Minor, a condition which has never, in fact, been fulfilled. The treaty was justified in the British Parliament on the ground that Cyprus would be of great value as a *place d'armes* for the British army in the event of attack by Russia on the Asiatic provinces of Turkey or of an attack from any quarter on Egypt. The Porte was guaranteed by the British Government an annual tribute so long as the occupation should last, based on the average revenue which it had received from the island. The proceeds were assigned for payment of the interest on the loan raised by Turkey during the Crimean War, guaranteed by England and France. The arrangement was made hastily and without due inquiry, with the result that the island has been burthened with a charge far in excess of its past payments to the Porte, and the British taxpayers have been compelled to bear a part of the burthen. An occupation such as that of Cyprus was almost certain to become permanent, and in 1914, during the existing war, the island was permanently annexed by the British Government.

Looking back at the events which led to the liberation of Bulgaria from Ottoman rule and to all the other changes sanctioned by the treaty of Berlin, it must now be fully admitted that the agitation which Mr. Gladstone promoted against the Turkish Government had a great ultimate effect. It averted the use of armed force by Great Britain for the purpose of preventing the intervention of Russia on behalf of the Christian population of the Balkans. In a great speech in the House of Commons in review of the treaty of Berlin, Mr. Gladstone delivered himself of this verdict on it:—

Taking the whole provisions of the treaty of Berlin together, I must thankfully and joyfully acknowledge that great results have been achieved in the diminution of human misery and towards the establishment of human happiness and prosperity in the East.

- 261 -

As regards the conduct of England at the Congress he added these weighty words:—

I say, Sir, that in this Congress of the Great Powers the voice of England has not been heard in unison with the constitution, the history, and the character of England. On every question that arose, and that became a subject of serious contest in the Congress, or that could lead to any practical results, a voice has been heard from Lord Beaconsfield and Lord Salisbury which sounded in the tones of Metternich, and not in the tones of Mr. Canning, or of Lord Palmerston, or of Lord Russell.... I do affirm that it was their part to take the side of liberty, and I do also affirm that, as a matter of fact, they took the side of servitude.[45]

Lord Salisbury himself lived to make the admission that England in its Eastern policy "put its money on the wrong horse."

The three years which followed the treaty of Berlin were spent by the Great Powers in the endeavour to give effect to its provisions, by settling the boundaries between Turkey and its *disjecta membra*, and other important details. Two of these questions led to great difficulty. The Porte, as was to be expected, put every obstruction in the way and resorted to its accustomed dilatory methods. By the treaty Montenegro had been guaranteed a port in the Adriatic. It was not till 1880, after the return of Mr. Gladstone to power in England, that effective pressure was put on the Porte. He induced the other Powers to join in sending a combined fleet to the Adriatic to blockade its coast as a demonstration against the Porte. This, however, was not effective for the purpose. It mattered little to the Porte that its coast in the Adriatic was blockaded. It was not till the British Government threatened to send its fleet to Asia Minor, and by seizing some custom houses there to cut off supplies of money, that the Sultan was brought to book. Eventually the port of Dulcigno and the district round it were ceded to Montenegro and its claim for access to the Adriatic was conceded.

The case of Greece caused even greater difficulty. The treaty of Berlin, it has been shown, contained no specific promise or guarantee of a cession of territory to Greece. It merely made a recommendation to that effect, leaving it to the discretion of the Porte whether to accede to it or not. As Greece had taken no part in the war of liberation of the Balkans, it had no special claim, except such as arose from a wish of the Powers to avoid complications in the future. It was admitted, however, by the Porte that something should be done in the way of rectifying its frontier in this direction. Another conference of the Powers at Berlin reported in favour of drawing the frontier line so as to include in the kingdom of Greece the whole of both Thessaly and Epirus. This was gladly assented to by Greece, but was rejected by the Sultan. The Powers, however, were not willing to back up their proposals by armed force. The French Government, which had supported the claim of Greece at the Congress, now drew back. Eventually, after two years of diplomatic labour, a compromise was arrived at, mainly at the instance of the British Ambassador to the Porte, Mr. Goschen, who showed infinite skill and patience in dealing with the Sultan. A line of frontier was agreed to, which conceded to Greece the whole of Thessaly and about a third part of Epirus. This line excluded Janina and other districts inhabited by Moslem Albanians, and also other districts where Greeks predominated, but under the circumstances it was the most which could be effected without a resort to arms. Greece had to wait some years before a more complete settlement could be secured to her.

As regards the organic local reforms in administration and law which, under the treaty of Berlin, were to be carried out in the European provinces of the Empire, a Commission was appointed by the Great Powers in 1880. The British representative was Lord Edmund Fitzmaurice, later Lord Fitzmaurice. He took the leading part in drawing up a large and complete scheme of reform, which was agreed to by the Commission and was presented to the Sultan for his approval in accordance with the treaty.

There followed, after these proceedings, a period of twenty-eight years, up to 1908, during which Turkey, under the rule of Abdul Hamid, was free from external war, and opportunity was therefore afforded for giving effect to the promises by the Porte, guaranteed by the treaty of Berlin, of reforms and improved administration in Macedonia and other Balkan provinces left in its possession, and also in Crete and Armenia. Except as regards Crete, not a single step, however, was ever taken by the Porte to give effect to these promises. The scheme of organic reform was never approved by the Sultan. It was treated as waste-paper, like every other promise of reform in Turkey. Disorder and misgovernment continued unabated.

Several events soon took place which showed that the disintegration of the Ottoman Empire was still slowly but surely proceeding. The most important of these was in relation to Bulgaria. The reduced and mutilated province under that name, as settled by the treaty of Berlin, chose as its ruler, with the consent of the Powers, Prince Alexander of Battenberg, a young man of great merit and promise. Eastern Roumelia, cut off from Bulgaria, was also constituted as a separate province, more immediately dependent on the Porte, but with autonomous government, under a Christian governor nominated by the Sultan. But this ingenious scheme of Lord Beaconsfield did not work in practice. Economic difficulties, arising from separate tariffs, equally with national aspirations, necessitated union. The representative chambers of both provinces were incessant in their demands for this.

The union of the two States was now opposed by Russia. But, strange to say, it was supported by Great Britain, at the instance of Lord Salisbury, who had been associated with Lord Beaconsfield at the Congress of Berlin in insisting on the severance of the two provinces. He had since been persuaded by the British Ambassador at Constantinople, Sir William White, a far-seeing statesman who had intimate knowledge of the Balkans, that a united and strong Bulgaria would, in the future, be a bar to the ambitions of Russia against what remained of Turkey.

Fortunately for the Bulgarians, the Sultan arrived at the same conclusion. When, therefore, in 1885, the two provinces insisted on union, and a Bulgarian army occupied Eastern Roumelia, with the full assent of its population, who deported the Turkish governor to Constantinople, the Sultan made no real opposition. He was persuaded to accept the union as a *fait accompli*. The diplomatic difficulty arising out of the treaty of Berlin was evaded by the Sultan in 1886 nominating the Prince of Bulgaria as governor of Roumelia. Thenceforth the representative chambers of the two States met as one body at Sofia, and the union was practically effected. This caused great discontent in Serbia, which was jealous of the aggrandizement of its neighbour and demanded territorial compensation. War consequently broke out between Serbia and Bulgaria. After a three days' battle at Slivnitza, the Bulgarians, contrary to all expectations, were completely successful, under the able generalship of Prince Alexander. Belgrade lay open to the victorious army. But the Great Powers then again intervened and insisted on terms of peace between the belligerents, based upon the *status quo* before the war. The Emperor of Russia deeply resented the action of his relative, Prince Alexander. The Prince was kidnapped and was forcibly conveyed out of the country and compelled to abdicate. There ensued a strong movement in his favour in Bulgaria. He was recalled from exile. But at this critical moment of his career the Prince appears to have lost his nerve, and instead of standing firm and relying on the support of the people, for whom he had done so much, he gave way to the demands of the Czar, and retired into obscurity as a cavalry officer in the Austrian army. In his place Prince Ferdinand of Saxe-Coburg was elected as ruler of the united province, subject to the nominal suzerainty of the Sultan.

Another cause of frequent international difficulty during the reign of Abdul Hamid was that of the island of Crete. The Powers at Berlin had refused to include it in the kingdom of Greece or even to recommend this course to the Porte. They contented themselves with a provision in the treaty guaranteeing to the island a reformed administration under a Christian governor. In compliance with this, Photiades Pasha, a Greek subject of the Porte of administrative capacity, was appointed governor, and a representative chamber was constituted. For a few years the island enjoyed peace and prosperity. But later, on the retirement of Photiades, the Sultan endeavoured to restore his authority in the island by appointing a Moslem governor and suspending the national assembly. Insurrection followed in 1896. The Greeks of the island, who formed by far the greater number of its inhabitants, were supported by the Government and people of Greece. War broke out in 1897 between the Porte and Greece. It was the first occasion on which the Turkish army, which had been trained by German officers, under command of General von der Goltz, was able to show its quality. In thirty days it completely defeated the Greek army and occupied Thessaly and Epirus. The Powers thereupon intervened and prevented the Porte from taking advantage of its success. Peace was again insisted upon between the belligerents. Greece was compelled to submit to a small rectification of its frontier and to pay the cost of the war, estimated at four millions sterling.

The Turks thereupon evacuated Thessaly, and with them departed the last of the Moslem beys or landowners. Though Greece had at the time a navy superior in strength to that of the Porte, it effected nothing in the war by sea. Turkish troops had been able to invade Crete, and were in practical occupation of it. The four Powers, not including Germany, whose Kaiser was already coquetting with the Sultan, with a view to a future military alliance, then blockaded the island, occupied ports on its coast, and ultimately compelled the Turkish troops to evacuate it. In 1898 Prince George of Greece, a son of the King of Greece, was appointed governor of the island at the suggestion of the Powers, and the native assembly was recalled into existence. This arrangement was obviously of a temporary nature. It lasted with growing friction till the revolution in Turkey in 1908. When Austria annexed Bosnia and Herzegovina, the Cretan Assembly proclaimed annexation to Greece, and thenceforth the union of the island to the present kingdom was complete and was fully recognized by the Powers.

The Great Powers were less successful in securing performance of the promises of the Sultan under the treaty of Berlin in the case of the Armenians. The Porte had undertaken by the treaty to carry out, without delay, "the amelioration and reforms demanded for provinces inhabited by Armenians and to guarantee their security against Kurds and Circassians." Periodic reports showing what reforms were effected were to be laid before the Powers, who were also to superintend their application. These provisions were the more important as they were practically the conditions on which the provinces of Erzerum and Bayezid, which had been occupied by the Russians in their invasion of the Asiatic provinces of Turkey in 1877, were restored to the Porte. It may be taken that, if the Powers had conceived it possible that these promises would not be carried out, they would not have been so cruel as to restore these two provinces, inhabited so largely by Armenians, to Turkish rule. Lord Salisbury in 1888 did, in fact, use strong language to the Porte on the subject of Armenia, and threatened armed force if reforms were not carried out. In spite of this threat, no reforms were effected. Mr. Gladstone, when he came into power again in 1892, endeavoured to bring pressure on the Porte in favour of the Armenians, but he met with no support from other Powers. Bismarck at last intimated to him that the subject had better be allowed to drop. Russia, it seems, was at that time engaged in the effort to induce the Armenians inhabiting the districts round Kars, which had been ceded to it under the treaty of Berlin, to give up their national Church and to join the Greek Church. It was little disposed to give support to the Armenians who remained subjects of the Porte.

As a result, the Armenians obtained no valid protection, and the Kurds and Circassians continued their raids against these peaceful people. Later, suspicion of Armenian insurrection arose in the mind of Sultan Abdul Hamid. There were a few isolated cases in which insignificant numbers of Armenians, prompted by their compatriots across the frontier in Russia, formed conspiracies against the Turkish Government. But these feeble sparks were extinguished by the Turkish officials on the spot without difficulty. They were made the excuse, however, by the Sultan for a new policy of massacre directed against these unfortunate people. Massacres on a small scale began in 1889.

In 1890, when the writer was at Constantinople, he was favoured with an interview by the Sultan, who spoke on the subject of the Armenians, and sent a message to Mr. Gladstone, conveying his most positive assurances that he was animated by none but the most friendly feelings towards these people, and that he was determined to secure to them good government. Such assurances from this quarter were but proofs of malevolent intentions. Certain it is that the tale of official massacres was thenceforth for some years a continuous one. Abdul Hamid appears to have deliberately made up his mind, if not to settle the Armenian question by extermination of the Armenians, once for all, at least to inflict such a lesson on them as would never be forgotten. This policy culminated in 1894. Commissioners were then sent into the country inhabited by Armenians with directions to summon the Moslems of the district to the mosques and to inform them of the Sultan's wishes and plans. They were to be told that liberty was given to them to take by force the goods of their Armenian neighbours, and if there was any resistance to kill them. It was not an appeal to the fanaticism of the Moslems, but rather to their greed for loot and to their jealousy of their more prosperous neighbours.

At the same time every precaution was taken to prevent the news of these wholesale acts of rapine and massacre from being known to the outside world. No strangers or visitors were allowed to enter the country where these scenes were taking place, and the most rigorous censorship was applied to all letters coming from them. Save in a few rare cases where the mollahs refused to obey, in the belief that the Koran did not justify such acts, the instructions were acted on and the policy of murder and robbery was preached in the mosques. In the province of Bitlis twenty-four Armenian villages were destroyed by Zeki Pasha. Their inhabitants were butchered. Zeki was decorated by the Sultan for this infamy. In 1895, and again in 1896, wholesale massacres of Armenians took place, organized by Sultan Abdul Hamid, and effected through the agency of Shakir Pasha and other officials, civil and military. It was estimated that a hundred thousand Armenians were victims of these massacres, either directly or indirectly by starvation and disease which followed them. Constantinople itself, on August 22 and 28, 1896, was the scene of an organized attack on the Armenian quarter. It was invaded by gangs of men armed with clubs, who bludgeoned every Armenian to be found there. In vain did the ambassadors protest and appeal to the treaty of Berlin. In vain did Mr. Gladstone issue, for the last time, from his retirement and appeal to public opinion on behalf of these people, designating the Sultan as Abdul the Great Assassin. No Power was willing to use force or even to threaten force on behalf of the Armenians. Even Russia was disinclined to do so. These people had no wish to be absorbed by Russia. An Armenian of good position and wide acquaintance with his countrymen in Asia Minor, when questioned by the writer on this point in 1890, said that the Armenians had no desire to become subjects of Russia. They would prefer to remain under the Turks, if England would hold a big stick over the Sultan; but if England would not do this, they would prefer Russia, or the devil himself, to the Turk.

It need not be said that those massacres of 1890-5 have been completely put into the shade by the far more extensive and bloody massacres of 1915, and that the policy of deporting the whole population of Armenians has been carried to a terrible conclusion.

There remains the case of the Macedonians and other people of the Balkans who were replaced by the treaty of Berlin under Ottoman rule. The difficulty of dealing with them was aggravated by the fact that the population of these districts was not homogeneous. Bulgarians, Greeks, and Serbians were in many districts mixed up, each with separate villages or communities, so that no definite geographical lines could be drawn between them. The neighbouring States of Bulgaria, Serbia, and Greece were furiously jealous of one another, each claiming these intervening districts. This, however, was no excuse to the Porte for the continued misgovernment of these provinces. Their unfortunate populations, while enduring the evils of misrule, were able to compare their position under Turkish rule with that of their more fortunate neighbours who had been liberated from it by the treaty of Berlin, and were enjoying all the benefits of self-government in Bulgaria, Serbia, and Greece.

The writer had the opportunity of personally forming an opinion on this subject. In 1887 and 1890 he paid visits to Greece, and in 1890 he visited Bulgaria on his way to Constantinople, staying a few days at Sofia and Philippopolis. In both cases he was able to compare the new condition of things with what he recollected of his previous visits to these districts in 1857. Nothing could be more striking and more satisfactory to those who had felt confidence in the principle of self-government and of democratic institutions. The change in Bulgaria was the more remarkable as it had been effected in the twelve years which had elapsed since the treaty of Berlin. In these few years the Bulgarians had equipped themselves with the machinery of a progressive democratic community, with schools and colleges, and with compulsory education. Roads, harbours, and improvements of all kinds were in course of construction. The Tartars and Circassians who had been planted in Bulgaria by the Porte after the conquests by Russia of the Crimea and the Caucasus, and who were the main instruments of the horrors of Batak, had again been transplanted by the Porte in Asia Minor. But the indigenous Moslems, whether of Slav or Turkish race, in spite of vehement exhortations of their mollahs, remained and were well treated by the Christian population now in possession of power. They had no cause for complaint. They were represented in the National Assembly of Bulgaria by not a few men of their own religion.

The Bulgarian peasants, who, under Turkish rule, had in many parts been driven from the fertile plains into the Rhodope Mountains and had there formed congested districts, had migrated again into the plains and were extending cultivation. A member of the Bulgarian Chamber of Deputies, when asked by the writer what his constituency of peasants thought of the change since old Turkish times, replied that they all admitted that though taxation had not been reduced there was this great difference: Under the Turkish régime the taxes went into the pockets of the Turkish officials and of the Sultan's gang of robbers at Constantinople, and the peasants who paid got no return for them. But under the new régime they had full return for their money in schools and roads, with other improvements, and in the protection of life and property. Brigandage, which used to be rampant, had wholly ceased, and justice could be obtained from the magistrates without bribes.

In Greece there was everywhere the same story, the same comparison of the present with the past, to the immense advantage of the existing state of things. Brigandage had entirely ceased. Athens had become a capital worthy of the nation—remarkable for the number and character of its public buildings and institutions, for its museums, colleges, and schools, founded for the most part by wealthy Greeks in all parts of the world.

There remains to consider what had been the relative and contemporaneous changes in the Balkan provinces still remaining under Turkish rule and in the (mainly Moslem) countries of Asia Minor, Syria, and Mesopotamia. To inquiries of the writer in all quarters, in 1890, there was but one answer, that since the treaty of Berlin the condition both of Christians and Moslems throughout the Turkish Empire had gone from bad to worse. In the Christian Balkan provinces still under Turkish rule misgovernment was more rampant. Brigandage had increased. The rapacity and exactions of the Turkish officials were worse than ever. Discontent was seething in all directions—the more so when the populations compared their fate with that of their more fortunate neighbours across the frontiers who had been liberated by the armies of Russia and by the treaty of Berlin. Nor were the reports as to the condition of the Moslem subjects of the Porte in any way better. The exactions of Turkish officials had increased on people of all races and religion. The concurrent testimony from all quarters was that the condition of the Moslem peasants had greatly deteriorated.

The writer, on his return from the East in 1890, in the following paragraph described the danger to Turkey resulting from this state of things:—

The danger to Turkey in its Eastern provinces of Asia Minor and in its European provinces in Macedonia and Epirus is the comparison between the condition of those who were freed in 1878 from the Sultan's rule, and who have become self-governing, as in the case of the Bulgarians, or have gone under the rule of Austria, Russia, or Greece, with those who remain the subjects of Turkish rule. When, on one side of mere geographical lines, without any physical difference, the populations are flourishing and improvements of all kinds in roads, railways, harbours, schools, etc., are being effected; when brigandage is at an end, and the cultivation of land is extending; when justice is equally administered, and security to life and property is afforded by the authorities; and when all these improvements date from the time when they ceased to be under Turkish rule; and when, on the other side of these lines, the conditions are the same as formerly, or even worse, and no improvement of any kind has taken place, the contrast must inevitably lead to fresh aspirations of the peasantry, to renewed political difficulties, to threats of intervention, and to further schemes for disintegrating the Empire at no distant date. The real defects of the Turkish Government appear to be the same as ever, not so much in the laws themselves as the administration of them, or the want of administration, the excessive centralization, the want of honest and capable governors, the corruption which infects all official classes, the want of money to supply the needs of the central Government and the extravagance of the Sultan, the consequent excessive taxation, the complete absence of security for life and property.[46]

For seventeen more years these evils continued unabated in the Ottoman Empire under Abdul Hamid, while the condition of the liberated provinces was continually improving and the contrast was becoming every year more striking. Discontent and disaffection to the Turkish Government, and contempt and hatred of the Sultan, the head of it, increased not only among his Christian subjects, but equally among the Moslems throughout the length and breadth of the Empire.

The provinces of the Empire which had attained virtual independence under Moslem rulers, such as Egypt and Tunis, were little more fortunate in their experience. They were infected with the same radical defects and misgovernment as the suzerain Power. In Egypt the enlightened despotism of Mehemet Ali had degenerated into the corrupt administration of his grandson, Ismail Pasha. Egypt fell into the hands of French and English moneylenders, and millions of borrowed money were squandered by the Pasha with little or no benefit to his country. Bankruptcy ensued to the State, and the bondholders persuaded the French and English Governments to interfere on their behalf and to insist on a financial control through their Consuls. Later, in 1881, a popular movement arose in Egypt against this foreign control, and the army, under Arabi Bey, revolted. France refused to join with England in putting down the revolt and in maintaining the dual control. England alone undertook the task. It sent an army to Egypt, defeated Arabi and his native army, and restored the nominal rule of the Khedive. The dual financial control of Great Britain and France was maintained. But a virtual protectorate by the former was established, with the result that it became eventually the master of Egypt.

In no case was the action of Abdul Hamid more fatuous and more opposed to the real interests of his Empire than in dealing with this Egyptian question. It was the policy of Great Britain, at the time we are referring to, pursued by both political parties in the State, to maintain as far as possible the authority of the Sultan in Egypt and the integrity of the Turkish Empire. When, in 1881, Mr. Gladstone's Government proposed to send an army for the temporary occupation of Egypt in order to put down the rebellion of the Egyptian army, it was most anxious to do so with the consent and support of the Porte. It invited Abdul Hamid to send troops there to act in concert with the British army and in support of his own sovereign rights. The Sultan refused to do so. He could not be brought to believe that, in the event of his refusal, the British Government would act without him. But this was precisely what it did. A British army was landed in Egypt and put down the rebellion without any support from the Sultan. When it was too late, Abdul Hamid discovered the supreme error of his policy.

Later again, between 1885 and 1887, when Lord Salisbury was Prime Minister, he was most anxious to come to an arrangement with the Porte for the ultimate withdrawal of the British army in occupation of Egypt. He sent a special envoy (Sir H. Drummond Wolff) to Constantinople, with the offer of a treaty to the Sultan, under which the British army was to be wholly withdrawn from Egypt within seven years, but with the condition that if, later, armed intervention should again become necessary, British troops should be employed for the purpose in preference to those of any other Power. This most friendly and advantageous proposal was agreed to by all the ministers of the Porte and was favoured at first by the Sultan, but, after long negotiation, he refused to sign the treaty. Later, when he perceived the mistake which he had made, he offered to reopen the negotiations, but met with a rebuff from Lord Salisbury. The two incidents are important as showing that Egypt became a dependency of Great Britain mainly through the perversity, folly, and stupidity of Abdul Hamid.

In Tunis analogous agencies had been at work in favour of France. The occupation of this province had been the subject of conversations between the Powers at the Congress of Berlin. Prince Bismarck himself suggested it to the representative of France, hoping perhaps that it would be the cause of ill-feeling between that country and Italy, and would widen the breach between them to the advantage of Germany. The British delegates expressed themselves as not unfavourable to this project. It followed that, between 1881 and 1883, the Government of France forcibly assumed a protectorate over Tunis and a control of its finance and administration, with the acquiescence, if not the full approval, of the British Government. In the case of Tunis, however, its connection with the Turkish Empire had been virtually severed three centuries earlier.

Both in Egypt and Tunis, European control effected great improvements in the condition of the native populations, especially the peasantry, and afforded illustration to the people of Turkey of the grave defects of their own Government and its corrupt administration. A party was gradually formed in the first decade of the present century among Moslems in Turkey in favour of constitutional reform. It was known as the Party of Union and Progress. Its members were called the Young Turks. It had its origin with Turks exiled abroad and chiefly living in Paris, and thence it began to permeate Turkey and find influential support in Constantinople. It obtained adherents in great numbers in the Turkish army. It established a Committee at Salonika, where it was in close touch with the officers of the Turkish army, which had its headquarters there. By the year 1908 this movement had enormously increased. Among its ablest members were many Jews and crypto-Jews of Salonika.

There was universal discontent. The system of espionage which the Sultan had set up, and which was his main engine of government, was odious to people of every rank, high and low. The army shared in the discontent. It was not till they were certain of the support of the army that the Committee of Union and Progress attempted any overt act. But when assured of this they boldly proceeded with their plans. On July 23, 1908, at Salonika, Enver Bey, on behalf of the Committee, proclaimed a revolution, and on the same day the 2nd and 3rd Army Corps, stationed there, declared their intention of marching to Constantinople and compelling the Sultan to reform the Constitution. It was decided by the Committee that Abdul Hamid should not be deposed, but that he should be allowed to remain on the throne, provided he accepted the Constitution in good faith. The Committee had further made certain of the support of the Albanian soldiers who formed the bodyguard of the Sultan, and who had been looked upon by him as his most reliable supporters. Abdul Hamid, when he found that the army was against him and that he had no friends on whom he could rely, even among his bodyguard, announced his willingness to concede the demands of the revolutionary party. Never was a revolution effected with so little bloodshed and with more complete success. The Sultan dismissed his corrupt and hated ministers and appointed others, dictated to him by the Committee. He agreed to summon again the Parliament which he had dismissed in 1877. He issued a firman abolishing the system of espionage. He publicly swore fidelity to the new Constitution. For a time the people of Constantinople were willing to believe in his sincerity. The Sheik ul Islam pronounced that there was nothing in the demands of the people which was opposed to the laws of Islam. A general election took place of members for a National Assembly under a process of double election. Men of all races and religions were equally admitted to the franchise.

There were everywhere great rejoicings over the new Constitution, though very few people beyond Constantinople and Salonika had any conception of what it meant. There was for a time great enthusiasm for England, and the new ambassador, Sir Gerard Lowther, on arriving at Constantinople to take up the post received a great ovation. On December 10th the new Parliament met, and was opened by the Sultan with a speech, in which he promised to safeguard the Constitution and to protect the sacred rights of the nation. The various Christian and other subject races were well represented in the Chamber of Deputies. Its members showed an unexpected ability in the conduct of its proceedings and in their speeches.

It was not long, however, before difficulties began to arise, and reaction reared its head again at the secret instigation of the Sultan. There was an outbreak in Albania against the Committee of Union and Progress. The bodyguard of Albanians was won back to the support of Abdul Hamid by profuse bribery. Disorder broke out in many parts of the Empire. It was at Constantinople, however, that the gravest dangers to the new order of things arose. The first act of the new Government was to dismiss the host of spies, who had been maintained at a cost of £1,200,000 a year. It was said at the time that if three persons were seen talking together in the streets one of them was certain to be a spy in the employment of the Sultan. These people found their occupation gone. The new ministers also cleared the public departments of a vast body of superfluous and useless employés, most of them hangers-on of the palace. These two classes of people made a formidable body of malcontents, who conceived that their fortunes depended on the restoration to the Sultan of his old powers of corruption. They were supported by a small body of fanatical mollahs, who believed, or pretended to believe, that the new Constitution was in opposition to the sacred law. But more important than these agencies of reaction were the personal efforts made by Abdul Hamid to tamper with the fidelity to the new Government of the troops at Constantinople by the profuse distribution of money from his private stores. The new ministers had also made the mistake of releasing from prison, not merely great numbers of persons imprisoned at the will of the Sultan for political reasons, but also all the prisoners convicted of serious crimes. These formed an element of disorder in the city and caused alarm and distrust among the well-disposed citizens.

On April 13, 1909, nine months after promulgation of the new Constitution, a revolt broke out among the troops at Constantinople, and a counter-revolution was proclaimed. It had no ostensible leader of any repute or influence. Abdul Hamid avoided committing himself openly to the movement. But for the moment, backed by elements of discontent, it was successful. The new ministers, the members of the Committee of Union and Progress, and the members of the new Assembly were compelled to seek safety by flight. If Abdul Hamid had boldly come forward as the champion of the reactionaries and fanatics, he might have crushed his enemies and have restored the old régime. But he lacked the courage for a desperate game. He contented himself with the secret supply of money in support of the movement.

Meanwhile the Committee of Young Turks met at Salonika, and determined to put down the counter-revolution by force. They called on Mahmoud Shefket Pasha, in command of the 3rd Army Corps, to support them. He said that he had sworn to maintain the Constitution, and agreed to march his army to Constantinople. At San Stefano he met the members of the

Assembly and the ministers who had fled from the city. By the 24th of April the army had overcome the feeble opposition of the rebellious troops and were in occupation of the most important parts of the capital. The counter-revolution was suppressed at a very small cost of lives. The National Assembly met again, and the first question for their decision was what should be done with Abdul Hamid. They put the following question to the Sheik ul Islam:—

"What should be done with a Commander of the Faithful who has suppressed books and important dispositions of the Sharia law; who forbids the reading of, and burns, such books; who wastes public money for improper purposes; who, without legal authority, kills, imprisons, and tortures his subjects and commits tyrannical acts; who, after he has bound himself by oath to amend, violates such oath and persists in sowing discord so as to disturb the public peace, thus occasioning bloodshed?

"From various provinces the news comes that the population has deposed him; and it is known that to maintain him is manifestly dangerous and his deposition is advantageous.

"Under these conditions, is it permissible for the actual governing body to decide as seems best upon his abdication or deposition?"

The answer was the simple word 'Yes.'

Never was a sovereign condemned by a more emphatic and laconic word. Upon this the National Assembly unanimously decided on the deposition of Abdul Hamid. They sent a deputation to the palace to inform him to this effect. He appears to have taken the sentence of deportation very quietly. "It is Kismet," he said. "But will my life be spared?" He who had been so merciless to others was chiefly concerned now in claiming mercy for himself. He pleaded that he had not put to death his two brothers, Murad and Réchad. The question was reserved for the National Assembly.

Abdul Hamid found himself deserted and friendless. He was execrated by his subjects and despised and distrusted by all his fellow sovereigns in Europe, unless it were the German Emperor, who, of late years, had given a support to him in all his misdeeds at home and abroad. In his hour of peril the Emperor gave him no support, but the reverse. When he found how the wind was blowing, William II commenced an intrigue with the Committee of Union and Progress through Enver Bey, who had received a military training in Germany and was personally known to him. It is said that the Emperor insisted as a condition of recognition of the new order that the life of Abdul Hamid should be spared. There was another reason for doing so— namely the hope of the Young Turks to squeeze his hidden wealth from the deposed Sultan. However that may be, Abdul Hamid's life was spared. He was deported with a few of the more favoured members of his harem to Salonika, where he was detained as a virtual prisoner, but not otherwise maltreated. After his departure money and diamonds to the value of over a million pounds sterling were found in his palace, a small part only of his ill-gotten wealth. Two millions sterling were deposited with German banks and very large sums were in the hands of the Emperor William. Thus ended a reign of thirty-three years, more disastrous in its immediate losses of territory and in the certainty of others to follow, and more conspicuous for the deterioration of the condition of his subjects, than that of any other of his twenty-three degenerate predecessors since the death of Solyman the Magnificent.

XXII

THE YOUNG TURKS
1909-14

MEHMET RÉCHAD was proclaimed Sultan in place of his brother, under the title of Mahomet V, at the age of sixty-four. He had spent the whole period of his manhood as a virtual prisoner, the last thirty-four years of it under the close surveillance of his brother. He was never allowed to have friends or even to read newspapers. His servants were in the pay of Abdul Hamid and acted as spies on him. He devoted his life to his harem. It was not surprising that he lost what little intellect he was originally endowed with. A diplomatist who had many opportunities of seeing him since his elevation to the throne thus describes him:—

The very appearance of Mahomet V suggests nonentity. Small and bent, with sunken eyes and deeply lined face, an obesity savouring of disease, and a yellow, oily complexion, it certainly is not prepossessing. There is little or no intelligence in his countenance, and he never lost a haunted, frightened look, as if dreading to find an assassin lurking in some dark corner ready to strike and kill him.... Abdul Hamid hated and despised him, but was afraid to have him killed—perhaps through fear that a stronger man might take his place.[47]

The new Sultan had not been a party to the conspiracy which dethroned his brother. No one in his senses would have entrusted him with so important a secret. It was said of him that he simulated the mannerisms of an idiot in order to allay suspicion in the mind of Abdul Hamid that he took any interest in politics. He lived in constant fear of being put to death. A portrait of this degenerate would explain better than words, if it were not too cruel, the depth to which the once proud race of Othman has fallen. It was probable, however, that the cunning men who engineered the revolution thought it would better serve their purpose to have a cipher as the figure-head of the Empire than a man with a will of his own.

After the defeat of the reactionaries and the deposition of Abdul Hamid, in 1909, the Young Turks had another spell of power, during which they had the opportunity of effecting reforms in the administration of the Empire. They made a bad use of it. It soon became evident that there were two sections in the Committee in violent antagonism to one another. That which succeeded in getting the upper hand was chauvinistic, vehemently national in its objects and methods, aiming at the enforcement of unity throughout the Empire by Turkifying everything, without regard to local customs or to difference of race. They endeavoured to impose the Turkish language on the many subject races who spoke only their own language. They forbade the teaching in schools of the Albanian language in Albania, and of Arabic, the sacred language of Islam, in Arabia. They introduced compulsory service for the army, and forced the Christians of the Balkan provinces to serve in its ranks, with the result that thousands of young Bulgarians, Greeks, and Serbians, inhabitants of Macedonia, fled the country and sought refuge in the neighbouring States. The Young Turks availed themselves of the opportunity which this afforded them of strengthening the Moslem population of Macedonia by inviting thousands of the lowest class of Moslem Bosnians to migrate there. These men were the cause of grave disturbance and disorder. No provision was made for their employment. Committees of Young Turks were formed there, who incited the Turkish local authorities to deeds of arbitrary tyranny rivalling, if not excelling, the infamies of Abdul Hamid's rule. The autocracy of that tyrant was broken at Constantinople and his system of espionage, which had caused such indignation, was suppressed, but hundreds of local Abdul Hamids came into existence in the provinces.

The central Government at the capital followed the method of the late Sultan in minute interference with every detail of administration. There can be no doubt that the condition of the Christian provinces of the Empire became worse than ever. Meanwhile the enthusiasm for England and for the principles of the British Constitution cooled down at Constantinople. Whatever may have been the cause, the fact was certain that British influence at the Porte fell to a vanishing point, while that of Germany rapidly rose. The military alliance which has been so valuable to Germany in the existing great war was then formed. The period was also marked by repeated changes of the Grand Vizier, according as one or other section of the Young Turks got the upper hand.

It was not long before the process of dismemberment of the Empire was renewed and the wolves were gathered round it to share in the spoil. The Young Turks were less successful in resisting them than Abdul Hamid, who, at least, had kept them at bay by his cunning and shifty diplomacy during the many years which had elapsed since the Congress of Berlin, though it may well be said of him that the pent-up evils of his long misgovernment were in great part responsible for the dismemberments which followed in the régime of the Young Turks.

Very soon after the revolution of 1908, on October 7th, before there was experience of the new Constitution, the Austro-Hungarian Government took advantage of the crisis and proclaimed the annexation of Bosnia and Herzegovina, in defiance of the treaty obligations imposed by the Great Powers at Berlin. There was no attempt to justify this. The annexations made little or no difference to the people of the two provinces. They were already, for all practical purposes, under the rule of Austria-Hungary. The main difference was that the Bosnian soldiers discarded the fez which they wore as the symbol of Ottoman suzerainty. The annexation, however, caused great indignation among the Turks, who regarded it as an insult to their Empire. It was also the cause of ill-feeling in Russia, and did something to bring about the great war of 1914. The Austrian Government gave up its occupation of the Sandjak of Novi-Bazar and agreed to take over a share of the Ottoman debt, to the amount of about four millions sterling. As these concessions were accepted, the Porte must be held to have condoned the offence. Prince Ferdinand of Bulgaria very soon followed the example of the Austro-Hungarian Government. He proclaimed himself an independent sovereign. This also made very little practical difference to his subjects. On October 12th the Cretan Assembly proclaimed the union of the island with Greece.

The next blow to the Ottoman Empire came from a very unexpected quarter, from Italy, which made a sudden and unprovoked attack on Tripoli. This province in Africa had never been autonomous. It was an integral part of the Ottoman Empire, governed directly from Constantinople. Its population was purely Moslem—Turks and Moors in the city of Tripoli and other places on the coast, and with semi-independent Arabs in the hinterland. There was no demand on the part of these natives for a change of government. Italy had no valid cause of complaint on behalf of its few subjects who resided in the province, though it trumped up something of the kind. It was a case of pure aggression, prompted by jealousy of France in respect of Tunis, to which, geographically and economically, Italy had a stronger claim. It may be confidently assumed that the French Republic gave its consent to the seizure of Tripoli by Italy, and that Great Britain acquiesced in it, if it did not formally approve.

Up to the end of 1910, the Italian Government had constantly professed the desire to maintain the integrity of the Turkish Empire. When rumours arose of an intention to grab Tripoli, its Foreign Minister, so late as December 2, 1910, emphatically denied them in the Italian Chamber. "We desire," he said, "the integrity of the Ottoman Empire and we wish Tripoli always to remain Turkish." Nothing had since occurred to disturb the relations between the two countries. But in September 1911 the Italian Government sprang a mine on the Porte by declaring its intention to occupy Tripoli. On October 26th it notified to the Powers of Europe its intention to annex that province. It sent an army of fifty thousand men for the purpose. Its fleet bombarded the Turkish town of Prevesa, in the Adriatic, and drove the Turkish fleet to seek refuge within the Dardanelles. It took possession of several of the islands in the Ægean Sea.

The Porte was caught at a disadvantage. Abdul Hamid had for many years completely neglected his navy. He owed it a grudge for having taken part in the deposition of his predecessor. He feared that its guns might be trained on his palace. He had allowed the Minister of Marine, the most corrupt and greedy of all his Pashas, to appropriate to his own use the money allotted by the budget for the repair of warships. For many years the battleships never left the Golden Horn. But for this the Ottoman navy, which in the time of Abdul Aziz had been the third most powerful in Europe, might have made the landing of an Italian army in Africa impossible. The garrison in Tripoli, which Abdul Hamid had always maintained in strength, had been greatly reduced by the Young Turks. The reinforcement of it after the declaration of war, when Italy had command of the sea, was a very difficult task, the more so as the British Government proclaimed the neutrality of Egypt, though it was still tributary to the Porte, and forbade the passage of Turkish troops into Tripoli.

In spite of these obstacles, the Porte made a gallant fight for its African province, with the aid of the Arabs of the hinterland. Both Turkish and Italian armies committed the most horrible atrocities in this war, and there was little to choose between them in this respect. The war lasted till October, 1912, and was only brought to an end when the Porte found itself confronted by danger from a quarter much nearer home.

There can be little doubt that the war with Italy, the consequent engagement of a large Turkish army in defence of Tripoli, and the blockade of Turkish ports by the Italian navy, making it difficult for the Porte to transfer its troops from Asia direct to the Balkan States, precipitated the intervention of Greece, Bulgaria, and Serbia on behalf of the Christian inhabitants of the remaining provinces of the Porte in Europe, which were now on the eve of revolt.

The condition of these Christian provinces had in no way improved under the régime of the Young Turks, but very much the reverse. The governors and other Ottoman officials were as corrupt, rapacious, and arbitrary as they had ever been. There was no security for life or property. The Turkish soldiers plundered the villages of Christians which they were sent to protect. Bands of brigands, sometimes wearing the uniforms of Greek, sometimes of Bulgarian soldiers, devastated the country. No attempt was made by the Young Turks to put in force any part of the reforms which had been proposed by the Commission appointed by the Great Powers after the Congress of Berlin.

Lord Fitzmaurice's scheme remained as much a dead letter as it had been for over thirty years under Abdul Hamid. The Young Turks had added new difficulties and more causes of complaint by their attempts to Turkify everything, and by their extension of conscription to the Christian population. The physical situation of Macedonia made it impossible that its people would willingly submit to this continued misgovernment and tyranny. Their immediate neighbours were Bulgarians, Serbians, and Greeks, of kindred race, all of whom, with the assistance of Russia and other European Powers, had obtained freedom from Turkish rule. The peoples of Greece, Bulgaria, and Serbia sympathized with their compatriots who were still under the detested yoke.

If ever intervention by neighbouring States was justified for the purpose of restoring order and securing good government in accordance with treaty obligations, this was a case for it. The crisis was precipitated by massacres of Bulgarians at Kotchana, in Macedonia, and of Serbians on the borders of Montenegro.

Early in 1912 negotiations for armed intervention in Macedonia took place between the Governments of Greece, Bulgaria, and Serbia, at the instance mainly of the able and patriotic Premier of Greece, M. Venezelos. For the first and only time in their history a combination was effected between these three States against the Turkish Empire. It will be seen that, though it was most effective for its immediate purpose of defeating the Turks and expelling them from nearly the whole of their European possessions, it broke down, with most unfortunate results, almost immediately after this great success.

On March 18, 1912, a treaty was signed between Bulgaria and Serbia for mutual military aid to one another in war with Turkey. A secret clause provided that in the event of any portion of Macedonia being conquered the parts respectively nearest to the two States should be annexed to them, and that the intervening territory should be divided between them by the arbitration of Russia. This clearly showed that the intervention aimed at territorial conquest. Two months later another treaty was signed between Greece and Bulgaria, binding the two States to aid one another if attacked by Turkey, or in the event of systematic violation of rights by that Power. Nothing was said in this as to the division of spoil after the war. Montenegro later came into the chain of alliances, and, in fact, was always eager for war with Turkey.

When it became known to the Great Powers that these alliances were formed, and that war was imminent, they made every effort to allay the storm and to maintain peace. A strong protest was addressed, on September 25th, by Russia and Austria on behalf of all the Powers. They endeavoured to resuscitate the treaty of Berlin, which had so signally failed, to secure order and good government in the remaining Christian provinces of Turkey. They undertook, by virtue of the twenty-third article of that treaty, to insist on the realization of the promised reforms in the administration of these provinces, but with the reservation, which made the promise futile in the eyes of all concerned, that the reforms should not in any way diminish the sovereignty of the Sultan or impair the integrity of the Ottoman Empire.

The allied Balkan States, in a very dignified despatch of October 15th, declined to act on the advice of the Powers.

The Governments of the Balkan States [they said] consider that after so many promises of reform have been so often and so solemnly given by Turkey, it would be cruel not to endeavour to obtain in favour of the Christian population of the Ottoman Empire reforms of a more radical and definite nature which would really ameliorate their miserable condition if applied sincerely and in their integrity.

They enclosed a copy of an ultimatum which, on the same day, they addressed to the Porte, insisting on the carrying out of a series of reforms specially detailed.

If [they said] the Porte desires to accept these proposals, order and tranquillity will be reinstated in the provinces of the Empire, and a desirable peace will be assured between Turkey and the Balkan States, which have hitherto suffered from the arbitrary and provocative measures adopted by the Porte to them.

Among the list of reforms insisted on was the ceding and confirmation of the ethnical autonomy of provinces of the Empire, with all its consequences. The ultimatum was presented to the Porte, which treated it as a declaration of war. Its first and most important act was to come to terms with Italy in order to free its hands for the more important war at its very portals. A treaty of peace was signed on October 15th, by which the Porte agreed to withdraw its troops from Tripoli, and thus virtually recognized the acquisition of that province by Italy. Italy, on the other hand, agreed to withdraw from the islands of the Ægean Sea which it had occupied—a promise which, in fact, it did not perform.

Meanwhile hostilities had already commenced in the Balkans. Montenegro declared war on October 8th. The three other States followed suit on October 18th, and each of them sent its army on the same day, or nearly so, across its frontiers to invade Turkey. Beyond the desire for the better government of the Christian provinces of Turkey, there were doubtless *arrières pensées* on the part of all the allied States. Greece coveted Crete and other islands in the Ægean Sea, and hoped to extend its frontiers on the mainland. Bulgaria yearned for the big Bulgaria as defined by the treaty of San Stefano. Serbia had ambitions for a revival of its wide boundaries under Stephen Dushan, and aimed at access both to the Ægean Sea and the Adriatic. Montenegro wished for a part of Albania and for extensions in the Adriatic. Each State had large populations of a kindred race beyond its frontier suffering from cruel misgovernment and tyranny and crying for help. But it seems improbable that they could have expected to realize their full hopes, or to achieve such a *dénouement* as actually occurred.

The allies between them had seven hundred thousand men under arms. Turkey had no more than four hundred thousand in Europe. It had, however, great reserves in Asia, and its aggregate force largely exceeded that of the allies. It was to be expected that the Turkish armies in Europe would make a good fight, and would at least afford time for these reserves to come up.

The Greek army, under the command of the Crown Prince Constantine (the present King of Greece), who had received a military education in Germany, crossed the northern frontier and, in four days, on October 22nd, encountered a Turkish army, under Hassan Pasha, at Sarandoporus. The Turks held a very strong position and were little inferior in numbers. In spite of this, they were worsted, and were compelled to retreat in the following night. The next day the Greeks renewed their attack. The unfortunate Turks, disheartened by their defeat at Sarandoporus and wearied by the long night march, were caught unawares in a ravine which offered no possibility of defence. Terror-stricken and demoralized, they fled before their foe. They left behind them the whole of their artillery and transport.

The retreating Turks, despite their panic, found time to wreak their vengeance on the unfortunate Christian inhabitants on their route and mercilessly butchered them. What remained of their army retired on Veria, where it was reinforced by fourteen fresh battalions. On the 28th the Greek army resumed its march. In front of Veria it again came in contact with the Turks, who were posted in a very strong position. The issue was not long in doubt. The unhappy Turks were mown down by the Greek guns. Officers and men again fled like a beaten rabble. After these signal defeats the remainder of the Ottoman army crossed the River Vardar on November 3rd, within a few miles of Salonika. On the 8th that city capitulated to the Greeks, not without suspicion of treachery. Hassan Pasha and twenty-five thousand men, the remains of his army, were made prisoners. On the next day a division of the Bulgarians, detached from their main army in Thrace, appeared on the scene at Salonika, after a forced march, in the hope of being able to claim a share in the capture of that important city. At the request of its general, the Greeks gave permission to two regiments of Bulgarians to enter the city. In spite of this limitation, ten regiments were sent there, and were the cause of much subsequent trouble.

While these great and unexpected successes were being achieved by the Greeks, the Serbians were advancing from the north. A Turkish army of a hundred thousand men, under Zeki Pasha, had marched up the valley of the Vardar River to meet them. The two armies, about equal in numbers, met at Koumanovo on October 23rd, the day after the victory of the Greeks at Sarandoporus. The Turks were well supported with all modern implements of war, with machine guns, aeroplanes, and wireless telephone apparatus, but they had not a staff competent to make use of them. Their artillery was the best which Krupps' celebrated German works could turn out, and was superior in number to that of the Serbians. The French Creüsot guns, however, of the latter proved to be the better in action. But, worst of all, the commissariat arrangements of the Turks were of a most primitive character. They relied mainly on their men feeding themselves at the expense of the peasantry on their route, with the result that they were underfed. The weather was most inclement and the troops were only provided with light summer clothing. The best of soldiers cannot fight with empty stomachs and scanty clothing. As a result, in spite of a vigorous resistance in the great battle, the Turkish lines were broken by the splendid infantry of the Serbians. There resulted a rout and the precipitate retreat of the Turkish army. It lost the whole of its artillery—a hundred and twenty guns. Of the hundred thousand men, only forty thousand survived as a military force. Uskub, the ancient capital of Serbia, was captured. Another Serbian army advanced towards the Adriatic and captured Durazzo.

After the fierce and decisive battle at Koumanovo, what remained of the Turkish army retreated down the Vardar Valley to Veles, and thence, instead of marching to Salonika, where it might have been in time to save that city from the Greeks, it marched westward to Prilip, on the route to Monastir. The Serbians, after a brief delay, followed it up and came in contact again at Prilip, where the Turks held an immensely strong position. It was taken at the point of the bayonet, a striking proof of the superb quality of the Serbian infantry.

The Turks retreated thence to Monastir, where they found reinforcements. On November 17th and 18th, another great battle was fought in front of Monastir, in which the Turks were again defeated, with the loss of ten thousand prisoners. The remains of the army retreated into Albania, where it was too late in the season for the Serbians to follow them. They were ultimately, in the following spring, brought back to Constantinople by sea from the Adriatic. There could not have been a more completely victorious campaign for the Serbians. Zeki's army was virtually extinguished.

While these critical events were pending in Macedonia the Bulgarians were equally successful in the east. They invaded Thrace on October 18th in great force, and on the 22nd encountered a Turkish army at Kirk Kilisse and, after a two days' battle, defeated it. On the 28th they fought the main Turkish army, under Nazim Pasha, which was drawn up in a line from Lulu Burgas to Viza. The Turks made an obstinate resistance, but after forty-eight hours of fierce assaults by the Bulgarians they gave way and retreated in terrible disorder, till they found themselves behind the lines of Tchatalja, the celebrated fortifications which protect Constantinople at a distance of nineteen miles on a line from the Black Sea to the Marmora. On their advance through Thrace the Bulgarian soldiers, assisted by irregulars of Bulgar race, committed atrocities and cruelties on the Turkish population which rivalled all that the Turks in the past had perpetrated.

On November 17th the Bulgarians attacked these lines of Tchatalja with great vigour. But the Turks had brought up fresh troops from Asia. The lines were well defended with Krupp guns, and several successive assaults were repelled.

On December 3rd, at the instance of the Great Powers, an armistice was agreed upon between Turkey and Bulgaria and Serbia. War, however, was continued with Greece and Montenegro. As a result of the campaign the Turks had been defeated in every engagement by Greeks, Serbs, Bulgars, and Montenegrins. They were driven from Macedonia and from nearly the whole of Thrace and Epirus. They still, however, retained Adrianople, Janina, and Scutari. It was only when in defence of such cities, or behind such lines as those of Tchatalja that the Turkish soldiers showed the tenacity and courage for which they had been famous. Whenever they met the enemy in the open field they were always defeated.

It is almost incomprehensible [wrote Mr. Crawford Price, who was a witness of this *débâcle* of the Turkish army] that this warlike nation, the stories of whose valour fill the most thrilling pages of the military history of the world, could have degenerated into a beaten rabble flying before the onslaught of despised Serbians and Greeks, people who, till yesterday, scarce dared to lift their voices when questions affecting their interests were discussed and settled. The Greeks most effectually wiped out the stain of 1897. They showed themselves the superior of the Turk in organization, strategy, and even in personal courage.... I do not wish to dwell too strongly on the lack of courage exhibited by the Ottoman soldiers. Words fail me to describe the utter demoralization I found in the ranks of the Turkish troops after their defeat.[48]

Among the chief causes of this demoralization of the Ottoman armies was the complete absence of preparation for feeding them. It was the rule, rather than the exception, for the troops to be left three or four days without food. Another cause was that the Ottoman armies in this campaign in Europe had in their ranks a large proportion of Christian natives of the district who had been conscripted for the first time. Their sympathies were all in favour of the enemy, and they undoubtedly assisted in promoting the stampedes when the Turkish lines were broken. The survivors fled to their homes.

The winter of 1912-13, after the conclusion of the armistice, was spent in futile negotiations for peace at a Conference in London. The main cause of failure was Adrianople. The Bulgarians insisted on its cession to them as a condition of permanent peace. The Porte, in the first instance, was not unwilling to give way on this. But a military *émeute* occurred at Constantinople. A deputation from the army, headed by Enver Bey, insisted on entering the chamber where the Council of Ministers were deliberating on the question, with the object of protesting against the surrender of the stronghold. Nazim Pasha, the Minister of War, and his aide-de-camp were killed in the endeavour to resist this inroad. The Grand Vizier was thereupon terrorized into resignation. In his place Mahmoud Shefket, who had proved to be so loyal to the Young Turks at the early stage of their movement, was appointed. He refused to surrender Adrianople. The negotiations in London were broken off.

Early in 1913, on January 4th, the Bulgarians gave notice of the termination of the armistice. War was renewed. On February 4th the Bulgarian army commenced an attack on Adrianople, supported on this occasion by fifty thousand Serbians. On the same day they fought a battle near Bulair, defeated the Turks, and captured that important fortress, threatening the command of the Dardanelles. The Greeks also renewed the war. They sent an army into Epirus and, on March 6th, captured Janina, making prisoners thirty-three thousand Turks and seizing immense stores of guns and ammunition. On the 10th of the same month their fleet captured the island of Samos.

On March 28th the Bulgarians captured Adrianople and its garrison of twenty thousand Ottomans, and on April 21st the Montenegrins succeeded in getting possession of Scutari, which they claimed as the capital of their State. After these serious reverses the Porte was desirous of coming to terms, and was willing even to cede Adrianople and almost the whole of Thrace. It invited the mediation of the Great Powers. The allied States agreed to this. A second Conference was held in London on the basis that the Porte was to give up all its possessions in Europe, save the small part of Thrace south of a line drawn from Enos, in the Ægean Sea, to Media, in the Black Sea, a few miles north of the Tchatalja lines. Crete was to be ceded to Greece, and the destination of the islands in the Ægean Sea lately in the possession of Turkey, and some of which were necessary for its defence, was to be left to the decision of the Powers. A treaty was effected between the Porte and the Powers to this effect. But there was far greater difficulty in determining how the ceded districts were to be divided between the victorious Balkan States. The position was aggravated by Roumania coming into the field and claiming compensation in territory, in consideration of the important changes impending in the balance of power in the Balkans.

The four States so lately in alliance against the common enemy, Turkey, were now madly jealous of one another in the division of the spoils. Serbia, which had contributed so largely to the result by the splendid valour of its army against the main body of Turks under Zeki Pasha, was not content with the small slice of Macedonia which it had agreed to in the treaty with Bulgaria in 1912, before the war. The decision of the Powers that Albania was to be an independent State deprived Serbia of the much-hoped-for access to the Adriatic. The acquisition by Bulgaria of Thrace, including Adrianople, would greatly alter the balance of power in the Balkans to the disadvantage of Serbia and justified its claim to a larger share of Macedonia. It was already in occupation of nearly half of that province. Bulgaria was equally ambitious to revive the big Bulgaria of the San Stefano treaty, and could also appeal to long past history in favour of it. It was determined to get possession of Salonika, and was madly jealous of Greece. The Greeks, on their part, were in possession of that city and of the southern half of Macedonia. They had got hold of these districts by force of arms and were determined not to give them up. No agreement could be come to in London. Russia in vain did its utmost to compose these differences. It offered to act as arbitrator and invited the Balkan States to send representatives to Petrograd to settle the questions.

We now know that the Bulgarian Government had no intention whatever to make concessions to the other Balkan States. The pacific section of its ministers were overborne by the more bellicose members. M. Gueshoff, the able Premier, who had been responsible for the policy which preceded the war, and who was now in favour of a peaceful settlement, was compelled to resign. King Ferdinand, a most unscrupulous and ambitious intriguer, backed up the war party, and was mainly responsible for the treacherous policy pursued, which was fraught with so much misfortune to his State. In spite of the warnings from Russia that, if force were resorted to, Bulgaria would find itself confronted by a Roumanian army, and that the Porte would also join in the war against it, King Ferdinand and his Government decided on war with their late allies. They had unbounded and arrogant confidence in their army, and despised those of Greece and Serbia.

On June 29, 1913, at midnight, the Bulgarian army in Macedonia made a sudden and unprovoked attack on the Greek and Serbian outposts, without any warning or declaration of war. This treacherous action was followed up the next day by an advance of the Bulgarian army of a hundred thousand men on the right flank against the Serbian army, which was nearest to them. For the moment this seemed to promise success, and the Serbians were compelled to fall back. But on July 1st the Serbians, whose forces, supported by the Montenegrins, were almost equal in number to the Bulgarians opposed to them, rallied and decided on a counter offensive. On July 2nd they attacked the Bulgarians on the Bragalbabza River, defeated them, and captured many of their guns. On July 4th another battle took place with much the same result. Istib was captured on the 8th, and the Bulgarians were then compelled to retreat towards their own frontier.

Meanwhile the main army of the Greeks, which was concentrated at Salonika, a day's march from the Bulgarians on the left flank, advanced to attack them. The two armies were equal in numbers, each of about seventy thousand men. They met at Kiltich, about half-way between the Rivers Vardar and Struma, and a day's march from Salonika. The Greeks inflicted a very severe defeat on their foes. This was followed up a few days later by victories at Doiran and Strumnitza. In the fortnight which followed the Bulgarians were defeated in a series of engagements as they retreated to their own frontier.

The prediction and warnings of the Russian Government were now verified. The Roumanians, when they found that the Bulgarians were involved in war with the other Balkan States, announced that they were dissatisfied with the small concession of territory made to them at the Conference in London— namely the fortress of Silistria and a belt of land on the Danube. They insisted on a further cession of territory to them in the Dobrudscha. They sent an army across the Danube, on July 10th, to support this demand. It advanced without opposition to within a few miles of Sofia. The Turks also saw the opportunity of retrieving out of the scramble something of their recent great losses of territory. They determined to tear up the treaty of London, signed only a few weeks ago. They sent an army, under Enver Pasha, into Thrace, on July 15th, to attack Adrianople. It had no difficulty in recapturing that most important city, from which the Bulgarians had withdrawn nearly the whole of its garrison in order to strengthen their armies against Greece and Serbia. It also reoccupied Demotika and Kirk Kilisse.

The Bulgarians found themselves in a most perilous position. Their armies had everywhere been defeated and driven back. They were surrounded by invading armies. They were compelled to sue for terms. On July 31st an armistice was agreed to, and a Conference was decided on, to be held at Bucharest, between the representatives of the Balkan States, without the presence of those of the Great Powers. At the Conference the Bulgarians found themselves in the position of being hoist with their own petard. They were compelled by *force majeure* not only to give up all their ambitious projects, but also to make serious concessions to all their rivals. Had they been willing to come to terms at the Conference at London or, later, to submit to the arbitration of Russia, they would undoubtedly have secured for themselves a large slice of Macedonia. They would have retained possession of a great part of Thrace, with Adrianople and Demotika, and the only concessions they would have made were Silistria and the small belt of land on the Danube. They were now compelled to agree to the division of the whole of Macedonia between Greece and Serbia. They had to surrender a part of the Dobrudscha to Roumania, and the larger part of their conquests in Thrace, including

Adrianople, to the Turks. All that remained to them in return for their stupendous efforts in the recent wars was a small portion of Thrace with a narrow frontage to the Ægean Sea, but without a port of any value or importance. Never was there a case in which base treachery and overweening arrogance were followed by more fatal retribution.

Greece got the larger share of the spoil of Turkey in the two years of war. It obtained rather more than half of Macedonia—namely 17,000 square miles, with a population of 1,697,000. It also secured the final cession to it of the important island of Crete, and of Samos, and other islands in the Ægean Sea. Its territory and population were increased by more than one-half. Serbia obtained 15,000 square miles, with 1,656,000 inhabitants, Bulgaria only 9,600 miles and 125,000 inhabitants. Roumania secured 2,600 square miles, with 286,000 inhabitants, and Montenegro 2,100 square miles and 251,000 population; while the Turks lost 54,000 square miles, inhabited by a population of 4,239,000. But the recovery of Adrianople, Demotika, and Kirk Kilisse was a great coup for them. It redounded to the prestige of the Young Turks and their leader, Enver Pasha, who soon became Minister of War.

The German Emperor telegraphed his congratulations to the Sultan on the recovery of Adrianople, and to the King of Roumania on the success of his intervention. He also conferred on the King of Greece, his brother-in-law, the bâton of a Field Marshal in the German army. The King received this honour in person at Berlin in the presence of a great gathering of German generals. In a speech on the occasion, he attributed his success in the recent war, in the first place, to the bravery of his army, and in the second to the training which he and many of his officers had received in the military schools of Berlin. Thenceforth, till the outbreak of the great war in Europe in 1914, the influence of Germany in the Near East, and especially in Turkey, was continually on the increase. Enver Pasha, who now predominated in the councils of the Porte, was devoted to the interests of Germany, and was probably in its pay. At his instance the Turkish army, which had so conspicuously failed in the recent wars, was put under the control of the German General Von der Goltz, and large numbers of officers were lent by Germany for its better training. Secret drillings of troops took place in many remote parts of the Empire. These measures were well timed to coincide with the outbreak in 1914 of the great war, which, it is now very certain, had been already determined on by the General War Staff at Berlin.

It only remains to add that when, soon after the commencement of the war, the Porte, at the instance of Enver Pasha, declared itself against the Allied Powers, the British Government at once proclaimed the independence of Egypt, under its protectorate, and the annexation of Cyprus. These were the last territorial losses of the Ottoman Empire which can be counted as *faits accomplis*. It has been shown that, in the past, there were due to the régime of the Young Turks, during the six years of its predominance, from 1908 to 1914, the loss in Europe of Macedonia, Epirus, and Albania, and of a large part of Thrace; of Crete, Cyprus, and many other islands in the Ægean Sea; and the suzerainty of Bulgaria, Bosnia, and Herzegovina; and in Africa of the province of Tripoli and the suzerainty of Egypt. These great losses rivalled in extent of territory and population those incurred either by Mahmoud II or by Abdul Hamid II. It needs no prophet to predict a further shrinkage of territory, or loss of independence, after the conclusion of the existing war in Europe, whatever may be its other results.

London: T. Fisher Unwin. Ltd.   *Stanford's Geog.¹ Estab.¹ London.*

SOUTH EASTERN EUROPE
AND ASIA MINOR
1914.

XXIII

A RETROSPECT

IT has been shown in preceding chapters that the two great historic movements of the growth and decay of the Turkish Empire extended over periods not differing much in length. Reckoning its birth from the accession, in 1288, of Othman, as chief of a small tribe of Turks in Asia Minor, nearly three hundred years elapsed before the Empire reached its zenith. During these years ten eminent Sultans and one Grand Vizier (Sokolli) of a degenerate Sultan were concerned in its extension. It was a period of almost continuous victory and conquest. The Ottoman armies, during these years, met with only a single serious disaster, that at Angora in 1402 at the hands of Timur and a host of Mongolian invaders, which seemed at first to have struck a fatal blow to the Empire. But it soon rallied, and the process of aggrandizement was renewed. With this exception the Ottomans were almost uniformly successful. The number, however, of pitched battles in the field, which decided the fate of States successively invaded, was not great. Thrace was won by the defeat of the Byzantines by Murad I at Eski Baba in 1361. The Bulgarians were conquered at Samakof in 1371, and the Serbians at Kossova in 1389, by the same Sultan. The Hungarians were overthrown at Mohacz in 1529. The Persians were defeated at Calderan, 1514, near Tabriz, and the Egyptians at Aleppo, 1516, and Ridania, near Cairo, under Selim, 1516. The crusaders from Europe were defeated in three great battles—at the Maritza, 1363, Nicopolis, 1396, and Varna, 1444. At most of these battles the Ottomans had great superiority of numbers, and as against the Persians and Egyptians they were provided with a powerful artillery, of which their opponents were wholly deficient. The other very numerous campaigns consisted mainly of successions of sieges by invading armies of Ottomans, where the invaded, with inferior forces, protracted the defence, often over long terms of years.

The Ottomans were almost equally successful at sea, with one notable exception, at Lepanto, at the very end of the period we are referring to, when they met with a terrible disaster from the combined navies of Europe, much inferior in numbers of ships and men. But before this their naval supremacy had enabled them to extend the Empire over Algiers and Tunis. Nothing resulted from the great battle of Lepanto except loss of prestige to the Ottomans. The combination against them was dissolved, and for many years they maintained supremacy in the Eastern Mediterranean.

At the close of this period of growth the Ottoman Empire reached its zenith and extended over the vast countries described in the chapter on the Grand

Vizier Sokolli. The whole of its immense area, however, was not in full ownership of the Ottomans. Parts of it, such as North Hungary, were autonomous States with native rulers paying tribute to the Porte. Other parts, such as the Crimea, Wallachia, and Moldavia, were vassal States, whose princes were appointed by the Sultan, and which were bound to send contingents in support of the Ottoman armies when at war. The really integral parts of the Empire in Europe were Thrace, Macedonia, Bulgaria, Greece, Serbia, Bosnia, and Albania; in Asia, Anatolia, Mesopotamia, Syria, and a great part of Arabia; and in Africa, Tripoli. Egypt, Tunis, and Algiers very early acquired a practical autonomy under the suzerainty of the Porte, though they were still nominally integral parts of the Empire. The Empire thus constituted was one of the greatest in the then world. It may be worth while briefly to review the causes which led to its aggregation.

It was the common belief in Europe, confirmed by many historians, up to recent times, that the Ottoman armies which invaded Europe from Asia Minor were composed of pure Turks, and that the motive which impelled them in their conquest was the fanatical desire to extend Islam. But these views have been modified of late years. It has been shown that the armies which Sultans Orchan and Murad led across the Straits into Europe were not pure Turks, but were very largely composed of subjects of the East Roman Empire from the northern parts of Asia Minor, who, after the defeat there of the Byzantine armies, had embraced Islam. They were welded with the Turks by religion into something approaching to a nation. They called themselves Osmanlis, or Ottomans, from the founder of the Othman dynasty. It may be doubted whether the Turks alone were capable of effecting the conquests in Europe. It is certain that they could not have maintained the Empire when formed.

The Turks of Anatolia had many valuable qualities as soldiers. They were, and are to this day, brave, hardy, sober, frugal, and cleanly in their habits, as inculcated by their religion, a strong point in their favour in days when sanitary arrangements were completely ignored by armies. They bore the hardships of long campaigns without complaint. But they were deficient in intelligence and education, which count for much in war as in civil life. In this respect they were very inferior to subjects of the East Roman Empire and to many of the Christians with whom they came in conflict. But the Ottomans who first invaded Europe were not simply Turks. Later, the most effective corps in the Ottoman army was formed exclusively of the sons of Christian parents in the Balkans, conscripted at an early age and forcibly converted to Islam. It was with forces thus constituted that the Ottomans extended their Empire up to and beyond the Danube. The conquests of the larger part of Asia Minor, of Mesopotamia, Syria, and Egypt, were also effected, by composite forces, to which Serbia and Wallachia sent contingents by virtue of treaties with the Porte. The greater number of Ottoman generals who distinguished themselves in these early days of conquest were not of Turkish race, but were Greeks, Albanians, Slavs, and Italians, who had embraced Islam or whose forbears had done so. It was the same with almost all the naval commanders. They were of foreign origin, who had gained experience as pirates and had embraced Islam. The crews who manned the Ottoman navy were mainly Greeks from the islands in the Ægean Sea.

With respect to the objects and motives of the Ottoman conquests, a careful review of the history of the early Sultans has shown that there was very little, if any, of missionary enterprise on behalf of Islam. It will be admitted that there is no pretence for concluding that the vast conquests in Asia and Africa had any such motive. The populations there were already Moslems. The motives for conquest were the ambition to extend the Empire at the expense of neighbouring States and the hope of plunder on the part of the soldiers. Religious zeal had nothing to do with it. What reason is there to suppose that conquests in Europe had any different object than those in Asia? As a matter of fact, there was no very large extension of Islam in Europe as a result of Ottoman conquest. When cities were captured and their inhabitants were massacred, or when districts were conquered and the people were carried away as captives to be sold as slaves, they do not appear to have had the alternative offered to them of embracing Islam.

In some few districts, as in Bosnia and parts of Albania and the Morea, the landowners, or some of them, were allowed to avoid the confiscation of their property by becoming Mussulmans. But these were exceptions. The general rule was that the land of the conquered districts was confiscated without the option to the owners of changing their religion and saving their property. As regards the labouring people, the rayas, there does not appear to have been any desire that they should adopt the religion of their conquerors. They were wanted for the cultivation of the land as serfs or slaves. It seems to have been a matter of indifference what their religion was.

There is also nothing to show that the Ottoman soldiers were animated by any religious zeal in their campaigns in Europe. The main cause of their military efficiency was the organization of the army effected by Orchan and perfected by Murad I. It offered immense rewards to the soldiers for victories in battle and for personal valour, in the share of booty and plunder levied in the conquered districts, of captives to be sold as slaves, of women for wives or concubines or to be sold for harems, and of lands to be distributed as fiefs. These rewards appealed to the predatory instincts of the Moslem soldiers, whether Turks or others of alien origin. In the rare intervals of peace the soldiers soon wearied of life in barracks, and yearned for active campaigns. At such times the Janissaries and other soldiers were a danger to

- 292 -

the State from their turbulence and disorder. It was necessary to find employment for them at a distance. This acted as a constant incitement to war and to fresh conquests. It was one of the causes of the continuous growth of the Empire.

A second main cause of success to the Ottoman armies in Europe was the want of union for resistance on the part of the people of the Balkan States. There can be little doubt that if the Greeks, Bulgarians, and Serbians had combined to resist the invading Moslems their efforts would have been successful. But Greeks and Bulgarians, Greeks and Serbians hated one another more than they feared and hated the Ottomans. In the six centuries dealt with in this volume there was only a single occasion when Greeks, Bulgarians, and Serbians formed a combination against the Ottomans. This was not till 1912. The combination was successful and drove the Turks out of Macedonia, Epirus, Albania, and the greater part of Thrace. But we have shown that it broke down on the division of the spoil, with the result that the Turks recovered a small part of their lost territory. The case illustrates our contention that want of union of the Christian States was a main cause of the servitude of all of them for nearly five hundred years under Turkish rule.

Lastly, in appreciating the causes of the wonderful growth of the Ottoman Empire, we must not lose sight of the personal element, of the fact that, for ten generations, the Othman family produced men capable of leading their armies in the field to victory, and almost equally remarkable as administrators and statesmen. This succession of a single family, father and son, for ten generations without a break, culminating in the greatest of them, Solyman the Magnificent, is quite without precedent or example in history. The Othman family were pure Turks in their origin. But the Turkish blood was very soon diluted. The mothers of future Sultans were either captives taken by corsairs or slaves bought on account of their beauty. They were of every race—Greeks, Slavs, Italians, or Russians. But in spite of this mixed blood the type of Sultans remained much the same for ten generations. The prestige acquired by the family in these three hundred years, as founders and maintainers of the Empire and as generals who led their armies to victory, was such that it has impressed itself on the imagination of all Ottomans, and has survived to this day, in spite of the long subsequent degeneration of the family. Unquestionably, the foundation and growth of the Empire were largely due to the personal qualities of the Othman dynasty.

After the death in 1578 of Grand Vizier Sokolli, who carried on the traditions of the first ten Sultans for a few years under the worthless Selim II, the pendulum of Empire swung in the opposite direction. Thenceforth, down to the present time, there were successions of defeats and disasters to the Turkish Empire, with but few intermissions. Provinces were torn from it periodically, like leaves from an artichoke, till all but a small fraction of it in Europe, the whole of its possessions in Africa, and a large part in Asia have been lost to the Empire. What remains to it is the core of Turkish and Arabic provinces in Asia, and in Europe only its capital, Constantinople, and a small portion of Thrace to the north of it.

Five of the Great Powers of Europe have had their share of the spoils, and six independent States have been resuscitated out of the remaining débris of it. It is hard to say which of the Great Powers gained most. Austria recovered by force of arms Hungary, Transylvania, Dalmatia, Croatia, and Slavonia, and by artful policy Bosnia and Herzegovina. Russia obtained by conquest the Crimea, Bessarabia, Podolia, and a part of the Ukraine in Europe, and the Caucasus, and a great part of Armenia, in Asia. France has possessed itself of Algiers and Tunis. England has secured the suzerainty and practical possession of Egypt and complete possession of Cyprus and Aden. Italy has seized Tripoli. Of the six smaller independent States, Bulgaria and Roumania owe their revival solely to Russia, Greece mainly to Great Britain and France, Albania to the concert of the Balkan States in 1912, and Serbia and Montenegro alone owe their freedom mainly to their own valour. It need not be said that gratitude forms no part of the ethics of modern statecraft, and a few only of the above States have recognized that they owe anything to the Powers who rescued them from Turkish rule.

During the last three hundred years, when these vast changes were being effected, the Ottoman army lost all the prestige it had acquired during the previous three hundred years. With the single exception of the battle of Cerestes, fought against the Hungarians in 1646, when a *débâcle* of the Turkish army was averted by the splendid cavalry charge of Cicala Pasha, which saved to the Ottoman Empire the larger part of Hungary for another term of seventy-two years, its armies were defeated in almost every battle of any importance. In nearly all of them the Ottomans had the advantage of very superior numbers, but this did not save them from disaster. The armies opposed to them were led by a succession of generals who were masters of the art of war, such as Sobieski, King of Poland, Prince Eugène of Savoy, Prince Charles of Lorraine, Generals Munnich, Loudon, Kutusoff, Suvorov, Diebitsch, Paskievitch, Skobeleff, and Gourko. Compared with these, the Turks had not a single general of eminence and only a few valiant leaders in battle.

To what causes, then, are we to attribute the decay and dismemberment of the vast Empire, and the complete failure of its armies to maintain prestige for victory and valour? It is more easy perhaps to suggest causes for downfall than for the birth and growth of the Empire. First and foremost of the causes has unquestionably been the degeneracy of the Othman dynasty. It could not have been by a mere chance coincidence that the growth of Empire was synchronous with the reign of the first ten Sultans, and that its decay and dismemberment were extended through the reign of twenty-five successors, of whom all but two, or possibly three, were degenerates and wholly incompetent to rule. The Ottoman State was an autocracy in which all military, civil, and religious faculties were centred in its head. It needed autocrats competent for the task, and in the absence of such it was certain that the State would take the road to ruin. Whether the degeneracy of the dynasty was due, as has been hinted, to a break in the true succession, and the introduction of alien blood after Solyman the Magnificent, or not, the fact remains that we can discern no trace of the eminent qualities of the family in those who succeeded him.

The deterioration of the race, which began with Selim 'the Sot,' was confirmed and accentuated by what occurred after three more Sultans had succeeded father to son—all of them equally unfit to fill the throne. The original law of succession, which had been set aside by the cruel practice of fratricide, was then reverted to, and the eldest male of the family, and not the eldest son of a defunct Sultan, was recognized as his successor. Thenceforth, by way of precaution against conspiracy and rebellion, the reigning Sultans, in lieu of putting their brothers to death, immured them as virtual prisoners in the building of the Seraglio known as the Cage, where they were allowed little or no communication with the world. They were permitted to maintain their harems, but by some abominable process the women were sterilized so as to prevent their giving birth to possible claimants to the throne. Of twenty successors to Mahomet IV, seventeen were subjected to this degrading treatment, and only left prison on succeeding to the throne. Three Sultans escaped this treatment, two of them by succeeding their fathers, in default of other male heirs of an older age. Only one of these three was better equipped to fill the throne than the average of the other seventeen. It is evident, therefore, that the dynasty was worn out. It would have been well for the Empire if the Othman race had long ago come to an end, and had been replaced by some more virile and competent stock.

It followed, from the degeneracy of this long succession of Sultans, that the supreme power of the State fell into other hands, either of viziers who were able to dominate the reigning Sultans and to secure themselves against intrigues of all kinds, or more often of the harem. It would be difficult to exaggerate the evils which resulted from the intervention of the Sultan's harem in affairs of State. The harem consisted of a vast concourse of women and slaves, of concubines and eunuchs, maintained at a huge expense—a nest of extravagance and corruption. It was always in antagonism to the official administration of the Porte, which ostensibly carried on the administration of the State under the direction of the Sultan. The favourite concubine for the time being, or the ambitious mother of a Sultan, or not infrequently the principal eunuch, gained the ear of the Sultan and overruled the more experienced advisers of the Porte. The harem was the centre from which corruption spread throughout the Turkish Empire, as officials of every degree, from the highest to the lowest, found it expedient to secure their interest with its inmates by heavy bribes. It has been shown in previous pages that the sale of offices, civil and military, became universal. This was largely responsible for the decay and dismemberment of the State. An illustration of this was to be found in the cases of Egypt, Algiers, and Tunis. The incompetent pashas, who had obtained by purchase the governorships of these important provinces, were unable to control the local Mamelukes in Egypt, or the local Janissaries in Algiers and Tunis, with the result that these provinces became practically independent and later were lost to the Empire.

A second main cause of the decadence of the Empire was undoubtedly the deterioration of its armies. We miss altogether in the many great battles of the last three hundred years the élan and the daring spirit by which the Ottomans won their many victories in the period of accretion of the Empire. Two main explanations may be offered for this. The one that the armies in the later period were formed more exclusively from the Turkish and Arabic subjects of the Empire, and that the proportion of men of Greek or Slav descent was far less, if it was not wholly absent. When the Empire was extended over the whole of Asia Minor, Mesopotamia, and Syria, the Moslem population was enormously increased. In 1648 the corps of Janissaries ceased to be levied from Christian youths and was recruited from Moslems. There was wanting, therefore, to the army the spirit given to it in the past by the Greeks and other Christian races. This difference was probably more serious in the case of the officers than with the rank and file. The Turks supplied very poor material for officers.

The other explanation is to be found in the absence of incentive to military ardour in the later period. If we have been justified in the conclusion that there was little or no motive for the Turkish army in the shape of religious fanaticism and the desire to spread Islam, but that plunder and the hope of acquiring lands for distribution among the soldiers was its main inducement, it followed that this incentive to victory and valour was almost entirely absent in the later period when the Empire was on the defensive, when it was no longer a question of making fresh conquests, but of retaining what had already been won. The army could not expect to get loot and plunder or captives for sale as slaves, or land to be confiscated for fiefs, when engaged in war for the defence of some tributary or vassal State or of some more integral part of the Empire. Nor could there be the feeling of fighting for their own homes and property when defending a subject Christian province. Yet another partial explanation is to be found in the fact that the general corruption had infected the army, as well as the civil administration of the

State. Promotions through all the ranks went not to merit, but to the highest bidders. The civil branches of the army also, such as the commissariat and those for the supply of munitions, which in the earlier period were well provided for, fell into disorder and confusion owing to the universal spread of corruption.

In view of these many serious changes, it is not difficult to appreciate the causes for the falling off of the *morale* of the Ottoman army and for its failure to maintain the reputation it had achieved in the three centuries of conquest and extension of the Empire. The war which is now raging in the Near East has shown that the Ottoman soldiers, when organized, and in part led, by competent foreign officers, when fighting *pro aris et focis*, and especially when in defence of well fortified lines, have a great military value.

A third cause, however, for the failure of the Ottomans to maintain their Empire in Europe is undoubtedly to be found in the continually worsening conditions of the Christian populations subject to it. In the earlier period there is good reason to conclude that the average condition of the rayas in the Christian provinces subjected to Ottoman rule and law was somewhat better than that of the peasants in some neighbouring States, such as Hungary, Austria, and Russia. There was something in the way of fixity of tenure accorded to the rayas which was absent from the feudal serfs.

It was alleged that peasants from Hungary not infrequently migrated into the Balkan States in order to enjoy this better treatment, and it is certain that the Greeks of the Morea and Crete preferred the rule of the Ottomans, bad as it was, to that of the Venetians, who were even more cruel and rapacious. However that may have been, it is certain that everywhere under Turkish rule, during the last three hundred years, the conditions of the Christian populations became more wretched and intolerable, and relatively far worse than in neighbouring States. This was greatly due to the degeneracy and corruption of the central Government at Constantinople, and to its evil example and influence throughout the Empire. Governors of provinces and all local officials became more corrupt and rapacious. There was no security for life or property. Justice was not obtainable in the local tribunals. Arbitrary exactions were levied on the peasantry. Brigandage everywhere increased. Money levied in the provinces was never expended for the benefit of their populations. Turkish rule acted as a blight on the districts subject to it. Provinces liberated from it improved in condition beyond recognition. The comparison with them was an ever present object-lesson to those who remained under Turkish rule. The efforts of the combined Powers of Europe to induce or compel the Porte to effect improvements in the government of its subjects proved to be futile and impotent. Treaty obligations with this object were habitually disregarded by the Porte and were treated as waste-paper. Provinces thus conditioned were always on the brink of rebellion.

They were kept in subjection, not by the maintenance of any large armed forces there, but by periodic massacres of a ruthless character. These were not the product of religious fanaticism, as has often been suggested, but of deliberate policy, and were instigated by orders direct from the Porte, with the hope of inspiring terror in the minds of the subject races.

Foreign intervention, incited not so much by territorial ambition as by popular sympathy for the oppressed, was resorted to for the purpose of redressing grievous wrongs and for preserving the peace of Europe. As a result of these causes, extending over more than three hundred years, the Turkish Empire, so far as Europe is concerned, and in the sense of a dominant Power over subject races, has ceased to exist. In countries which it held in subjection for over five hundred years it has left no trace that it ever existed. The very few Turks and the Tartars and Circassians who had been planted there by the Porte when the Crimea and the Caucasus were subjected by Russia have departed bag and baggage from Europe. They have migrated to Asia Minor at the instigation of their mollahs. The few Moslems who remain behind in these districts are not of Ottoman or Turkish descent; they are of the same races as their neighbours. Their ancestors adopted Islam to save their property.

The Young Turks, who of late years have controlled the Empire, have signally failed to arrest the great movement which we have above described. They have further developed their policy of Turkifying what remains to them of the Empire during the existing war. Their massacres and deportations of Armenians in Asia Minor have been on a scale and with a cruelty without precedent in history. Whether responsibility for this indelible crime will be enforced on them, and whether, as it richly deserves, the Turkish Empire will suffer further reductions, will depend on the issue of the colossal struggle in which the nations of Europe are now engaged. Whatever the future may have in store in these respects, there is one certain moral to be drawn from the story which has been told in these pages, namely that an Empire originally founded on the predatory instincts of an alien military caste, and whose rulers during the last four hundred years have never recognized that they had any responsibility for the good government and well-being of the races subject to them, could not, if there be any law of human progress in the world, be permanent, and was destined ultimately to perish by the sword.

APPENDIX

GENEALOGY OF THE OTTOMAN SULTANS.

			1. OTHMAN (accession as Emir atat Sugut), 1288.	
		ALAEDDIN.	2. ORCHAN, 1326.	
			3. MURAD I, 1360.	
			4. BAYEZID, 1389.	JACOUB.
SOLYMAN.	MUSA.	ISSA.	5. MAHOMET I, 1402.	MUSTAPHA.
			6. MURAD II, 1421.	
			7. MAHOMET II, 1451 (deposed).	
			8. BAYEZID II, 1481.	DJEM.
	KHORKAND.	AHMED.	9. SELIM I, 1512.	
			10. SOLYMAN I, 1520.	
	MUSTAPHA.	BAYEZID.	11. SELIM II, 1566.	
			12. MURAD III, 1574.	
			13. MAHOMET III, 1595.	

		14. AHMED I, 1603.							15. MUSTAPHA 1617 (deposed).	
		16. OTHMAN II, 1618 (murdered).			17. MURAD IV, 1623.				18. IBRAHIM, 1640 (deposed).	
		19. MAHOMET IV, 1648 (deposed).			20.SOLYMAN II, 1687.				21. AHMED II, 1691.	
		22. MUSTAPHA II, 1695 (abdicated).							23. AHMED III, 1703 (deposed).	
		24. MAHMOUD I, 1730.			25. OTHMAN III, 1754.					
		26. MUSTAPHA III, 1757.							27. ABDUL HAMID I, 1773.	
		28. SELIM III, 1789 (deposed)								
		29. MUSTAPHA IV, 1807 (deposed).							30. MAHMOUD II, 1808.	
		31. ABDUL MEHZID, 1839.							32. ABDUL AZIZ, 1861 (deposed).	
		33. MURAD V, 1876			34. ABDUL HAMID II, 1876				35. MAHOMET V, 1908.	

FOOTNOTES:

[1] Von Hammer, i. p. 28 (French translation).

[2] Cantemir, p. 20.

[3] Mr. Gibbons refuses credence to this interesting story on the ground mainly of its inherent improbability. His argument does not convince me. The succession of the younger brother to the Emirate without a fight for it, on the part of the elder one, was an event so remarkable, and so contrary to all experience in Ottoman history, as to make the explanation given a reasonable one. The probabilities seem to me to be all in its favour. Alaeddin died in 1337. It is admitted that for seven years he acted as the first Grand Vizier of the Ottoman State. It may well be, therefore, that he commenced, if he did not complete, the important organization of the army with which he has been credited by Turkish historians.

[4] This was not the corps of Janissaries, which, as Mr. Gibbons has shown, was created not by Orchan but by his son Murad.

[5] Mr. Gibbons in his account of the origin of this corps disputes the figures as reported above from previous writers, and also the alleged motives for its constitution. After careful consideration of the question, I have preferred to adhere to the version given by Sir Edwin Pears, who has investigated the subject with great care in the early Greek and Turkish histories. I have, however, followed Mr. Gibbons in one point, namely, in attributing the constitution of the force to Murad I rather than to Orchan. Mr. Gibbons's account of the corps of Janissaries is to be found on pp. 118-20 of the *Foundation of the Ottoman Empire*, and that of Sir Edwin Pears in his work on the *Destruction of the Greek Empire*, pp. 223-30.

[6] Pears, p. 228.

[7] Knolles, i. p. 139.

[8] Gibbons, p. 221.

[9] Froissart, xvi. 47.

[10] Boucicaut in 1399, with four ships and two armed galleys and twelve hundred knights and foot soldiers, after defeating an Ottoman fleet in the Dardanelles, arrived at Constantinople and gave assistance to the Emperor in defence of the city.

[11] Gibbon, viii. p. 114.

[12] This story of the cage, which forms the subject of a scene in Marlowe's play of *Tamerlane*, has been discredited by some historians of late years. But

Mr. Gibbons, after a full and careful examination of all the records of the time, has re-established its veracity.

[13] Gibbon, viii. p. 242.

[14] Von Hammer, ii. p. 379.

[15] Sir Edwin Pears, *Destruction of the Greek Empire*, p. 217.

[16] The four pages which Gibbon devotes to a description of this attempted union of the two Churches are masterpieces of irony and scorn (Gibbon, viii. pp. 287-91).

[17] The writer, in 1890, had the advantage of viewing what remained of these walls in the company of Sir Edwin Pears, who has fully described them in his admirable account of the great siege.

[18] Stone balls of considerable size were used by the Turks to defend the Dardanelles up to a late date. When in 1855 the writer visited the forts there, he observed that they were still provided for some of the guns.

[19] Speech of Mahomet recorded by the historian Christobulus, quoted by Sir Edwin Pears, pp. 323-4.

[20] Quoted by Pears, p. 303.

[21] Von Hammer, vii. p. 4.

[22] *Sir T. Roe's Embassy*, pp. 66-7.

[23] Ibid. p. 178.

[24] Ibid. p. 206.

[25] Ibid. p. 243.

[26] Von Hammer, xi. p. 378.

[27] Schimmer, *Two Sieges of Vienna*, p. 137.

[28] Von Hammer, xii. p. 372.

[29] See the *Mémoires de Morosini*, iii. pp. 112, 113.

[30] Whitworth to Leeds, January 10, 1781; Record Office.

[31] Ranke's *History of Serbia*, p. 115.

[32] Moltke, p. 257.

[33] Moltke, p. 443.

[34] Finlay, vii. 59.

[35] The above conversations are reported in Parliamentary Papers, 1854, Eastern Question, House of Commons, 84.

[36] *Life of Lord Stratford*, ii. p. 442.

[37] *Life of Lord Stratford*, ii. p. 436.

[38] The above is from notes of conversations with Lord Stratford made at the time.

[39] *Life of Lord Stratford*, ii. p. 449.

[40] Lord Morley's *Life of Gladstone*, ii. p. 555.

[41] It may be well to add, what has not been mentioned by his able biographer, doubtless because Lord Stratford's daughters were alive when the book was published in 1888, that the Great Elchi gave testimony of his belief in the permanence of the Turkish Empire by investing the greater part of his personal property and savings in Turkish Bonds. In 1874, when the Porte became bankrupt and repudiated payment of interest on the debt, some friend at Constantinople wrote to Lord Stratford giving timely information of what was coming and advising him to sell his bonds while there was yet time. Lord Stratford, however, thought it was inconsistent with his sense of honour to act on this advice. His means were greatly reduced by the bankruptcy of the Porte. After his death and the cessation of his pension, his daughters would have been in very reduced circumstances if it had not been for the generosity of a personal friend of their father, the late Lady Ossington, who made up to these ladies, for their lives, the amount of the pension from the State which had lapsed by the death of Lord Stratford.

[42] *The Bulgarian Horrors and the Question in the East*, 1876.

[43] House of Commons, April 24, 1877.

[44] Bismarck induced Lord Beaconsfield to propose this to the Congress.

[45] Parliamentary Report, House of Commons, July 30, 1878.

[46] *Nineteenth Century Review*, December 1890. This article, which contained other severe criticisms on the rule of Abdul Hamid, was translated into the Turkish language, for his perusal, by the late Professor Arminius Vambéri, who was the guest of the Sultan at the time of my visit to Constantinople in 1890, and who had suggested to him that he should favour me with an audience. The Professor backed up my statements by remonstrances on his own behalf, with the result that the Sultan took grave offence. He withdrew the pension which he had annually paid to the Professor and put an end to their long friendship.

[47] *The Near East from Within*, p. 38.

[48] *The Balkan Cockpit*, G. M. Crawford Price, p. 102.

Milton Keynes UK
Ingram Content Group UK Ltd.
UKHW030902151124
451262UK00006B/1073